European Financial Systems
in the Global Economy

European Financial Systems in the Global Economy

Beate Reszat

John Wiley & Sons, Ltd

Copyright © 2005   John Wiley & Sons Ltd, The Atrium, Southern Gate, Chichester,
West Sussex PO19 8SQ, England

Telephone   (+44) 1243 779777

Email (for orders and customer service enquiries): cs-books@wiley.co.uk
Visit our Home Page on www.wiley.com

Other Wiley Editorial Offices

John Wiley & Sons Inc., 111 River Street, Hoboken, NJ 07030, USA

Jossey-Bass, 989 Market Street, San Francisco, CA 94103-1741, USA

Wiley-VCH Verlag GmbH, Boschstr. 12, D-69469 Weinheim, Germany

John Wiley & Sons Australia Ltd, 33 Park Road, Milton, Queensland 4064, Australia

John Wiley & Sons (Asia) Pte Ltd, 2 Clementi Loop #02-01, Jin Xing Distripark, Singapore 129809

John Wiley & Sons Canada Ltd, 22 Worcester Road, Etobicoke, Ontario, Canada M9W 1L1

Wiley also publishes its books in a variety of electronic formats. Some content that appears in print may not be
available in electronic books.

Library of Congress Cataloging in Publication Data

Reszat, Beate.
  European financial systems in the global economy / Beate Reszat.
    p. cm.
  Includes index.
  ISBN 0-470-87056-7
  1. Finance—Europe. 2. Financial institutions—Europe. 3. Monetary policy—Europe. I. Title.
  HG186.A2R47 2005
  332.1′094—dc22   2004027310

British Library Cataloguing in Publication Data

A catalogue record for this book is available from the British Library

ISBN 0-470-87056-7 (PB)

Typeset in 10/12pt Times by Integra Software Services Pvt. Ltd, Pondicherry, India
Printed and bound in Great Britain by Antony Rowe Ltd, Chippenham, Wiltshire
This book is printed on acid-free paper responsibly manufactured from sustainable forestry
in which at least two trees are planted for each one used for paper production.

Contents

About the Author

Dr Beate Reszat is head of research on International Financial Markets at the Hamburg Institute of International Economics. She is also lecturer on a course on the Japanese economy at the University of Hamburg, teaches a course on European and International Financial Markets as part of the Master of European Studies Programme at Hamburg University, and a general Macroeconomics course at Nordakademie, a private university directly supported by business partners. She has worked for the International Monetary Fund, Washington, D.C., the Economic Planning Agency, Tokyo, and as Visiting Scholar with the Bank of Japan, Tokyo. She has published widely on international financial relations, exchange rates and Japan's financial markets. She is author of *The Japanese Foreign Exchange Market* and co-editor (with Lukas Menkhoff) of *Asian Financial Markets – Structures, Policy Issues and Prospects*. Her research interests include international monetary policy cooperation, the relationship between financial systems and economic development and the role of international finance for world city growth.

1
Introduction

Financial markets are generally regarded as the forerunners of globalisation. Leading banks and investment houses have a presence in financial centres all over the world. There is 24-hour trading in foreign exchange and other financial instruments, and advances in communications and computer technologies allow anyone with a PC and telephone, even in the remotest parts of the world, access to financial information and trading and investment opportunities as has never been known before. The financial industry has long completed the transition from internationalisation to globalisation, from the central operation and control of worldwide activities to the dispersion of central functions to all major nodes of the world economy and their constant interaction within large networks. Globalisation has not only revolutionised the way in which financial instruments are traded but also a wide spectrum of activities from information gathering and price discovery, through portfolio and risk management, to clearing and settlement and mergers and acquisitions.

So why study European financial markets, which are embedded in this worldwide net of financial relations and activities, as a special entity? There are at least three reasons. The first is *history*: many financial systems, institutions and techniques in today's markets have their roots in early Europe. Examples are bonds, shares, techniques of forward trading, exchanges and central banks – but not banks, since bank-like institutions existed in other regions and eras too. Another aspect is that there are many peculiarities in Europe which represent a competitive advantage or disadvantage in the world system and that are rooted in the past. Those include institutions, legal systems and the role of governments in financial sector development.

The second reason is *diversity*: focusing on European financial markets offers the opportunity to study a wide range of institutions and systems, to make comparisons and learn to distinguish the main characteristics of, say, universal banking systems and specialised ones, strongly and less strictly regulated financial markets with direct or indirect policy interference, or the implications of different norms and rules.

The third reason is *specialty*: Europe is special among the world's regions. This does not only refer to the monetary union, this unique experiment in history. With the introduction of the Internal Market Programme for financial services the European Union has become the largest financial market worldwide. It has a unique system of regional bank supervision, and the centre of international supervision is located within Europe too. Europe is the location of what is in many respects the largest financial centre in the world; the European Central Bank is one of the world's leading central banks and the euro ranks second in the league of world currencies behind the US dollar. Besides all this, the experience with, and constant challenge of, integrating new entrance candidates into an existing framework of monetary and financial cooperation may provide many lessons to other regions.

This little book is thought of as a first introduction to Europe's financial markets and institutions, their performance and overall position in the world financial system. Although requiring some familiarity with basic principles of economics it is designed for students without prior knowledge of international finance. Since it developed from materials for a master course on European and International Financial Markets in an international university programme it may also be useful for readers outside Europe with no direct experience of European financial markets and systems. The text is a mixture of fundamentals and empirics with boxes giving short explanations of basic economic terms or referring to related case studies. Several appendices provide in-depth discussions or examples of related aspects of general interest that are not covered in the main text. Each chapter typically includes a brief summary, a set of exercises and a list of links and references at the end. The aim of the exercises goes beyond recapitulating the contents of the chapters; they are directed at stimulating discussion and further reading, and reflecting on arguments, in order to gain deeper insights into circumstances and developments that can be only briefly sketched here.

The book is organised as follows. Chapter 2 gives a short overview of the history of financial markets in Europe and explores the rise of centres and peripheries and the emergence of financial institutions and instruments. Chapter 3 examines market structures; European financial markets are characterised by a diversity of arrangements, products, assets and market types and in the first part of this chapter the reasons for this diversity are studied, while the second part deals with financial market typology in detail. It starts with various forms of financial intermediation focusing on the markets for money, credit and foreign exchange as well as for capital and derivatives. Attention then turns to financial systems discussing the main characteristics of bank-based and market-based systems as they are found in various parts of western Europe. Another focus is the development of financial systems in eastern European countries and here, in particular, in the new accession countries. The last part of this chapter turns to external markets, including traditional markets such as the Euromarkets and offshore centres, but also the virtual market places that have emerged with the internet revolution and the development of electronic finance in Europe.

Chapter 4 examines the role of European markets, systems and institutions in the world economy. One focus here is on the performance of banks and exchanges and the role of clearing and settlement systems for the international competitiveness of European markets. Another is on the consolidation process that is underway in the European financial industry and the way this changes the global position of European institutions. Chapter 5 focuses on market mechanisms and prices: in which ways do the choices and behaviours of investors, borrowers and lenders determine market conditions? Which are the main motives and strategies behind their actions and which role do expectations play in the process of price formation? How does the interplay of various groups of actors affect prices? What kinds of characteristic price patterns can be found in financial markets in Europe and elsewhere?

Containing price volatility and spill-over effects in times of crisis is one major policy issue these days. Others are overall financial stability and the relationship between finance and economic growth. Chapter 6 examines these and other topics in detail within the European context. One special aspect here is the efficiency of policy instruments in a globalised environment; as a rule, globalisation is weakening national sovereignty and limiting the use of policy instruments. In this it provides a strong rationale for policy cooperation. The European example demonstrates that agreement on cooperation, and a balance between national interests and international necessities, is easier to reach on a regional level than worldwide. However, as will also be shown, financial integration in Europe, too, is still fraught with uncertainties and hindered by countless impediments, and the introduction of the common currency, albeit an important element in the integration process, so far contributed less to the development than expected.

The book concludes with some general remarks on the prospects and challenges of the future of European monetary and financial integration.

2
European Financial Markets in History

Thinking of financial markets in Europe big financial metropoles like London, Paris, Frankfurt, Zurich or Amsterdam come to mind.

In contrast to developments on other continents, European financial history has always been a history of *places* where those in search of capital and those with idle funds came together. The European financial landscape has always been characterised by *centres and peripheries*.

Early financial activities stretching beyond the boundaries of the local town or village were rooted in long-distance trade. The earliest centres of the Middle Ages developed almost simultaneously with the rise of big *merchant empires* in the north and south of Europe. Before that time, up to the twelfth and even thirteenth centuries, European trade and finance was largely regionally limited. There was an infinity of states, sub-states, duchies, church-controlled territories and city states. Merchants' activities were restricted by the need to have personal knowledge of people and economic circumstances, limiting their business horizons to several days' walking distance and journeys along the major trade routes.

The first changes came when preferences for particular goods from remote places emerged, for example for salt from the Atlantic coast or wines from southern regions. Emerging crafts resulted in a rise in purchasing power in northern Europe and a taste for wines and other products from southern regions. Italian merchants introduced Flemish wool fabrics to the Mediterranean. Long-distance journeys such as pilgrimages and crusades heightened the awareness of other regions and aroused partiality to luxuries and exotic products such as ebony, silk and spices.

From the twelfth century onwards, increasing business activities led to the emergence of a threefold *division of labour* in Europe. Sedentary merchants, above all from northern Italy, specialised in the financing and organisation of trade. Specialist carriers then transported the goods from principals to agents by land or by sea. Full-time agents resident in foreign places engaged in sales and purchases according to the instructions sent by their principals.

The nascent merchant empires developed sophisticated business methods and forms of credit, ringing in what has been called *the classic succession of dominant cities*: Venice, Antwerp, Genoa, Florence, Amsterdam and London.

Each of those financial centres is known for the *innovations* they contributed to the development of European and international finance. This is particularly true for the financial instruments and practices introduced by Italian merchants:

- *Bills of exchange*, the essential form of foreign exchange in the Middle Ages, were traded at Italian fairs from the twelfth century. Those allowed for the avoidance of the physical transport of precious metals; it was safer to send a courier with bills than to dispatch specie or bullion under the guard of an armed convoy – and it was faster.

- From at least the tenth century, the *contratto di commenda*, a form of limited-liability partnership to share economic risks, whereby people could use their savings to invest in long-distance trade, was in use in Italy. The contratto di commenda (known in Venice as *collegantia*, in Genoa as *societas maris*) is widely regarded as a forerunner of the joint-stock companies.
- Florence and Genoa were the first European cities to mint their own *coins*, the Fiorino and the Genovino, in 1252. The Fiorino and later the Venetian ducat soon replaced the dinar, becoming the 'dollar of the Middle Ages'.
- The earliest surviving *cheque* was drawn in 1365 in Florence to pay a draper for black cloth for a family funeral.
- Genoa and Venice introduced the instrument of *public debt* to finance infrastructure and military projects before 1200 with the first *government bonds* issued in Venice.
- Prototypes of *marine insurance* date back to thirteenth-century Genoa, which remained the centre for this type of activity until the seventeenth century when London took the lead.
- Florence between the twelfth and the fourteenth centuries was the origin of great banking families, such as the Peruzzi, Bardi and Acciaiuoli, and later the Medici, all of whom had large capital stocks and wide *networks* of subsidiaries and relations in western Europe, north Africa, and the Levant.

However, Italians were not the first to have a flourishing money-based economy. The Italian city states owed much of their success to early relations with the Islamic world. There, credit instruments were highly developed before they became known in Europe, social functions such as 'bankers' were much older than the Italian 'benches', and Islamic traders knew sophisticated techniques for pooling capital much earlier than their Italian counterparts. Up to the thirteenth century Italian merchants continued to rely on the gold coins of Constantinople, and later Egypt, which at that time were the preferred specie for international transactions in Europe, the Middle East and India.

The first financial intermediaries in western Europe were *pawnbrokers* and *money changers*. First, the latter largely conducted business in exchange of currencies, with no element of credit involved. Given the great variety of coins in circulation in the Middle Ages, they played an indispensable role in major trading centres. The terms '*banks*' and '*bankers*' first appeared in the twelfth and thirteenth centuries; they are rooted in the benches or 'bancos' Italian merchants established at European trade fairs. *Deposit banking* evolved in reaction to the inconvenience involved in making all payments in specie and to the waste of time involved in counting coin. *Bank money* based on a fractional reserve dates back to the early fourteenth century when money changers discovered that in taking deposits and making payments on behalf of depositors it was not always necessary to keep cash covering the total value of deposits. As a consequence, they began keeping a small fraction of that amount, lending out the rest at interest to third parties or investing it directly in other businesses.

Trade and financial activities among European merchants were largely facilitated by the rise of organised fairs. In the thirteenth century, the *Champagne fairs* became an important financial centre in the European heartland. Located in north-eastern France, they lay midway between the two poles of economic activity in Europe at that time: the Italian cities and the industrially developing textile region of Flanders. Trading in money and foreign exchange became the true specialty of the fairs, but there was a divide between 'local' and international bankers: traditional money changers and local transfer banks in those places usually neither dealt in bills of exchange nor did they have correspondents abroad. This was left to the – mostly Italian – international merchant bankers.

Bill of Exchange

The Bill of Exchange was a contract defining an agreement between a deliverer and a trader by which the *deliverer* advanced a sum of money to the *trader* and, in return, received from him a 'letter missive', the bill of exchange, payable in a distant place and in another currency. Usually, the implementation of the contract required two other parties or agents to be involved in the location where the payment took place. These were the *payor* and the *payee*. The letter would specify the amounts and currencies in which funds were to be received and repaid, as well as the exchange rate and the time at which the bill was to be paid. The latter was known as *usance*.

The length of the usance was not only determined by the time it took to deliver the bill. At a time when financial activities in wide parts of Europe were limited by the *prohibition of usury*, bills of exchange were often used as credit instruments with exchange and re-exchange only concealing an interest-bearing loan (Appendix A). In this, a loophole in the law was exploited: Under a rule endorsed by most scholastic writers, buying and selling bills issued in terms of a foreign currency, and payable in a foreign country, was not considered usury. The practice of using a bill as a credit in disguise helps explain why merchant custom with regard to usance remained practically unchanged for several centuries – long after communication methods had improved considerably.

In the fifteenth century the overall economic supremacy of the Italians came to an end and the centre of financial activities in Europe shifted to the Low Countries, first to *Bruges*, and later to *Antwerp* and *Amsterdam*. They, too, became important centres of financial innovation:

- Among Bruges's wealthiest residents was the van der Beurs family, inn-keepers who allegedly gave their name to the later *bourse* or *stock exchange*.
- Bruges also became known for being the first place to establish *brokers*, called 'makelaer' or 'couretier', as intermediaries as early as the thirteenth century.
- In Antwerp, the *bond*, or *debenture*, was invented, where assets and liabilities were settled by an issuer committing himself to pay an agreed sum at maturity to the owner of a paper that could be sold by the borrower in the meantime.
- Another Flemish invention was the *rentes*, an alternative to loans to governments, which were strongly controversial in the usury debates of the Middle Ages. Antwerp's *Beurs*, founded in 1531, was the first bourse providing a physical presence for such papers.
- Amsterdam largely contributed to the wide acceptance of *stock trading*. The first known share worldwide dates from 1602, and was issued there by the Dutch East India Company (Vereenigte Oost-Indische Compagnie, or VOC). The Amsterdam bourse was Europe's leading securities market for many years.
- Also in Amsterdam, *forward transactions* as a specific form became a common tool of exchange trading.

In the sixteenth and early seventeenth centuries there was a short interlude between Antwerp's supremacy and Amsterdam's reign in which *Genoa* took the lead as Europe's financial centre,

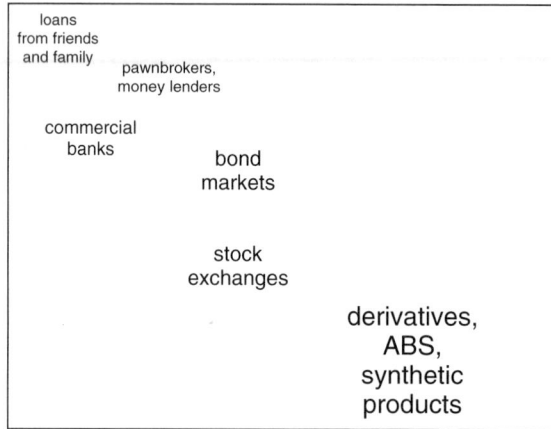

```
loans
from friends
and family
              pawnbrokers,
              money lenders

       commercial
         banks
                         bond
                        markets


                    stock
                 exchanges
                                      derivatives,
                                         ABS,
                                       synthetic
                                       products
```

Figure 2.1   Development of finance

following the example of Florence in earlier years with its merchants' wide international networks of subsidiaries and relations. Then, after Amsterdam's decline in the seventeenth and eighteenth centuries, *London* became the financial centre, first of Europe and then of the world, and kept this role until the First World War. It temporarily lost it to New York, only to regain it in the 1960s with the advent of the Euromarkets, and has maintained it ever since.

In literature, financial development is often regarded as a *linear, stepwise process* from simpler to more sophisticated forms. In this view, financial relations start from informal borrowing and lending arrangements with friends and family, followed by a rise of pawnbrokers and professional money lenders, developing into a system dominated mainly by commercial banks in which bond and stock markets slowly play an ever-growing role, with more sophisticated financial services and increasing specialisation emerging still later on (Figure 2.1). While this picture may hold true for countries in an early stage of economic development, it is misleading for the highly advanced economies of western Europe for two reasons at least. On the one hand, in these countries financial products of varying complexity often emerged in parallel in reaction to the needs of trade and commerce. On the other, as the German example demonstrates, even highly advanced economies long made do without a fully developed system. In addition, many examples can be found showing that the process from lower to higher sophistication is *not irreversible*. For instance, this holds true for some of the EU accession countries in eastern Europe such as Poland and Hungary which at the end of the nineteenth century already had well-developed stock markets. The origin of the Budapest Stock Exchange dates back to 1864, and the Warsaw Stock Exchange, which re-opened in April 1991 after half a century of interruption, had first been established in 1817.

Hierarchy also prevails in views of the history of *money* itself. Here, the development started with individual barter and then proceeded from crops and cattle – mankind's 'first working capital asset' (Davis 2002) – to cowrie shells, the world's oldest and most widely spread currency which began to be used in China around 1200 BC and up to the early twentieth century was still accepted in some parts of Africa. The next step was metal coins, then paper currency and, most recently, electronic money (Figure 2.2). But, again, history shows that the process is not irreversible. One example from outside Europe is Japan, where mintage of coins started in the eighth century only to be abandoned again in 958 when the government

barter

cattle and
crops

cowrie
shells

metal
coins

paper
currency

electronic
money

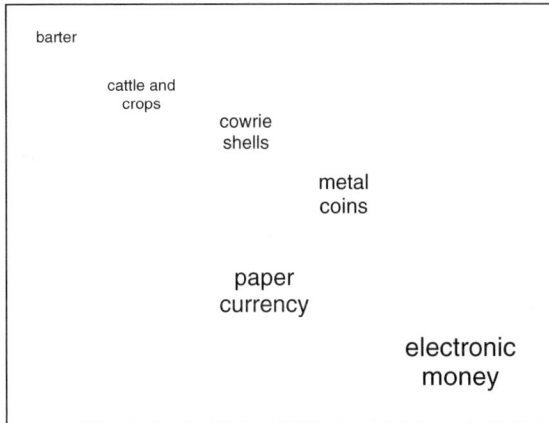

Figure 2.2   Development of money

forbade all circulation of coins after 250 years of mixed success and the country returned to rice and fabrics as mediums of exchange. This situation lasted until merchants and smugglers introduced foreign coins in the twelfth and thirteenth centuries and these soon became widely used and remained the main pillars of the Japanese currency system for the next 500 years.

Regarding the history of *financial centres* in Europe, development was stimulated by many influences. Long-distance trade first created the backbone along which, together with wines, wool and exotic products, money and credit travelled. The high risks involved established the need for inventing cashless means of payment, capital pooling and insurance. Frequent failures as the result of excessive loans to finance wars and other rulers' ambitions, speculative bubbles and the circumvention of the prohibition of usury were other sources of inspiration for financial innovations. Precious metals from the New World found their ways to markets in Europe, reshaping its financial landscape and altering cities' comparative advantage as financial centres, as did the process of industrialisation much later.

There were many reasons why a place became a centre in the world of European finance, why it kept that role for a while, or lost it to other places. *Political and economic influences* played their parts, but so did *natural disasters* and what economists like to call 'historic accident'. The Spanish–Dutch conflict that put an end to Antwerp's supremacy, or the decline of Amsterdam during the French wars, is an example of the first. Economic prosperity is the main explanation for the rise of Italian cities in the Middle Ages. *Institutional influences* help explain the rise and fall of German centres in the eighteenth and nineteenth centuries. Those were rooted in two different developments: in the general market activities of trade fairs in towns like Nuremberg and Augsburg, and in the guilds and merchant cooperatives found in Frankfurt, Cologne, Hamburg, Berlin and elsewhere. Bruges in the early twelfth century is often named as an example for a 'historic accident': when a storm opened a deep channel allowing the navigation of big commercial ships the town became the biggest trading port on the North Sea Coast, a position it held for many years. However, some authors argued convincingly that other influences added to its attractiveness, too.

These days, the financial landscape in Europe is determined both by a fierce *competition* between places like London, Frankfurt, Paris, Zurich and Amsterdam, and by mergers and acquisitions and other efforts to jointly exploit synergies. London is still the Number One among all European centres, although its position is no longer unchallenged. Its rise dates back to the seventeenth and eighteenth centuries when England brought a large part of the transatlantic trade under its flag and foreign commercial and banking families settled in the town as they fled from war on the continent. In later years, the strength of the Bank of England, the range of financial instruments available and the constant flow of financial demand resulting from industrial expansion and government debt became the pillars of the city's success.

Scale Economies and Lock-in

Broadly defined, *scale economies* are benefits arising from a production of more, rather than less, allowing maintenance of a low share of fixed costs per unit. For example, if inventing or adapting a new product or production technique requires significant setup costs, larger firms would perform better than smaller ones. Scale economies may also arise from agglomeration effects and a concentration of activities in one place. A concentration of financial institutions in one location leads to improved information flows, greater liquidity and higher efficiency in organised markets, and a centralisation of support services that all contribute to reducing costs.

Scale economies are special sources of rigidities in an economy giving rise to *path-dependence* and *lock-in*. The former broadly means that history matters. The current international status of a financial place depends on the advantages – and disadvantages – it has acquired in the past and the way in which those have influenced financial firms' location decisions. Lock-in stands for an inflexibility resulting from this process. Even if they offer high incentives for financial institutions to change location, due to long-established bonds and customs newly emerging competitors will find it hard to succeed in challenging the status of the Number One. Lock-in effects may offer one explanation why, despite the fundamental changes of financial systems, structures and techniques that Europe has experienced in recent years, and the introduction of the common currency outside the UK, the European hierarchy of centres with London at the top has remained widely unchanged.

Nowadays, there are additional factors underpinning London's status both in Europe and worldwide. They include

- a concentration of firms with the resulting *scale economies* and *lock-in effects*;
- the existence of *high quality professional and supporting services* such as accounting, actuarial and legal services and IT;
- an efficient *infrastructure* including office accommodation and telecommunications;
- the use of the *English language*.

Compared to other world regions, the spatial pattern of centres and peripheries found in European finance is quite unusual. In America the phenomenon of a financial centre is a very recent one, dating back to the nineteenth century. Even in Asia, the origin of one of the oldest informal money transfer systems (known as *hawala*), until fairly recently there was no need for a city hosting a bourse or fair to serve as a central place for financial activities.

In times of *electronic trading* and the *internet*, in Europe and worldwide, the rationale for financial institutions and activities to 'cluster' in centres seems to be waning. Relations between information technology and financial location are, however, more complex than generally assumed. Unlike in many other sectors, in international finance IT is *not an entirely new phenomenon*. Since the invention of the telegraph in the early nineteenth century, financial services have always been bridging distances using every available new medium and technology, from telephone, telex, video and fax to email and the internet, for speeding up communication and trade. On the other hand, many financial activities continue to require *proximity*. One aspect here is risk considerations and the experience that electronic surveillance is no substitute for human management. Others are the role of *trust building* that is crucial to many financial transactions and the need to become familiar with a special *context* before making financial decisions. Further arguments for an ongoing centralisation are *innovation and networking* and the desire to benefit from the constant presence, exchange and communication with others. In general, the less financial activities require spatial proximity in order to manage risks, gain access to information, establish social contacts or get impulses from the creative milieux of local communities, the greater the scope for dispersion and virtualisation.

Summary

- In contrast to other world regions, the history of finance in Europe is a history of centres and peripheries.
- Long-distance trade and the rise of big merchant empires laid the foundations for the success of cities like Venice, Antwerp, Genoa, Florence, Amsterdam and later London.
- The rise and decline of financial centres was influenced by political and economic developments, but also by what economists call 'historic accident'.
- Organised fairs facilitated early exchange beyond local boundaries with money changers and bankers playing a decisive role for their functioning.
- Financial innovations were stimulated by the risks related to long-distance trade and by the lessons learned from financial failures and speculative bubbles.
- London's present status as the leading financial centre, both in Europe and worldwide, is in part explained by advantages gained from scale economies and lock-in effects rooted in history.
- In the age of electronic trading and the internet, the role of financial centres is weakened, but an ongoing need of proximity to enhance trust building, innovations and networking still provides a rationale for 'clustering'.

Exercises

1. Discuss the reasons why

   - long-distance trade
   - wars and crusades
   - overseas colonies and
   - technological progress

   stimulated financial innovation and the rise of financial centres in history.
2. Explain the following activities and their origins:

   - money changing
   - deposit banking
   - banking based on fractional reserve.

3. Trace the origins of

   – bond trading
   – stock markets
   – credit and foreign exchange
   – insurance

   in Europe.
4. Name the comparative advantages of London as a financial centre in the seventeenth and eighteenth centuries and explain their relative importance today.
5. Discuss possible determinants of the relations between information technology and international finance.

Additional Links and References

Sources dealing with the early history of money and finance are:

Davis, Glyn (2002) *A History of Money: From Ancient Times to the Present Day*, Cardiff: University of Wales Press.
Einzig, Paul (1970) *The History of Foreign Exchange*, London: Macmillan.
Favier, Jean (1998) *Gold and Spices: The Rise of Commerce in the Middle Ages*, New York: Holmes & Meier.
Spufford, Peter (2002) *The Merchant in Medieval Europe*, London: Thames & Hudson.

A source of working papers, links and references to the economic and financial history of later-medieval and early modern Europe can be found at:

http://www.economics.utoronto.ca/munro5/

Later centuries are well captured in:

Ferguson, Niall (2001) *Cash Nexus – Money and Power in the Modern World 1700–2000*, London: Penguin Books.
Hamilton, Adrian (1986) *The Financial Revolution*, Harmondsworth: Penguin.
Kindleberger, Charles P. (1993) *A Financial History of Western Europe*, Oxford: Oxford University Press.

The influence of developments outside Europe on early European financial activities is discussed in:

Abu-Lughod, Janet L. (1989) *Before European Hegemony – The World System A.D. 1250–1350*, New York: Oxford University Press.

The role of information technologies, both old and new, in international finance is described in:

Reszat, Beate (2002) Information technologies in international finance and the role of cities, in: *GaWC Research Bulletin 74*: http://www.lboro.ac.uk/gawc/publicat.html, 26 February.

A lively demonstration of the history of money and banking in London is found on this interactive museum site of the Bank of England:

http://www.bankofengland.co.uk/museum/walkthrough/timeline_flash.asp

A picture of 'the mother of all banks', an Italian money changer's cabinet or 'banco', can be found on the fascinating site of the National Bank of Belgium's numismatic and historical collection. As is explained there: 'This 16th century item of furniture already had an ingenious security system: secret compartments and a drawer which can be locked with an impressive key. Such tables were sometimes the object of popular rage, especially when their owners were no longer able to meet their financial obligations. A destroyed moneychanger's table is a "banco rotto" ': its owner is then bankrupt.' See:

http://www.nbb.be/Sg/En/Contact/33_1e.htm

3
Market Structures

Europe's financial landscapes are characterised by a diversity of arrangements, products, assets and market types, and the following sections give an impression of the facets of this diversity. However, before turning to individual markets and systems, there is an overview of the motives and actions driving supply and demand in general and the emergence of financial instruments and institutions.

3.1 FINANCIAL SYSTEMS, MARKETS AND INTERMEDIARIES

These days, the head of a *private household* in western Europe looking to finance the purchase of a new car, a house, or other consumer durables, has several options. These include:

- taking a loan from her bank;
- looking for special finance, for example turning to a bank or building society for a mortgage, or to the car producer for a consumer loan;
- using a credit card; or
- spending her own savings.

Except for the last alternative she would need a *financial intermediary*, that is, for example, a bank or a credit card company, to provide the money, without knowing the ultimate source it comes from.

On the other hand, if she has money available and wants to save it instead of spending it immediately, again there are several alternatives. For example, she could put the money into a savings account, buy bonds or shares, speculate in foreign exchange, invest in derivatives or buy insurance, or simply keep the money under the mattress. For most of these activities, too, she would need a bank or another financial intermediary, that is, for instance, she would not turn directly to the share-issuing firm but instruct a bank or a broker.

In short: financial intermediaries take the money from one source and give it to another in exchange for a small fee or another form of compensation, or arrange for capital demand and supply to meet in organised markets. These days, banks are only one kind of provider of financial services. Others include investment funds, insurance companies, credit card companies and new types of non-bank financial firms such as GE Capital or Ford Motor Credit Company.

A *business firm* looking for the means to finance either an investment or its daily expenses, to actively manage financial risks or to engage in a financial transaction in search for profits, usually has far more options than a household, depending, among other things, on *size*. For instance, a large enterprise can issue short-term papers, bonds or shares and even engage directly in money market or foreign exchange transactions and derivatives trading. Size largely influences costs and returns of financial transactions. As a rule, a large customer gets better conditions both as a borrower and an investor, and has a wider spectrum of financial instruments available as well as better market access than a smaller one.

Among non-bank corporations, so-called *institutional investors* play a special role in financial markets; these include mutual funds, life insurance companies and pension funds. One common characteristic of these firms is the weight they have in the markets due to their financial strength. Collecting contributions from countless employees and small savers, they have large funds at their disposal that need to be invested regularly. Another characteristic is that, forced by law or voluntarily, many of them follow strict prudential rules for asset allocation. In particular, life insurers and pension funds differ in their investment strategies from many others in that they seek long-term engagements, following more of a buy-and-hold strategy. They are conservative investors with a strong preference for stable markets and smooth trading. Being constantly aware of the risk of reverse price movements in smaller or illiquid markets they largely focus on traditional debt instruments and equity. Professional management of collective portfolios, a long-term view of investments and emphasis on stability make institutional investors large and reliable sources of finance that are much sought after, in particular in developing countries and transition economies, where they are expected to significantly contribute to financial development.

Table 3.1 gives an overall impression of the *financial structure* in the euro area compared to the United States and Japan. It shows that in all three regions households have a large positive net position in financial asset holdings that makes them the ultimate providers of funds for non-financial corporations and governments while, as expected, financial corporations merely function as intermediaries between the two groups, as their net position close to zero indicates. What the table does not show is the marked differences that exist within Europe.

Table 3.1 The financial structure in the euro area, Japan and the United States[1]

	Assets	Liabilities	Net position
Euro area			
• Households	202	57	145
• Non-financial corporations	147	240	−93
• Financial corporations	371	369	2
• Government	28	80	−52
• Total	748	746	2
Japan			
• Households	281	78	203
• Non-financial corporations	140	250	−110
• Financial corporations	596	598	−2
• Government	86	146	−60
• Total	1104	1072	32
United States			
• Households	322	80	242
• Non-financial corporations	112	132	−20
• Financial corporations	334	332	3
• Government	20	62	−42
• Total	788	606	182

[1] In 2001, as percentage of GDP.

Source: Hartmann, Philipp, Angela Maddaloni and Simone Manganelli (2003) The euro area financial system: structure, integration and policy initiatives, European Central Bank, *Working Paper No. 230*, http://www.ecb.int/pub/wp/ecbwp230.pdf, Table 1.

Table 3.2 How people save and invest[1]

	Europe	Japan	United States
Mutual funds	8	4	11
Securities	28	10	37
Pensions	15	9	32
Life insurance	17	18	3
Deposits	32	59	17
Total	100	100	100

[1] In percent.
Source: Sallard, Delphine (1999) Risk capital markets, a key to job creation in Europe. From fragmentation to integration. *Euro Paper No. 32*, Brussels: European Commission, Figure 7, http://Europa.eu.int/comm/economy_finance/publications/Euro_papers/2001/eup32en.pdf.

For example, companies in France, Germany, Italy and Spain are generally less indebted than those in the Netherlands, Portugal and Finland.

The figures in Table 3.2 show how people *save and invest* in Europe. Compared to the United States they appear more *risk averse*. Their share of deposits is much higher and they spend comparably more on life insurance and less on securities and mutual funds. In addition, these figures include the UK, Europe's biggest financial centre. For continental Europe the difference to the US would be even more striking. On the other hand, a comparison with Japan shows that the European case is not extreme.

Financial preferences differ by sector. As Table 3.3 demonstrates, in general, European households rely entirely on *loans* for external funding and invest their money above all in shares and bank accounts. For companies in Europe, the *stock markets* are the most important source of external finance, followed by bank loans, while bonds and other debt securities play a negligible role. The latter, for example, is in strong contrast to the US and one aspect to be discussed will be the reasons behind this phenomenon. A second aspect is the marked differences that exist between European countries. Other features not shown in the table are the strong importance of *internal funding* and of *private equity*, i.e. unquoted shares, which seems a European characteristic, too. Both can be explained at least in part by the comparably high percentage of *small and medium-sized firms* in the region.

The characteristics discussed indicate that in order to derive some sort of overall financial market typology, several criteria can be chosen. The first, and the one applied here, is the *range of financial products and services* available. These include classic financial instruments such as bank loans, bonds and shares, and also highly sophisticated innovations such as synthetic assets or credit derivatives. Traditionally, in literature, distinctions are found between markets for debt and equity, money and capital, domestic and foreign currency, or derivatives and their underlyings, focusing on features such as ownership, maturity, denomination and substance. However, in recent years, with increasing business complexity and growing competition worldwide, these distinctions have become more and more blurred. Debt is easily converted into equity, loans are becoming securitised and structured instruments are developed in order to mimic the characteristics of all sorts of financial products to meet investors' needs.

According to the classification in the following sections, three broad groups of financial products can be distinguished (Figure 3.1). The first consists of financial claims and liabilities that, traditionally, are *not transferable and not tradable*. For instance, this holds true for bank

Table 3.3   Sources of financing and investments in the euro area[1]

	Sources of financing	Investments
Households		
• Loans	52	
• Debt securities	0	19
• Shares	0	67
• Currency and deposits	0	61
Non-financial corporations		
• Loans	68	
• Debt securities	8	9
• Shares	132	77
• Currency and deposits	0	15
Financial corporations		
• Loans	12	
• Debt securities	50	80
• Shares	75	69
• Currency and deposits	170	77
Government		
• Loans	15	
• Debt securities	57	2
• Shares	0	9
• Currency and deposits	4	6
Total		
• Loans	95	
• Debt securities	115	110
• Shares	207	222
• Currency and deposits	174	159

[1] In percent of GDP.
Source: Hartmann, Philipp, Angela Maddaloni and Simone Manganelli (2003) The euro area financial system: structure, integration and policy initiatives, European Central Bank, *Working Paper No. 230*, http://www.ecb.int/pub/wp/ecbwp230.pdf, Tables 2 and 3.

Non-transferables	Securities	Derivatives
• loans	• equities	• forwards
• deposits	• bonds	• swaps
• mortgages	• notes	• options
• ...	• ...	• ...

Figure 3.1   Financial market products

loans and deposits or mortgages. However, the latter is already an example of the changing nature of even classic markets. With the rise of the Pfandbrief, a type of bond backed by mortgages or local government loans, tradability has entered this area by means of securitisation, i.e. by pooling the loans and backing tradable, standardised securities.

As a rule, the products in the second category, *securities*, are transferable. Securities include long- and short-term debt instruments such as bonds and notes, as well as equities, which are claims to share in everything a company owns after allowing for its debt, and the profits it makes. A third, wholly different category is *derivatives*. These do not exist in their own right but their substance and value is related to (derived from) another financial product.

Why are there so many different types of markets and instruments? The *diversity* of products reflects the variety of needs and preferences of financial market participants as well as the inherent dangers and limitations. Finance theory emphasises a constant *trade-off* between risk and return underlying all financial transactions. In general, financial prices contain a *risk premium* to compensate the investor for the uncertainties related to the investment. The lower the risks the greater the willingness of investors to provide funds and the more favourable the conditions for the borrower or equity issuer.

Figure 3.2 gives an idea of the relation between risks and returns and their effects on borrowing and investment. If overall risk in a market rises from A to A', investors become less inclined to invest funds in this market and will demand a higher return for doing so. In this example, they are risk averse. As a consequence, returns will have to rise higher than the perceived risk increase to attract them or make them stay in the market. However, higher returns mean higher borrowings costs which will drive some of the borrowers out of the market, leading to a decline in borrowings from C to C'. In addition, some investments will not be made at all at the higher risk. As a consequence, total investment declines from D to D'.

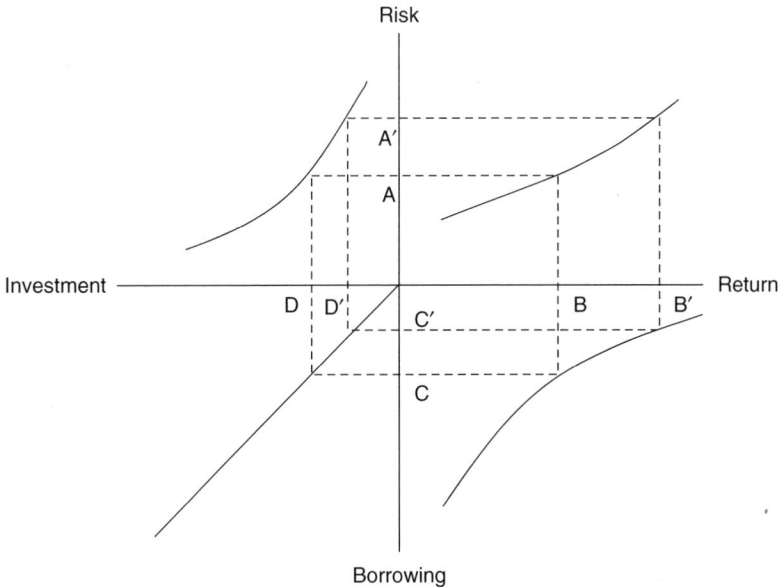

Figure 3.2   Risk and return relations

In the literature, different classes and components of risks are distinguished that will be discussed in detail in Chapter 5. However, there are situations where the dangers are perceived as too high or transparency is lacking. In these cases, a market for the respective product may not appear at all and the existence of non-market financial intermediaries providing the link between financial demand and supply may become of overwhelming importance for financial and economic development. In recent years, debates about 'bank-based' versus 'market-based' financial systems have been highly critical of the role of banks, often neglecting the fact that in many circumstances, and many parts of the world, banks provide the only reliable source of finance. On the other hand, there are even circumstances when banks shun the risks of intermediation, or, vice versa, financial institutions themselves are perceived as too risky to attract the savings they need for granting loans.

In general, different financial markets and institutions fulfil different functions in an economy and face different *risk and return profiles*. For example, stock markets give shareholders a strong position and great flexibility, compensating them for the high risks corporate ownership bears. Should they be dissatisfied with a firm's performance, they may sell their shares. Alternatively, they may choose to use their ownership to influence board and management to change their strategy. The high risks in stock markets are accompanied by comparably high expected returns. Other suppliers of financing, such as bond holders and bank lenders, bear less risk as they have prior claim on the firm's assets in case of failure. However, they also have no direct vote in the operation of the firm and a lower expected return on their investment.

Intermediation is but one of numerous *financial services* provided in an advanced economy. Others include custody, research, technology provision and advice. In addition, there are related activities, such as clearing and settlement, and related industries such as advertising, accounting, management consulting, legal services and many more. These days, many of the latter so-called *producer services* are no longer provided in-house by financial institutions, whose reliance on them makes a financial centre act like a magnet, dragging respective industries to the place and thereby enhancing its overall attractiveness and growth prospects.

Products and services are one way to classify markets; another is the *ways* in which these are offered (Table 3.4). Trades are done *over the counter* (OTC), on organised exchanges and

Table 3.4   Financial market classification

Criterion	Features	Examples
Products	Tradability, transferability, ownership, maturity, denomination, substance	Equity, debt instruments, derivatives
Services	Technical, advisory, information and knowledge-based, administrative	IT support, research and analysis, custody
Ways of trading	Physical, electronic, virtual	Over the counter, exchange, internet
Actors	Professionals, non-professionals, institutions, individuals, officials	Banks, central banks, non-bank financial companies, institutional investors, business firms, households
Origin	Domestic, cross-border, regional, international	National markets, regionally integrated markets, Euromarkets, domestic/foreign currency markets, onshore/offshore markets

via the internet. Seen as a whole, the bulk of trading in financial products takes place over the counter. On the one hand, this includes trading by screen and telephone in the huge interbank markets for money and foreign exchange. On the other, it makes up most customer business as well. By contrast, despite the overall attention it gets and the fact that it is catching the headlines more frequently than others, trade on *organised exchanges* is reserved to a comparably small share of products. Exchange trading may take different forms; while in the United States, trading by *open outcry* on an exchange floor – where dealers shout using particular calls and gestures – is still in wide use, in Europe, almost all exchange dealing is done *electronically*.

A new dimension was added to the world of finance by the emergence of the *internet* with the rise of new market segments and structures. Its most dramatic effect was the virtualisation of retail finance; suddenly, everyone with a PC and telephone had access to financial information worldwide and trading opportunities never known before. The speed of change has been impressive. For example, in Europe in early 2000, an average of 466 new online accounts was being opened in Sweden every day, 685 in Britain and 1178 in Germany. In 2003, with 84.7 websites per 1000 people, Germany ranked first in Europe and worldwide, followed by Denmark and Norway with 71.7 and 66.4, respectively. By comparison, the EU average at that time was slightly under 40 while in both the UK and the US there were more than 60 sites per 1000 people.

Besides products and places, there is still another possible classification criterion, this being the type of *actors* involved. At one end of the spectrum there are first-rate borrowers and lenders in wholesale markets. These markets are characterised by large trading volumes, high transparency, few clear and binding rules and a high degree of standardisation. As in product markets, wholesale trading serves to provide funds to those professionally acting as intermediaries. On the other end are the retail markets for investors and borrowers where most transactions are small, conditions are fixed individually and each case is judged carefully. As a rule, in these markets, overall transparency is low, personal relations matter a lot and products and services are often tailor-made, perfectly suiting counterparts' purposes. There are markets where fund seekers' *quality and creditworthiness* are high as is the case with blue chip companies listed on the world's biggest exchanges. In other markets, this is rather low as the example of start-up entrepreneurs targeting venture capitalists demonstrates. Markets may be very *liquid* and thereby highly efficient in pricing products, with major participants acting as market makers, but, more often, liquidity is low, with larger transactions containing the risk of adverse price movements.

In the era of *financial globalisation*, the options for both borrowing and investing are far more numerous than in earlier times, and are no longer restricted to domestic markets. These days, big corporations and financial institutions shop around the world for a loan with a low interest rate, borrow in foreign currency, issue stocks or bonds in international capital markets and choose from a variety of financial products worldwide for hedging and risk management purposes. At the same time, banks, securities firms, mutual funds and insurance companies from foreign countries penetrate home markets thereby exerting strong competitive pressures on the domestic financial industry. However, some financial market segments are more internationalised than others and access to global markets, again, is often a matter of size.

Why do financial institutions, borrowers and lenders go abroad? One argument is *market access*. Actors may be excluded from sources in one place that are available to them in others. Another aspect, again, is risk and return. For individual investors and lenders, *conditions* in international markets may be more favourable than in national ones, processes of risk monitoring and management may be simpler or more reliable and opportunities for diversification more numerous. In Europe, for instance, these are some of the advantages listed for the Euromarkets that are described in the next section. For financial institutions, extending business activities beyond national borders offers an opportunity for growing and for realising additional economies of scale.

However, despite an increasing international interdependence, there are *limits to convergence*, and regional differences still show remarkable persistence. The impediments to integration are numerous. Official rules and regulation play an important role, but in many cases, even in the age of electronic trading and the internet, distances simply remain insurmountable, proximity to clients and competitors is still indispensable and local peculiarities continue to dominate. In addition, as in markets for other products and services, establishing a financial business abroad brings higher costs and additional risks. As a rule, these require a certain critical size in order to succeed, which perhaps remains the single most important barrier to cross-country financial activities on a broader scale.

Domestic and foreign financial markets offer a wide range of risk and return combinations allowing for choice and combination of products depending on factors such as size, market access, creditworthiness and individual preferences. Actors usually engage in a variety of activities; investors in one market are borrowers in another. As is discussed later, this allows them to compensate for individual risks and increase overall expected returns. One consequence is the *interconnectedness* of markets. To give an example, imagine a decline in shareholders' trust in a company's future performance in reaction to shrinking profits (Figure 3.3). This is likely to draw investors' attention to the size of the firm's outstanding debt and related risks, which may easily result in a fall in bond prices; with declining share and bond prices, access to the short-term fixed-income market may no longer be available to the company. At the same time, with banks becoming increasingly aware of the build-up of tensions the company's

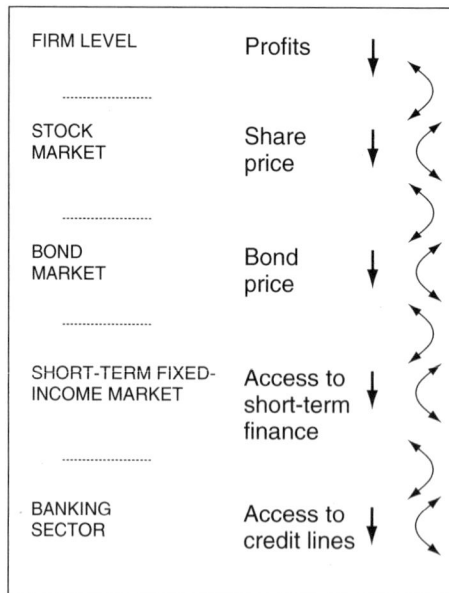

Figure 3.3 Micro-independencies

bank relations may worsen as well and it may become increasingly difficult to negotiate lines of credit. In addition, market conditions may not change in steps but, as indicated by the little curved arrows in the figure – at least from a certain moment onwards – simultaneously influence and reinforce one another. And, of course, the relations described hold true in the opposite direction, too. A firm with shining growth prospects and a rising share price will have few difficulties getting other forms of finance at attractive conditions.

Linkages do not exist only across markets but also within and between industries. When a big company tumbles, the whole sector may face financial strains, which may spread to related industries and affect the financial conditions of banks and investors exposed to them. Another example for the interdependence of markets is the relation between cash instruments and their derivatives, and between different categories of derivatives. The most famous phenomenon in this context is the *triple-witching hour* four times a year when the S&P 500 futures contract expires at the same time as the S&P 100 index option contract and option contracts on individual stocks.

Summary

- Europe's financial landscapes are characterised by a diversity of markets, systems and intermediaries.
- Compared to the US, Europeans appear more risk averse, investing less in securities and mutual funds and more in life insurance, and holding a higher share of deposits.
- Traditionally, internal funding and private equity play a more important role in Europe than elsewhere, which can be explained by the region's high share of small and medium-sized firms.
- With the emergence of securitisation and synthetic assets, traditional distinctions between financial markets and products have become increasingly blurred.
- The diversity of products reflects the variety of needs and preferences of financial market participants who face a constant trade-off between risks and returns.
- In the age of financial globalisation, borrowing and investment opportunities are no longer restricted to domestic markets. However, for various reasons, in some markets regional differences show remarkable persistence.

Exercises

1. Describe various sources of finance

   - for a private household
   - for a business firm

   and the role they play in a European context.
2. Try to broadly categorise financial markets and instruments showing their common features and differences.
3. Discuss the role of risks in financial markets and their implications for investors, borrowers and lenders.
4. Describe the interdependencies of markets for equity, bonds and short-term finance and the inherent dangers for finance-seeking firms.
5. Discuss the reasons of various groups of actors in financial markets to go international.

Additional Links and References

A broad general introduction to financial markets and products and related theories and concepts is provided by:

Allen, Franklin and Anthony M. Santomero (1996) The theory of financial intermediation, Wharton Financial Institutions Center Working Paper 96–32, http://fic.wharton.upenn.edu/fic/papers/96/9632.pdf
Bodie, Zvi, Alex Kane and Alan J. Marcus (2002) *Investments*, New York: McGraw-Hill/Irwin.
Mishkin, Frederic S. and Stanley G. Eakins (2000) *Financial Markets and Institutions*, Reading, MA: Addison Wesley Longman.

An important site for latest research of these issues in general is that of the Wharton Financial Institutions Center of the Wharton School of the University of Pennsylvania:

http://fic.wharton.upenn.edu/fic/

There is a financial economics website managed by James R. Garven listing internet resources that provide substantive information concerning finance-related topics:

http://finance.baylor.edu/weblogs/garven/

Important sources of information about financial topics are the research departments of central banks and monetary research institutes worldwide. An exhaustive list is provided by Mark Bernkopf:

http://patriot.net/~bernkopf/

3.2 FINANCIAL MARKET TYPOLOGY

Following the market typology suggested in Figure 3.1, a distinction is made between securities, derivatives and traditionally non-tradable and non-transferable products. Why stick to this classification if, as described, it is fraught with so many ambiguities these days? The reason is that in their purest form the products in each of these categories share some fundamental characteristics that distinguish them from all others, defining a unique set of opportunities and risks. As a rule, for one reason or the other, in *markets for non-tradable and non-transferable products*, compared to returns the risks are too high to be borne by non-specialists. On the one hand, this holds true in the wholesale markets, where amounts traded, and flexibility required, are high and standardisation holds down costs. On the other, it is also valid for the retail business where low standardisation, long maturities, individual performance and the amount of information needed for decision making require professional expertise.

By contrast, in *securities markets*, techniques and mechanisms prevail that allow a distribution of risks among a wider public, thereby opening up additional sources of financing. However, in order to attract investors and to compensate them for providing funds, accepting a lower liquidity and higher risks than with other uses, as a rule, expected returns in these markets have to be correspondingly higher. In the third category, *derivatives*, the nature of transactions differs fundamentally from the other two in that they are entirely forward looking allowing an unbundling and separate trading of the risk related to a financial product (Table 3.5). Again, this dominance of risk asks for compensation via a higher expected return, which is normally achieved by means of leverage. The latter is defined in this context as the amount of money invested in relation to notional amounts and expected profits (or losses).

Table 3.5   Financial product categories in comparison

Category	Risk determinants	Expected returns	Main actors
Non-tradables and non-transferables	In wholesale money markets: transaction volumes In retail markets: low transparency, lack of standardisation, low creditworthiness In foreign exchange markets: high volatility, change of currency	In wholesale money markets: low In credit markets: low In foreign exchange markets: high	In wholesale money markets: banks In retail markets: banks and non-bank firms and households In foreign exchange markets: financial institutions, companies
Securities	Market volatility, individual risks and failures	Comparably high	Banks and non-bank firms, individuals
Derivatives	Market volatility, leverage	Very high	Banks and non-bank firms, individuals

Studying these different categories, the main questions are:

- Why did particular markets develop and who are the main participants?
- Which role do these markets play in individual European countries and in the European financial system?
- What are the causes for the rise or decline of markets and why have some of them become more popular than others over time?

3.2.1   Non-tradables and Non-transferables

Non-tradable and non-transferable claims and liabilities are among the earliest and most common forms of financial relations. Loans granted or taken both in wholesale and retail business establish individual borrower–lender relations. In these markets, unwinding the transaction, or stepping in for another counter-party, is rare and, as a rule, only possible at high cost, if at all.

In general, these sorts of contracts and financial relations are common in three types of markets, differentiated by actors, maturity and/or currency denomination. These are the markets for money, credit and foreign exchange (Table 3.6). These days, in all three, tradable products are also found – and in the money markets they have a substantial share. These will be discussed in the next sections, while this one focuses on traditional elements.

The difference between the money and credit markets is largely in maturities. *Money markets* allow for the provision of short-term liquidity of usually less than one year. Money market instruments are low risk and very liquid which, together with their short-term nature, makes them close to being money – hence the name. These are *wholesale markets* with very large transactions where traders buy and sell the equivalent of millions of US dollars in a few seconds every day. For example, in the European market, transactions of €500 million to €1 billion are common and deals over €1 billion are not unusual. Credit risk in these markets is minimised by limiting access to high-quality counter-parties; participants are mainly *banks*. In addition, central banks use the money markets to steer the economy's supply of liquidity by means of interventions and by fixing the terms at which they provide money to the banks.

Table 3.6   Markets for non-tradables

Market	Features	Main participants
Money market	Short term (less than one year), wholesale, large amounts traded, high trading volumes, high liquidity, standardised	Banks, central banks
Credit market	Medium to long term, retail, varying amounts, low liquidity, tailor-made contracts	Banks, firms, individuals
Foreign exchange market	Short and long maturities, both standardised and tailor-made, in standardised trading high market volume, high liquidity in main currencies	Banks, big companies, central banks in wholesale markets, tailor-made contracts for small firms and individuals without direct market access in retail markets

In recent years, the importance of the traditional money market has decreased with the rising tendency to finance short-term needs by issuing securities such as commercial paper and certificates of deposit. One explanation is the steady shift to off-balance-sheet instruments in reaction to the introduction of capital rules for internationally operating banks under the auspices of the Bank for International Settlements. Another is that high-quality customers increasingly recognise the advantages of this form of finance that offers an opportunity to diversify borrowing, reduce costs and borrowers' dependence on bank loans and circumvent credit limits.

A similar tendency is observed in *credit or loan markets*. In contrast to the money market, these markets deal with longer maturities, with loans and deposits stretching over a much wider time frame. They are less transparent, risks are higher and market participants are more diverse. This reduces the possibilities of securitisation and a shift to off-balance-sheet trans-actions. As a rule, individual borrowers are evaluated very carefully before a new loan is granted. Often, repayment is guaranteed by collateral as in the case of a *mortgage*, which is a long-term loan secured by real estate. Until the emergence of credit derivatives, which are a very recent phenomenon, credit markets had been among the least liquid, most complicated to price and most costly financial markets, and in many ways they still are. This helps explain why actors with sufficient financial strength and economic performance look for alternatives that are less costly, less complicated (more standardised), and more liquid, such as markets for bonds and equities.

Whenever means sought or to be invested are denominated in foreign currency, borrowers and investors have to turn to the *foreign exchange markets* where currencies are bought and sold. These are not markets for foreign coins and notes, but for book values, i.e. assets and liabilities denominated in foreign currency. Again, as a rule, transactions are very large. The foreign exchange market, too, is largely an interbank market, although there is a remarkable share of customer trading; it is, accordingly, rather a money market than a credit market in that most of the trades are very short term by nature.

However, this has not always been the case; by its very nature, the foreign exchange market is a hybrid between the highly standardised interbank money markets and the customer-oriented credit markets. Initially it served the purposes of both sides equally; in its beginning, demand for, and supply of, foreign exchange was largely determined by foreign trade. It was only when cross-border capital flows were liberalised in many countries in the 1970s and 1980s, and currencies became freely convertible for both trade and financial transactions, that cross-border portfolio investments and proprietary trading by professional dealers started to dominate market activity. Meanwhile, foreign exchange trading has been the domain of a small group of large, internationally operating banks, with customer business – whether for commercial purposes or portfolio investments – making up only a small fraction of the market (see Appendix B). In addition, the majority of trades is no longer done on the spot markets but on the forward and swap markets which, as part of the derivatives markets, are discussed later.

The foreign exchange market has become a two-tier system. There is a wholesale market which, in principle, is a money market in foreign currencies, and a retail market for smaller banks, firms and individuals in need of, or with surplus amounts of, foreign currency, that have no direct market access but must turn to a bank. While for them bank fees make foreign exchange transactions costly, easily eating up expected currency gains, for financial institutions and others with direct access, trading is most profitable. The reason is volatility: as a rule, fluctuations in exchange rates are much higher than in interest rates or even share prices, and information and computer technologies and sophisticated trading techniques allow for the exploitation of even the smallest price movements.

In the past there were many policy efforts to limit currency fluctuations either by unilateral central bank interventions or by regional and international monetary policy cooperation. In Europe, there was a linear development from the liberalisation of currency trading via the introduction of limits to exchange rate volatility to the shift to a single currency. Since January 1999, there has been a new European currency, the *euro*, which in early 2002 replaced national currencies in 12 countries: the French franc, German mark, Italian lira, Dutch guilder, Spanish peseta, Irish punt, Portuguese escudo, Finnish markka, Austrian schilling, Greek drachma and Belgian/Luxembourg franc. In addition to the immediate impact this had on markets in participating countries, a number of non-participating countries were affected, too, because, for example, they had pegging arrangements formerly involving one of the member currencies.

Euro Territories

The introduction of the euro was not limited to the 12 member states but extends to a number of countries which can be categorised into three groups:

1. Territories outside Europe. These include the French overseas departments of Guadeloupe and Martinique, part of the little Antilles north of Venezuela, French Guyana, located between Brazil and Surinam in the north of South America, and Réunion which lies east of Madagascar. In addition, the euro was also introduced in the Portuguese Azores, Madeira in the North Atlantic and in the Spanish Canary Islands.
2. Third countries that are surrounded by members of the euro zone and do not have their own currencies. These include Andorra, Monaco, San Marino and the Vatican.
3. Areas that do not belong to one of the former groups but have introduced the euro as official means of payments such as Montenegro and Kosovo.

In addition, some 30 countries currently have exchange rate regimes involving the euro in one way or another. These include:

- countries whose currency is pegged to the euro, such as Denmark (participating in the Exchange Rate Mechanism of the European Monetary System), Cyprus or Macedonia;
- countries with euro(formerly D-mark)-based currency boards (Bosnia-Herzegovina, Bulgaria and Estonia);
- countries that peg their currency to a basket of currencies including the euro or one of the currencies it replaced. Examples are Hungary and Iceland and the African countries still forming a Franc zone or CFA (see Appendix C);
- countries having adopted a system of managed floating using the euro informally as a reference currency such as the Czech Republic, Slovakia and Slovenia.

During its first years in existence, the euro has gained widespread acceptance outside member states and, in some cases, became a *serious rival to the US dollar*. For example, the results of a tri-annual survey of foreign exchange turnover from April 2001 show that the euro captured a dominant market share in some eastern European countries such as the Czech Republic and Hungary, although it was still outweighed by the dollar in others such as Poland and Russia. The latter is partly explained by the fact that, in the past, these countries had a high foreign debt denominated in dollar (Table 3.7).

Since the introduction of the European System of Central Banks (ESCB) there has been a common monetary policy and a *common money market* in Europe. The most significant money market segments are the unsecured deposit market, the short-term repo market and the swap market (Figure 3.4). All three differ in their conditions for providing short-term finance: in the *unsecured deposit market*, banks exchange short-term liquidity without the guarantee of collateral. Banks able to offer collateral may turn to the market for short-term repurchase agreements, or *repos*. In the *swap market*, participants take advantage of individual differences in the conditions they get exchanging fixed for floating interest rate payments. In 1999, unsecured deposits accounted for 53% of the money market in the euro area, foreign currency swaps for 23% and repos for 24%.

The traditional markets for money, credit and foreign exchange described in this section are the main targets of financial innovation today, in an attempt to overcome related inefficiencies and circumvent existing financial regulations. All these markets have one common characteristic in that they establish *individual borrower–lender relations* whose claims on one another, as described, are usually neither transferable nor tradable. This differs markedly from a second category of markets, securities.

3.2.2 Securities

In securities markets, assets and liabilities are traded, anonymity is the rule and ownership may change frequently. One distinction made is between *primary and secondary markets*. In primary markets, new securities are issued for cash while in secondary markets existing ones are sold by one investor to another. There are two major forms of capital provision in these markets, differing by the status of those providing the finance: equities, i.e. claims to share in the net income and assets of a corporation, and fixed-income securities. The latter include, among others, bonds, notes, bills and short-term commercial paper (Table 3.8).

Table 3.7 Foreign exchange turnover by country and currency in April 2001* (daily averages in billions of US dollars)

Country	Total	US dollar	Euro
Austria	7950	6670	5594
Belgium	10051	8815	6010
Denmark	23294	19473	7920
Finland	1597	1211	1336
France	47972	44466	34917
Germany	88469	75808	56368
Greece	4778	3220	3994
Ireland	8287	6925	5800
Italy	16950	14060	12948
Luxembourg	12908	11233	7840
Netherlands	29985	25565	22247
Norway	12841	11282	4266
Portugal	1708	1263	1461
Spain	7579	6919	6583
Sweden	24076	15297	7723
Switzerland	70824	60793	31571
Turkey	1042	993	704
UK	504429	462094	207268
Czech Republic	2028	1357	1036
Hungary	581	401	468
Poland	7534	5346	291
Slovakia	676	572	321
Slovenia	91	9	50

* As two currencies are involved in each transaction, the sum in individual currencies is twice the total reported turnover.
Source: Bank for International Settlements (2001) *Triennial Central Bank Survey: Foreign Exchange and Derivatives Market Activity in 2001*, Basle, March 2001, Annex Table E.4.

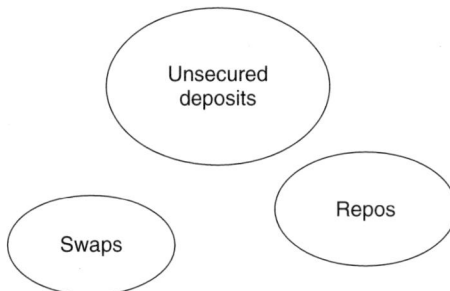

Figure 3.4   Money market segments in the Euro area

Table 3.8 Fixed-income markets

		Market	Features	Issuers
Long term		Bonds	Long-term obligations to make a series of fixed payments	Governments, firms
		Convertibles	Bonds that can be swapped for equity at pre-specified conditions	Firms
		Asset-backed securities	Securitised 'receivables' presenting future streams of payments	Financial institutions, firms
		Preferred stock, subordinated debt	Debt and equity hybrids	Firms
Medium term		Notes	Medium-term obligations	Governments
		Floating-rate notes	Medium-term instruments with interest rates based on LIBOR or another index	Firms
Short term		Bills	Short-term obligations	Governments
		Commercial paper	Short-term debt instruments	Firms
		Certificates of deposit	Short-term debt instruments	Banks

(a)   Fixed-income markets

In *fixed-income markets*, in principle a loan is granted to those in need of finance and this loan is securitised and traded in secondary markets. Nevertheless, the status of the holder of the security remains that of a lender, who is entitled to a set amount of interest payments at periodic intervals and who, at maturity, has the right of a return of the money. These products are claims on some *nominal* amount of debt.

As in the money and credit markets, a distinction is made between short-term and longer term instruments. *Short-term* ones include government securities, i.e. Treasury bills with maturities of up to one year, and private securities such as commercial paper (CP) and certificates of deposit (CDs). CDs are issued by banks, while CP are short-term securities issued by corporations.

Throughout the euro area, the supply of *Treasury bills* is unevenly distributed. At the start of Stage Three of the European Monetary Union there were only four significant and relatively mature markets, in Belgium, France, Italy and Spain, that had substantial amounts outstanding, conducted regular auctions and had a primary dealership system, that is a system of selected credit institutions authorised to buy and sell original issuance of government securities in direct dealing with the Treasury. In Germany, there are regular quarterly auctions for 'Bubills', but outstanding volumes and issuance remain comparatively small. Since German securities play a benchmark role in other market segments in the euro area, this is a considerable impediment to the development of the euro Treasury bill market and also helps explain why non-European investors tend to stay out of this market.

Before the introduction of the common currency, *CDs* and *CP* were instruments that, in Europe, were rarely used. Only very large European firms operating internationally issued securitised money market instruments for short-term financial operations. At the end of the first half of 1999, the amount of CDs outstanding in the euro area was €226 billion, that of CP €86 billion. By comparison, the figures for the United States at the same time were €977 billion and €249 billion, respectively. 53% of all CDs and CP in the euro area were concentrated in one country – France.

Recently, however, it has been possible to see a changing trend in issuing activities, with privately issued securities overtaking the short-term government paper market. This has four main reasons: one is the direct influence of the euro on firms' financial environment that has fostered the growth of the CP market. The second is a rise in mergers and acquisitions that were to some extent financed by CP issuance. Third, the attractiveness of the euro market as a whole has encouraged non-resident issuers to enter it and establish regular issuing activity. And fourth, the CP market has benefited from an overall tendency towards securitisation and a rising preference for collateralised lending.

CDs and CP are not standardised; issues are often tailor-made to meet the needs of investors, indicating their importance in replacing bank loans in a changed regulatory environment. The most common maturities are three, six and 12 months, but shorter maturities are also common, notably in France. In some countries, CP issuance is part of the business relation between banks and corporations and banks are the main buyers of CP. This explains why funding is still globally intermediated by banks, with two consequences: one is the very short maturity of most banks' CDs and CP as both appear as an alternative to bank deposits for the investment of temporary liquidity surpluses. The other is the strong relation between the private paper market and other forms of short-term funding such as credit lines.

With the introduction of the euro the second largest market worldwide for long and medium-term *bonds* has emerged in the region. At the beginning of 1999, its volume was almost 50% of the US bond market and 128% of the Japanese one. The most important segment in practically all countries is government bonds, although in Europe, for reasons to be discussed later, their share has diminished gradually over recent years. For the corporate sector in Europe, the impression is very much the same as for short-term maturities: as a rule, only large firms with high ratings issue corporate bonds. A comparison with the US market shows that there is still a considerable growth potential in this respect (Table 3.9).

In general, compared to markets for short-term debt, risks in the bond market are high, in particular the risk of defaults. In order to assess these risks, bonds are rated by investment advisory firms or *rating agencies* (Appendix D). The biggest three worldwide are Moody's Investors Service, Standard & Poor's Corporation and Fitch. The higher the default risk, the

Table 3.9   Corporate bond issues classified by ratings[1]

Rating	Europe	US
Aaa/Aa	72	12
A	15	28
Baa	5	22
Sub-Baa	8	38
Total market volume[2]	598	510

[1] 1997–July 1998, in percent, excluding financial institutions.
[2] In billions of US dollars.
Source: Sallard, Delphine (1999) Risk capital markets, a key to job creation in Europe. From fragmentation to integration. *Euro Paper No. 32*, Brussels: European Commission, Figure 6.

higher the *risk premium* the debtor has to pay. *Investment-grade* securities have a relatively low risk. Bonds with low ratings are called speculative-grade or *junk bonds*.

Firms that have sunk from investment-grade to junk are also called *'fallen angels'*. Becoming a fallen angel matters because it may increase a firm's refinancing cost dramatically. The reason is that, for institutional investors in particular, there are asset-allocation rules that prevent them from buying bonds lacking an investment-grade rating. As a consequence, mere rumours that a firm may lose its investment-grade status may considerably increase the rate of interest it must pay on new debt.

In national and international financial markets, bonds serve many *purposes*:

- Investors hold them because of their low risk profile and long maturities.
- Government bonds are widely used as hedging instruments, in the expectation that their development may compensate for losses in other markets.
- Investment funds often take short positions on some types of bonds betting that their price will fall and, at the same time, take long positions on other securities whose prices should rise.
- Macro funds which base investments on expected changes in global economies instead of focusing on individual firms and industries, speculate in currency, equity and bond movements.
- Developments in bond markets also affect mortgage funds as the amount of income owners of mortgage securities receive changes with fluctuations in bond yields.
- In addition, there are managed futures funds, which use statistical models to track market trends; their performance also depends on bond market developments.

In national markets government bonds usually serve as *benchmarks*. As a rule, benchmark status is highly attractive to issuers because it reduces borrowing cost. Markets for benchmark securities are characterised by low risks, highly efficient functioning and a high degree of liquidity making fund raising comparatively cheap.

Government debt is special in many respects; it is considered to be essentially free of the risk of default. Trading is facilitated by the often large amount of debt outstanding and the fungibility of issues. Large borrowing needs and a long life enable governments to offer a wider range of maturities than many other borrowers which, in turn, facilitates the construction of yield curves. And, as a rule, in advanced economies well-developed repo and derivatives markets exist for government securities, allowing market participants to take short and long positions that reflect their expectations of future interest rate movements.

In addition, securities with benchmark status provide a couple of *positive externalities*. Besides serving as orientation for pricing and quoting yields on other securities, and as hedging instruments, they are the most common form of collateral in financial markets; investors tend to choose them as 'safe havens' during periods of financial turmoil. In addition, the infrastructure of government securities markets, including the legal and regulatory framework, trade execution arrangements and clearing and settlement systems, are considered as enhancing the development of non-government markets. This is one reason why, for example, governments with a history of financial surpluses such as Hong Kong, Norway and Singapore were issuing debt even when it was unnecessary.

For longer maturities, the private *repo market* bridges the gap between the money and bond markets; in this market, longer term liquidity is provided in exchange for securities. Market participants are banks, corporations and institutional investors; repos play an important role in portfolio decisions, allow efficient management of liquidity and help avoid possible squeezes in derivatives trading.

In recent years, bond markets have gained some impetus from the growing interest of investors in hybrid equities in the form of *convertible bonds*. These initially have a bond structure but offer the option of being converted into equity if share prices reach a certain level; investors pay for the call option by forgoing some interest on the debt. The main determinant of the value of the option is the volatility of the underlying asset over the life of the option: the more volatile the price of the share, the more the option is worth.

Hedge Funds

Hedge funds are private investment funds that take highly leveraged speculative positions or engage in arbitrage, i.e. in the exploitation of price differences in different markets. Although, in recent years, some of them have set up operations in London, Paris and elsewhere, their roots are in the United States, where they have a long history; the oldest is AR Jones, founded in 1949.

It is the high leverage and a lack of regulation – most of them are located in offshore places such as the British West Indies and the Dutch Antilles – that distinguish these funds from other institutional investors. Hedge funds were brought to public consciousness with the currency turmoils in Europe in September 1992 when George Soros' Quantum Fund became 'the villain of the piece' (Copeland 2000) in which the British pound was forced out of the Exchange Rate Mechanism. During the EMS crisis, the Quantum Fund group was reported as having established a short sterling position of $15 billion that made a profit of $1 billion out of sterling's fall with a $10 billion 'bet' on it. When the pound left the system within a few days its rate fell by more than 10%. In those days, fund traders could become very rich very quickly. For example, in 1993, one UK hedge fund manager, in his first year on the job, was said to have made more than $30 million. These and other success stories created some lasting myths around hedge funds and the men running them. However, hedge funds are dwarfed by other institutional investors such as pension funds or mutual funds. For example, in the third quarter of 1997, at the height of the Asian crisis, their capital was some $100 billion, compared to the more than $20,000 billion held by other institutional investors.

Convertibles allow companies to raise money by issuing equity without tapping the stock markets directly (which might upset existing shareholders) and to reduce their interest payments on debt. Major investors in convertibles are *international hedge funds* engaged in convertible-bond arbitrage. They buy the convertibles and sell the debt component, keeping the call option. They then sell the company's shares short – they do not own the securities they sell, but plan to buy them at a later stage – giving them a hedge against movements in the share price. As the share price moves up and down, the fund adjusts its short position, a tactic known as delta hedging. The hedge fund makes money if the shares turn out to be more volatile than was assumed by the issuer of the convertible (Figure 3.5).

With a decline in the commercial paper market in 2000 and 2001, a special form of convertible bond, known as *quasi-commercial paper*, has become increasingly popular. This comes with a put option allowing investors to force companies to repurchase the bonds at their original price at a fixed future date. However, these instruments have turned out to cut both ways. When issuers' prospects worsen and share prices fall, the likelihood of conversion

Buy ...   Sell ...

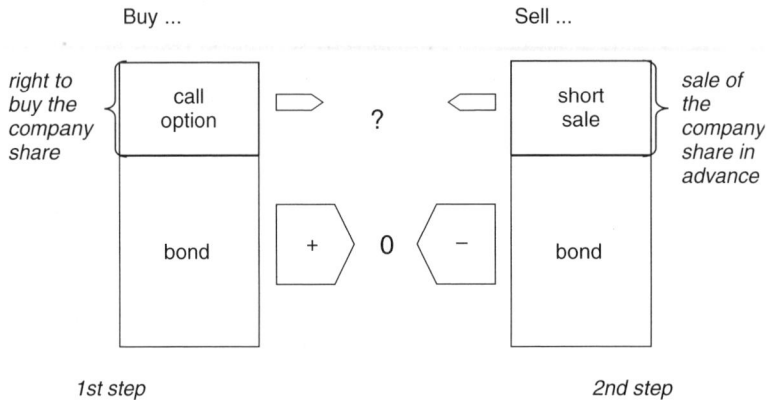

right to buy the company share — call option ⇨ ? ⇦ short sale — *sale of the company share in advance*

bond + 0 − bond

1st step   *2nd step*

Figure 3.5   Convertible-bond arbitrage

of debt into equity declines and bondholders become less willing to keep the bonds. In addition, credit considerations may make them want to sell anyway. This means additional strains in a situation where a company's need for cash is growing and sources are drying up.

Another form of finance of growing importance in Europe is *asset-backed securities* (ABS). This is a way to raise funds from the bond market by securitising 'receivables', claims of seller firms that arise from the sale of goods and services and present future streams of payments. Asset-backed securities add value by making otherwise illiquid assets liquid, and greatly broadening the pool of potential investors both domestically and globally. Examples are credit card revenues, residential mortgages, loans made to customers and even goods such as barrels of maturing whisky. Investors prefer ABS transactions because they are highly rated – often they are assigned Triple A credit ratings. For them the advantage is twofold: an additional level of security from owning bonds backed by assets and higher interest payments than on similarly-rated regular bonds.

Asset-backed securities were one of the most dynamic markets in the US for almost 30 years. In Europe, however, with one exception there have been no successes so far. There are a variety of reasons, such as fragmentation of national markets, regulators and taxation barriers, and the lack of interest of large institutional investors for risk considerations. However, even in the US, investors have become more cautious recently in reaction to downgradings and a number of bankruptcies among ABS issuers. For example, according to the rating agency Moody's, in the first half of 2002 there were 502 downgrades in the ABS market, but only eight upgrades. Most of the downgrades were in *collateralised debt obligations* (CDO) backed by bonds, loans or derivatives with poor performance. Other securities downgraded were backed by franchise loans, aircraft leases and mutual fund fees. Investors worldwide also increasingly worry about securities backed by complex or unusual assets. One example, to which the bankruptcy of healthcare financier National Century in autumn 2002 drew attention, is securitisation of healthcare receivables. The latter are expected billing payments paid by more than one entity and the payment cycle is complex because payments securitised have a life of only about 90 days. As a consequence, these receivables are hard to value and to track.

The one ABS market segment which is growing strongly in Europe is the *Pfandbrief* market. Originating in Germany, from where it spread to other European countries, this is a market in bonds backed by mortgages or local government loans and usually issued by state-controlled savings banks and mortgage institutions. Pfandbrief debt, which in bond market statistics is counted as part of the corporate bond sector, is highly rated and combines low levels of risk with comparatively high returns. The market has achieved its current predominant status not least as a result of the introduction of the Jumbo Pfandbrief in 1995, with a minimum issuance volume of €500 million. At the end of 2000, with business worth more than €1000 billion, the Pfandbrief market had become the largest bond market in Europe, exceeding the total amount of sovereign debt outstanding of France, Germany and Italy combined.

In addition to these debt instruments there are *medium-term notes* issued by firms and governments. With the rise of the Euromarkets, companies started to issue *floating-rate notes*. The interest rate on these instruments is not fixed, but is adjusted at regular intervals, based on the London-Interbank Offered Rate (LIBOR) or another index.

(b)   Equity markets

In contrast to markets for fixed-income instruments, in *equity markets* the provider of the money becomes one of the owners of the firm. In general, there are different forms of ownership (Table 3.10). In particular small and medium-sized companies – but also some very large firms – are organised as partnerships or private limited companies whose shares are not traded publicly. In these cases, in contrast to exchange-traded shares, liability may possibly not even be limited to the amount of capital contributed but may extend to total private wealth.

In principle, these activities are part of the wide spectrum of *private equity*, a form of equity investments made through private placements. This category has gained importance in Europe among big institutional investors since the late 1990s. The most prominent forms are venture capital investment and leveraged buyouts. *Venture capital firms* are financial intermediaries that pool their partners' resources, using the funds to help entrepreneurs start up new businesses. *Leveraged buyouts* spread from the US to Europe in the 1980s; 'leveraged', in this context, means 'geared up' and refers to the relationship between the company's own funds and borrowed money. The principle behind is that the purchase of a (listed) company is financed with a small proportion of share capital and a large proportion (80% or more) of debt provided by banks and others. In these cases, interest charges absorb

Table 3.10   Equity markets

Market	Features	Investors
Stock market	Corporate ownership	Firms, financial and non-financial institutions, individuals
Preferred stock	Hybrid security combining features of debt and equity	Financial and non-financial institutions, individuals
Private equity	Investments made through private placements, organisation as partnerships or private limited companies	Venture capital firms, institutional investors, wealthy individuals

most of the profits and there are great pressures to dispose of parts of the businesses to raise cash, thereby reducing borrowings, as quickly as possible. In Europe, where the concept of private equity investment is only slowly gaining ground, the main sources of private equity funds are pension funds, insurance companies and banks, many of them from the United States.

What is traded on organised equity markets is shares of *public limited companies* or *stock corporations*. As in the bond markets, activities here are not limited to national investments. In Europe, there is a long tradition of *international* or *cross-border equity investing*. Years ago investors tended to follow the expansion of empire; these days, above all, the incentives are twofold. Either there are *expected value gains* resulting from inefficient or segmented markets in foreign countries, or the motive for investing abroad is *diversification* in order to reduce risk for a given level of returns – or increase returns for a given level of risk – along the lines of modern portfolio theory.

Some corporations are listed on more than one exchange: in Europe, there is fierce competition between major stock exchanges which strive to attract foreign listings in order to increase trading volumes and business opportunities to exploit scale economies. As a rule, companies *listing abroad* are expecting to benefit from securing cheap capital for new investment, preparing for foreign acquisitions or enhancing their reputation.

Table 3.11 shows the comparative advantages and disadvantages of debt instruments and equity. Unlike in fixed-income markets, in equity markets there is *no time limit* to the financial engagement. If the investor wants her money back she has to sell the shares in the secondary market at a price that is not predictable. If the firm goes bankrupt, she risks losing the money invested. The owner of an equity share may receive dividends or distributions denominated in nominal values, but what the share truly represents is a claim on the *real* assets of the firm and all accruing cash flows once all creditors have been paid.

Loans and bonds, but also medium-term and short-term notes, bills and comparable instruments, are *external funds* – outside claims that need to be serviced with interest paid at regular intervals. In contrast, equity investments are a firm's own *capital*. The firm keeps the right to decide whether to pay dividends or not, and stock markets, or, more generally, the interplay of supply and demand, decide on nominal value. As a rule, to equity investors returns earned from dividends are far less important than expected value gains.

Table 3.11   Debt versus equity

	Debt	Equity
Characteristic	Borrower–lender relation, fixed maturities	Ownership, no time limit
Advantages		
• for the firm	Predictability, independence from shareholders' influence	Flexibility, low cost of finance, reputation
• for the investor	Low risk	High expected return
Disadvantages		
• for the firm	Debt servicing obligation	Shareholder dependence, short-sightedness, market volatility influencing management decisions
• for the investor	Low returns	High risk

A hybrid between these two categories is *subordinated debt*, which in a company's capital structure ranks between shareholder funds and senior debt, that is, for interest and repayment it comes after all other borrowings of the company. This means that for issuers it is a more expensive source of funding than senior debt. Its attractiveness is partly explained by the fact that it is treated by rating agencies and regulators as shares rather than debt, thus supporting the firm's capital base. For investors it promises higher returns than senior debt of comparable credit quality.

A major driving force in falling stock markets in particular is *short selling*, i.e. the selling of stocks the investor does not own in the hope to buy them back later at a lower price. Thus, short selling allows an investor to earn profits from falling prices. Usually, this involves an arrangement with a broker to borrow the securities that are to be sold and later replace them by the purchased ones. This explains the role of *securities lending* in the markets. Long-term owners of shares such as pension funds and life insurers earn valuable fees from lending to hedge funds and other investors engaged in short selling.

Short-selling is but one forward looking activity in financial markets. Others are found in the derivatives markets.

3.2.3 Derivatives

Derivatives differ from both credit and capital market instruments, in that they are financial contracts whose value is closely related to, and largely determined by, the value of a related instrument. This can be a security, but also a currency, an index, a commodity or any other item the contracting parties agree upon.

There are three broad categories of financial derivatives: forward contracts, swaps and options (Table 3.12). Common to all of them is that they are *forward-looking transactions* tied to an underlying instrument or – as, for example, in the case of stock index futures – to a bundle of instruments.

Table 3.12 Derivative markets

Category	Features	Advantages/Disadvantages
Forwards/Futures	Agreements to buy or sell an asset at an agreed-upon price for future delivery	Hedge instrument, for speculative purposes in some markets only for actors without direct access to the spot and swap markets, low flexibility, low leverage, comparatively costly
Swaps	Agreement to exchange two financial instruments for a specific period and reverse that exchange at the end of the period	Allows exploitation of individual comparative advantages in different markets, hedge instrument, speculative tool to prolong open positions in cash or forward markets
Options	Contingent claims, giving the buyer the right to buy or sell a particular financial product in the future at a pre-specified price	High leverage, highest possible flexibility, high uncertainties, asymmetric risk, unreliable pricing models

All three allow an *unbundling of price risks* making it possible to hedge exposures against price movements or to deliberately exploit the inherent profit opportunities thereby giving investors and firms a high flexibility in structuring trading and investment positions. Another common feature is *leverage*. This allows the holder to get the same potential return an outright buyer of the underlying asset may receive for a much smaller investment. The extent of the leverage depends on the instrument chosen.

A *forward contract* is an agreement to buy or sell a specific asset at a predetermined future date and price. Traditionally, forward contracts are traded over the counter (OTC). However, since the early 1970s, there have also been organised futures exchanges. The first was the International Money Market of the Chicago Mercantile Exchange (CME), established in 1972. In Europe, the leading ones are the London International Financial Futures Exchange (LIFFE) and Eurex. *Futures* are standardised exchange-traded forward contracts with comparatively few fixed amounts and maturities: the exchange specifies all contract terms except the price. A trader taking a long position – committing to purchasing the instrument on the delivery date – is buying a contract, a trader taking a short position – committing to delivering the instrument at maturity – is selling the contract.

Futures exist for a wide variety of financial and non-financial products such as currencies, bonds and stock market indices, and also pork bellies, oil platforms and even weather conditions. In Table 3.13, *advantages and disadvantages* of forwards and futures for comparable products are listed. Although information and computer technology have brought dramatic changes in recent years it still holds true that while the futures industry seeks to attract private individuals, forward markets in the same kind of instrument are largely a domain of professional traders and business firms.

As a rule, forwards are tailor-made, with individual contract terms varying widely. This makes them highly illiquid and hard to unwind before maturity. By contrast, on a futures exchange all a trader needs to do to unwind a position is to buy or sell a respective, compensating contract. In traditional forward markets counter party risk is high; on futures exchanges, by comparison, it is low because for each contract between the buyer and the seller there is a clearing house acting as counter party for both of them.

There are several reasons why trading in traditional forward markets still dominates despite the advantages described. One is transaction volumes: in forward markets, the risk that large trades trigger reverse price movements is lower. Another is the anonymity of OTC trading. A third is the benefits of receiving a tailor-made contract. Standardised contracts do not only come at a cost when they do not fully meet investors' need; if they are intended as hedging instruments they may leave the buyer or seller exposed to a considerable amount of risk.

Table 3.13   Forwards and futures in comparison

Characteristic	Forwards	Futures
Contracts	Tailor-made	Standardised
Trading places	Inter-bank market, OTC	Centralised exchanges
Transaction volumes	Large	Comparatively small
Maturities	Up to several years	Short term
Unwinding of positions	Difficult to impossible, expensive	Easy
Market liquidity	Low	High
Counter parties	Varying	Clearing house

A *swap* is an exchange of two financial instruments for a specific period and a reversal of that exchange at the end of the period. In the foreign exchange market it may consist either of a combination of a spot and a forward leg or of two forward trades with differing maturities. For example, in a yen/dollar foreign exchange swap a dealer may buy the yen for delivery in two days at an agreed spot rate, simultaneously selling it back for delivery in a week, a month, or three months.

Swaps may be used to exploit *comparative advantages* that individual participants have in different markets. For example, assume that a Spanish firm faces a higher interest cost for borrowing in the US dollar market than a German firm, while the German firm may only receive less favourable conditions than the Spanish one in the euro market. In this case, it may pay for both of them to borrow in the currency in which they face the lower cost and then simply exchange currencies for the period of the contracts. Apparently, these opportunities always arise when financial markets are *segmented*, evaluating firms differently. This may happen for various reasons; inefficiency and lack of transparency are two of them. However, yet another explanation is saturation: investors tend to hold a portfolio of assets from a broad range of borrowers, setting limits to the share for individual ones. An issuer who has not saturated the market in this sense may enjoy better conditions than another.

Swaps are also used for several other purposes: combined with an outright position they may serve to assume, or hedge against, market risks, offering much higher flexibility for certain market participants than other available strategies. Again, currency markets may serve as an example; a foreign exchange swap is defined as an exchange of two currencies for a specific period and a reversal of that exchange at the end of the period. It consists either of a combination of a spot and a forward leg or of two forward trades with different maturities. For example, a British bank buys euros against US dollars for spot value – with delivery within two working days – and at the same time agrees to buy back the dollars against euros in three months. This foreign exchange swap *per se* is by definition without risk: it contains both a long and short position of equal amount in the same currency and of the same maturity. However, in currency markets this type of contract is frequently used to prolong an open position, either for hedging purposes or to exploit expected price movements. A trader with an open minus position in euro may buy the currency spot, thereby closing the initial position at maturity and at the same time sell the euros again to the same counter party against dollars for a future date. This new open currency position may serve to hedge an existing exposure or to benefit from an expected rise in the exchange rate. Keeping maturities short – the bulk of foreign exchange swaps is for seven days or less – and renewing swaps continuously, traders gain high flexibility to react to market events (Figure 3.6).

Options are contracts sold for a premium that give the buyer the right, but not the obligation, to buy (in case of a call option) or sell (in case of a put option) a financial asset in the future at a specified price. In contrast to other financial instruments, options are so-called *contingent claims* based on the insurance principle with an asymmetry in the related risks. For instance, the worst that can happen to the buyer of a call option is that in not exercising her option (if the expected price movement does not take place) she loses the premium. In contrast, for the seller who has the obligation to deliver if the option is exercised, in principle, the risk is unlimited if he does not already own the underlying asset and so needs to buy it in the market.

Option trading has inherent uncertainties that distinguish it from other derivatives markets resulting from the way in which options are valued. Standard approaches in one form or another rely on a formula developed by Black, Merton and Scholes in the early 1970s for the stock markets, which subsequently found many applications in other markets as well.

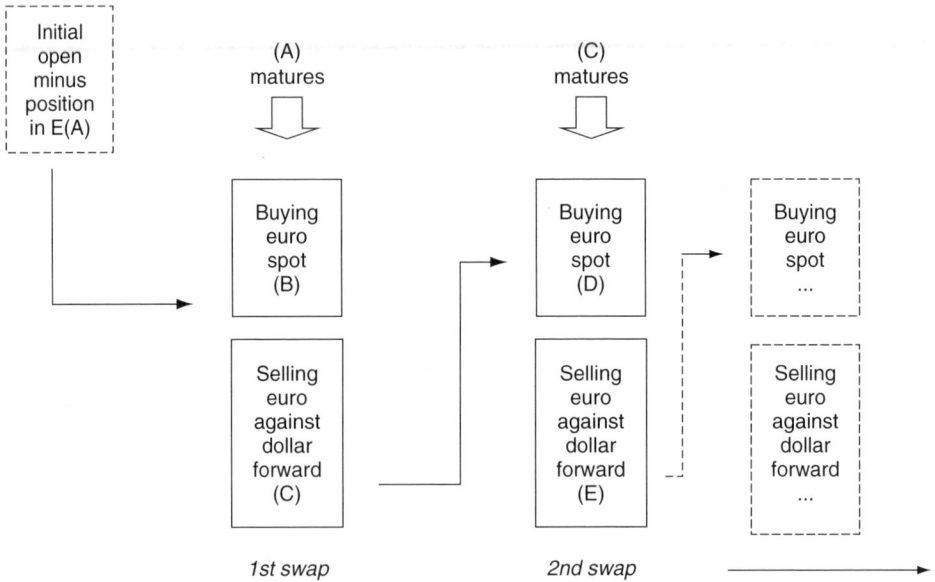

Initial position (A) was established to hedge expected euro cash inflow that will not arrive in subsequent stages, requiring prolongation of the hedge ....

With each new swap, the initial open position is closed with the spot leg, and re-established with the forward leg

Figure 3.6   Hedging with a foreign exchange swap

According to this formula the value of a stock option depends on the share price today, its volatility, a risk-free interest rate, time to maturity, strike price at which the option is exercised, and the probability that it will be exercised as described by a normal distribution function. In principle, all components of the formula can be observed – except volatility which, in practice, poses financial traders and analysts insurmountable difficulties.

These difficulties result from the fact that, as a rule, financial time series have a non-constant variance – the standard measure of volatility. Daily, monthly and yearly data, and data for different time periods, give a different picture of volatility. One solution is to calculate 'implied volatilities' derived from observed options prices of other market participants. However, implied volatilities do not always exist and if they do they may include price components, such as transaction costs or risk premiums, that are hard to judge. Another problem is that implied volatilities for options that are far in or out of the money – with the exercise price highly above or below the asset's value – have much higher implied volatilities, a phenomenon known as the 'volatility smile' (Figure 3.7).

Experienced traders have various means to cope with the resulting uncertainties, not relying on one formula alone, but errors occur frequently – at times with dramatic consequences for the firms. In addition, there are two assumptions on which options pricing models are based. These are continuous trading and the absence of large price jumps. However, experience shows that in practice these two are regularly violated, and as a result models become particularly unreliable in periods of market stress and low liquidity when they are most needed.

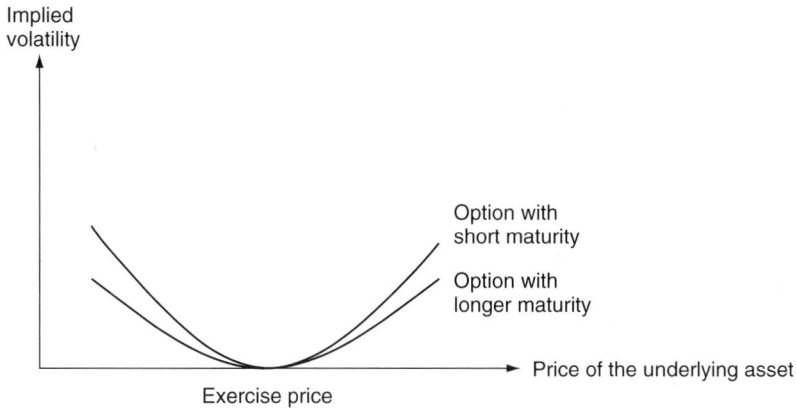

Figure 3.7   The smile effect

The late 1990s saw a dramatic rise in the volume of two kinds of derivatives in the European markets in reaction to financial crises, repeated market failures and changing investor preferences. One is *interest rate swaps*: these are contracts that allow parties to exchange streams of interest payments. The pricing of swaps is typically based on the London-Interbank Offered Rate, LIBOR, and for euro-denominated instruments on EURIBOR. The rise of these instruments is partly explained by the introduction of the euro and the resulting process of integration and standardisation. Interest rate swaps increased by more than 60% during the first year after the introduction of the euro. Above all, the EURIBOR three-month futures contract, traded simultaneously on the LIFFE in London, the Eurex in Frankfurt and the French Matif, became very liquid, representing more than 80% of the total daily LIFFE trading volume. In a sense, the contract inherited the success of the former 'Eurodem' LIFFE contract.

However, market growth is in parts also the result of the rising interest of market participants in off-balance-sheet instruments. Swaps *spare capital* in not consuming large amounts of credit limits and, as a consequence, are increasingly replacing deposits as a source of funding and as a means of establishing hedge positions in fixed-income instruments. Still another explanation is the deficiencies of traditional hedge instruments that has become apparent in recent years. Until the late 1990s, dealers routinely hedged positions in non-government securities with government bonds and related derivatives, taking advantage of the usually stable relationship between yields in both markets. Then a number of events highlighted the risks of this strategy. One was the near-collapse of Long-Term Capital Management (LTCM) in September 1998; another was occasional squeezes in German government bond futures contracts. These and other events demonstrated that the features accounting for the uniqueness of government bonds – quality and liquidity – may cause their prices and those of other credit products to move out of sync, during periods of financial turmoil in particular. This reinforced the search for new hedging vehicles and made market participants increasingly turn to derivative products to construct yield curves; one obvious solution was interest rate swaps.

In principle, an interest rate swap is a contractual agreement between two counter parties to exchange a fixed rate instrument for a floating rate instrument. No principal amount changes hands. Instead, basically, a series of payments is calculated by applying a fixed interest rate to a notional principal amount, and another stream of payments using a floating rate of interest, and then both are exchanged. Interest rate swaps are used by a wide range of financial intermediaries and corporations, government agencies and sovereign states, for a variety of reasons. These include the reduction of funding costs, the hedging of interest rate exposures and the creation of types of assets not obtainable otherwise. Between 1998 and 2000 the interest rate swap market expanded by 34% in notional terms to $48.8 trillion. In the euro area, average daily transactions grew by 72% in the second quarter of 1999 compared to the fourth quarter 1998. The average transaction size increased to €50 million with amounts of €5 billion no longer being exceptional.

The emergence of *swaps as benchmarks* added a new element of credit risk. Usually, benchmark government debt has a triple-A credit rating. In December 2002, Germany caught the headlines when its status as benchmark in the euro zone debt market came under threat after leading rating agencies expressed concerns about the country's fiscal position. By contrast, banks in the LIBOR contributor panels are mostly rated double A. This can be an advantage: swap rates tend to move more closely with prices of other credit products, including during periods of financial turmoil.

Another advantage is the *absence of an underlying asset*. There are no limits to entering into swap contracts, and reverse price movements due to supply and demand imbalances are rare. However, there are also disadvantages that help explain why, so far, government securities have not lost their dominance. Debt issued by the government of an industrial country is still one of the most liquid instruments. As a consequence, transaction costs for hedging with government securities are often lower than those associated with other hedges, in particular over shorter periods where the risk of widening spreads between government and non-government securities (credit spread risk) is low. Also, swaps have a credit risk in that the counter party may default at the end of the agreement.

Another instrument of growing importance in Europe is *credit derivatives*. Originating in the early 1990s, by 1997 the total global credit derivatives market was $180 billion. In 2001, it was over $1 trillion, with London and New York as the main centres of activity. There are estimates that in 2004 this number will have risen to $4.8 trillion. The most common form of credit derivative is the *credit default swap*, a contract which enables one party to buy protection against the risk of default of an asset paying a fee or premium for the cover, until a credit event occurs or – if this does not happen – until maturity. *Credit events* include bankruptcy, failure to pay interest or debt and restructuring of obligations, but the documentation of these instruments, and of what counts as a credit event, is still fraught with uncertainties.

Market participants on the demand side are, above all, banks that have made a loan or investors who have bought a bond, searching to reduce their exposure by buying credit insurance. Credit derivatives are particularly popular with banks that have a long-running relationship with clients they are reluctant to offend by selling on part or all of their exposure. Instead, they pay a premium in return for the seller of a credit derivative. The latter is often an insurance company or a hedge fund. However, as the market has developed, credit derivatives have moved beyond simply serving as hedging instruments; they are traded in their own right, too, and used as the basis for more complex financial instruments. In a sense, they have become 'commoditised'. As a result, the market has become very liquid with competitive quotes available from most investment banks. This means prices in this market are often a truer reflection of risks associated with a particular lender or investor than credit margins.

Although the market for credit derivatives is still only a fraction of the size of the interest rate swap market it has been growing strongly, rising by 25% to $2,690 billion worldwide in the first six months of 2003, compared with 24% growth in interest derivatives to a total of $123,900 billion. By 2004, the market for portfolio products, known as *collateralised debt obligations* (CDOs), is expected to increase to about a quarter of the global market in credit derivatives. These come in two variants: traditional 'cash flow' CDOs are securities backed by pools of debt such as high-yield corporate bonds and loans. They have existed since the 1980s and are still the dominant variety in the US. As a rule, a *special-purpose entity* (SPE) is set up, which issues securities to investors, using the money to establish a portfolio of assets. The returns these assets generate are passed through to the investors. The securities are broken up into *different tranches* representing different levels of risk and reward. As a broad range of assets of different quality are required for diversification purposes, the top tranche of a CDO may achieve a triple-A credit rating even though the individual assets have a far lower ranking.

In Europe, *synthetic CDOs* dominate, with London as the market leader. Synthetic CDOs use credit derivatives instead of bonds and loans. In the simplest form, the SPE issues notes to investors and sells credit protection on a notional 'reference pool' of assets. The buyer of the credit protection pays a premium to the SPE that is passed through to the investors. One explanation for London's worldwide dominance in this area is that, compared to the US, in Europe the market for bonds from which a CDO pool can be assembled is much smaller and more transparent. One advantage of synthetic CDOs is the high degree of flexibility they offer. Instead of being sold to a large number of investors, they are increasingly customised for one big client such as an insurance company or pension fund, who wants exposure to credit markets or to hedge its bond portfolio. Another advantage is investors' influence over the assets held in the portfolios: compared to traditional CDOs with synthetic CDOs, investors are much more involved in the profile of the risks they are assuming and the selection of credits in the reference portfolios.

The rise of interest rate swaps and credit derivatives in recent years indicates how structures and preferences in the markets are changing. They are part of a consolidation process which, in Europe, is altering financial systems, depriving them of many of their special characteristics and making them more integrated into global markets. However, as becomes apparent in the next chapter, 'plus ça change, plus c'est la même chose' and the systems' fundamental nature remains largely unchanged, reflecting persistent European institutional influences and European historic legacies.

Summary

- Distinguishing between non-tradable and non-transferable products, securities and derivatives allows for the unique set of opportunities and risks in each of these categories.
- Markets for non-tradables include traditional money and credit markets and the foreign exchange market, which, nowadays, have become the main targets of financial innovation to overcome inefficiencies and to circumvent existing financial regulation.
- In securities markets, government bonds play a special role, serving as benchmarks for other debt instruments.
- While fixed-income markets establish borrower–lender relations, in equity markets the providers of funds become capital owners.

- Derivatives are traded over the counter and on centralised exchanges with each form having its own advantages and disadvantages.
- Forwards, swaps and options differ with respect to market liquidity, flexibility and expected risks and returns.
- In recent years, there has been a dramatic rise of interest rate swaps and credit derivatives which indicate changing market structures and preferences.

Exercises

1. Describe the main markets for non-tradable financial instruments in Europe.
2. Bonds as benchmarks in financial markets – characteristics and advantages.
3. Discuss the advantages and disadvantages of

   – private equity
   – convertible bonds
   – asset-backed securities

   and give examples.
4. Describe the various forms of private equity and explain their importance in European financial markets.
5. Describe various techniques of forward looking financial market activities and their relevance in European markets and discuss possible implications

   – for risk-averse investors
   – of market volatility
   – of monetary policy.

6. Discuss the role of swaps in financial markets and give examples.

Additional Links and References

Books on international financial markets are:

Dufey, Gunter and Ian Giddy (1994) *The International Money Market*, Englewood Cliffs, NJ: Prentice Hall.
Levich, Richard M. (1998) *International Financial Markets – Prices and Policies*, Boston: Irwin McGraw-Hill.
Melvin, Michael (2004) *International Money and Finance*, Boston, MA: Pearson Addison Wesley.
Walmsley, Julian (1996) *International Money and Foreign Exchange Markets: An Introduction*, Chichester: John Wiley & Sons Ltd.

Publications about the foreign exchange market in theory and practice include:

Copeland, Laurence S. (2000) *Exchange Rates and International Finance*, London: Prentice Hall.
Kettell, Brian (2000) *What Drives the Currency Markets*, London: Prentice Hall.

Bond market developments are discussed in:

Study Group on Fixed Income Markets (2001) The changing shape of fixed income markets, BIS Paper No. 5, October, http://www.bis.org
Turner, Philip (2001) Bond markets in emerging economies: an overview of policy issues, BIS Papers No. 11, December, http://www.bis.org

The implications of 'missing markets' for a financial system with a special focus on the bond markets are described lucidly in:

Herring, Richard and Nathporn Chatusripitak (2001) The case of the missing market: the bond market and why it matters for financial development, Wharton Financial Institutions Center Working Paper 01–08, http://fic.wharton. upenn.edu/fic/papers/01/0108.pdf

There are many excellent publications on derivatives markets and products. Here are two examples:

Hull, John C. (2002) *Options, Futures, and Other Derivatives*, London: Prentice Hall.
Kolb, Robert W. (2002) *Futures, Options, and Swaps*, New York: Blackwell.

A challenging general overview of the derivatives industry is given by:

Steinherr, Alfred (2000) *Derivatives – The Wild Beast of Finance*, Chichester: John Wiley & Sons Ltd.

The role of producer services for financial places is emphasised in:

Sassen, Saskia (1991) *The Global City – New York, London, Tokyo*, Princeton: Princeton University Press.

With the introduction of the euro there has been a flood of research studies, working papers and publications with a special focus on its impact on European financial markets. Here is a short selection:

Galati, Gabriele and Kostas Tsatsaronis (2001) The impact of the euro on Europe's financial markets, BIS Working Paper No. 100, July, http://www.bis.org/publ/work100.pdf
Gros, Daniel and Karel Lannoo (2000) *The Euro Capital Market*, New York: John Wiley & Sons, Inc.
Hartmann, Philipp, Angela Maddaloni and Simone Manganelli (2003): The euro area financial system: structure, integration and policy initiatives, European Central Bank, Working Paper No. 230, http://www.ecb.int/pub/wp/ecbwp230.pdf
Santillán, Javier, Marc Bayle and Christian Thygesen (2000) The impact of the euro on money and bond markets, European Central Bank Occasional Paper No. 1, July, http://www.ecb.int/pub/pdf/scpops/ecbocp1.pdf
Walter, Ingo and Roy Smith (2000) *High Finance in the €uro Zone – Competing in the New European Capital Market*, London: Prentice Hall.

See also Giancarlo Corsetti's web page on the euro:

http://aida.econ.yale.edu/~corsetti/Euro/

For special financial products mentioned in this chapter see:

Kiff, John and Ron Morrow (2000) Credit derivatives, *Bank of Canada Review*, autumn, 3–11, http://www.bank-banque-canada.ca/publications/review/r005-ea.pdf
Mastroeni, Orazio (2001) *Pfandbrief-style Products in Europe*, BIS Paper No. 5, October, http://www.bis.org

A survey of international financial services in London which is regularly updated is:

International Financial Services London (IFSL) (2003) *International Financial Markets in the UK*, http://www.ifsl.org.uk

Regular coverage of markets also can be found in the following journals and periodicals:

The Banker: http://www.thebanker.com/
Euromoney: http://www.Euromoney.com/
OECD: Financial Market Trends

One of the leading centres in Europe for academic research into financial markets is the Financial Markets Group of the London School of Economics:

http://fmg.lse.ac.uk/

An informative annotated link list is provided by the Global Finance site of the International Economics Network, maintained by Jamus Jerome Lim:

http://www.internationaleconomics.net/bizfinance.html#finance

See also the related site on financial research:

http://www.internationaleconomics.net/research-finance.html

A useful link list is the *Worldwide Directory of Finance* jointly sponsored by the Ohio State Department of Finance and the American Finance Association, for locating phone numbers, addresses and home pages of finance faculty in academic institutions and finance professionals in non-academic institutions worldwide:

http://www.cob.ohio-state.edu/fin/findir/

3.3　FINANCIAL SYSTEMS IN EUROPE

These days, the lines between credit, capital and derivatives markets have not only become more and more fuzzy, finance has also become a *high-technology business* where loans, securities, derivatives, and also insurance policies, exchange-traded commodities and other tools are regarded as part of a continuum of products with one characteristic in common: they all *price risks*. Price differences may depend, among other factors, on liquidity and maturity, on market volatility, on the development of another instrument considered as a benchmark, or on individual size and estimates of future costs and returns. In some markets, such as retail housing loans, decision making is still a cumbersome process involving many people and taking into consideration a whole range of individual influences and circumstances. In others, trades are initiated in seconds by computer programs without any human involvement at all.

The changing nature of the financial business has also altered the rationale for the existence of financial institutions. Traditional theories of financial intermediation stress the role of *transaction costs* and *asymmetric information*. Institutions take deposits and channel funds to individuals and firms; evaluating assets gives rise to fixed costs that intermediaries can share, thereby giving them an advantage over individuals. Transaction costs also arise in association with direct finance when the primary securities issued by firms are transformed into indirect financial securities sold to the final investor, or when short-term liabilities to customers are transformed into long-term loans.

Synthetic Assets

Synthetics are securities that allow combinations of assets to be obtained with low transaction costs. Synthetic stocks can be constructed by buying a stock index future contract and a riskless security. Synthetic securities – assets or liabilities – denominated in one currency can be constructed by combining a security denominated in another currency

> with a forward foreign exchange contract of similar maturity and a spot contract. A forward foreign exchange contract that does not exist can be replicated by using a spot contract combined with borrowing and lending in the two currencies involved. A synthetic option is built from a set of transactions replicating a portfolio of the traditional financial claims it corresponds to. Common to all these instruments is that they are so-called *redundant securities*. Their cash payoffs may be replicated by a set of transactions in other financial instruments. Synthetic assets mimic the payoffs, but not necessarily the risk profile of the desired product which, in practice, may differ considerably from those combined. This observation refers to the underlying distribution of returns for various instruments and also to the assumption of continuous price movements and liquid markets that is usually made.

In addition, intermediaries are said to have a comparative advantage in *screening and monitoring* borrowers. In financial markets, information asymmetries are a common phenomenon. As a rule, borrowers have better information about the riskiness of their financial situation and repayment prospects than do their lenders, and managers know more about the profitability of their firm than shareholders and lenders. Information asymmetries may give rise to *adverse selection*: as soon as lenders and shareholders are unable to differentiate between those in search of finance, the average financial conditions available in a market will attract below-average candidates, while those above average may find them inadequate. As a consequence, bad borrowers may crowd out better ones and firms with below-average profitability may come to dominate the market. Information asymmetries offer an explanation for the emergence of financial institutions that represent an attempt to overcome the resulting deficiencies.

In recent years, financial intermediation has become less and less restricted to the traditional bank business. Not only have banks started securitising loans in searching for a way to not keep all the money they lend on their balance sheets, but companies developed their asset management capabilities beyond their core competences and begin widening their activities to the financial realm, so new types of intermediaries have emerged. In addition, today most trading of financial instruments takes place among financial institutions without any customers involved at all.

Some of the changes observed cannot be explained by traditional arguments. For example, although recent advances in information technology have substantially reduced information costs and asymmetries, the need for financial services has not declined to a similar extent – direct lending is still the exception and not the rule. Another unresolved puzzle is the large share of trades among intermediaries. More recent concepts therefore stress the ability to *distribute risks* as an additional rationale for banks. Financial intermediaries transact at near zero cost and can create a large number of synthetic assets through dynamic trading strategies, allowing them to create products with very safe payoffs and/or with varying degrees of complexity according to their own needs and to those of their customers.

Market volumes differ markedly. Among all financial market segments worldwide the foreign exchange market is by far the largest one. To give a few numbers: in 2001, according to a tri-annual survey conducted under the auspices of the Bank for International Settlements (BIS), estimated *daily* global foreign exchange turnover was about $1.2 trillion. This far outweighs the *annual* volume of world merchandise exports of $6 trillion. It is also much larger than *quarterly* foreign consolidated bank claims worldwide, which were $11.3 trillion. The total world market value of domestic equity markets in August 2001 was $27 trillion,

Table 3.14   World financial markets in figures*

Volume of estimated daily global foreign exchange turnover in April 2001	1.2
Foreign consolidated bank claims worldwide, first quarter 2001	11.3
Domestic equity markets, world total of market value, August 2001	27.1
Outstanding value of world bonds markets, June 2001	>29.3
In comparison: world annual merchandise exports for 2001	6.0

* In trillions of US dollars.
Sources: BIS, IFSL, WTO.

Table 3.15   European financial markets in comparison[1]

	UK	France	Germany	US	Japan
Branches and subsidiaries of foreign banks (March 2003)	287	179	129	224	84
Cross-border bank lending (March 2003)	19	6	11	9	9
Foreign equities turnover (January–September 2003)	45	–	3	32	–
Foreign exchange dealing (April 2001)	31	3	5	16	9
Derivatives turnover[2]					
– exchange-traded (January–August 2003)	6	3	13	27	3
– OTC (April 2001)	36	9	13	18	3
International bonds (2002)					
– primary market	60	–	–	–	–
– secondary market	70	–	–	–	–

[1] If not otherwise stated, as percentage share of world total.
[2] Based on the volume of contracts.
Source: IFSL.

while the outstanding value of world bonds markets in June the same year was more than $29 trillion (Table 3.14).

As Table 3.15 demonstrates, in Europe, much of this and other financial activity takes place in London. The *City of London* has by far the highest number of foreign banks and the highest share of equity turnover, foreign exchange dealing and OTC derivatives trading, and it is the most important centre of international bond trading in both primary and secondary markets. Major *financial customers* tend to show similar patterns of centralisation. There are more corporate headquarters in London than in any other European centre: one-third of Fortune Global 500 companies have their European headquarters there, compared with 9% in Paris, 6% in Brussels, 3% in Düsseldorf and 3% in Frankfurt. Over 65% of the Fortune Global 500 companies are represented in London – more than in any other European city.

On the other hand, the table also demonstrates that other places, too, attract a considerable share of international financial institutions and activities, and in some market segments are even taking the lead. This holds true, for example, for exchange-traded derivatives, which are primarily traded in Frankfurt, or (not shown in the table) for mutual fund management, of which the world's second-largest market behind the US is in France. Another example not shown in the table is the insurance industry, which is largely concentrated in Munich where total premium income exceeds those in both New York and London, the Numbers Two and Three, respectively. Dispersion is also observed for the activities of key market firms; while

Table 3.16 Bank-based versus market-based systems in percent

	Germany		US	
	1990	2001	1990	2001
Equities	9	15	25	38
Bonds	27	30	51	46
Bank assets	64	55	24	16
Total	100	100	100	100

Source: Milken Institute.

international treasury and risk management is often centralised in London, and euro foreign exchange, international bond and equity trading and research is mainly based there, other activities are not. Money and government bond trading is more widely spread, and sales teams for non-government bonds and equity sales and M&A are decentralised across the euro area. The tendency towards concentration is rather weak in these cases and, apparently, local factors and the need for proximity to individual markets and customers have a greater influence than in other markets.

In recent years, together with the line between credit and capital markets, the borders between various types of national financial systems in Europe have become blurred, too. Traditionally, a distinction is made between *bank-based systems* and *market-based systems*. In Europe, both can be found: the US and the UK are market-based systems, while France and Germany are examples of bank-based systems.

A look at the relative importance of banks and securities markets in the US and Germany shows the difference (Table 3.16). In the US, banks are relatively unimportant compared to equities and, in particular, bonds, which play by far the largest role. In Germany, the contrary holds: here, apparently, banks are relatively important and bond and equity markets less so. The data also show that, in the 1990s the importance of bank finance has declined in both systems, while the share of equities has risen markedly. This indicates a worldwide structural change in financial markets rather than an adjustment or convergence of systems.

3.3.1 Bank-based Systems

In countries with bank-based systems like Germany, firms' external financial funds are primarily provided by banks with which they have long-term relationships. As a rule, banks are *universal banks* that are allowed to offer a wide range of financial services. Banks take deposits and lend directly to firms and individuals and, at the same time, trade in equities and provide underwriting services. In contrast, in market-based systems, there are more or less strict 'firewalls' separating different kinds of financial services such as taking deposits and granting loans on the one hand and underwriting and trading equities on the other.

However, the lines are not clear-cut and the limit of what is allowed or forbidden varies from country to country. As Table 3.17 demonstrates, in the mid-1990s the differences in various areas of financial business in and outside of Europe have been considerable. Many of these differences still persist, although, over recent years, European countries have experienced some convergence in the course of the implementation of the single market programme, which will be discussed later. The table also shows that among all bank activities, the most

Table 3.17   Permissible banking activities in Europe, the United States and Japan*

	Securities	Insurance	Real estate	Commercial bank investment	Nonfinancial firm investment
Very wide powers					
Austria	UR	PM	UR	UR	UR
Switzerland	UR	PM	UR	UR	UR
United Kingdom	UR	PM	UR	UR	UR
France	UR	PM	PM	UR	UR
Netherlands	UR	PM	PM	UR	UR
Wide powers					
Denmark	UR	PM	PM	RS	UR
Finland	UR	RS	PM	UR	UR
Germany	UR	RS	PM	UR	UR
Ireland	UR	PH	UR	UR	UR
Luxembourg	UR	PM	UR	UR	RS
Portugal	UR	PM	RS	PM	UR
Spain	UR	PM	RS	UR	PM
Somewhat restricted powers					
Italy	UR	PM	RS	RS	RS
Sweden	UR	PM	RS	RS	RS
Belgium	PM	PM	RS	RS	UR
Greece	PM	RS	RS	UR	UR
Restricted powers					
Japan	RS	PH	RS	RS	RS
United States	RS	RS	RS	RS	RS

* As of 1995.
Definitions:
Securities activities include underwriting, dealing and brokering all kinds of securities and all aspects of mutual funds business.
Insurance activities include underwriting and selling of insurance products/services as principal and as agent.
Real estate activities include investment, development and management.
Unrestricted (UR): the full range of activities can be conducted directly in the bank.
Permitted (PM): the full range of activities can be conducted, but some or all only through subsidiaries.
Restricted (RS): less than the full range can be conducted in the bank or its subsidiaries.
Prohibited (PH): the activities cannot be conducted at all.
Source: International Monetary Fund (1997) *International Capital Markets – Developments, Prospects and Key Policy Issues*, Washington, DC, Table 44.

sensitive cases seem to be involvement in real estate business, which is restricted in a large number of countries, and mutual investments, both of banks in non-bank financial firms and vice versa. Other aspects worth mentioning are that for European banks, in contrast to those in the US and Japan, securities trading is widely unrestricted and that, although overall restrictions on insurance are low, they exist among others in the country with some of the largest insurers worldwide, Germany.

A practice which is widespread in bank-based systems – but not exclusive to them – has become known as *relationship pricing*: banks offering credit to investment-grade companies tend to charge very little in the hope of being rewarded later with more lucrative work such as underwriting securities. Often they use this instrument to survive in an ever-increasing investment banking competition worldwide. Many of these commitments are based on the assumption that the related costs are low because companies would rather sell commercial paper than draw down credit lines, which are more expensive. However, this way of competing contains a systemic risk: under changing economic conditions, companies may become unable to raise funds in the markets and the demand for credit may rise. In such a situation, repricing – which would be a normal reaction – may be prevented because the banks find themselves too close to the firms.

Relationship pricing is but one of the inefficiencies inherent in bank-based systems. Admittedly, relationship finance has many *advantages*. On the one hand it is said to promote *cooperative behaviour*, in that a firm that defaults on a bank loan risks being excluded from further credit in the future. A related argument is that in bank-based systems risks can be contained by *intertemporal smoothing*: in accumulating low-risk, liquid assets, banks reduce the need for cross-sectional risk sharing through markets. In a market-based system, competition from financial markets where risks are actively managed and traded would rule out this possibility. A third advantage is *information*: banks in long-term relationships with their customers are necessarily better informed, so goes the argument, than stock market investors.

However, as so often, these arguments have to be put into perspective. The overall efficiency of a bank-based system depends on the extent to which the advantages are realised. In international debates on investor relations and shareholder value, bank-based systems are usually equated with financial backwardness. By most measures financial markets in the US and UK are more developed than in France, and far more developed than in Germany, raising concerns about *corporate governance and control*.

The *German hausbank system* may serve as an example. In Germany, besides lending, there are three kinds of activities that are not reflected in banks' balance sheets which, according to critics, taken together, are giving them an undue scope of influence that has become a source of major inefficiencies over the years:

- First, control of *equity voting rights* by the banks, which allows them to considerably influence the outcome of shareholder meetings. The banks derive their strategic advantage in these meetings not only from direct holdings of equity but also from *proxy votes* from client shareholders.
- Second, banks' substantial representation on firms' *supervisory boards*. Germany has a system of co-determination (*Mitbestimmung*) for companies with more than 2000 employees. These have two boards, the management board and the supervisory board. The latter is the controlling body supervising the management board's activities. Half of its representatives are elected by shareholders and the other half by the employees. However, usually, its chairman, who has a casting vote in the event of a tie in the voting of the supervisory board, is from the shareholder side which, in a sense, gives shareholders ultimate control.
- Third, the *underwriting* of new share issues of large listed stock corporations. In Germany, this is often concentrated in the hands of a few big banks that have an informational advantage over potential competitors with no relationships whatsoever to the companies. Critics say this allows the banks to earn monopoly rents as is indicated by the comparatively high fees they receive.

Philipp Holzmann

An example of the cracks in the German financial system is the Holzmann case. Philipp Holzmann, founded in 1849 and once Germany's second-biggest construction group, went bankrupt in early 2002. In 1999, the group had already been the subject of a rescue operation when it announced potential losses of DM 2.4 billion ($1.26 billion) on property deals. Among its 20 core creditors were leading German banks with the role of Deutsche Bank widely regarded as exemplary of German relationship finance. The bank's links to the group had a long tradition; Hermann Josef Abs, later Deutsche's chairman, had been chairman of the Holzmann supervisory board from 1939 for over 30 years. In 1999, too, the head of the supervisory board was a member of Deutsche's management board. The bank was the group's biggest creditor, with loans totalling almost DM 2.2 billion. With a 15% stake it was also its biggest shareholder and widely seen as its 'quasi-manager'. In this role, in 1997, Deutsche had already installed new management at Holzmann in an effort to stem losses. Then, in 1999, the group was rescued by political intervention from the newly elected Chancellor Schröder, only to go bust three years later.

The abuse of these and other instruments of power in bank-based systems is widely held responsible for outdated structures, high costs and a great deal of red tape that deter investment and make venture capital scarcely available, thereby adding considerably to the structural weaknesses of the economy. In bank-based systems, corporate governance and control is largely exerted behind closed doors; for example, changes through a stock market takeover are rare.

However, the systems in continental Europe are no longer bank-based in the way they were in the past. In countries such as Belgium, France and Italy in particular, but also elsewhere, with regulations of investment funds and pension funds having become more permissive, and tax advantages created for investors in life insurance products, the traditional bank business is in decline and other financial intermediaries such as investment funds, pension funds and insurance companies are gaining ground. Banks themselves, on the other hand, are increasingly becoming *all finance companies*, involved in insurance (bancassurance) and pension fund business, and to a wide extent managing and marketing mutual funds. This indicates that their role in the intermediation process is changing rather than diminishing.

3.3.2 Market-based Systems

Market-based systems are widely regarded as a cure to the failures observed in bank-based systems. The *arm's length finance* they provide functions according to mechanisms which, in principle, ensure better transparency and control. Publicly listed firms face extensive *disclosure requirements*, offering a great deal of information about firms' activities. In addition, many analysts working for institutional investors and other intermediaries gather private information that then becomes reflected in market prices. In addition, traditionally, managers of corporations tend to consider themselves as ultimately more responsible to the shareholders than to firms' employees or to particular owners' interests.

In general, this superiority is reflected in performance. An analysis of profits and interest margins in international comparison shows that banks in open competition with other sources of finance obviously work more efficiently than those sheltered in bank-based systems

(Table 3.18). Again, however, the argument has to be put into perspective: even in market-based systems, shareholders' rights rarely go beyond electing directors, and no mechanism ensures that managers do not pursue their own interests. As a consequence, there is a problem known in the literature as *moral hazard*: since managers cannot be held fully liable for the consequences of their decisions they may be inclined to take greater risks than the owners of the firm would.

There are other drawbacks to market-based systems (Table 3.19). That most often cited is *short-sightedness* of company decisions as a result of dependence on shareholders' attitudes. Stock markets are driven by *fads and fashions*, they rarely allow firms to pursue long-term strategies that include temporary failures and losses. While internal information may make banks inclined to support and finance company decisions, in stock markets performance is judged by external *analysts* whose background and intentions are not always beyond doubt.

Critics also emphasise that, apparently, neither disclosure requirements and controls nor market research from outside can prevent failures such as the Enron case, which will be

Table 3.18   Profitability of major banks in international comparison*

	Pre-tax profits	Net interest margin
US (10)	1.66	3.11
UK (4)	1.11	2.02
France (4)	0.58	1.03
Germany (4)	0.05	0.80
Italy (6)	0.48	2.16
Spain (4)	0.93	2.66
Sweden (4)	0.70	1.48
Switzerland (2)	0.08	0.84

* In 2002, as percentage of total average assets.
Number of banks included in parentheses.
Source: BIS.

Table 3.19   Bank-based versus market-based systems

Bank-based systems	Market-based systems
Relationship finance	Arm's-length finance
Advantages:	Advantages:
• Cooperative behaviour	• Transparency
• Intertemporal smoothing	• Efficient pricing
• Information	• Efficient risk allocation
• Long-term planning horizons	• High competition
Disadvantages:	Disadvantages:
• Intransparency	• Short-sightedness
• Inefficient corporate governance	• Dependence on fads and fashions
• Inefficient pricing	• Dependence on analysts
• Low competition	• Low management liability

discussed later, or Barings and AIB. In February 1995, *Barings Bank*, one of the oldest British merchant banks, went bankrupt after one of its traders at Baring Futures (Singapore) Ltd, Nick Leeson, lost about $850 million on the Singapore and Osaka futures exchanges. These losses stemmed mostly from positions in Nikkei 225 futures; when the Japanese city of Kobe was hit by an earthquake in January 1995, and Japanese stock prices became highly volatile, falling more than 15% in two months, Barings' fate was sealed. The losses were made worse by the sale of options implicitly betting on a stable market. In the end, the trader was unable to make the cash payments required by the exchanges and the bank was ruined.

In the case of the *Allied Irish Bank* (AIB), in February 2002, its US subsidiary, Allfirst, announced a loss of $750 million in currency dealings. One of its two currency traders, John Rusnak, who had been with Allfirst since 1993, had made losses in yen–dollar spot and forward exchange contracts and generated the cash needed to cover these losses by selling undeclared option contracts. In one instance, he sold call options that entitled his counterparty at a future date to buy dollars at about ¥70 – significantly below the market rate.

Barings and AIB are but two – extreme – examples of the *agency costs* associated with the monitoring of activities in cases where participation in derivative and other speculative markets offer extraordinary trading opportunities. One reason for these and other failures – which, in principle, holds for both market-based and bank-based systems – is that in a global environment where firms' businesses are more and more complex, stretching over a vast range of regions and activities, the influence of the home country financial system is clearly limited and electronic systems installed to bridge distances cannot replace the human factor and personal communications required for effective internal supervision.

In principle, neither bank-based nor market-based systems exist in a pure form, which makes it difficult to come to a final conclusion about their respective advantages and disadvantages. Inefficiencies are found in both of them (Table 3.20). In addition, these days, even market-based systems are changing. The most obvious example is the increasing role of *institutional investors*, which is fundamentally altering the traditional environment for corporate governance and control in these systems. Institutional investors are a relatively new phenomenon in market history – they differ from other market participants above all in two respects. First, they are answerable not only to shareholders, but – as they are not as anonymous as other private shareholders – also in a sense potentially to public opinion. Second, as a rule, they are too big to simply walk away if they do not like a management strategy or a firm's prospects; in contrast to other shareholders exit is rarely an option. As a consequence, they have begun to cultivate a 'capitalism of voice' (Loriaux 2003) which is characterised by a constant dialogue with the companies.

Given their readiness for dialogue, financial strength and investment strategies largely focusing on stability and long-term engagements, institutional investors may play a decisive role in the development of financial markets in developing countries and transition economies. This is of particular interest to the Central and Eastern European Countries (CEEC) on the brink of EU membership, and discussed in the next section.

The debate on bank-based versus market-based systems easily eclipses the fact that in many countries *internal finance* is still the most important source of funds for firms. In these countries, the nature of the financial system is less important than the overall economic and institutional environment allowing generation of profits that may be used for this purpose. However, studies have shown that this does not necessarily hold true for emerging economies – an aspect that has received very little attention so far.

Table 3.20   Sources of inefficiencies in bank-based and market-based systems

Feature	General description	In bank-based systems	In market-based systems
Asymmetric information	One person or one group of people knows more than another	Borrowers know more about the repayment prospects for a loan than the banks	Management knows more about the firm's performance than analysts and shareholders
Adverse selection	With imperfect information, discrimination between underperforming and overperforming actors is not possible. Average conditions favour the former and put the latter at a disadvantage. Result: underperformers will dominate	Bad borrowers take out loans, good borrowers will find them too expensive. Result: the overall riskiness of banks' credit portfolios is too high compared to returns	Badly performing firms face a higher demand for their shares, higher liquidity and better financing conditions than justified under full information. Better performing companies face worse conditions than expected and thus are driven out of the market
Moral hazard	Initially, a market failure associated with the provision of *insurance*: someone who has insurance or enjoys another form of protection against bearing the full consequences of a decision may take greater risks than otherwise	In a system with deposit insurance, or central banks willing to act as lender-of-last-resort, banks may be more willing to take risks than otherwise in search of higher returns	Managers not wholly liable for the consequences of their decisions may be more willing to take risks than otherwise
Agency cost	Whenever a person (the principal) hires somebody else (the agent) to carry out a task, conflicts of interests may arise for the latter. This is a *principal–agent problem* where costs arise for the principal from the agent acting selfishly	Under insufficient monitoring dealers may become tempted to take more risks than justified in search of profits and promotion	A principal–agent problem may arise in the relationship between shareholders or firm owners and managers if owners want managers to run the firm maximising share values, while managers' priorities are elsewhere

3.3.3   Financial Systems in Eastern Europe

Emerging economies are special in that to them external finance is often more important than internal finance, and their reliance on the nature and quality of the financial system is much greater than that of developed countries. In May 2004, besides Malta and Cyprus, eight countries from Central and Eastern Europe became EU members. These are Poland, the Czech Republic, Estonia, Hungary, Latvia, Lithuania, Slovakia and Slovenia. Bulgaria and Romania are expected to follow in 2007. The accession of these countries is posing huge challenges to the EU and, in particular, to Europe's financial markets and currency relations. Not only will their membership alter rules and regulations in these countries, but more importantly will intensify competition and structural transformations with repercussions on Western markets and systems.

EU membership requires the countries to implement the *acquis communautaire*, a set of laws that underpin the common market. In the course of this process, despite being still largely underdeveloped (Table 3.21), financial systems and markets in the CEEC have made great progress over recent years. The *banking sectors* were transformed from a single-tiered system under the communist rule of the late 1980s, where the state bank had a quasi-monopoly on banking and credit, to a two-tiered one. Bank legislation along the lines of the EU rules has been implemented everywhere. In all countries, except Slovenia, major banks have been

Table 3.21 Comparison of financial systems in 'old' and 'new' EU member states

	CEEC	EU
Banking		
• Historic experience	Single-tiered system, planned economy, monobanks providing loans based on decisions in planning bureaux	Two-tiered structure of central bank and commercial banks, market economy
• Role of banks	Low degree of monetisation, low bank penetration	High degree of monetisation/ bank penetration
• Foreign ownership	High penetration of foreign banks	Low penetration of foreign banks
Equity markets		
• Stage of development	Underdeveloped, delistings in favour of listings abroad not uncommon	Highly developed
• Privatisation	Vouchers, management and employee buy-outs, initial public offerings	Initial public offerings, mergers and acquisitions
• Market capitalisation	Low	High
• Market dynamism	High at first	Low
Bond markets		
• Government debt	Low level of available securities	Deep and liquid internal and external markets
• Corporate debt	Negligible, crowded out by banks, preferences for listing abroad	Growing internal and external markets
Common institutions	Developing with EU integration	Common regulatory framework, single-market programme, FSAP
Monetary policy		
• Main transmission channel of monetary policy	Exchange-rate channel	Interest-rate channel
• Monetary regime	Hard and soft currency pegs, floating	Exchange-rate mechanism, common currency

privatised. Foreign banks have entered the region's markets, buying domestic banks and stepping up retail networks where these already existed. In Hungary, Bulgaria and the Czech Republic, foreign banks hold a share of between 60 and 70% of total bank assets; in Slovakia the share is even higher.

The degree of *monetisation* in these countries is low compared to EU standards. In 2002, money in circulation plus deposits in the CEEC as a percentage of GDP was only about two-thirds the EU level. Bank intermediation, measured as bank claims on the domestic sector as a percentage of GDP, is about one-third of the respective EU measure. The use of *bank accounts* is less widespread than in Western Europe. This is the case for Bulgaria and Romania in particular, where less than 10% of the population have bank accounts; even in Poland the share is only 34%, while in Slovenia it is close to 80%. The difference between old and new member states is even greater for the total of bank assets. While in the euro area, bank assets amount to 265% of GDP, in the CEEC they range from 30 to 100%.

In contrast to many other countries, in the CEEC, *foreign investors* control a large part of the banking sectors. The advantage is that they bring capital and know-how and contribute to establishing best practices in bank business. Furthermore, they strengthen competition, enhance financial sector restructuring and help the banks to adjust to international standards. On the other hand, in many cases, foreign-owned institutions in these countries have lost important functions in recent years as trading and other key activities were shifted to the investors' headquarters. Another drawback is the possibility of disinvestment as a result of a worsening domestic environment or a change in the owner's commercial strategy, as has already occurred in a few cases.

In the formerly planned regimes, financial markets were *non-existent*, which is one explanation for the still prevailing low level of market activity in the CEEC. Another is the importance of foreign direct investment in the transition process as an alternative to domestic financing. A third explanation is the renewed recession several countries experienced after the initial output decline following the collapse of the planned economic system. Despite the fact that in the first few years of their existence exchanges in Eastern Europe regarding market dynamics – measured as growth in market capitalisation, traded value and number of listed companies (Table 3.22) – clearly outperformed not only those in developing countries outside Europe but also Western European exchanges, *market capitalisation* in these countries remained low. The combined annual turnover on the stock exchanges of Prague, Budapest and Warsaw is said to equal that on the Frankfurt stock market in 10 trading days. In an international context, only the markets of Poland and, to a lesser extent, the Czech Republic and Hungary, play some role. The dire state of the exchanges makes it easy to forget that before the Second World War some countries such as Poland and Hungary had vibrant financial markets and a long tradition of stock trading.

The development of stock markets in the CEEC was strongly influenced by the *privatisation strategies* chosen (Table 3.23). In principle, three different privatisation strategies were pursued – voucher privatisation, management and employee buy-outs and initial public offerings including direct sales to strategic investors. In countries with mass privatisation schemes, such as Bulgaria, the Czech Republic, Lithuania, Romania and Slovakia, at first a large number of companies were listed rapidly, but liquidity remained low and corporate governance structures were insufficient as the result of widespread ownership. The consequence was an equally rapid delisting. In countries where privatisation took place in the form of initial

Table 3.22 Stock market dynamics in Eastern and Western Europe in international comparison[1]

Rank in Europe	Market capitalisation[2]	Highest growth in market capitalisation[3]	Highest growth in value traded[3]	Highest growth in number of listed companies[3]
1	United Kingdom (3)	Bulgaria (1)	Romania (2)	Romania (1)
2	France (4)	Romania (2)	Iceland (4)	Bulgaria (2)
3	Germany (5)	Belgium (5)	Latvia (5)	Spain (4)
4	Italy (7)	Latvia (6)	Finland (6)	Cyprus (5)
5	Switzerland (9)	Slovenia (9)	Cyprus (8)	Poland (9)
6	Spain (11)	Greece (12)	Bulgaria (12)[4]	Finland (13)
7	Netherlands (12)	Poland (15)	Italy (13)	Malta (14)
8	Sweden (15)	Finland (16)	Greece (15)	Iceland (16)
9	Finland (18)	Iceland (17)	Lithuania (16)	Latvia (17)
10	Belgium (20)	Malta (18)	France (19)	Slovenia (19)
11	Denmark (26)	Portugal (29)	Portugal (20)	Greece (27)
12	Greece (27)	Cyprus (19)	Malta (23)	Germany (29)
13	Ireland (29)	Ireland (25)	Spain (24)	Turkey (31)
14	Norway (32)	Italy (27)	United Kingdom (26)	Hungary (37)
15	Turkey (34)	France (29)	Netherlands (28)	Sweden (41)
16	Portugal (35)	Hungary (31)	Hungary (30)	Switzerland (42)
17	Poland (39)	Spain (33)	Sweden (37)	n.a.
18	Austria (40)	Portugal (34)	Turkey (38)	n.a.
19	Luxembourg (42)	Germany (38)	Denmark (41)	n.a.
20	Hungary (47)	n.a.	Slovenia (42)	n.a.

[1] World rank in parantheses.
[2] End of 2001.
[3] In dollar terms, percentage increase 1996–2001.
[4] 1998–2001.
Source: The Economist (2004) *Pocket World in Figures*, London.

Table 3.23 Privatisation in Central and Eastern European countries

Country	Privatisation strategy
Bulgaria	Mass privatisation
Czech Republic	Mass privatisation
Estonia	Initial public offerings
Hungary	Initial public offerings
Latvia	Initial public offerings
Lithuania	Mass privatisation
Poland	Initial public offerings
Romania	Mass privatisation
Slovakia	Mass privatisation
Slovenia	Initial public offerings

Source: Caviglia, Giacomo, Gerhard Krause and Christian Thimann (2002) Key features of the financial sectors in EU accession countries, in Christian Thimann (ed.) (2002) *Financial Sectors in EU Accession Countries*, Table 1, http://www.ecb.int/pub/pdf/other/financialsectorseuaccessionen.pdf.

public offerings, such as Estonia, Hungary, Latvia, Poland and Slovenia, firms were only listed after a framework for securities trading had been established.

Currency Board Arrangements

Currency boards exist in countries as diverse as Argentina, Hong Kong and Estonia. They are widely regarded as a strategy to prevent or withstand foreign exchange market speculation and to maintain or restore international investors' confidence in a currency. A currency board strongly limits the scope of monetary policy. It is a constitutional guarantee of a currency's foreign value that goes beyond a mere fixing of the exchange rate and comprises explicit restrictions on the government's ability to print money. Under such an arrangement, currency can be issued only in exchange for the foreign currency against which its rate had been fixed – which may be another currency such as the euro or the US dollar, or a basket of currencies. The advantage of such a system is credibility: the central bank can no longer provide free liquidity to banks; financial sector reforms which are otherwise difficult to implement will be forced and discretion will be removed from corrupt and incompetent economic managers.

However, there are considerable disadvantages as well. Monetary policy is determined in the country of the reserve currency and fiscal policy can no longer print money to finance a deficit by borrowing from the central bank. As a result, the authorities lose the means of shielding the economy from shocks and can become very restricted in their economic policy. They cannot raise interest rates to defend the value of their currency or to fight inflation. They cannot act as a lender of last resort in the local currency. If there is a bank run, banks cannot turn to the central bank. The mandatory use of foreign exchange reserves to back the rate at which the currency is fixed requires reserves large enough to cover a chosen money supply. Experience has shown that movements in a crisis out of the local currency, reducing liquidity, may easily lead to rising interest rates and fears of a credit crunch in the interbank system, thereby increasing overall uncertainty and worsening the economic situation. In addition, there are two further general criticisms of currency boards: first, fully backing a currency with foreign exchange reserves is costly. Second, fixed exchange rates may not always be appropriate, given a country's terms-of-trade development.

CEEC *bond markets* are dominated by government bonds and are still small, accounting for between 5 and 20% of GDP, compared to an average of 50% in the euro zone. Even in the Czech Republic, where the non-government bond market is larger than the government market, liquidity is higher in the latter. In many countries, government bonds are mostly bought and held until maturity with liquid secondary markets existing only in the Czech Republic, Hungary and Poland. In addition, in recent years, foreign currency-denominated bonds have gained significance as spreads on these instruments have fallen considerably against the background of reforms and the prospects of EU accession.

Foreign exchange markets developed rapidly after the transition to full convertibility of CEEC currencies, often providing the most important transition channels of monetary policy. This particularly holds true for countries with a currency board arrangement such as Bulgaria, Estonia and Lithuania strongly limiting the possibility of conducting monetary policy (Table 3.24). In general, there is a risk related to the existence of these and other currency

Table 3.24   Currency regimes in Central and Eastern Europe

Country	Currency	Regime
Bulgaria	Lev (BGL)	Currency board arrangement based on the euro
Czech Republic	Koruna (CZK)	Managed float
Estonia	Kroon (EEK)	Currency board arrangement based on the euro
Hungary	Forint (HUF)	Crawling peg based on the euro
Latvia	Lats (LVL)	Currency peg based on SDR (39% US dollar, 32% euro, 18% yen, 11% pound sterling)
Lithuania	Litas (LTL)	Currency board arrangement based on the US dollar
Poland	Zloty (PLN)	Floating
Romania	Lei (ROL)	Managed float, segmented foreign exchange market
Slovakia	Koruna (SKK)	Managed float
Slovenia	Tolar (SIT)	Managed float

regimes in Eastern Europe. After EU entry, the countries are obliged to wait for a transition period of two years before joining the euro. So far, Poland and Slovakia are planning to adopt the common currency in 2008, while the Czech Republic and Hungary are aiming for 2009/10; during this period, their currencies will be exposed to a heightened *risk of speculative attacks* – Hungary's currency troubles in 2003 were a foretaste of the looming dangers. The EMS crises of 1992/93 have demonstrated the force of such attacks and, given the volume of foreign exchange trading in global markets, there are strong doubts as to whether the new member states will be able to stand the pressures. They will have no opportunity to avoid this situation, by shortening the transition period for example, because that would mean a breach of the rules. The only alternative left was unilateral 'euroisation' – the lonely decision to adopt the euro from the start – but the resulting economic effects which could aggravate existing problems and increase the costs of EU membership are a strong argument for not following this course.

The currency risks of EU enlargement are not necessarily limited to accession countries. There is a danger of *contagion* to the three existing EU countries outside the euro. With EU enlargement, traders in the markets may treat the EU area as an entity and not discriminate between 'new' and 'old' members. In this case, a speculative attack would not spare the UK, Denmark and Sweden. In addition, in contrast to the monetary relations of members within the euro area, those countries would have to face the possibility of destabilising cross-rate effects.

The Maastricht Criteria

The convergence criteria are five conditions countries must meet before taking part in full economic and monetary union. These are:

- Inflation must stay below 1.5% above the average inflation rate of the lowest three inflation countries in the EU.
- Their long-term interest rate should be no more than 2% above the average of the three countries with the lowest inflation rates.

- Budget deficits must not exceed 3% of GDP.
- National debt must not exceed 60% of GDP.
- Exchange rates should have been within the 15% fluctuation range from parity of the exchange rate mechanism (ERM) without realignments for at least two years.

On the other hand, experience with former enlargements demonstrates that crises need not occur despite major weaknesses in accession countries' economic performance before entry. One example is the *Maastricht criteria*: when in December 1991 the leaders of the 12 EC countries met at Maastricht in the Netherlands to negotiate a treaty on the European Union, they not only set out a detailed timetable for economic and monetary union (EMU) but also convergence criteria for economies wanting to join in EMU, which referred to the level of public budget deficits and debt among others.

The idea behind this was that, for a single currency to work, the economies need to be following similar patterns of growth and similar policies of aiming at becoming an *optimum currency area* (see Appendix E). However, a look at the performance of old and new member countries shows that large deviations from the criteria before the beginning of the transition period were not unusual (Table 3.25). The prospect of joining the common currency may help to force governments into fiscal discipline, as happened in Spain, Portugal and Italy. On the other hand, much depends on the nature of the budget deficits; in Portugal and Italy, for example, these were mainly caused by high interest payments on public debt whose reduction was easy to justify and to achieve with the prospects of declining interest rates in the course of monetary unification. In contrast, CEEC deficits are largely due to high social spending, investment and tax reductions, which are much harder to reduce.

Table 3.25 Budget deficits and debt before EMU[1]

Country	Year	Budget deficit	Public debt
Italy	1994	−9.1	124
Spain	1994	−6.6	66
Portugal	1994	−6.0	64
Greece	1994	−7.4	111
Czech Republic[2]	2002	−3.9	27
Estonia[2]	2002	+1.3	6
Hungary[2]	2002	−9.2	56
Latvia[2]	2002	−3.0	15
Lithuania[2]	2002	−2.0	23
Poland[2]	2002	−4.1	42
Slovakia[2]	2002	−7.2	43
Slovenia[2]	2002	−2.6	28

[1] As percentage of GDP.
[2] Preliminary.
Source: *The Economist*, country data.

Summary

- In recent years, the rationale for the existence of financial institutions has altered with a greater emphasis on the ability to distribute risks.
- Traditionally, a distinction is made between bank-based and market-based financial systems.
- Bank-based systems are characterised by relationship finance and cooperative behaviour between borrowers and lenders.
- Market-based systems provide arm's length finance with bond and equity markets playing an important role.
- Financial systems in the 'new' EU member states from Central and Eastern Europe are characterised by a low degree of monetisation and underdeveloped banking sectors.
- Equity markets in CEEC countries showed high dynamism in the first years of their existence but market capitalisation remains low.

Exercises

1. Explain the following terms and try to give examples:

   - transaction costs
   - information asymmetries
   - securitisation.

2. Explain how, these days, banks contribute to the distribution and reduction of investment risks. Take a special look at the role of:

   - information for both borrowers and lenders
   - market access
   - technical assistance.

3. Discuss the advantages and disadvantages of a bank-based system considering the German example.

4. Describe the moral hazard firms' shareholders face and discuss possible solutions taking into account such factors as:

   - the firms' size
   - the role of banks
   - the role of market research.

5. Compare financial systems in old and new EU member states. Where do you see the main hindrances to full financial integration of an enlarged Europe?

6. Discuss the foreign exchange risks related to an enlargement of the euro area for both old and new EU member states.

Additional Links and References

For a general overview of different financial systems see:

Allen, Franklin and Douglas Gale (2001) Comparative financial systems: a survey, http://fic.wharton.upenn.edu/fic/.

For a vivid description of the changes the UK system experienced since the 1980s see:

Augar, Philip (2001) *The Death of Gentlemanly Capitalism*, London: Penguin Books.

For a survey of the theoretical and empirical literature on financial intermediation see:

Gorton, Gary and Andrew Winton (2002) Financial intermediation, NBER Working Paper No. 8928, May, http://www.nber.org/papers/w8928

For a discussion of the future role of banks in the euro area, for example, see:

Hartmann, Philipp, Angela Maddaloni and Simone Manganelli (2003): The euro area financial system: structure, integration and policy initiatives, European Central Bank, Working Paper No. 230, http://www.ecb.int/pub/wp/ecbwp230.pdf

The consequences of the emergence of institutional investors in capitalist systems is discussed in:

Loriaux, Michel (2003) France: a new 'capitalism of voice'? in Linda Weiss (ed.) *States in the Global Economy – Bringing Domestic Institutions Back In*, Cambridge: Cambridge University Press, pp. 101–20.

For a survey of the German bank-based system see:

Edwards, Jeremy and Klaus Fischer (1994) *Banks, Finance and Investment in Germany*, Cambridge: Cambridge University Press.
Reszat, Beate (2003) Financial reform in Germany, in Maximilian J.B. Hall (ed.) *The International Handbook of Financial Reform*, Cheltenham: Edward Elgar, pp. 88–112.

Fads and fashions are the topic of a research area called 'behavioural finance'. Two of its main proponents are Robert J. Shiller, author of *Irrational Exuberance* (Princeton University Press 2001), and Richard H. Thaler, author of *The Winner's Curse* (Princeton University Press 1994) and of the well-known 'Anomalies' articles published in the *Journal of Economic Perspectives*. See also Robert Shiller's very informative web page:

http://www.econ.yale.edu/~shiller/

Adverse selection, moral hazard and other inefficiencies rooted in asymmetric information have long been – and still are – a vital field of economic research. In 2001, three researchers received the Nobel Prize for their work in this field: George A. Akerlof (author of the famous essay 'The market for "lemons": quality uncertainty and the market mechanism', in *Quarterly Journal of Economics*, August 1970), A. Michael Spence (who focused on the role of 'signalling' for avoiding the phenomenon of adverse selection) and Joseph E. Stiglitz (who complemented the works of Akerlof and Spence on informational asymmetries). For further information see their respective web sites:

George A. Akerlof: http://emlab.berkeley.edu/users/akerlof/
A. Michael Spence: http://gobi.stanford.edu/facultybios/bio.asp?ID = 156
Joseph E. Stiglitz: http://www-1.gsb.columbia.edu/faculty/jstiglitz/index.cfm

3.4   EXTERNAL MARKETS

As a rule, financial markets are located in a particular place and subject to the jurisdiction of their home country. However there are three exceptions. One is the Euromarkets that emerged in the early 1960s, the second is the offshore centres worldwide that have become notorious as financial havens and the third is the virtual market places arising with the growing popularity of electronic trading and the internet.

3.4.1 Euromarkets

The Euromarkets have shaped the way international financial business is done, not only in Europe but also worldwide. Euromarkets, unlike conventional financial markets, occupy no fixed location but rely on international telecommunications networks linking financial centres throughout the world. Their beginnings date back to the post war period when the widespread use of the US dollar as a vehicle currency for making payments in international transactions, the easing of exchange restrictions in major European countries and the overall growth in European business after the formation of the Common Market contributed to the need for external markets for currency deposits and loans. However, their true take-off is often related to the 1960s and to the restraints on foreign portfolio investment in the United States (the interest equalization tax), and on US bank lending abroad.

The introduction of the Eurodollar market in the 1960s marked the first step towards the internationalisation of financial markets on a broad scale. In general, a *Eurocurrency* is a currency deposited in a bank outside its country of origin. Examples are US dollar deposits outside the United States or pound sterling deposits outside the UK. Participants in the Euromarkets are banks that accept deposits and make loans in Eurocurrencies. These days, Eurocurrencies and Euromarkets are not restricted to the European area. For instance, there are Euroyen traded outside Japan, and several countries have set up special regulations to permit Eurocurrency deposits within their national borders. An example is the International Banking Facilities (IBFs) in the United States. These are dollar deposits that are subject to less regulation than ordinary dollar deposits in US banks, available only to non-residents and not allowed for use in conducting transactions within the United States.

The Euromarkets introduced two principles that changed the world of finance. One is the principle of *revolving credit facility*: although long commitment periods exist in the markets, in general, lenders are unwilling to carry the interest rate risk normally associated with those kinds of engagements. Thus, typically, for short-term borrowing a line of credit is prearranged determining the maximum amount that can be borrowed within the commitment period, which is usually one year but renewable, with drawdowns carrying interest charges based on current short-term market rates that are adjusted every one, three or six months. Medium-term lending is usually done in the form of a revolving loan facility. In this case, commitment periods are up to 15 years or longer – the majority of loans are in the range of three to seven years – but the pricing period rarely exceeds six months.

The second principle is loan *syndication* in large-scale, medium-term financing for which *Luxembourg* became a centre in Europe (Appendix C). Loan syndication works in the same way as bond or share underwriting. In syndication it is not an individual bank but a group of knowledgeable and well-capitalised institutions that provide the entire loan and then sell portions of their share of the credits to a wide range of smaller or less knowledgeable banks. The aim is risk reduction. Syndication exposes firms to a far wider audience and allows them to have a more diversified base of lenders. In contrast to traditional bank business, in the Euromarkets lenders come from many nations; instead of doing a thorough credit analysis and monitoring and control of issuers from countries with diverse regulations and accounting norms the banks reduce risks by taking a smaller amount of more diversified assets and relying on the monitoring role of the lead banks.

Besides Eurocurrency markets there are markets for other financial instruments such as Eurobonds, Eurocommercial paper and Euroequities. The most important one is the *Eurobond market* which is the market for long-term debt instruments issued through international

International Bonds		National Bonds
Eurobonds	Foreign Bonds	Domestic Bonds
Issued through an international syndicate, sold outside the country of the currency in which the bonds are denominated	*Issued by a foreign borrower in the currency of the country in which they are sold*	*Issued by a domestic borrower in the home country*

Figure 3.8   The international bond market

syndicates of financial intermediaries and sold outside the countries of the currency in which the bonds are denominated. One example is bonds denominated in US dollars that are sold in London. Eurobonds must not be confused with *foreign bonds*, which are sold in a foreign country and denominated in that country's currency; the definition of 'foreign' refers to the nationality of the issuer in relation to the market place (Figure 3.8).

The difference between a domestic and a foreign bond is that the issuer of the latter is a foreign entity which may be beyond investors' legal reach in the event of default. For example, a US dollar bond sold in the United States by the Swedish car producer Volvo is classified as a foreign bond while one issued by General Motors is a domestic bond. Foreign bonds sometimes have colourful names, for example: sterling-denominated bonds issued in the UK by foreign borrowers are called bulldog bonds – the bulldog is a national symbol of England. Bulldog bonds are the UK equivalent of Samurai bonds (Japanese yen obligations of non-Japanese firms) and Yankee bonds (US dollar bonds issued by non-US firms). A name used for both Eurobonds and foreign bonds is *international bonds*.

The fact that Eurocurrencies, Eurobonds and other instruments are traded outside national boundaries with financial intermediaries from many countries involved raises the question of *reference rates*. In general, in debt markets the reference rate for a financial instrument is the interest rate available for the best borrowers in the most liquid market segment. Traditionally, in national markets, for short-term loans and deposits these are the banks with direct access to the national money market and to central bank money. In the markets for medium- and long-term debt it is the government. Rates for other debtors or borrowers are derived from these depending on risk and liquidity.

In the Eurocurrency markets, prior to the introduction of the euro, the primary benchmark used by banks, securities houses and investors to determine the cost of borrowing was the London-Interbank Offered Rate, *LIBOR*. Traditionally, this was fixed daily for 12 currencies (and still is for euro-out currencies) for maturities up to one week and from one month to 12 months inclusive by the British Bankers' Association (BBA). There is a panel of Contributor Banks selected by the BBA on the basis of market activity and perceived market reputation with each bank contributing the rate at which it could borrow funds in the interbank market prior to 11 a.m. each working day.

Since the introduction of the euro, the BBA fixes the *EURO BBA LIBOR*, which is a measure of the cost of euro funds based on the offer rates quoted by 16 of the most active banks in the London market. However, the European Monetary Institute, the forerunner of the European Central Bank (ECB), was unhappy with the money market reference rate for the euro being set outside the euro area, and a new benchmark sponsored by the European Banking Federation was introduced: the *EURIBOR*. This is the rate at which euro interbank term deposits within the euro zone are offered by one prime bank to another. The rates for the EURIBOR are fixed by a panel of 57 banks: 47 selected by national banking associations and 10 international banks active in the euro market with an office in the euro area. While the EURIBOR is fixed for maturities from one month to 12 months the most important one is the three-month rate. The EURIBOR serves as a basis for derivatives such as interest-rate futures and swaps and contracts with variable interest rates (floaters).

There is also a new overnight reference rate that replaced those formerly designated prior to the introduction of the euro: the Euro Overnight Index Average or *EONIA*. The EONIA is calculated by the ECB with the panel of reporting banks being the same as for the EURIBOR. The euro-out zone equivalent to the EONIA is the *EURONIA*, which is the average interest rate, weighted by volume, of all unsecured overnight euro deposit trades arranged by eight money brokers in London. The spread between EONIA and EURONIA is very small.

Short term	EONIA	Euro Overnight Index Average
	EURONIA	Euro-out zone equivalent to the EONIA
	LIBOR	London-Interbank Offered Rate
	EURIBOR	Euro Interbank Offered Rate (European Banking Federation)
	EURO BBA LIBOR	Euro Interbank Offered Rate (British Bankers' Association)
Medium and long term	Government bond yields	
	5–7 years:	France
	10 years:	Germany
	15 years:	France
	longer maturities:	Greece, Italy, Spain
	Interest-rate swaps	

Figure 3.9   Reference rates in the euromarkets

The Yield Curve

Risk and liquidity are but two factors influencing interest rates. Another is the term to maturity. A plot of the yields on bonds with differing terms to maturities but the same risk and liquidity is called a yield curve. The yield curve describes the term structure of interest rates for a particular type of financial instrument such as government bonds. The numbers on the vertical axis indicate the interest rate, the numbers on the horizontal axis the maturity. Yield curves are mostly upward-sloping reflecting the higher cost of borrowing for longer periods (a). When yield curves slope downward (b), long-term interest rates are below the short-term ones, which is usually interpreted as short-term interest rates being expected to fall, on average, in the future. Curve (c) shows a humped term structure with short-term rates expected to rise and longer rates to fall. As a rule, when short-term interest rates are low, yield curves are more likely to have an upward slope. When short-term rates are high, yield curves are more likely to slope downward.

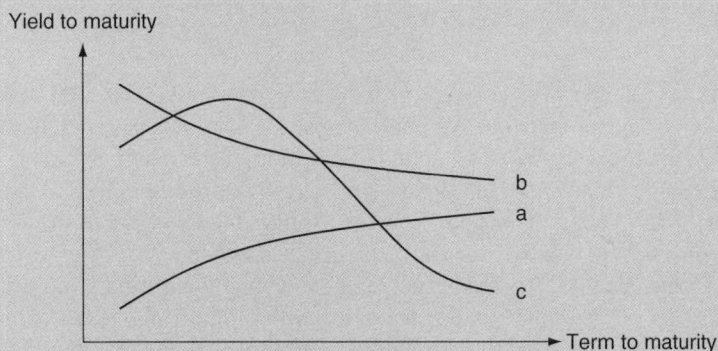

Yield to maturity

b
a
c

Term to maturity

In the discussions about the eurozone benchmark yield curves play an important role in several respects. Lower yields reflect higher creditworthiness and liquidity, the traditional conditions for benchmark status. Another aspect is completeness and a country's ability to issue bonds with low yields at a variety of maturities. These days, in Europe different countries have become dominant on different parts of the yield curve offering a window of opportunity for smaller countries as well as for issuers in other asset classes such as highly rated corporate debt.

In the Euromarkets for medium- and long-term debt the introduction of the euro raised the question of which country would assume *benchmark status* or whether, with the elimination of exchange-rate risks, investors would regard government bonds of different EMU countries as complete substitutes. It turned out that the latter is not the case. Besides exchange-rate considerations yield spreads are influenced on the one hand by liquidity and the capacity of a market to absorb shocks and large fluctuations in supply and demand, and on the other hand by credit differences among sovereign bonds in the euro area usually reflected in credit ratings (Table 3.26). Both still exist. Since countries continue to be responsible for their own issuing activity, and wholly liable for their government debt, national differences in rating and liquidity continue to matter. In addition, there are other factors which are possibly relevant in this context such as the nature of the primary dealer system, order flow and issuance arrangements.

Table 3.26   Ratings of Western European government bonds*

Country	Date	Foreign currency rating	Local currency rating
Austria	21 Sep 2000	AAA	AAA
Belgium	17 Jun 2002	AA	AA
Finland	21 Sep 2000	AAA	AAA
France	21 Sep 2000	AAA	AAA
Germany	21 Sep 2000	AAA	AAA
Greece	20 Oct 2003	A+	A+
Ireland	21 Sep 2000	AAA	AAA
Italy	17 Jun 2002	AA	AA
Luxembourg	21 Sep 2000	AAA	AAA
Netherlands	21 Sep 2000	AAA	AAA
Portugal	21 Sep 2000	AA	AA
Spain	10 Dec 2003	AAA	AAA

* Long-term ratings, as of 26 February 2004.
Source: Fitch.

Nevertheless, yield spreads *did converge* narrowing from more than 300 basis points for certain maturities to fewer than 30 basis points across the maturity spectrum. Furthermore, no individual government's securities have turned out to offer the depth and range of issuance that would be required to assume benchmark status across all maturities. Instead, the benchmark yield curve is made up of more than one issuer. As well as the interest-rate swaps described in the last chapter, German bunds represent the undisputed benchmark at the 10-year maturity, benefiting from the country's Triple A rating and the highly liquid bund futures market, while France has staked a position in the mid-range of maturities from five to seven years. For longer maturities, the French 15-year bond is a widely accepted benchmark, but in this group, and even for longer maturities, countries like Italy, Spain and Greece are also competing for investors' demand.

A phenomenon worth mentioning in this context is the convergence of bond spreads for *Eastern European countries* while they were negotiating for EU entry in 2004 with the prospects of joining the euro zone in 2007. For example, in March 2002, euro-denominated bonds of Slovenia and Hungary were yielding 45 to 50 basis points over the German bund and Poland about 70 basis points. By comparison, Sweden's bond yields at the same time were 46 basis points over the German bund, Greece's 33 basis points. In November 2002, Moody's eliminated the gap between foreign and domestic government debt ratings of the eight countries treating them as though they were already full members of the eurozone. Agencies normally assign a lower rating to a country's foreign debt on the ground that, in contrast to domestic debt, it cannot print its own currency for debt service and repayment (Table 3.27). However, Moody's said this foreign currency risk could be expected to fall and be eliminated completely by the time the states joined the euro. The case indicates how much the introduction of the common currency has changed Europe's financial landscape. Four years before its introduction, Italy, Spain and Portugal were yielding about 500 basis points over the German bund while Greece was not even able to issue domestic bonds of 10-year maturity until 1997.

In general, changes in bond yields in leading industrial countries in Europe and worldwide are increasingly *correlated* indicating a growing international interdependence of markets.

Table 3.27   Ratings of East European government bonds*

Country	Date	Foreign currency rating	Local currency rating
Bulgaria	24 Jul 2003	BB+	BBB–
Czech Republic	20 Jun 2003	A–	A
Estonia	22 Oct 2003	A–	A+
Hungary	15 Jul 2003	A–	A+
Latvia	4 Nov 2003	BBB+	A
Lithuania	28 Jan 2004	BBB+	A
Poland	4 Nov 2003	BBB+	A+
Romania	18 Dec 2003	BB	BB+
Slovakia	22 Jan 2004	BBB+	A
Slovenia	4 Nov 2003	A+	AA

* Long-term ratings, as of 26 February 2004.
Source: Fitch.

Table 3.28   Stock indices in Europe

Country	Name	Index value[1]
Austria	ATX-INDEX VIENNA	1805.42
Belgium	BEL20 INDEX	2389.56
Czech Republic	PX50 INDEX	790.50
Denmark	KFX TOP20 INDEX	268.12
France	CAC 40 INDEX	3620.11
Germany	XETRA DAX PF	3862.37
Italy	MIBTEL INDEX	20286.00
Netherlands	AEX-Index	341.57
Norway	OSE ALL SHARE GI	203.21
Slovakia	SAX INDEX	183.64
Spain	MADRID GEN INDEX	820.04
Sweden	SAX ALL SHARE	208.42
Switzerland	SWISS MARKET INDEX	5654.20
United Kingdom	FTSE 100 INDEX	4441.30
European index	DJ Euro Stoxx 50	2788.30

[1] As of 15 March 2004.

The same holds for equities. In equity markets, there is no benchmark comparable to the German bund. Investors in these markets tend to judge the performance of individual stocks in relation to overall market performance as measured by an *equity index*. Major European equity indices are the London FTSE 100, the French CAC, the German DAX and the Dow Jones Euro Stoxx (Table 3.28).

3.4.2   Offshore Centres

Euromarkets are one category of external markets. Another is *offshore financial centres*. Traditionally, these centres offer *preferential treatment* such as low or zero taxation and high financial privacy to foreigners helping them attract financial business and high-quality professionals and support personnel. Many of them have carved out niches by specialising in specific types of financial services or regions. Multinational corporations and high-net-worth persons are among their most frequent users.

In general, financial activities undertaken in offshore centres include:

- *International banking*. Most banks located in offshore centres are branches or subsidiaries of international banks. Many are specialised in *private banking*, offering services such as asset management, estate planning, foreign exchange trading and pension arrangements for wealthy clients.
- *Collective investment schemes* such as mutual funds and hedge funds. Related activities are asset allocation and management, fund distribution and administration, custodian services and back-office work.
- There are many *special purpose vehicles* (SPVs) registered in offshore centres which are established by both financial and nonfinancial corporations. While the former use the SPVs mainly for securitisation purposes, for nonfinancial corporations they have the advantage of lowering the cost of raising capital.
- *Insurance business* is another niche exploited by offshore centres. In particular, as a consequence of innovative regulatory and legal environments, some have attracted a large share of the world's reinsurance market.
- Still another service offered by offshore centres is *asset protection*, including trusts. Among the reasons why assets are managed in these centres are protection from weak domestic banks or currencies, tax avoidance and protection from lawsuits in the home jurisdictions.
- Loose financial regulation and supervision provide incentives for a whole range of *criminal financial activities* of which money laundering and the financing of terrorism attracted a growing international attention in recent years.

There are growing concerns about the potential risks posed by offshore centres. The OECD has started a global initiative to improve financial transparency listing four criteria for identifying a preferential regime:

1. The regime imposes low or no taxes on the relevant income from geographically mobile financial and other services activities.
2. It is ring-fenced from the domestic economy.
3. It lacks transparency and regulatory supervision or financial disclosure are inadequate.
4. There is no effective exchange of information with respect to the regime.

Based on these and other criteria, the OECD in 1998 began to evaluate jurisdictions identifying an initial group of 47 countries as *tax havens*. In 2000, the organisation published a 'blacklist' of 30 countries refusing to lift the veil of secrecy surrounding their tax and regulatory systems. In the meantime, most of these have agreed to improve financial transparency. In 2002, among the seven countries still listed were six offshore centres. They risk pariah status, and there are moves afoot to punish uncooperative centres by imposing financial sanctions such as the abolition of favourable tax treaties with the OECD's 30 member countries.

Most of the European offshore centres are small countries (Figure 3.10). They have few sources of income outside financial services, which explains why they resist becoming more transparent. However, there are two notable exceptions: Switzerland and Luxembourg. Both

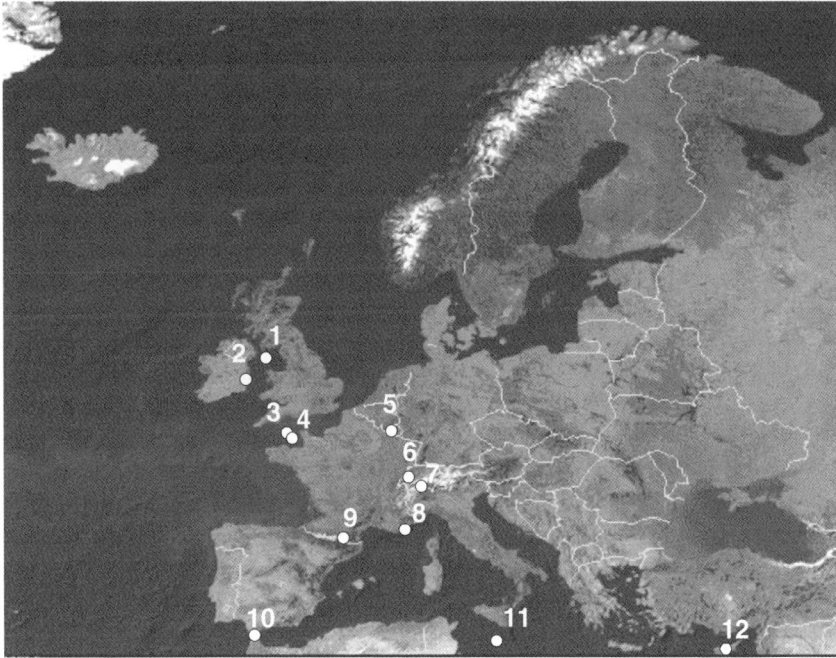

1 Isle of Man, 2 Dublin, 3 Guernsey, 4 Jersey, 5 Luxembourg, 6 Switzerland,
7 Liechtenstein, 8 Monaco, 9 Andorra, 10 Gibraltar, 11 Malta, 12 Cyprus.

Figure 3.10   European offshore centres

are not on the list and – both OECD members – did not approve the OECD's 1998 report, refusing to commit themselves to the same standards demanded of those on the blacklist. European offshore centres say complying with the OECD's demands could harm their competitive position relative to these two, which maintain high levels of financial privacy despite international pressure.

Some progress was made, when Switzerland in 2003 reached a compromise deal with the European Union on access to non-residents' financial information which might help revive the issue in talks with the OECD. However, under the arrangement EU demands for free exchanges of information were dropped. Instead, Switzerland, which handles an estimated one-third of all money held in private accounts in offshore centres, will levy a withholding tax on non-residents' savings and transfer it to their relevant tax authorities.

Tax evasion is but one of the concerns of international observers. Besides the OECD and the EU, there are several international forums focusing on the compliance of national supervisory and regulatory systems with international standards and, in particular, the effectiveness of *anti-money laundering measures* and the regime for *combating the financing of terrorism* (AML/CFT). Those include the Financial Stability Forum (FSF) and the Financial Action Task Force on Money Laundering (FATF).

The *Financial Stability Forum* brings together senior representatives of national financial authorities (e.g. central banks, supervisory authorities and treasury departments), international financial institutions, international regulatory and supervisory groupings, committees of central bank experts and the European Central Bank. In April 2000, the forum published a report on

Table 3.29 Offshore centres in Europe[1]

Centre	Population[2]	Number of licensed banks
Group I		
Dublin (Ireland)	n.a.	54
Guernsey	0.07	77
Isle of Man	0.07	67
Jersey	0.09	79
Luxembourg	0.42	221
Switzerland	7.10	n.a.
Group II		
Andorra	0.06	n.a.
Gibraltar	0.03	32
Malta	0.38	20
Monaco	0.03	n.a.
Group III		
Cyprus	0.77	46
Liechtenstein	0.03	11

[1] List of jurisdictions that have significant offshore activities. The list is organised according to the FSF's groupings, which are defined as follows: The first group (Group I) would be jurisdictions generally viewed as cooperative, with a high quality of supervision, largely adhering to international standards. The second group (Group II) would be jurisdictions generally seen as having procedures for supervision and cooperation in place, but where actual performance falls below international standards, and there is substantial room for improvement. The third group (Group III) would be jurisdictions generally seen as having a low quality of supervision, and/or being noncooperative with onshore supervisors, and with little or no attempt being made to adhere to international standards.
[2] Million.
Source: International Monetary Fund (2000) Offshore financial centres, IMF Background Paper, June 23, http://www.imf.org/external/np/mae/oshore/2000/eng/back.htm#table2.

offshore centres, which laid the foundations for further official activities in this area, highlighting prudential and market integrity concerns and listing countries with significant offshore activities, many of which are located in Europe (Table 3.29). In the same year, the *Financial Action Task Force on Money Laundering* undertook a first initiative to identify noncooperative countries and territories in the fight against money laundering. The FATF was established by the G-7 Summit that was held in Paris in 1989. The recommendations published by the FATF became the international standard in the fight against money laundering and the financing of terrorism. In addition, the *International Monetary Fund* (IMF) has developed an *assessment programme* which is based on two pillars: financial supervision and technical assistance helping jurisdictions upgrade supervisory laws and implement them and develop reform programmes. In an effort to safeguard their reputations and protect their niche markets, most offshore centres cooperated and participated in the programme.

3.4.3 Virtual Market Places

A wholly different category of external markets emerged with the spread of electronic trading and the internet. The meaning of 'electronic trading' depends on context. In principle, it may contain three main functions, electronic order routing, i.e. the delivery of orders to the execution system, automated trade execution and electronic dissemination of trade-related information.

The beginnings of electronic trading date back to the early 1970s and the introduction of videotext and screen trading. A series of companies emerged providing equipment that placed the information directly on dealers' desks thereby threatening the traditional role of the trading floor as the centre of activity. The terminals of Telerate and Quotron in the United States, and Reuters, Extel and Datastream in Europe, displayed prices fed to them by banks, brokers and dealers and allowed updates to information to be made live, or online, at the originator's request.

There was another revolution in the US stock markets with the development of *NASDAQ*, which was installed in 1971. NASDAQ first consisted of 20,000 miles of leased telephone lines connecting dealers' terminals with a central computing system that recorded prices, deals and other information. An even earlier system, which started in 1969, was *Instinet*, which aimed at providing a low-cost trading network along the lines of foreign exchange trading for institutions buying and selling *shares in bulk*. This later quoted not only US stocks but also foreign stocks and options on stocks and currencies from the CBOE (Chicago Board Options Exchange).

The latter was a first step towards *automation of derivatives trading* – a market which had traditionally been considered most resistant to being removed from the exchange floors due to the large sums involved and the volume brought by 'locals' or independent floor traders – revolutionising it worldwide. In Europe, the *London International Financial Futures Exchange* (LIFFE), founded in 1982, is one example. Although long keeping the open-outcry system of floor trading, from the beginning LIFFE had a high degree of automation in quotation and settlement.

The 1970s and 1980s saw a *convergence* of two initially distinct technologies, of *communications technology* concerned with the transmission of information on the one hand and *computer technology* concerned with the processing of information on the other. Computers and telecommunications became integrated into a single system of information processing and exchange affecting a wide range of areas and activities such as management information systems, professional databases, integrated text and data processing, professional problem solving, transaction clearing systems and online enquiry and electronic mail.

The changes for the financial industry were substantial. The new technologies allowed financial institutions the transition from internationalisation to globalisation – from the central operation and control of worldwide activities to the dispersion of central functions to all major nodes of the world economy and their constant interaction within large networks – and, at the same time, revolutionised not only the way in which financial instruments are traded but a wide spectrum of activities from information gathering, price discovery and trading via portfolio and risk management to clearing and settlement and mergers and acquisitions.

One example is *communication and networking*. Before the advent of the internet, only very large organisations and firms fully utilised the new technologies. For example, transnational corporations (TNCs) are the main users of international leased telecommunications lines for electronic data interchange (EDI) and *electronic fund transfer* (EFT), which are regarded as key factors for speeding innovation, mobility of capital and competitive advantage within organisations. In general, international EFT encompasses a wide range of payment systems and services differing among others by ownership, user access and geographical extent.

For interbank transactions *SWIFT* (Society for Worldwide Interbank Financial Communication) became a cheap, reliable and secure alternative to public services. The SWIFT network was founded in 1973 as a cooperative non-profit organisation with headquarters in Brussels. In the beginning, it had 239 member banks from 15 countries. Operation began in May 1977 with 15 banks in Belgium, France and Britain. Today there are over 7000 members from 194 countries. SWIFT is a private international telecommunications service for member banks and qualified participants that provides an international network for a large range of interbank communications including money transfers, letters of credit and much more. For *intraorganisational communications*, large TNCs and transnational banks alternatively use their own networks with lines leased from PTT (postal, telephone and telegraph) authorities. They are motivated by reliability and availability concerns as well as cost and control considerations.

Another example is *customer services*. Traditional modes of business were first altered by automatisation and the possibilities of home banking. The first *automated teller machines* (ATMs) – unmanned terminals used to dispense cash, take instructions on fund transfers and summarise information on the state of the account and other features – emerged during the 1970s and early 1980s. The greatest investments in this field were made in the United States, followed by France where the nationalised banks were encouraged by government to introduce the new technology. With respect to *home banking* Scandinavia, Finland in particular, led the development. This was explained by high labour cost and the isolation of the rural population. Another novelty was *credit cards* which, again, were first introduced in the United States.

The emergence of the *internet* had two main effects. First, it allowed substantial *cost reductions*. One credit card company estimated the cost of processing purchase orders to have declined from $125 to $40. In 2000, the cost of a financial transaction for a US bank was $1.27 for a teller, $0.27 for an ATM and $0.01 for an online transaction. Costs in back-office operations and brokerage transactions were reduced too, leading to online brokerage fees of below $5 compared to those of traditional discount brokers exceeding $50.

Second, new market segments and structures arose. Banks, securities houses and non-traditional players started to set up *trading platforms* and offered all sorts of financial services online. In Europe, there are about 100 online brokers with many of the largest based in Germany. Today most are facing difficult times since online trading by individuals has ground almost to a halt after the near-collapse of the market in new-economy stocks in the year 2000 and the concomitant sharp decline in profit margins. As a consequence, pressures to consolidate and find partners rose, and those pursuing a multi-channel banking approach, keeping voice-broking elements as well as their electronic systems, have fared best.

Perhaps surprisingly, there is not much *cross-border e-finance* in Europe despite the fact that low transaction costs potentially facilitate cross-border electronic banking. One explanation may be that the risks associated with the new medium are perceived as higher for cross-border transactions than within national borders. The use of electronic financial services is most widely spread in *Scandinavia* which is also one of the regions with the highest internet and PC usage in general (Table 3.30). For example, in Sweden the percentage share of both bank customers using online banking and electronic brokerage transactions is much higher than in Germany and the UK. In 1999, the respective numbers were 31% for online banking (Germany 12%, UK 6%) and 55% for electronic broking (Germany 32%, UK 26%). A comparison with countries from Eastern Europe shows that, here too, disparities are wide, although the distance from the European average does not seem as large as in other areas (Table 3.31).

In *wholesale financial markets*, in general, the penetration of electronic trading has been uneven across both sectors and regions. It is strongest in *equity markets* where the liquidity and relative homogeneity of major equities favoured the development and, above all, in the *inter-dealer spot foreign exchange market*. In London, in April 2004, electronic trading accounted for 55% of total foreign exchange activity and 76% of spot business (67% of

Table 3.30   PC and internet usage in Western Europe*

Country	Internet hosts per 10,000 Inhabitants	Internet users per 10,000 inhabitants	PCs per 100 inhabitants
Austria	450.95	4093.64	36.93
Belgium	325.04	3283.17	24.14
Denmark	1559.74	5128.15	57.68
Finland	2343.12	5089.30	44.17
France	232.86	3138.32	34.71
Germany	314.32	4119.38	43.13
Greece	145.97	1547.41	8.17
Ireland	347.21	2709.23	42.08
Italy	119.13	3524.37	23.07
Luxembourg	387.00	3699.55	59.42
Netherlands	1937.14	5063.29	46.66
Norway	561.79	5026.08	52.83
Portugal	159.36	1935.07	13.49
Spain	145.02	1563.01	19.60
Sweden	949.54	5730.74	62.13
Switzerland	770.34	3510.38	70.87
UK	485.03	4230.98	40.57
Europe	230.38	2164.47	21.40

* In 2002.
Source: ITU.

Table 3.31   PC and internet usage in Eastern Europe*

Country	Internet hosts per 10,000 inhabitants	Internet users per 10,000 inhabitants	PCs per 100 inhabitants
Bulgaria	42.28	807.59	5.19
Czech Republic	223.21	2563.09	17.74
Estonia	467.63	3276.75	21.03
Hungary	191.59	1576.04	10.84
Latvia	152.39	1331.04	17.17
Lithuania	157.70	1444.04	10.97
Poland	170.30	2299.98	10.56
Romania	18.90	830.22	6.92
Slovakia	159.91	1604.38	18.04
Slovenia	179.31	3757.52	30.06

* In 2002.
Source: ITU.

which is inter-dealer business) compared with 46% forward and swap. The majority of spot trading is via automated order-matching systems.

In *fixed-income markets* electronic trading advanced more slowly. One explanation is that fixed-income products are far less homogeneous and less liquid with many variations in coupon and maturity and frequency of interest payments. Trading in government bonds, where standardisation and liquidity are high, dominates in this sector. The most successful trading platform is *MTS* (Mercato Telematico dei titoli di Stato), an electronic quote-driven market based on a two-tiered structure: a central market for European government bond benchmarks (EuroMTS) and a combination of domestic markets for national issuers. Market-makers and a common electronic trading platform (Telematico) guarantee liquidity, while decisions about conditions of access, obligations of market-makers and list of traded securities are left to the national level.

One European characteristic is exchanges' *institutional design* of electronic trading. In contrast to the United States where many markets, including the two largest – the New York Stock Exchange and NASDAQ – have broadly maintained traditional arrangements such as floor trading and telephone-based screen trading, in Europe, many established exchanges in the course of demutualising (turning themselves into companies) or merging have moved their own systems to electronic trading. One explanation is less regulatory environment and the stronger competitive pressures prevailing in Europe. The advantages for the exchanges are considerable, since new market entrants find it difficult to compete with the range of services and sophistication they offer.

In recent years, in both retail and wholesale trading worldwide brokers and exchanges faced increasing competition from so-called *electronic communications networks* (ECNs) or alternative trading systems (ATS). ECNs include professional trading systems such as Instinet, which has become the world's biggest electronic broker trading in about 40 markets with offices in London, Frankfurt, Paris, Zurich, Hong Kong, Tokyo and Toronto, and order-matching services such as Posit and E-Crossnet. Most are owned by traditional market participants or brokers and regulated as investment companies rather than exchanges. In Europe, except in the foreign exchange markets where they led to a considerable reduction in search costs and trading, ECNs so far have played a minor role.

In bond and equity markets the advent of electronic trading strengthened competition enforcing a tendency towards *alliances, mergers* and pan-European and worldwide *24-hour trading* (Figure 3.11). One example is the merger of the bourses of Paris, Amsterdam and Brussels to form Euronext, which then won the battle for LIFFE in October 2001. Others are the (failed) hostile takeover bid for the London Stock Exchange by OM Gruppen of Sweden, and the (equally failed) plan to create iX by merging the London and Frankfurt stock exchanges and possibly Madrid and Milan.

Worldwide alliances include the creation of markets in various countries with local partners using a common technology, a strategy applied, for instance, by NASDAQ, which, with varying success, established NASDAQ Europe, NASDAQ Japan and NASDAQ Canada. Another example is the Globex Alliance which, as well as the CME and SIMEX, includes Euronext, Brazil's Bolsa de Mercadorias & Futuros (BM&F), the MEFF Renta Fija Spanish Exchange for Fixed Income Derivatives and MEFF Renta Variable Spanish Exchange for Equity Derivatives and the Montreal Exchange. In addition, there is a CME-LIFFE Partnership.

Summary

- There are several external markets outside national jurisdictions. Those include the Euromarkets, offshore centres and virtual market places.
- The Euromarkets developed important principles such as revolving credit facilities, syndication and underwriting that enabled financial institutions to cope with the increased risks of financial business in an international environment.
- In addition, special benchmarks emerged in the markets accounting for the fact that for financial products traded outside national boundaries other than traditional reference rates are needed.

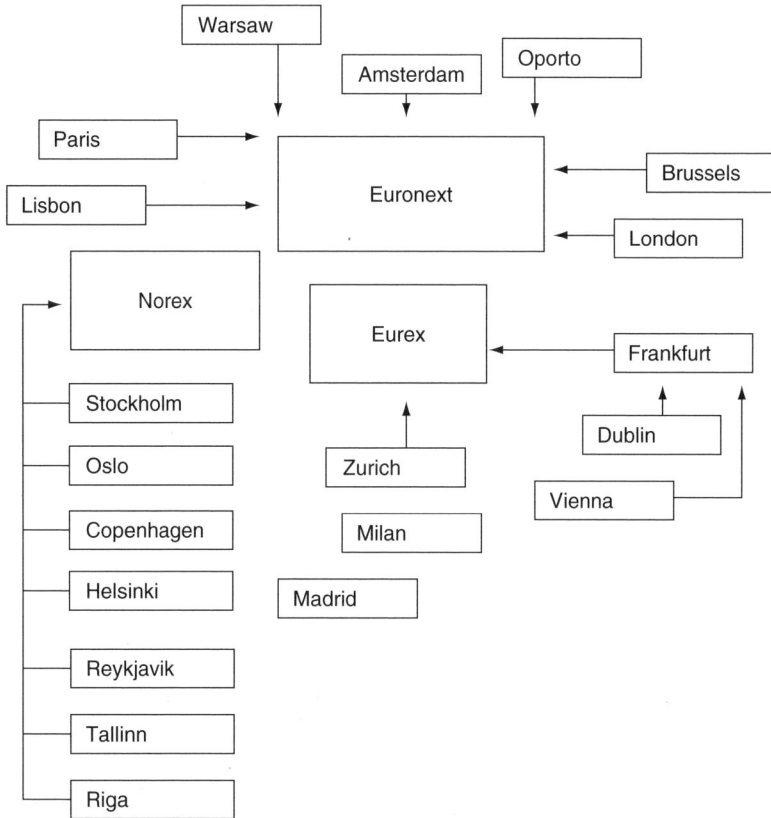

Figure 3.11   European exchange links and alliances

- Offshore centres offer preferential treatment such as low taxation and high financial privacy.
- There are international efforts to improve financial transparency in offshore centres and reduce the possibilities of tax evasion.
- There are also growing concerns about other risks related to offshore centres including money laundering and other criminal activities.
- Electronic trading is altering financial relations in Europe. Its influence is largest in wholesale markets for foreign exchange and equities.
- In retail banking and customer relations the scope for e-finance penetration differs widely across countries both in Western and Eastern Europe.

Exercises

1. Describe the main Euromarket segments and discuss the advantages of the principles of revolving credit facilities and syndication.
2. Why do reference rates in the Euromarkets differ from national benchmarks and which are the impediments in fixed-income markets for individual countries to assume benchmark status across all maturities?
3. Discuss the advantages of offshore centres in the age of globalisation and financial market integration.

4. Discuss the advantages and disadvantages of small countries in their role as offshore centres to comply with international transparency standards.
5. How did the convergence of communications technology and computer technology influence the world of European finance with respect to:

   – customer services?
   – communication and networking?
   – electronic trading?

Additional Links and References

See for an overview of the history and functioning of the Euromarkets:

Dufey, Gunter and Ian Giddy (1994) *The International Money Market*, Englewood Cliffs, NJ: Prentice Hall.

The role of offshore financial centres in a changing environment and related concerns are discussed in:

Darbar, Salin M., R. Barry Johnston and Mary G. Zephirin (2003) Assessing offshore financial centers, *Finance & Development*, September, 32–5.

For more information about the Financial Stability Forum, the FATF and the IMF assessment programme for offshore financial centres see:

http://www.fsforum.org
http://www1.oecd.org/fatf/
http://www.imf.org/external/np/mae/oshore/2003/eng/073103.htm

For a survey on various forms of electronic finance and related aspects see:

Sato, Setsuya and John Hawkins (2001) Electronic finance: an overview of the issues, http://www.bis.org/publ/bispap07a.pdf

Data on internet and PC usage in international comparison can be found on the International Telecommunication Union (ITU) site:

http://www.itu.int/ITU-D/ict/statistics/

There have been many approaches to visualising information and internet traffic flows within and between countries which give an impression of the unequal access to electronic and virtual market places. A list can be found at Martin Dodge's site *Atlas of Cyberspaces*:

http://www.cybergeography.org/atlas/atlas.html

4
European Financial Markets
in the World Economy

In many respects, European financial institutions and activities have followed the overall trend towards globalisation and are strongly integrated both at a regional level and in the world financial system. But in some market segments *national structures and characteristics* still dominate. In parts, they are rooted in historically grown institutional factors and the legal environment, partly the reasons are diverging preferences and attitudes across countries.

4.1 BANKS

Western European banks are among the *leading financial institutions* in the world (Table 4.1). Among the Top 20 in Europe, the biggest one is the British HSBC Holdings with a capital of more than $35 billion. It is followed by a French bank, Crédit Agricole, and a German bank, Deutsche Bank, with a capital of nearly $29 billion and $22 billion, respectively. However, these are by far not the biggest banks in the world. The Number One and Two worldwide are two US banks, Citibank and Bank of America, followed by a Japanese bank, Mizuho Financial Group. Each of these has a capital exceeding $40 billion, Citibank's is almost $60 billion. HSBC ranks only fifth internationally and the next two Europeans rank 7 and 12 in the world, respectively. There are strong differences among countries: the *biggest European banks* are from the UK, France, Germany, Switzerland, the Netherlands and Spain. The first Italian bank in this ranking is Number 34 in the world, the biggest one from Belgium ranks 38. No banks from other European countries are found in this league.

In the euro area, Germany has by far the largest *number of banks*, followed by France, Austria and Italy (Table 4.2). More than one-quarter of all EU financial institutions, and almost 30% of those in the euro area, are located in Germany. Like Spain and Austria, the country is usually considered as heavily overbanked with a population per branch of 1450. Differences in *banking density* have many reasons. There are geographic factors such as population density and regional population distribution. Other explanations are historic – one example is the evolution of many small credit cooperatives in Germany – or the ways and speed with which structural adjustments have taken place.

There are also huge differences in *bank concentration* among European countries. For example, in Austria, France and Ireland the market share of the five largest banks together does not reach 50%, while in Belgium, Finland and the Netherland it is around 80% and in Spain it amounts to 88%. However, these numbers have to be taken with caution in fragmented markets like those of Germany and Italy. For instance, some observers argue that the low share of the Top Five in Germany, which is 20%, does not reflect an intense competition. Instead it is hiding the fact that savings banks and credit cooperatives, which together

Table 4.1   Western European banks in the world economy

Company	Country	Capital*	World rank
1. HSBC Holdings	United Kingdom	35 074	5
2. Crédit Agricole Groupe	France	28 876	7
3. Deutsche Bank	Germany	21 859	12
4. Royal Bank of Scotland	United Kingdom	21 830	13
5. BNP Paribas	France	21 748	15
6. HypoVereinsbank	Germany	19 154	16
7. HBOS	United Kingdom	18 086	19
8. Barclays Bank	United Kingdom	18 046	20
9. UBS	Switzerland	17 482	21
10. ABN-Amro Bank	Netherlands	16 942	22
11. Banco Santander Central Hispano	Spain	15 209	24
12. ING Bank	Netherlands	15 070	25
13. Rabobank Nederland	Netherlands	14 961	26
14. Société Générale	France	13 516	30
15. Lloyds TSB Group	United Kingdom	13 297	31
16. Banco Bilbao Vizcaya Argentaria	Spain	13 107	33
17. Intesa Bci	Italy	13 041	34
18. Credit Suisse Group	Switzerland	12 613	36
19. Fortis Bank	Belgium	11 432	38
20. Crédit Mutuel	France	10 877	39
In comparison:			
Citigroup	United States	58 448	1
Bank of America Corp	United States	41 972	2
Mizuho Financial Group	Japan	40 498	3

* In millions of US dollars. Capital is essential equity and reserves. Figures for Mizuho Financial Group refer to the year ended 31 March 2002, for all other banks to the year ended 31 December 2001.
Source: The Economist (2004) *Pocket world in figures*, London.

account for more than three-quarters of the German market, are operating on the regional principle where competition is factually precluded.

Recently, European banks are facing mounting *challenges* both within the region and worldwide:

- The development of new *technology* is affecting the very core of bank business in all areas of information, processing and delivery.
- There is an erosion of *entry barriers* into banking services leading to mounting competitive pressures in the industry.
- The trend towards *securitisation and allfinance* in the industry is forcing banks increasingly to compete with money and capital markets and non-bank financial institutions.
- Competition is also strengthened by the growing *institutionalisation* of saving and investment business and the increasing role of institutional fund managers in financial markets and systems.
- In addition, banks are losing business because of the growing *internalisation* of banking operations by large corporate customers.
- A greater variety of financial instruments and sophistication of financial techniques are increasing the *complexity* of bank business.

Table 4.2   Banks in the euro area

Country	Number of banks[1]	Population per branch[2]	Concentration[3]
Austria	812	1500^4	43
Belgium	109	1785^4	78
Finland	365	2630^5	80
France	952	2375^6	47
Germany	2232	1450	20
Greece	61	4305^4	66
Ireland	83	–	45
Italy	808	2125^6	28
Luxembourg	176	1395^4	30
Netherlands	491	2315^4	82
Portugal	198	1820^6	60
Spain	349	1008	88

[1] In October 2003.
[2] In 2001.
[3] Market share of the five largest banks as pecentage of the total assets of domestic credit institutions in 2001.
[4] In 1999.
[5] In 1998.
[6] In 2000.
Source: Bundesverband Deutscher Banken.

- The ongoing process of *financial integration* is exposing banks more and more to competition from foreign institutions in their home markets.
- The introduction of the *common currency* in Europe resulted in a decline of profitable trading opportunities in foreign exchange markets that otherwise might have compensated for losses in other business areas.

These and other developments explain why many observers expect a *declining role* of banks in European financial intermediation. However, others argue that a distinction must be made between banks' lending business and the prospects of the banking industry and of *banks as firms*. The core competences banks have, for example, regarding information, monitoring and risk analysis can be used in very different ways beside making loans, and the described challenges include new *opportunities* as well.

Just as foreign financial institutions penetrate home markets, banks may *diversify into foreign markets* exploiting the advantages of European financial integration. In addition, just as other industries diversify into banking, so are banks diversifying into other areas, offering a wider range of services, *developing their off-balance-sheet business* and moving more and more in the direction of contract banking, acting as managers of internal and external contracts on behalf of their customers. However, there are limits to diversification. Financial integration in Europe is still hampered by national rules and regulations, and reciprocity does not always work. While, for instance, retail stores and car producers are offering a range of financial services, including loans, banks will not start selling clothes or cars.

As Table 4.1 demonstrates, European banks are not well positioned to meet the described challenges as far as *size* is concerned. In international competition, size matters in many respects. It allows banks to realise scale economies that enable them to operate at lower costs than their competitors and enhance their scope for strategies to secure or increase market shares. Size facilitates the entrance into new markets and business fields and the absorption of temporary shocks and losses. In many European regions, the sheer *number* of banks prevents the exploitation of scale economies. A related aspect is the excess capacity created by large *branch networks* of banks with their unnecessary duplication of banking infrastructure and fixed costs. In addition, in order to stay competitive banks must increasingly offer a *range of services and expertise*, which by far may be too broad and expensive for the small and medium-size institutions among them.

The question then is how smaller banks may survive and withstand the growing competitive pressures. To them *contract banking*, where the bank is not offering a full range of services but coordinating inputs from a variety of suppliers, is becoming an attractive alternative. Contract banking includes the *outsourcing* of important functions. Examples are mortgage processing, credit card administration, cheque processing, network operations and management, and securities safe-keeping. The advantages are that costs and risks are spread and skills and specialist knowledge can be used that cannot be provided in-house. However, there are also disadvantages. These include the costs of managing the contracts, the danger of loss of control and the risk that the bank may unwittingly introduce its customers to a potential competitor.

Outsourcing is one way for a bank to secure economies of scale if it is not big enough. Another is to grow by *mergers and acquisitions*. At first view, the European internal market for financial services offers a unique opportunity in this respect. However, beside some spectacular cases, the experience so far is rather disappointing. Most big European bank mergers have taken place domestically, and instead of investing in neighbour countries European financial institutions are increasingly turning to other world regions.

Generally, European banks are increasingly competing for an *international clientele*. Some of them are able to exploit cultural advantages. One example is Spanish banks' strong links to Latin America. Some European banks are highly successful internationally as the results of a poll conducted regularly by the magazine *Euromoney* indicate. In 2004, 11 of the Top 20 were European banks, and a German bank showed the best overall performance (Table 4.3). The poll distinguishes five categories reflecting the increasing complexity of international bank activities.

The category *Underwriting* comprises banks' overall capital-raising abilities as well as their skills in individual markets for debt and equity. *Trading* refers to the success of dealers in various markets. *Transactions processing* includes cash management services related to foreign exchange transactions and global custodial services. The category *Internet* refers to borrowers' nominations for the best websites used for capital raising, corporate treasurers' votes for the best websites used for risk management, and the capabilities for online execution, research and straight-through processing of foreign exchange transactions. The last category is *Advisory* which is related to foreign exchange research, risk management, credit research and M&A. Some European banks have successfully specialised in individual categories. For example, S-E-Banken from Sweden which is not among the Top 20 in the overall rating holds place 18 in Trading, and the Rothschild Group from the UK (overall place: 38) is Number 22 in Advisory.

In addition, European banks are following an international trend in increasingly looking for *new opportunities* to improve earnings in times of historically low margins and interest rates. Some of the biggest ones are taking more risks engaging in proprietary trading besides executing trades for customers. Some are actively contributing to the development of new highly successful financial instruments and related tools. One example is the market for credit derivatives, the development of a related legal framework and the establishment and management of a respective index for tracing market movements.

Table 4.3   European banks in a global environment

		Rank in the category				
Overall rank	Bank	Under-writing	Trading	Transaction processing	Internet	Advisory
1	Deutsche Bank	1	2	3	2	1
2	Citigroup	2	1	1	6	4
3	UBS	4	3	5	1	2
4	JP Morgan Chase	3	5	4	3	3
5	Goldman Sachs	6	4	33	7	5
6	Morgan Stanley Dean Witter	5	10	38	14	6
7	HSBC Group	9	11	2	10	9
8	Merrill Lynch	8	8	–	9	8
9	Credit Suisse First Boston	10	9	18	15	7
10	Barclays Capital	7	6	19	8	12
11	ABN Amro	11	12	8	5	13
12	Lehman Brothers	13	7	–	11	11
13	BNP Paribas	12	15	25	12	10
14	Dresdner Kleinwort Wasserstein	14	16	11	4	14
15	Bank of America	17	13	15	13	15
16	Société Générale	15	20	23	–	16
17	Royal Bank of Scotland	20	14	32	17	17
19	Crédit Agricole Indosuez	18	21	26	21	19
18	Royal Bank of Canada	26	17	14	38	24
20	Commerzbank	22	32	27	19	20

Source: *Euromoney* (2004) Poll of polls, February.

4.2   EXCHANGES

With the erosion of barriers between bank finance and capital markets the competition between the two intensified with European exchanges facing their own challenges in adapting to the changing environment. In Europe, competition of exchanges is a recent phenomenon. European capital markets were – and still are – *highly fragmented*. In 1998, there were 32 stock exchanges in Europe (compared to eight in the US) and 23 derivatives exchanges (seven in the US). In 2000, the largest European market, London, generated only about 23%, or €4.8 trillion, of the transaction volume in the largest US market, NASDAQ (€22.2 trillion). While in the US and Canada traditionally exchanges were functioning in a competitive environment, European institutions were *local monopolies* acting either as public entities, as at the continent, or as formally private bodies strongly regulated by public rules.

Technological developments, liberalisation, financial integration and the concomittant transformation of European securities markets brought a rapid *consolidation* of the industry with trading, clearing and settlement – albeit slowly – becoming more efficient. There were mergers and technological agreements among existing exchanges, and new institutions were created. Examples are the agreement of the Helsinki Stock Exchange and the Finnish Options Market (SOM) to form a new company, HEX Ltd (Helsinki Stock and Derivatives Exchange Clearing House) in July 1997, or the cooperation which in September 1997 led Deutsche Börse and the Swiss Exchange to merge their derivative exchanges into a single market,

EUREX. In addition, there were hostile takeover attempts and price wars as well as many forms of non-price competition. The latter includes process and product innovation, market architecture – such as LSE's switch from a dealer market to a quote-driven system – and advertisements. The most serious competitive move – and for some observers the first direct one in nearly 20 years – among European stock exchanges was the LSE's bid to become home of Dutch equities trading in signing up banks that represented more than half the market trading in Amsterdam-listed shares in 2004.

Consolidated pan-European stock exchanges emerged. In January 1998, Stockholmsbörsen and the Copenhagen Stock Exchange signed a cooperation agreement to form *NOREX*, a common nordic equity market. The two exchanges remained independent, but allowed cross-membership and used a single buy-and-sell order book for each security. In addition, they adopted common trading rules and a uniform trading platform, Stockholmsbörsen's SAX 2000. NOREX was later joined by the Helsinki Exchange and the Oslo Exchange and, more recently, by the exchanges of Reykjavik, Tallin and Riga. Another consolidation was the formation of an integrated European stock exchange, *Euronext*, by the Paris Bourse, the Amsterdam Exchange and the Brussels Exchange in March 2000. Euronext provides centralised trading and a uniform trading platform which establishes a single trade price. However, the different jurisdictions and local licenses of the individual exchanges are maintained and shares are listed at a national level.

Consolidation strongly increased the efficiency of European markets. An analysis conducted in 2001 showed that Euronext and Deutsche Börse, which are among the most efficient markets in Europe, are actually more efficient – measured in transaction and liquidity costs – than the New York Stock Exchange (NYSE) although the latter has a five to six times higher trading volume.

Virt-X

In June 2001, the blue chip section of the Swiss equity market was merged with Tradepoint, a London-based electronic exchange, to form Virt-X. The exchange's initial aim was more than simply dominating the domestic market. It wanted to become one of the leading European exchanges, setting itself the target of capturing 10% of trading in the 600 leading European stocks. However, after a year, it was forced to cut shares traded from 600 to 270 and then to 70. In December 2002, the Swiss Exchange took full control of Virt-X, buying out the stakes of the investment banks who had initially backed the Tradepoint venture. Following the move, Virt-X has been able to increase steadily the number of non-Swiss stocks traded on the platform to more than 150 at end of 2003. In 2003, the exchange introduced a central counterparty system, provided by two groups, the London Clearing House and SIS x-clear. The aim was to reduce costs at each stage of the trading. With success: Virt-X's share of trading in leading Swiss stocks has leaped from 71% in 2001 to 92% in 2003. At the end of 2003, the combination of the Swiss market, known as SWX, and Virt-X represented the fourth largest European stock exchange grouping by market capitalisation.

Electronic exchanges also attempted to evolve into pan-European exchanges – so far with mixed success. Two examples are Jiway and Virt-X. *Jiway*, a retail-focused centre was launched by OM Gruppen and Morgan Stanley Dean Witter in the year 2000 as an online cross-border exchange for retail investors. It was bought out by OM in September 2001 in an attempt to cut costs by integrating its exchange operations with those of the OM London Exchange, but finally had to be closed down due to financial losses. *VirtX* was formed in 2001 by a merger of Tradepoint, the UK electronic platform, and the Swiss Stock Exchange blue chips and specialised in cross-border trade, undercutting other exchanges with cheaper fees for trading and settlement. It is more successful than Jiway, but its main shareholders are said to continue to direct most of their share trading volumes through national stock exchanges which offer better liquidity.

Ownership structures of European exchanges were changing. Many institutions demutualised and some sought stock market listing to raise cash in order to keep pace with modernisation and the need to overhaul transaction-related technology (Table 4.4). As a consequence, European exchanges became equipped with the *latest electronic trading systems* which considerably strengthened their international competitiveness and, for example, made them less vulnerable to competition from those electronic communication networks (ECNs) that posed a growing challenge to their US counterparts still clinging to traditional floor-based trading. The NSC system was launched in Paris in 1995, the SETS in London and XETRA in Frankfurt in 1997. With demutualisation, pressure on the exchanges rose to make profits in order to meet share-holders' expectations. As a result, exchanges increasingly offer *extended services* at all stages of the value chain of the exchange business ranging from trading over clearing and settlement to depository work, or even try to expand their business lines in hope of generating new revenues.

In general, there are many influences determining the success or failure of an exchange. These are related either to the objects traded, the means of trading or the price dissemination process. The main function of stock exchanges is to provide a *trading system* which brings together buyers and sellers and enables the price discovery process to take place effectively. Trading systems differ by the trading technologies and trading rules applied. Other important services include software development and data dissemination.

Table 4.4   Demutualisation and listing of European stock exchanges

Exchange	Year of demutualisation	Listing
Stockholm Stock Exchange	1993	1993
Helsinki Stock Exchange	1995	
Copenhagen Stock Exchange	1996	
Amsterdam Stock Exchange	1997	
Italian Stock Exchange	1997	
Vienna Stock Exchange	1998	
Athens Stock Exchange	1999	2000
Deutsche Börse	2000	2001
Euronext	2000	2001
London Stock Exchange	2000	2001
Paris Bourse	2000	
Oslo Exchange	2001	
Budapest Stock Exchange	2002	
BME – Bolsas y Mercadores Espanoles	2002	
SWX Swiss Exchange	2002	

Source: OECD.

These days, exchanges face increasing competitive pressures regarding the traditional *economic functions* they fulfil. Those include:

- The *monitoring* of exchange trading to prevent manipulation and insider trading. On the one hand, experience shows that this function has not always been performed properly in the past. One example is specialist firms who executed market buy orders from clients by selling stocks from their own inventories at times of falling stock prices. On the other hand, competitors such as ECNs are developing sophisticated monitoring systems.
- The *signalling* to investors that an issuing firm's stock is of high quality thereby enhancing the company's prestige and reputational capital. This function is increasingly replaced by services of institutions such as accounting firms, investment banks, independent analysts and broker-dealer firms, which often have the advantage of providing customer-tailored services to their clients.
- The *clearing* function which ensures that the purchased stocks are delivered and cash is received. This is an aspect which deserves special attention and will be discussed later on.
- The function of *providing liquidity* in bringing together buyers and sellers. Liquidity allows the buying or selling of assets quickly and at a price similar to those of previous transactions under the assumption that no new information is available. In illiquid markets with few buyers and sellers, counterparties for a transaction may be difficult to find, and even small trades may trigger significant price fluctuations.

Given the declining role of monitoring and signalling, enhancing the liquidity of companies' shares has become the exchanges' main service in which they compete with one another. One aspect here is the ability to attract *institutional investors* with their desire to execute large transactions without triggering price reactions and to accommodate block trades.

Competition in this area is strongly influenced by the way in which trading is organised. In traditional exchanges, intermediaries such as *market makers and specialists* fulfil an important role as liquidity providers. By contrast, many electronic markets are organised as *limit order books* with liquidity entirely depending on the submitted orders of traders. These systems seem at a disadvantage when trading is concentrated on one side of the market, which is one reason why European exchanges using electronic limit order books introduced market-maker elements. One example is Deutsche Börse, which relied on *liquidity sponsors* for individual securities in the Neuer Markt.

It is only recently that in the literature exchanges are considered as *firms* instead of markets. These days, they derive their *incomes* from three major sources:

- trading fees for intermediaries trading on the exchange, including membership fees;
- listing fees, including the initial admission fee a company would pay when listing and an additional annual fee; and
- information and price-dissemination fees from property rights on prices formed on the exchange that are sold or given out to non-member firms.

However, fees are not only a source of income but also an important element of *international competition*. As Table 4.5 demonstrates there are considerable differences between European exchanges, although amounts are often smaller than in the US and Asia. Listing fees are one important argument for foreigners listing on an exchange. However, Table 4.6 shows that some exchanges manage to attract a high share of foreign companies despite comparatively high listing fees.

Table 4.5   Listing fees of European stock exchanges in international comparison*

Exchange	Admission fee		Annual fee	
	Minimum	Maximum	Minimum	Maximum
London	5 660	309 183	2 122	34 845
Deutsche Börse	846	n.a.	0	0
Borsa Italiana	8 464	423 226	5 501	211 613
Swiss Exchange	4 452	25 602	3 339	n.a.
Stockholm	55 368	n.a.	11 624	290 590
Wiener Börse	3 069	90 993	2 454	4 909
By comparison:				
NYSE	51 550	500 000	32 340	500 000
NASDAQ	29 525	95 000	10 710	50 000
Hong Kong	19 231	83 335	18 590	152 311

* As of early 2002, in million US dollars.
Source: OECD.

Table 4.6   Foreign companies listed on European stock exchanges in international comparison 2003

Exchange	Total companies listed	Share of foreign companies*
London	2 692	14.2
Luxembourg	242	81.8
Copenhagen	194	3.6
Deutsche Börse	866	21.0
Euronext	1 392	24.9
Helsinki	145	2.1
Borsa Italiana		2.9
Oslo	178	12.4
Spanish Exchanges (BME)	3 223	1.0
Stockholm	282	5.7
Swiss Exchange	419	31.0
Wiener Börse	125	16.8
by comparison:		
NYSE	2 308	20.2
NASDAQ	3 294	10.4
Hong Kong	1 037	1.0

* In % of total companies listed.
Source: WFE.

Thus, there are further *reasons for foreigners to list* on an exchange. Those include:

- Location of business activities. Corporations seek to get their stocks listed and traded in countries where most of their products are sold and their production activities are concentrated.
- Diversification. Companies are pursuing global financing (and investment) strategies in order to keep the costs of financing as low as possible and reduce refinancing risks.

- Trading costs.
- Market volume.
- Market liquidity.
- Own-industry listings.

Studies have found that the last three aspects seem particularly important to European corporations. Apparently, Europeans prefer large and liquid markets where other companies from their own industry are already cross-listed. *Market volume and capitalisation* means a broader set of potential investors, greater visibility and an improved reputation for the company and thereby additional prestige. Further exchange-specific incentives for foreign corporations are the presence of well-known companies in general, analysts' coverage, communication flows and institutional factors such as clearing and settlement. *Analysts' coverage* is considered as an advantage because it is exposing a company to the attention of a wider investor base. *Communication flows* do not only allow people 'to be with one's peers' but also create opportunities for companies to imitate the successful.

Besides, there are *country-specific factors* influencing an exchange's international attractiveness. These include the legal system and accounting standards, rules for investor protection and the enforceability of contracts, but also bureaucratic delays and the degree of red tape, the language and what is called cultural homogeneity. The latter is considered to reduce the costs of commmunication and frictions in legal and accounting matters. Table 4.7 summarises the main exchange- and country-specific influences.

The process of *consolidation* of European exchanges, which started in the late 1990s, brought many advantages (Table 4.8). On the one hand, there are *operational economies of scale* from the establishment of compatible or shared trading platforms: developing, upgrading

Table 4.7 Determinants of exchanges' international competitiveness

Exchange-specific	Country-specific
Trading costs	Investor protection
Listing fees	Enforceability of contracts
Market volume	Bureaucratic delays
Liquidity	Accounting standards
Own-industry listings	Language
Listings of well-known companies	Legal system
Analysts' coverage	Cultural homogeneity
Communication flows	
Institutional factors	

Table 4.8 Consolidation – advantages and barriers

Advantages	Barriers
Operational economies of scale	Product differentiation
Trading economies of scale	Legal and regulatory differences
Compatible/shared trading platforms	Information costs
Greater market liquidity	Home-country bias
Reduced market fragmentation	Fragmentation of clearing and settlement

and operating a trading system has substantial fixed costs that can be shared. A related aspect is the advantage consolidation has for cross-border transactions in reducing access costs. Consolidation enables investment banks and brokers to connect to a limited number of pan-European exchanges instead of maintaining connections with a large number of small local stock exchanges with incompatible trading systems.

Another advantage of consolidation is *trading economies of scale* arising from higher trading volumes and greater market liquidity. A further, rather long-run benefit may be the *reduction of market fragmentation* resulting from parallel trading of the same security on different exchanges. So far, the number of foreign companies listed on European stock exchanges is relatively modest and also includes non-European companies. However, with increasing market integration more companies can be expected to list on multiple exchanges making fragmentation a more pressing issue. Under a pan-European system, all buy and sell orders for a security could be concentrated enhancing price stability and more precise price discovery.

However, despite the potential benefits, barriers to consolidation of European exchanges are numerous. The most important is *product differentiation* in order to meet investor and company preferences. Smaller exchanges often find a niche in offering distinct products and targeting diverse clienteles making the emergence of a single pan-European institution rather unlikely. Another hindrance is *legal and regulatory differences* across countries. These include:

- differences in listing requirements;
- trading practices;
- antimanipulation laws;
- accounting and disclosure rules; and
- tax treatments.

Differences in tax treatments refer to taxes and mechanisms for tax collection as well as double-taxation treaties. In several European countries, policies lead to, or reinforce, a *home-country bias*: examples are pension funds required to invest largely in domestic government securities, or favourable tax treatments granted to domestic equity investment.

Another explanation for the prevailing home-country bias of European investors is *information costs* associated with cross-border trading. Geographic distance makes access to information on foreign securities difficult and expensive to obtain. In addition, cultural and linguistic barriers make it hard to interpret and evaluate this information.

One market where competition within Europe and worldwide has strongly increased in recent years is *exchange-traded derivatives*. This holds in particular for the relation between Liffe and Eurex. Liffe is the oldest financial futures exchange in Europe (Table 4.9). Established in 1982, its position as Number One in European trading was seriously threatened for the first time in October 1997 when DTB, one of the predecessors of Eurex, managed to win more than 50% of the market for German government bonds, known as Bunds, from Liffe. The development is a classical case of how a once established critical mass helps to lock in customers. In 1997, the authorisation from the US Commodity Futures Trading Commission enabled US-based members to trade Bund futures at the DTB giving the exchange a competitive advantage over its then dominant rival. As a consequence, DTB's market share went up to practically 100% within the year.

Recently, the competition between Eurex and Liffe is focusing more and more on innovative products instead of prices and on the improvement of remote access networks and there are indications that in the future it will further extend beyond Europe. Liffe started *challenging*

Table 4.9   A brief history of Liffe and Eurex

	Liffe		Eurex	
Established		1982		1998
Mergers/Predecessors	Merger with LTOM	1992	DTB	1988
	Merger with LCE	1996	SOFFEX	1988
Electronic trading	LIFFE CONNECT	1999	From the beginning	
Events	German Bund future accounting for 20% of total revenue	1997	Becoming the world's largest derivative exchange	1999
	End of Bund future trading	1998		
	Start of trading in euro interest-rate products	1999		
	Acquisition by Euronext to form Euronext.liffe	2002		
International advances	Launch of the US NQLX for trading single stock futures	2003	Start of Eurex US	2004
	Start of trading eurodollar derivatives	2004		

the US market in 2001 with the launch of single stock futures (SSF) in an initial joint venture with NASDAQ, NQLX. This ended in 2003 when NASDAQ decided to withdraw from joint ventures in Europe in general and Euronext.liffe acquired its 50% stake. Liffe's US rival is ONE-Chicago, a joint venture between the three main Chicago derivatives exchanges. Another advance challenging Chicago's exchanges was Liffe's announcement in 2004 of plans to trade eurodollar futures products, the mainstay of the Chicago Mercantile Exchange (CME). The Chicago exchanges are also the main rivals of *Eurex-US*, the electronic derivatives exchange launched by Eurex in early 2004 which, above all, is challenging the Chicago Board of Trade (CBOT) in trading in US Treasury derivatives.

Not all exchange-traded products are actually traded on an exchange. In some European stock and derivative markets, a substantial portion of trades is matched internally in cross trades at trading banks or other institutions. This is in contrast to the US where *internalisation* meets strong resistance in particular from floor brokers – an argument which, for example, was also raised by the CBOT in reaction to the Eurex-US advance. In London, in 2003, internalisation accounted for as much as 30% of equity trades. Nevertheless, there are exchanges in Europe, too, such as Paris and Milan, that require all trades to be done on the exchange.

Internalisation has been widely criticised by its opponents as *undermining market liquidity*. Banks that are crossing trades are bypassing the exchange. As a result, prices on the exchange may no longer reflect the true market and investors will lose out. On the other hand, the proponents of internalisation point out that without this practice certain trades would not get done at all or, as in the case of large block trades, only at less efficient prices.

One important element in the competition of exchanges and, more broadly, the development of capital markets in general is the presence of *institutional investors*. In this regard, it is important to note that the European Union is a fast-growing market for *investment funds*.

The UCITS (Undertakings for Collective Investment in Transferable Securities) Directive of 1985 intended to provide a 'passport' for pan-European sales of funds. But, so far, its success is limited. Market fragmentation is still high and national markets are dominated by domestic

Table 4.10   Eurex and Liffe core products

Eurex	Liffe
Fixed income derivatives • Euro Bund future • German yield curve from one month to 30 years • Swiss yield curve from eight to 13 years	Short-term interest-rate contracts • One-month Eonia future • Three-month EURIBOR future • Options on three-month EURIBOR futures • Sterling, Swiss franc, Euroyen interest-rate contracts
Market sector index derivatives • Automobile • Banks • Energy • Healthcare	Government bond contracts • Long gilt futures and options • Japanese Government Bond (JGB) futures • Two-year German Government Treasury Note (Schatz) futures
Equity derivatives • Futures and options on blue chip German, Swiss and Finnish indexes • Futures and options on European and global indexes • Options on Dutch, Finnish, French, German, Italian, Swiss and US stocks • Options on global stocks (DaimlerChrysler, Microsoft, Nokia)	Swap note derivatives • Futures and options on futures on euro-denominated swap notes • US dollar-denominated contracts Equity derivatives • Futures and options on equity indices • Individual UK, continental European and US equities contracts
Exchange traded funds (ETFs) derivatives	Commodities (futures and options on futures on cocoa, coffee, wheat, the weather)

fund companies. Only *three countries* (Luxembourg, Ireland and the UK) are selling their funds at least in two-thirds of all EU member countries. Even in countries where the number of foreign funds available is higher than that of domestic ones, this has to be put into perspective. Many of those foreign funds have their domiciles in Luxembourg, Dublin and other tax havens and are designed to target investors in specific national markets, thus being cross-border only in a formal sense.

Measured by the number of funds available, France is by far the *biggest fund market*, followed by Germany, Spain and the UK (Table 4.11). But, on average, EU funds are small in international comparison. For instance, at the end of the first quarter 2001 the average size of a EU fund was €176 million, compared to the average US size of €910 million. Size also differs considerably between EU countries. The *largest funds* are in Italy and the Netherlands, the smallest in Portugal, Spain and Finland.

With fund size being an important determinant of cost the differences indicate a considerable potential for scale economies by pooling funds in a unified EU market thereby strengthening European financial competitiveness. However, there are still many *obstacles to cross-border sales* of funds. Most are grounded in regulation and taxation. Some are related to advertising, others concern registration. For example, in Italy registration may take up to six months, Spain requires an official translation of the fund prospectus, the Netherlands asks for a fund's detailed tax history. Those and other obstacles are increasing the fixed cost for the

Table 4.11   The fund industry in Europe

Country	Number of funds available[1]	Average fund size[2]	Country share[3]	Significant discriminatory tax barriers to the sale of foreign funds
France	6 760	181	22	Plan d'Epargne en Actions ('PEA')
Germany	4 644	233	7	Existing foreign investment fund law Tax reform measures
Spain	4 233	71	5	None noted
UK	4 081	248	12	Offshore fund legislation UK imputation tax system
Austria	3 121	176	2	Existing income tax regime
Switzerland	2 922	n.a.	2	n.a.
Italy	2 828	417	13	Capital gains tax
Luxembourg	n.a.	167	23	None noted
Belgium	2 380	108	2	Tax on distributions to individual investors Participation exemption . Benefit from tax credits
Netherlands	2 352	389	3	Reclaim of foreign withholding tax
Sweden	2 096	172	2	None noted
Finland	1 163	56	n.a.	None noted
Ireland	841	118	4	Taxation of Irish investors in offshore UCITS
Norway	534	n.a.	n.a.	n.a.
Portugal	468	78	n.a.	Different income tax regimes for individual investors
Greece	401	126	n.a.	Investment funds legislation penalising foreign UCITS
Denmark	302	123	n.a.	Foreign fund legislation

[1] As of March 2001.
[2] In millions of euro, end of March 2001.
[3] Country share (domicile) in %, end of 2000.
Source: Heinemann, Friedrich (2002) The benefits of creating an integrated EU market for investment funds, ZEW Discussion Paper No. 02-27, ftp://ftp.zew.de/pub/zew-docs/dp/dp0227.pdf.

firms which helps explain why foreign funds are more present in the big markets than in the smaller ones.

4.3   VENTURE CAPITAL

One market segment which plays a growing role in Europe is venture capital. By definition, venture capital is sought after by fast-growing small and medium-sized entreprises (SMEs) that have specific financial needs. The projects they are engaged in usually have a high risk and the entrepreneurs rarely have collaterable assets. As a rule, banks consider these firms as costly, risky and difficult to monitor.

In general, several stages of entrepreneurial development are distinguished by which different forms of finance are available (Table 4.12). At the first stage, as a rule, the firm relies entirely on personal savings and money from friends and family. At later stages, venture

Table 4.12   Stages of entrepreneurial development and financing

Stage	Status	Financing
'Seed' or 'Concept'	The inventor stage. There is an idea and a concept, but no management plan, timetable or market research	High risk deters even traditional venture capital firms. As a rule, personal savings or friend and family money are the only funds available at this stage
'Startup'	At least one person is pursuing the project on a full-time basis. A business plan is set up, market analysis is undertaken and there is a management team	Fund raising becomes a major issue. Traditional venture capital firms may show a first interest. Other sources of finance are private placements and grants from foundations and government sources
First stage	Some company activity has taken place (first products are sold, services tried by customers). There have been first setbacks, marketing is being refined and the business plan is adjusted	This is the most preferable stage of traditional venture capital firms. Strategic partnerships may provide funding, too
Second stage	Business activities are growing as are assets and liabilities. The company is sporadically breaking even. Cash flow management becomes critical. Export marketing may be explored and management becomes more sophisticated	Venture capital financing becomes more sophisticated. Additional funds may come from larger companies that are looking for product distribution opportunities, institutional investors, venture leasing companies and additional strategic partners
Third stage (mezzanine stage)	All systems are working and the potential for major success is becoming visible. Pressures increase for proving second- and third-generation products, increase profitability records, improve the balance sheet and firmly establish market share and penetration	The company's financial choices are becoming broader: It has to decide either to take more venture capital, a bridge or mezzanine financing before going public, being acquired (possibly by a strategic partner) or selling out to another company
'Harvest'	The company is operating successfully	The company leaves the realm of private equity and is either going public, being acquired, selling out or merging

capital firms show a growing interest in its projects, more and more diverse sources of funds become available and a market for the firm's capital gradually begins to emerge. In the final stage at the latest, the firm leaves the realm of private equity and emerges as a public company.

For investors in these firms, *exit* may take several forms during the development process:

• Trade sales. These are outright, phased or partial sales of the company to a strategic investor or to an industrial or commercial company that aims at incorporating the target company's product lines as part of its own business. Trade sales are the predominant mode of exit in all venture capital markets.

- Private placement. Here the company is sold to an investor who is interested in gaining control over it without offering the shares to the public.
- Share repurchase by the entrepreneurs. In general, this form of exit is considered as indicating that the undertaking was less successful than expected.
- Public offering.

The latter is regarded as the most successful form of venture capital exit. Public offerings usually take place on so-called *growth exchanges*. In Europe, with the rising popularity of venture capital after the mid-1990s, several exchanges were established as special growth markets. Examples are the *Alternative Investment Market (AIM)* in London which included traditional small capitalisation companies and growth companies, the *Nouveau Marché* in France which was set up beside the traditional Second Marché functioning as a listing place for small companies with more modest growth potential, and the *Neuer Markt* in Germany which had a strong orientation towards technology companies and reached a high market capitalisation. By the end of 2001, about 20 growth markets were operating in Europe. Many of their activities were strongly driven back with the sharp falls in technology values in 2000–2001, and some of them never managed to recover. Neuer Markt was closed in 2002.

Some growth exchanges formed *international alliances*. The Nordic Growth market which existed as a joint exchange alongside national markets in Nordic countries is one example, another is the EuroNM, a loose alliance created by the growth markets in Germany, France, Italy, Belgium and the Netherlands, which was aimed at becoming a pan-European platform for growth stocks and was abandoned in 2001.

Beside the exchanges, a number of *electronic platforms* for trading growth equities across Europe emerged. One was NASDAQ Europe, owned by NASDAQ and designed to trade throughout Europe with links to its global trading platform. Another was EASDAQ, which was set up in Belgium, closely modelled on NASDAQ, and acquired by NASDAQ in 2001.

The venture capital sector, both in Europe and worldwide, was long a *quantité négligeable* in international financial markets (Table 4.13). It largely benefited from bullish '*new economy*' sentiment and a rush of investors into information and communication technologies and biotechnologies values in the second half of the 1990s, and was hit more hardly than traditional markets from the following downturn.

The *largest and most developed market* for venture capital in Europe is in the UK accounting for about 38% of venture investments. In contrast to other European countries the UK market is characterised by a strong preference for later-stage investments and larger

Table 4.13   Private equity and venture capital in the US and Europe*

	United States		Europe	
	Funds raised	Funds invested	Funds raised	Funds invested
1980	2.3 (2.1)	0.01 (0.6)	–	–
1985	6.3 (3.1)	2.1 (3.4)	–	–
1990	10.8 (3.1)	15.8 (3.3)	5.8 (–)	5.2 (3.0)
1995	41.8 (9.9)	21.9 (5.5)	5.7 (–)	7.3 (3.4)
2000	167.7 (92.9)	167.6 (103.5)	43.5 (20.4)	32.2 (18.1)

* In billions of US dollars, venture capital in parantheses.
Source: OECD.

transactions, and has a substantial share of capital from overseas, in particular from North America. For early-stage deals that require smaller investments transaction costs are comparatively high. As a consequence, even in this market, access to capital for smaller firms remains limited.

A comparison, for example, with the German market, shows further differences. One is *investment by sector* which reflects the different structures of both economies. While in Germany the focus of venture capital firms is on services and low-tech manufacturing, in the UK venture market there is a strong and growing orientation towards high-technology sectors with software and computer companies accounting for almost 30% of the number of companies receiving private equity financing followed by pharmaceuticals, health and IT hardware, in addition to newer sectors such as media and photography and the leisure industry. Another difference is *reliance on government sources*. This is greater in Germany while UK venture capital firms prefer public co-investments.

An annual survey conducted by the European Venture Capital Association (EVCA) shows that in many European countries *taxes and laws* need reforms to attract private equity (Table 4.14). This holds in particular for many new EU entrants but also, for example, for Austria, Denmark and Germany. The survey is based on criteria that are considered as key to a favourable environment for private equity. These include fund structures, merger regulations, tax rates and incentives. The UK is leading the league table with a virtually free reign for pension funds

Table 4.14   Private equity environment in Europe*

Country	Rating
United Kingdom	1.26
Luxembourg	1.49
Ireland	1.53
Greece	1.75
Netherlands	1.76
Portugal	1.81
Belgium	1.82
Hungary	1.86
Italy	1.86
France	1.89
Switzerland	1.95
Spain	1.96
Norway	2.04
Sweden	2.05
Czech Republic	2.12
Poland	2.13
Finland	2.30
Germany	2.37
Austria	2.42
Denmark	2.46
Slovak Republic	2.49

*National ranking of conditions for private equity, 2004.
1 = more favourable, 3 = less favourable.
Source: EVCA, *Financial Times*.

and insurance companies to invest in private equity and venture capital, tax relief for individual investors and no VAT on management charges and carried interest.

4.4   PAYMENT, CLEARING AND SETTLEMENT SYSTEMS

One area in which the European financial landscape is in constant change is payment, clearing and settlement. Initially created to meet purely *domestic needs*, national systems in Europe are usually organised around accounts held at the home central banks, and access to the local central securities depositories (CSDs), and differ in many respects. However, even before the advent of the common currency there had been *efforts to harmonise and consolidate* systems and to create pan-European institutions.

There are several ways in which systems for payment, clearing and settlement in financial markets can be categorised. One is according to the *nature of transactions*, for example, distinguishing between small- and large-value transfers or between systems for individual payments and bulk payments. Another approach contrasts *market participants* focusing on payment media used by non-banks on the one hand and interbank exchange and settlement on the other. Still another classification refers to financial market *segments*, for instance, distinguishing systems for settling trades in money and foreign exchange markets from those for securities and derivatives. In addition, there are differences in the *institutional design* of payment systems. The most important criterion here is the time it takes to reach finality. Further, risks are increasing when, instead of being kept within national borders, more than one country is involved in the payment and settlement process.

Real-time Gross Settlement (RTGS)

When in February 1995 one of the oldest British merchant banks, Barings Bank, went bankrupt after one of its traders had lost about ¥850 million on the Singapore and Osaka futures exchanges a widely unnoticed effect was a resulting problem in the then existing ECU clearing system. This threatened to block settlement of ECU50 billion of payments. Barings itself was involved in less than 1% of those payments. The case is a classic example of the systemic risk inherent in large-value net settlement systems. These systems are constantly keeping track of banks' net positions including thousands of payment instructions in the course of the day. At day's end the net amounts owed are settled. If clearing becomes impossible for one party, settlement between all participants is blocked and no payments take place.

In real-time gross settlement (RTGS) systems this risk is avoided. Funds transfers are settled individually as soon as orders are sent. These systems allow for *intra-day finality*, i.e. the certainty that transactions will not be unwound if a bank fails to settle. Funds received through the system are unconditional and irrevocable. However, RTGS systems have several disadvantages, too. The biggest is the *liquidity constraint* which poses a big challenge to both banks and central banks. With transactions settled individually instead of netting and bunching payments at the end of the day liquidity needs are much higher. Banks must fine-tune their use of liquidity during the day. There are special dangers involved in needing to provide cash several times a day which also has implications for central bank policy. On the one hand, intra-day credit available to banks should be sufficient to guarantee smooth payment flows. On the other hand, it should not be so cheap that banks are encouraged to take risks. Some central banks are charging for liquidity provision – and some of them do it not by the day but by the hour. Examples are the Bank of Japan which charges a flat rate every four hours and the US Federal Reserve charging Fed Funds even by the minute.

The smooth functioning of payment systems is essential for modern economies. This is one reason why it is of particular concern to *central banks*. Any malfunctioning threatens to undermine the stability of financial institutions and markets, to affect the confidence of its users and ultimately to erode public trust in the currency. In addition, payment systems are important vehicles for the implementation of monetary policy. This explains why payment and settlement services offered by the private sector are overseen by central banks that are concerned with system stability – in contrast to prudential supervisors looking at individual institutions – and why central banks also provide settlement services themselves and sometimes assume an operational role in payment systems. The latter holds in particular for the *European System of Central Banks (ESCB)* for which the dual role as overseer and service provider is explicitly stated in its statute.

To operate their own system, the Trans-European Automated Real-time Gross settlement Express Transfer, or *TARGET*, system, is one way for the central banks in the ESCB to promote the safe and efficient functioning of payment systems in the area. Established in 1999, TARGET is a real-time gross settlement (*RTGS*) system for the euro providing facilities for settlement in central bank money. Payment transactions are settled one by one on a continuous basis. It is a *decentralised* system consisting of 15 national RTGS systems, which are connected to the ECB payment mechanism (Figure 4.1). All countries that are adopting the euro must participate in TARGET. On the other hand, Denmark, Sweden and the UK, which are not taking part in the common currency, are connected to TARGET, too. TARGET is a

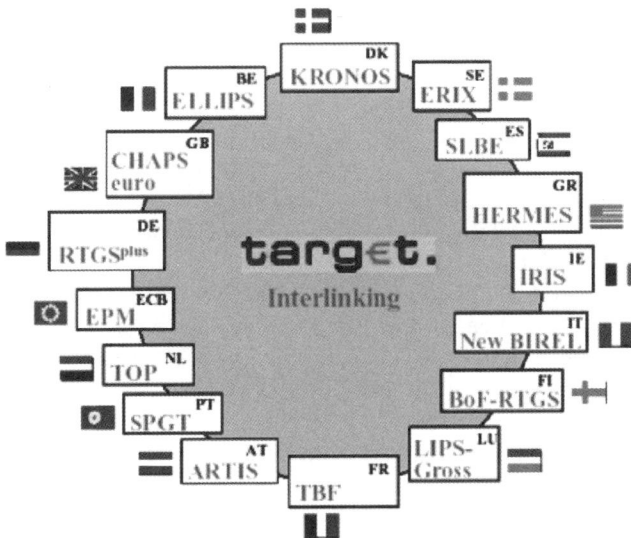

Figure 4.1 Decentralised structure of target. *Source*: European Central Bank: http://www.ecb.int/paym/target/current/view/html/index.en.html

settlement system for wholesale trading, i.e. for *large-value interbank payments*. In addition to banks there are several groups of participants that may be admitted to the related national systems. Those are:

- treasury departments of central or regional governments of member states active in money markets;
- public-sector bodies of member states which are authorised to hold accounts for customers;
- investment firms established in the European Economic Area which are authorised and supervised by a recognised competent authority; and
- organisations providing clearing or settlement services subject to oversight by a competent authority.

In the TARGET system, there is no central counterparty. Cross-border TARGET payments are processed via the national RTGS systems and exchanged *directly on a bilateral basis* between central banks. The national systems and the ECB payment mechanism (EPM) are connected via a telecommunications network called *Interlinking*. Credit institutions participating in this system are required to hold minimum reserves with their central bank, which can be used for settlement purposes during the day. In addition, intraday credit is provided free of charge. Both allow liquidity to be managed very flexibly and at low cost. From 2005 onwards, *TARGET2* will be operating as a follow-up providing a common centralised platform in particular for the new EU member states, which, for the foreseeable future, will not be able to run their own RTGS systems.

The only other EU-wide large-value payment system is *EURO 1*. This was established by the Euro Banking Association (EBA), an organisation of EU-based commercial banks and EU branches of non-EU banks, which is intended to be a forum for issues related to euro payments and the settlement of euro transactions. EURO 1 is operated by the *EBA Clearing Company* with administrative services and, in particular, human, technical and other support provided by the *EBA Administration Company*. All three have been established under French law.

In contrast to TARGET, EURO 1 is a net settlement system (Table 4.15). It is a true international system with participants from EU member states as well as Australia, Japan, Norway, Switzerland and the United States. Located in Paris it currently has 74 direct members and 38 connected as subsidiaries of member banks. The system settles at the end of the day in central bank money at the ECB. Credit and liquidity risk are contained by several rules and obligations. These include the establishment of credit lines and a standby liquidity pool held at the ECB. Table 4.16 shows the relative importance of both TARGET and EURO 1. The numbers demonstrate that, although transaction volumes are comparable, values differ markedly with TARGET playing a much larger role.

In addition to TARGET and EURO 1, there are three *other large-value payment systems* in Europe. These are the Pankkien On-line Pikasiirrot ja Sekit-järjestelmä (POPS) in Finland, Servicio de pagos interbancarios (SPI) in Spain and the Paris Net Settlement (PNS) system in France. All three are net settlement systems.

Initiatives to strengthen and harmonise payment systems and contain the risks related to cross-border transactions are not limited to the euro area. The strong growth of *foreign exchange markets* in the 1990s drew regulators' attention worldwide to the dangers and uncertainties of currency trading. Studies showed that these were far greater than previously thought. One element of risk in these markets is market concentration: in those years there were an estimated 30 to 40 banks in the world that were internationally active in a narrow sense – and numbers have shrunk again with recent financial crises and the advent of the euro – some

Table 4.15   Cross-border large-value payment systems in Europe

	Target	Euro 1
Participation	EU credit institutions, treasury departments of member state governments, public-sector bodies, investment firms, organisations providing clearing or settlement services	International participation; banks from EU member states and five non-EU countries; legal, financial and operational access criteria
Types of transactions handled	Credit transfers in euro: – payments connected with central bank operations – settlement operations of large-value netting systems operating in euros – interbank and commercial payments	Credit transfers, primary focus on processing large-value payments of EBA participants; balances of STEP 1
Settlement procedures	Real-time gross settlement	Net settlement at the end of the day in central bank money at the ECB
Credit and liquidity risk	Immediate finality Liquidity available at low cost Intraday credit provided free of charge	Payments cannot be cancelled once they have been processed by the system Each participant must establish credit lines for all other participants individually A standby liquidity pool is held at the ECB

Table 4.16   Transaction volumes and values of TARGET and EURO 1

	Transaction volumes[1]		Transaction values[2]	
	Target	Euro 1	Target	Euro 1
2000	188	97	1033	195
2001	211	113	1299	205
2002	253	135	1552	188
June 2003	264	154	1777	185

[1] In thousands of payments.
[2] In billions of euro.
Source: European Central Bank (2003) *Statistics Pocket Book*, September.

of which were settling routinely trades worth more than one billion dollars with a single trading partner on a single day. In London, the top 10 banks accounted for more than 40% of foreign exchange turnover. The main problem was that many institutions appeared unaware of the dangers, considering them as '*Cinderella risk*'. Payment and settlement were – and often still are – regarded as an administrative matter for the back office not concerning the boardroom.

Beside, foreign exchange settlement exposures were widely perceived as an intraday problem, ignoring the fact that the gap between the moment the trade is agreed on and the time the bank knows for certain that it is completed can take several days.

Being aware of the footloose nature of foreign exchange trading regulators shun an official solution. Instead, central banks and the Bank for International Settlements in Basle aimed for a private-sector arrangement. However, they threatened to impose legal frameworks on banks unless a global system was devised. The result is the *CLS Bank* which started operating in September 2002. CLS stands for continuous linked settlement. The founding 39 shareholders included the bulk of the world's leading trading banks and others soon joined. CLS replaced two-day settlement with a five-hour window each day covering the full process of funding, settlement and payment. Although a private-sector institution, by linking major central banks including the US Federal Reserve, the European Central Bank and the Bank of Japan, CLS requires unprecedented official cooperation. As a consequence, the central banks have connected their RTGS systems in a bank supervised by one of them, the New York Federal Reserve.

Herstatt Risk

On 26 July 1974, the then-German banking supervisory agency, the Bundesaufsichtsamt für das Kreditwesen, closed Bankhaus Herstatt in Cologne, a small bank which had been very active in foreign exchange dealing. The closure was announced in the early afternoon, German time, after settlement in all same-day interbank systems in Germany had taken place, and several of the bank's counterparties from the US and elsewhere had payed out D-mark to Herstatt to meet their obligations from D-mark/dollar trades.

Payment for the transaction of the dollar legs of these trades had been ordered by Herstatt's correspondent bank in New York, but could not be completed. In New York it was late morning when the bank failed and the settlement system was still closed leaving foreign exchange trades of over $620 million worth undone – a huge amount at that time. The markets were close to panic and, although eventually partial compensation for the losses was made, Herstatt risk, as this case of asynchronous settlement risk has become known, has been one of the major threats in international banking before the introduction of real-time gross settlement (RTGS) for major systems in the late 1990s.

Compared to large-value payment systems the development of *cross-border retail payment systems* within the euro area is rather unsatisfying. Cross-border retail payments are by far not as automated as domestic ones since often transaction data are missing or incomplete and costs are high. There are wide differences in both payment culture and settlement systems across countries. For example, *cash payments* play a small role in France where in 2000 they amounted to 3.2% of GDP, and an even smaller one in Luxembourg (1.9%) and Finland (2.2%). They are in wider use in Spain (8.9%), Germany (6.2%) and Italy (6.0%). Among non-cash payments *credit transfers* are the most widely used, but, again, there are differences across countries. While in Finland in 2000 they accounted for 57% of all non-cash payments, in Italy and the Netherlands their share was only 40%. Another difference concerns *direct debits* whose importance has grown in recent years with utility and retail companies increasingly offering this service. The use of direct debits ranges from 4.5% of all non-cash transactions in

Finland to 53% in Spain. In Luxembourg and Portugal non-cash payments are dominated by *payment cards* accounting for some 60% and 51% of transactions, respectively. In France and Ireland, *cheques* are the most widely used payment instrument. In 2000, 72% of all cheques in the euro area were used in France.

Despite the introduction of the euro, in all countries significant differences in quality, efficiency and price between domestic and cross-border services are still prevailing. Banks had few incentives to change this situation and initiate a Europe-wide system for cross-border retail payments. The share of cross-border payments of all payments is just 1% and the fees banks charged for cross-border transactions more than covered the costs. In addition, the banks use the large-value systems for their retail business as well.

It was only when *EU regulation on cross-border payments in euro* was introduced, with the explicit aim to bring prices of cross-border payments into line with those of similar domestic payments, that the need for banks to cut costs by integrating retail payment systems became manifest. Providers of payment services are now required to charge the same for the domestic and cross-border use of ATMs and card payments as well as for credit transfers up to a certain amount. In addition, transparency and efficiency were improved. Customers are provided with prior information on charges. In order to facilitate straight-through processing, institutions are obliged to communicate IBAN (International Bank Account Number) and BIC (Bank Identifier Code) to their customers on request.

In November 2002, EURO 1 launched an initiative for cross-border retail payments, called *STEP 1*, whose balances are settled via the EURO 1 system. STEP 1 so far is the only retail payment system which covers *the whole euro area* and is open to all banks. It is not operating in real time but needs two days for transaction processing. The system is intended to:

- reduce the execution time of cross-border retail payment instructions;
- foster the use of industry standards for messaging in order to enhance straight-through processing with banks; and
- develop and encourage the adoption of European business practices in the execution of cross-border retail payment instructions.

STEP 1 is one of several European retail credit transfer systems (Table 4.17). Based on the correspondent bank principle, most of them represent 'club solutions' of banking groups. For example, S-Interpay is a network initiated by, and consisting mainly of, savings banks in the EU and beyond. Eurogiro links postal and giro organisations.

Parallel to STEP 1, in April 2003, *STEP 2* started operating. Unlike STEP 1 it processes high-volume commercial and retail payments in *batches* and offers a clearing and sorting function. The participating banks may submit all their retail payments for one settlement day in a single file and then STEP 2 opens the file sorting the payments according to the recipients. The number of payments processed through STEP 2 is growing rapidly. In January 2004 it was 57,000, in March about 81,000. There are about 1100 banks with direct or indirect access to the system. The service provider is the Italian clearing company SIA. The fact that Italian banks agreed to process their domestic transactions through the system provided the critical mass for starting STEP 2 which so far processes bank transfers and from 2005 onwards will be able to process cross-border debits.

One area which has seen a marked acceleration of consolidation and integration in recent years is *securities clearing and settlement*. There are three principal steps in a securities transaction (Figure 4.2). The first is the process of *trade execution* which brings together the buyer and seller of a security. This can be done via a formal exchange, a broker or a matching

Table 4.17   Cross-border retail credit transfer systems in the euro area

System	Characteristics
STEP 1	An initiative of the EBA; covers the whole euro area; two-day processing using the technical platform of EURO 1
TIPANET	Network of cooperative banks from 18 countries in and outside Europe (the US and Canada); processes credit transfers, direct debits and cheques; settlement of payments via reciprocal correspondent bank accounts with conditions agreed bilaterally
Eurogiro	Network of the postal and giro organisations for the exchange of cross-border payments; bulk of business in low-value credits and cash payments; participants act as correspondents for each other; there are members in 39 countries including EU accession countries, the United States and Japan
S-Interpay	Initially an initiative by the German savings banks and their central institutions, the Landesbanken; network of correspondent banks in the EU and beyond; participants mainly from the savings banks sector with one bank in each country (in larger ones also two or more) acting as central correspondent for that country; high level of straight-through processing

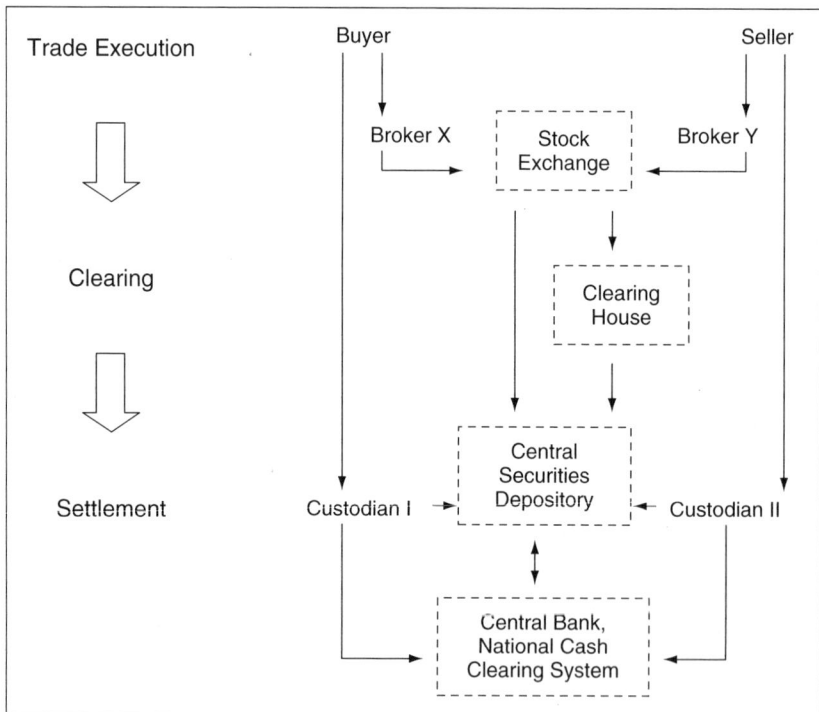

Figure 4.2   Principal steps in a securities transaction

system where both parties trade directly. The second step is *clearing* which is needed to properly complete the transaction. The clearing process consists of two elements. One is trade comparison confirming that the buyer and the seller have agreed on the transaction details such as price and quantity. Another is identification of the accounts to which the security and payment should be delivered.

Clearing may take place bilaterally or using a *central counterparty (CCP)*. Standing between buyers and sellers – and in effect, becoming the buyer to all sellers and the seller to all buyers – the CCP serves to minimise the risks of failure. These risks are further lowered if buy and sell trades are offset or netted. The benefits to market participants are obvious. Although not eliminating credit risk the CCP redistributes the risk making it easier for a firm to manage it by providing a single counterparty instead of several ones. Further, the CCP increases market liquidity by netting trades.

Since netting has a cumulative effect on all netting counterparties the risk reduction and liquidity effects are remarkable. *Netting* may take several legally distinct forms. In *netting by novation* market participants enter into a formal arrangement under which individual transactions are continuously automatically replaced with a single obligation for each future value date in each currency they trade. The second, and each subsequent, deal is netted with the first for that particular date and currency, and a new novated contract for the net amounts is effected. In the case that a CCP is involved it undertakes the novated net obligation as counterparty to each participant. Another form of netting is *close-out netting*. This is the right to cancel and liquidate obligations in an appropriate way in case of counterparty default.

However, establishing a CCP is also *costly*, in particular, because it needs to have a robust risk management system. The latter includes sound margining policies, collateral management procedures and strong capital cushions as well as regular monitoring of members. In addition, the CCP must be structured in a way that members have incentives to control risks. To be cost effective, the CCP should have procedures in place for the rapid – preferably real-time – evaluation of risks in order to guarantee the lowest-possible margins and efficient use of collateral. Like all insurance systems, the CCP is exposed to market failures due to information asymmetries such as moral hazard and adverse selection. Further, since the CCP concentrates on operational risk rather than on any individual actor in a decentralised market, the repercussions of incompetent management would be a greater threat.

In Europe, until recently, few clearinghouses operated as central counterparties. One explanation is that the value-added of netting services increases with market size so that small markets have few incentives to invest in a respective infrastructure. Cross-border mergers of stock exchanges and consolidation of clearing and settlement in the last years have resulted in the emergence of three 'poles' in major centres (Figure 4.3). One pole is the *London Clearing House (LCH)* which – although long maintaining separate ownership and governance structure – closely aligned its operations with those of the London Stock Exchange (LSE) and Crest, the UK securities depository. Recently, the CCP project has been established as a joint initiative by the London Stock Exchange, the London Clearing House and Crest to establish a central counterparty for stocks.

A second pole formed with the establishment of Euronext, the joint platform of the Paris Bourse, the Amsterdam Exchange and the Brussels Exchange, to which *Clearnet* became the central counterparty. The third pole is Deutsche Börse with *Eurex Clearing*. In addition, there are other smaller central counterparties such as MEFF in Spain, CC&G in Italy and X-Clear, which was established to offset positions traded at Virt-X.

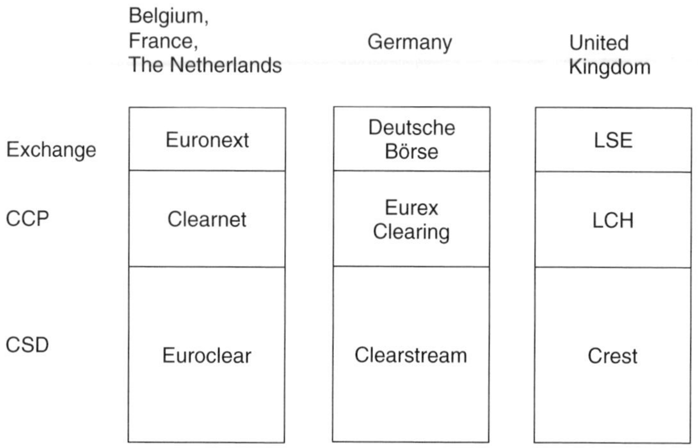

	Belgium, France, The Netherlands	Germany	United Kingdom
Exchange	Euronext	Deutsche Börse	LSE
CCP	Clearnet	Eurex Clearing	LCH
CSD	Euroclear	Clearstream	Crest

Figure 4.3 Major trading, clearing and settlement poles in Europe

Despite consolidation tendencies the European landscape remains fragmented and far away from the *US model* of one big country- or region-wide CCP. There were estimates that without a centralised system, in Europe, over 2050 linkages between existing entities were required in order to create a functioning network. Currently, two alternatives to such a *spaghetti model* based on multiple links are discussed for European securities settlement. One is the establishment of *a single Europe-wide institution*. The other is a *hub-and-spokes* system whereby all national institutions were linked to one single entity at European level.

According to estimates, investors and issuers in Europe face additional costs for cross-border trading and cross-border equity holdings of about €4.3 billion a year. Some 40% of these are explained by the need for *regulatory translation* accounting for differences in laws, taxes, rules for corporate actions and other peculiarities. However, another 20% are considered to be in the sphere of influence of intermediaries, exchanges, clearing houses and central securities depositories calling for measures like harmonisation of market practices and industry consolidation. The remaining 40% are the consequence of different languages and cultures and lower cross-border trading volumes because of investors' home bias and other attitudes and behaviours that are generally considered not influenceable. Further, there is a big difference between cross-border wholesale and retail trades with wholesale trades costing 30% more and retail trades 150% more than comparable domestic trades.

In the US, the Depository Trust and Clearing Corporation achieves as much as 97% netting thereby dramatically reducing the back office costs of trading equities. However, there are doubts whether a single CCP might work in Europe. The differences in legal, regulatory and tax systems between countries are too big. The alternative is *interoperability* or the linking of CCPs and exchanges as is already taking place.

The last step in the process of securities transaction after trade execution and clearing is *settlement*. At this stage, security and payment are exchanged. Instead of actually holding physical certificates, these days, ownership of publicly traded securities of most participants is tracked electronically through a book-entry system maintained by a *central securities depository (CSD)*.

There are big differences between *securities settlement systems (SSSs)* and *payment systems*:

- with payments often occurring among commercial banks central banks play a less active role in a payment system than securities depositories in a SSS;
- securities settlement requires the availability of both idle reserves of funds and securities thereby increasing the chance of queues;
- as a rule, unlike cash, securities are not fungible (exemptions such as cross-product netting are found in derivatives markets where no physical delivery is taking place) and similar products are needed for netting positions.

Figure 4.2 gave *an example* of a transaction process involving a stock exchange, a clearing house acting as CCP and a CSD. Both buyer and seller of the security turn to a broker. In addition, both use a custodian responsible for the safekeeping and administrative services related to the transfer and holding of securities. Custodians act on behalf of individual investors who do not hold accounts on the CSD where the securities are kept, monitoring the receipt of dividends and interest payments and providing a wide range of additional services.

Clearing and settlement systems are often referred to as the 'pipelines' of the securities markets which have to meet high standards of reliability and efficiency. Given the huge volumes of transactions processed every day each disruption hindering payments or securities to reach their destination, or delaying it, may cause severe liquidity pressures and losses, and in the extreme may destabilise the whole market.

In *cross-border trades* involving market participants buying and selling in non-domestic markets and undertaking transactions with counterparties in other countries, clearing and settlement becomes even more complex than in national markets. Securities located in different countries need to be delivered and received and related payments made. For *cross-border settlement*, in principle, five options exist (Table 4.18).

The most widely used option is to turn to a *local agent*, which, as a rule, is a financial institution with membership of a national CSD. The local agent provides the non-resident with a full range of services. Those with a sufficiently large customer base may even settle trades between customers internally. They may also offer this service as *indirect links* to CSDs and international central securities depositories (ICSDs).

Table 4.18   Channels for cross-border settlement

Option	Characteristics
Local agent	A financial institution which is member of a national CSD; most widely used option
Global custodian	Has a worldwide network of local branches and subsidiaries and local agents; large economies of scale and scope; option favoured by traders in equities
National CSD	Legal agreements and membership rules, technical requirements to be met; non-residents need to establish local branches or subsidiaries to get access
Bilateral links between CSDs	Most recent option available, so far not widely used
ICSD	Historically rooted in Eurobond markets; most widely used option for settlement of fixed-income products

An option favoured among traders in *equities* is the use of *global custodians*. Equities are more heterogeneous instruments than, for example, fixed-income securities and more complex to manage particularly with respect to corporate actions requiring continuous communication between the issuing company and the equity holder. This makes cross-border clearing and settlement particularly challenging. Global custodians are active world-wide through networks of sub-custodians which can be local branches or subsidiaries, but also local agents. In June 2004, the world's largest was State Street, a Boston-based bank with $9400 billion of assets under custody and administration, followed by Bank of New York ($8600 billion) and JP Morgan Chase ($8000 billion). The leading European banks in the asset-servicing business at that time were UBS, at sixth in the world, BNP Paribas, at eighth, and HSBC, at ninth.

Global custodians offer many advantages:

- They eliminate the costs of maintaining links to many local agents at a time.
- They are able to offer a wide range of services at low costs by exploiting economies of scope and scale.
- They benefit from a large pool of clients allowing them to settle transactions internally on their books.

In recent years, global custody has become an area of *intense competition* where smaller firms from continental Europe are increasingly threatened to lose against the big US banks which as leaders in this field are able to offer broad and sophisticated product sets to an expansive geographic reach. In general, the industry is benefiting from the growing tendency of fund management companies and their major clients, the pension funds, to *outsource administrative functions*. For global custodians settlement of cross-border trades is a most lucrative business. The charges for these transactions can be more than 10 times as much as for a domestic transaction. However, in particular in equity markets the local factor still matters. This may explain that, for example, in France, BNP Paribas Security Service settles about 90% of cross-border share trades.

Another option in settling a cross-border securities transaction – albeit one which, according to a survey conducted in the mid-1990s, is not widely used – is to turn directly to a *national CSD* in the country where the securities are issued. Access to a national CSD involves efforts such as signing legal agreements and complying with memberships requirements as well as investing in technological interfaces and access to a payment mechanism. Foreign institutions may gain access by establishing local branches or subsidiaries. Another not widely used option is the most recently available one, which is a *bilateral link between CSDs*.

The last option is using an *international central securities depository (ICSD)*. Originally, the two ICSDs established in Europe in the late 1960s to settle for the Eurobond market, Cedel and Euroclear, were intended to overcome the logistical difficulties related to the settlement of physical bond certificates across borders. They introduced two innovations. One was *book-entry registration* of transfers in place of the physical movement of certificates. The other was the concept of *fungibility* under which account holders in the ICSD could be credited with a certain amount of securities on deposit in the centralised custodial account without specifying the series number of the individual certificates.

In 2000, the Luxembourg-based Cedel merged with Deutsche Börse Clearing to form *Clearstream International* each holding 50%. In July 2002, Deutsche Börse acquired Cedel's 50%. The holding company has three main subsidiaries, Clearstream Banking Luxembourg (CBL), Clearstream Banking Frankfurt (CBF) and Clearstream Services

Luxembourg (CSL), with joint representative offices in the major financial centres. Clearstream International clears and settles securities transactions in 38 currencies in 33 markets.

The other big European ICSD, the Brussels-based *Euroclear Bank* is owned by Euroclear PCL which, in turn, has 121 institutional shareholders none of which with more than 5% capital. In 2000, all Irish government bond settlement activity was transferred to Euroclear. In January 2001, Euroclear took over Sicovam, the Paris settlement system, followed by the absorption of CIK and Necigef, the central securities depositaries of Belgium and the Netherlands, and is now settling all transactions of Euronext. By the end of 2001, the LSE reached an agreement with the London Clearing House and Euroclear allowing its international customers to use Euroclear to settle trades. In 2002, Euronext and *Crest*, the London-based settlement house merged to what became *Europe's largest equities settlement operation* handling about 60% of trades in leading European equities as well as more than 50% of fixed income trades.

Clearstream and Euroclear are still the most widely used option for settlement in the fixed-income market. Their customer base includes all the main participants in the cross-border markets enabling them to settle many transactions internally. Both benefit from their status of CSD *and* bank. In particular, Euroclear which owns four European CSDs, all of them monopolies, has drawn a lot of criticism and accusations by leading European banks claiming that it abuses its dual role as a market utility and a commercial operation mentioning cross-subsidies and the creation of unfair competition.

Considering the *costs* of securities clearing and settlement helps appreciate the advantages of this dual role. *Direct settlement costs* include safekeeping and transaction fees which have to be paid to a CCP or CSD, along with foregone interest income. There are estimates that these costs account for about 30% of post-trade expenses. In addition, there are *indirect costs* incurred by broker-dealers and investors using clearing and settlement systems. These are magnified by the redundancies and inefficiencies inherent in the fragmented nature of European systems where institutions and arrangements required to execute trades are replicated numerous times. For example, a broker wishing to settle foreign securities transactions may have to turn to foreign custodian banks, maintain business relationships and telecommunication links with settlement organisations and hold collateral at multiple clearing organisations. Of the estimated 70% indirect costs, there are 10% costs of unsynchronised settlement, another 10% costs related to operational and custody risk, 14% extra custodial and brokerage fees, 15% financing costs and 21% back-office costs.

Since 1980 there exists an '*electronic bridge*' between Clearstream and Euroclear which was substantially upgraded in 1993. While most links between CSDs allow the free transfer of payment orders only, this one is admitting settlement versus payment, too (Figure 4.4).

Different patterns of consolidation of trading, clearing and settlement in Europe have stimulated the discussion of the pros and cons of *horizontal and vertical 'silos'*. Vertical consolidation refers to the integration of various points in the securities transaction chain such as trading, clearing, settlement and custody services within a single institution. Vertically integrated exchanges control all stages of a transaction from trade to clearing and settlement. Its proponents argue that this makes exchanges more competitive allowing them to control new business opportunities more effectively. Horizontal consolidation includes mergers or alliances between systems providing similar services. Examples are Euronext and Norex. Deutsche Börse's acquisition of Cedel as part of a strategy to integrate all areas under the umbrella of one group is

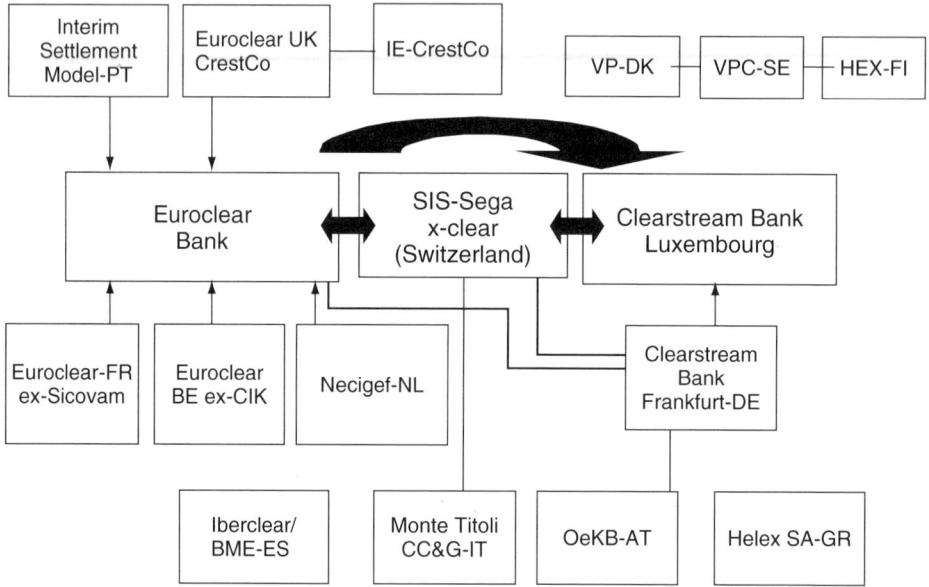

Figure 4.4 Settlement links between CSDs and ICSDs in Europe. *Source*: Hirata de Carvalho, Cynthia (2004): Cross-border securities clearing and settlement infrastructure in the European Union as a prerequisite to financial market integration – challenges and perspectives, HWWA Discussion Paper No. 287, Chart VII

an example of a vertical solution. Another example of a very competitive vertical arrangement is SIS-Sega which links the SWS Swiss Exchange trading platform with the SIS SegaInterSettle AG for clearing and settlement and the payment system of the Swiss Interbank Clearing AG. Untypical for an ICSD, 90% of SIS-Sega's international business is in equities. The main opponent of vertically integrated exchanges in Europe is the LSE which maintains that separate providers result in cheaper costs for users and separate charging of clearing and settlement makes them more transparent, leaving it to the exchanges to choose the best opportunity.

Clearing and settlement is one important element in the changing network of links and alliances between European securities and derivatives exchanges, which is becoming increasingly complex (Figure 4.5). This is an area in which major transformations are taking place widely unnoticed by the public. For example, in 2001, when the first *Giovannini Report* about the state of cross-border clearing and settlement arrangements in EU securities markets was published there were 21 settlement systems in the 15 EU countries widely separated from one another. Nowadays, many of them have established interfaces and the possibility of remote access to one another.

15 Jun 2004

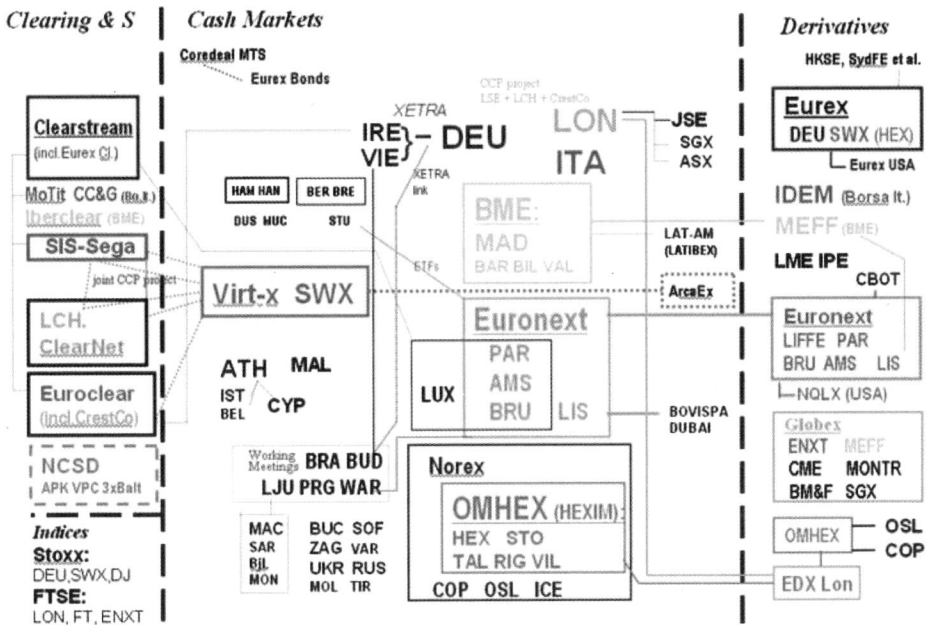

Figure 4.5 The European exchange landscape. *Note*: For the legend to this diagram see Appendix I. *Source*: Federation of European Stock Exchanges, http://www.fese.be/statistics/exchange_landscape

---

The Eurosystem

Many EU rules relating to monetary union, and most of the provisions of the Statute of the European System of Central Banks and of the European Central Bank, apply only to EU member states that have adopted the euro and/or their central banks and the ECB. For this group the name 'Eurosystem' was coined at the beginning of stage three of EMU. The decision-making bodies of the Eurosystem are the Executive Board and Governing Council of the ECB.

The national central banks of Denmark, Sweden and the United Kingdom, as well as of the new member states that are not yet participating in monetary union, are not part of the Eurosystem. The ECB and the central banks of all EU member states form the more general 'European System of Central Banks' (ESCB).

One important category of cross-border links is those used for the *transfer of collateral* for the Eurosystem's credit operations and for interbank operations. According to the Treaty establishing the European Community the Eurosystem's monetary policy and intraday credit operations should be collateralised. In addition, all collateral eligible for monetary policy operations of the central banks of the euro area must be usable by all monetary policy counter-parties. In order to create the necessary facilities for the cross-border transfer of securities the central banks set up the *correspondent central banking model (CCBM)*. In the CCBM, central banks act as correspondents for one another. In addition, with increasing need of cross-border transfers of securities, SSSs have established links for securities transfer.

One prerequisite of the functioning of this system is the guarantee of the safety and efficiency of transfer, settlement and custody of collateral. For this purpose, standards were developed that have to be met by SSSs in the EU in order to ensure a level playing field. In July 2001, 66 eligible links had been assessed and approved by the Eurosystem, although frequent and significant use was only made by 29 of these links. Activity is concentrating in a smaller number of countries than covered by the links and dominated by the two ICSDs Clearstream International and Euroclear.

Despite the progress achieved, there are a number of *open questions* related to the efficiency and reliability of securities settlement in Europe. One is CSDs' *risk controls and operational reliability*. This includes the existence of reliable, secure and adequate systems providing means to assess the impact of a member default, contingency plans and back-up facilities. Another topic is *delivery versus payment (DVP)* and *legal certainty*. The aim of DVP is to eliminate principal risk ensuring neither the seller nor the buyer being out of stock or cash at any time, and ownership, once transferred legally, not being challenged. In Europe, at a domestic level, DVP in central bank money has become standard. In cross-border trades the adoption of commercial bank money is increasingly advocated in order to facilitate transactions. Legal certainty aims at protecting the investor at all stages of the transaction process and includes the establishment of rules to define the jurisdiction for potential disputes regarding securities. Currently, in Europe, different legal arrangements apply in different jurisdictions requiring the CSD in every link established to understand the entire legal framework associated with it.

A third topic is the development of uniform international communication standards and procedures by securities clearing and settlement systems. In particular, this concerns the promotion of *straight through processing (STP)* as a uniform and efficient communications system for simultaneously transferring information electronically between all parties involved in a trade such as exchanges, intermediaries, investors, custodians and settlement and payment systems. The fully automated processing of a securities transaction from order to placement, over delivery versus payment, to the subsequent custody of the security is swift, safe and efficient.

Still another topic is the *shortening of settlement periods*. The shorter the settlement period the lower the exposure to the risks of settlement and system failure. In most countries, final settlement on the third day after the trade took place ($T+3$) is the rule. For the US, there are estimates that a move to $T+1$ that would reduce the amount of outstanding settlement exposure by two-thirds could lower risk exposure by $250 billion. However, there is general agreement that a shift to $T+1$ could not be considered as a positive step towards $T+0$. This would require a fundamentally different infrastructure implying all trades to be settled trade by trade on a real-time, gross-settlement basis thereby eliminating the benefits of netting and resulting in a huge increase in settlement volumes.

Summary

- Although European markets followed the overall trend towards globalisation in some market segments national structures and characteristics still dominate.
- European banks are among the world's leading financial institutions, but the challenges they face both within the region and worldwide are increasing.

- European capital markets are still highly fragmented.
- European exchanges are exposed to growing competitive pressures regarding the economic functions they fulfil such as monitoring, signalling and clearing.
- Given their changing role the provision of liquidity has become the exchanges' main service.
- Recent literature changed the way in which exchanges are perceived in economics considering them as firms instead of markets and studying the determinants of their overall performance.
- Exchanges' international competitiveness depends, among other things, on country-specific factors such as the legal system and accounting standards, rules for investor protection and the bureaucratic environment.
- One market segment, which despite recent setbacks is playing an increasing role in Europe, is venture capital.
- Activities of European growth exchanges were driven back strongly with the sharp falls of technology values of 2000–2001 and are recovering only slowly.
- Clearing and settlement systems are an important part of the process of exchanges' consolidation in Europe.
- Integration is strongest in systems for large-value interbank payments in Europe while development of cross-border retail payment systems is still unsatisfying.
- Although European securities clearing and settlement is still highly fragmented growing networks and alliances demonstrate that for Europe interoperability is an alternative to the US model.
- Open questions related to securities settlement in Europe concern CSDs' risk controls, delivery versus payment, legal certainty, straight-through processing and the shortening of settlement periods.

Exercises

1. Discuss the role of European banks in the world economy and their relative strengths and weaknesses.
2. Describe the various challenges European banks face in the region and worldwide and explain why despite various hindrances you would not expect a declining role of banks in financial intermediation in the region. Or would you?
3. Describe the role of contract banking for smaller financial institutions in a changing environment.
4. How were European exchanges affected by the increasing challenges to the financial industry in recent years and how did they react?
5. In which way did technology foster the regional and international competitiveness of exchanges? In which way did it influence:

   – the competitiveness of leading European exchanges in relation to financial institutions in other parts of the world?
   – the opportunities of smaller European exchanges?

6. Discuss the prospects of various forms of venture capital in Europe with a special emphasis on:

   – small entrepreneurs at different stages of development
   – the role of growth exchanges.

7. Discuss the advantages and disadvantages of net settlement and real-time gross settlement in large-value interbank payment systems.

8. Discuss the problems of consolidating cross-border retail payment processes in Europe.
9. Describe the comparative advantages of global custodians in securities clearing and settlement and discuss the alternatives.
10. Describe the role of ICSDs in securities clearing and settlement in Europe.
11. Describe the pros and cons of horizontally and vertically integrated exchanges.

Additional Links and References

The distinction of the future role of bank lending and banks as firms is elaborated by:

Llewellyn, David (1996) Banking in the 21st century: the transformation of an industry, http://www.rba.gov.au/PublicationsAndResearch/Conferences/1996/Llewellyn.pdf

The main characteristics of exchanges and influences of competition between them are discussed in:

Di Noia, Carmine (1998) Competition and integration among stock exchanges in Europe: network effects, implicit mergers and remote access, http://fic.wharton.upenn.edu/fic/papers/98/9803.pdf

The German Bund example of locking in customers, as well as many of the arguments concerning the costs and benefits of CCPs, is taken from:

Giordano, Francesco (2002) Cross-border trading in financial securities in Europe: the role of central counterparty, European Capital Markets Institute, December, http://www.ecmi.es/files/giordano.pdf

Data on the demutualisation of stock exchanges, listing fees, share of foreign companies and much more useful information about the consolidation process of stock exchanges in Europe and worldwide can be found in:

Schich, Sebastian and Gert Wehinger (2003) Prospects for stock exchanges, *OECD: Financial Market Trends*, No. 85, October.

The discussion of the advantages of consolidation of European stock exchanges and remaining barriers relies heavily on:

McAndrews, James and Chris Stefanadis (2002) The consolidation of European stock exchanges, *Federal Reserve Bank of New York: Current Issues*, **8**(6), http://www.newyorkfed.org/research/current_issues/ci8-6.pdf

A survey of 'Extended Exchange Services' under mounting competitive pressures in different regions and worldwide was prepared for the Working Committee of the World Federation of Exchanges (WFE) by the Taiwan Stock Exchange Corporation in March 2004 and is available at:

http://www.fibv.com/WFE/home.asp?action = headline&article = 88

There are some recent studies on the role of legal aspects such as investor protection and the enforceability of contracts for the development and competitiveness of markets. See for example:

La Porta, Rafael, Florencio Lopez de Silanes, Andrei Shleifer and Robert W. Vishny (1999) Investor protection and corporate governance, http://ssrn.com/abstract = 183908

See for a general overview of country performance in these and other respects the *World Competitiveness Yearbook*:

http://www02.imd.ch/wcy/

For an overview of private equity and venture capital development in Europe see:

OECD (2002) Risk capital in OECD countries: recent developments and structural issues, *Financial Market Trends*, No. 82, June.

Sallard, Delphine (1999) Risk capital markets, a key to job creation in Europe. From fragmentation to integration. Euro Paper No. 32, Brussels: European Commission, http://Europa.eu.int/comm/economy_finance/publications/ Euro_papers/2001/eup32en.pdf

See, in particular, for venture capital in the UK:

Baygan, Günseli (2003) Venture capital policy review: United Kingdom, OECD STI Working Paper 2003/1, http:// www.oecd.org/dataoecd/41/58/2491240.pdf

The Federation of European Securities Exchanges is regularly revising its diagrammatic representation of the linkups and alliances between European securities and derivatives exchanges:

http://fese.org/statistics/exchange_landscape/http://fese.org/statistics/exchange_landscape/

The Bank of England's latest annual small firms finance report 'Finance for small firms: an eleventh report' published in April 2004 is available at:

http://www.bankofengland.co.uk/fin4sm11.pdf

The latest study on benchmarking European tax and legal environments of the European private Equity and Venture Capital Association (EVCA) can be found at:

http://www.iban.it/ftp/biblioteca/evca.pdf

In autumn 2002 KfW conducted a survey of private equity companies in Germany and Great Britain together with a German–British group of researchers from the Universities of Cambridge, Edinburgh, Eichstätt and Hamburg. The study 'Private equity in Germany and Great Britain – A comparison of market structures' is available only in German:

http://www.kfw.de/DE/Research/Sonderthem68/Beteiligun15/Cambridge_Vergleich_Beteiligungsmaerkte.pdf

but an English summary is provided at:

http://www.kfw.de/DE/Research/Sonderthem68/Beteiligun15/private-equity-in-germany-and-great-britrain2.pdf

An overview of payment systems in Europe as well as in individual European countries is given in:

Committee on Payment and Settlement Systems of the Central Banks of the Group of Ten Countries (CPSS) (2004) Statistics on payment and settlement systems in selected countries – Figures for 2002, CPSS Publications No. 60, March, http://www.bis.org/publ/cpss60.htm

A detailed discussion of major incidents threatening the functioning of payment and settlement systems in the past is found in:

Committee on Payment and Settlement Systems of the Central Banks of the Group of Ten Countries (CPSS) (1996) Settlement risk in foreign exchange transactions, CPSS Publications No. 17, March, http://www.bis.org/publ/cpss17.pdf

The estimates of the differences in costs for domestic and cross-border equity trading in Europe and other useful information are presented in:

Clearstream International and Deutsche Börse Group (2002) Cross-border equity: trading, clearing and settlement in Europe, White Paper, http://www1.deutsche-boerse.com/INTERNET/EXCHANGE/zpd.nsf/PublikationenID/ AKLS-58TMV6/$FILE/White-Paper_online_d.pdf?OpenElement

The first and second reports of the Giovannini Group on EU clearing and settlement arrangements are:

The Giovannini Group (2001) Cross-border clearing and settlements arrangement in the European Union, November, http://europa.eu.int/comm/economy_finance/publications/giovannini/clearing1101_en.pdf

The Giovannini Group (2003) Second report on EU clearing and settlements arrangements, April, http:// europa.eu.int/comm/economy_finance/publications/giovannini/clearing_settlement_arrangements140403.pdf

Calculations demonstrating the advantages of bilateral and multilateral netting in securities settlement are presented in:

Hirata de Carvalho, Cynthia (2004) Cross-border securities clearing and settlement infrastructure in the European Union as a prerequisite to financial market integration – challenges and perspectives, HWWA Discussion Paper No. 287, http://www.hwwa.de/Publikationen/Discussion_Paper/2004/287.pdf

The estimates of direct and indirect costs of securities transactions in Europe and other useful information can be found in:

Goldberg, Linda, John Kambhu, James M. Mahoney, Lawrence Radecki and Asani Sarkar (2002) Securities trading and settlement in Europe: issues and outlook, *Federal Reserve Bank of New York: Current Issues in Economic and Finance*, **8**(4), April.

5
Market Mechanisms and Prices

In chapter 3 we saw that risks and returns determine the choices of investors, borrowers and lenders in financial markets. In this chapter, we will take a closer look at their behaviour and the resulting implications for market prices. The first section gives an overview of trading motives and strategies. The dynamics resulting from the interplay of different kinds of actors and the role of expectations will then be described. The third section presents selected price series in order to give an impression of the range of patterns prevailing in the markets.

5.1 DIVERSIFICATION, HEDGING AND ARBITRAGE

Only a small proportion of transactions in financial markets are of *original* nature and directly related to the real economy. Examples are the flow of liquidity to a company emitting a bond or issuing shares to meet its financial needs in order to conduct its core operations or make future investments, a currency demand or supply in the foreign exchange markets resulting from an export or import of goods or services, or a loan granted to a consumer. Most trades are *secondary by nature* in the sense that they aim at exploiting profit opportunities in financial markets or limiting financial risks. This includes phenomena such as securities trading in secondary markets, proprietary trading of financial institutions and non-financial firms and the large volumes of interbank trading of all sorts of financial instruments which are increasing constantly. Some trades produce *snowball effects* that are one explanation – albeit not the only one – why financial markets are so much bigger than goods markets: a bank granting a loan to a consumer hedges the resulting exposure by taking a loan from another bank which, in order to limit the resulting exposure, in turn takes a loan from a third one, and so on.

5.1.1 Diversifying Risks

Three kinds of activities dominate. These are diversification, hedging and arbitrage. *Diversification* has its roots in modern *portfolio theory*. The idea that financial alternatives come with different characteristics – those with high risks usually being associated with above-average returns in order to compensate for the inherent greater probability of loss – which can be exploited to create an optimal combination of assets was first developed in a formal theoretical framework by Harry Markowitz in the 1950s. In order to maximise the return of a portfolio of assets for a given risk level or alternatively, to minimise risk for a given return, the rule is *'not to put all of one's eggs into one basket'*, with the eggs being the number of financial instruments and the basket the portfolio of investments or securities chosen by the investor. The gain in risk reduction by combining securities depends on the way in which their returns are *correlated*. If a pair of securities have a negative correlation of returns, while one is performing badly the other is likely to be doing well and vice versa. As a consequence, the average return on these two in combination is likely to be 'safer' than investing in one of them alone.

In practice, one prerequisite for diversification to work is transparency and investors' ability to move freely between markets establishing both short and long positions. However, even in this case, not all kinds of risks can be diversified. As a rule, most securities will display a degree of *positive correlation* reflecting the influence of common factors. Generally, even after diversification, portfolios will be exposed to *market risk*, i.e. the risk inherent in market-wide developments which are not firm-specific. This kind of risk is also called *systematic risk* or *nondiversifiable risk*.

Portfolio theory as developed by Markowitz is based on a number of crucial assumptions with respect to investors' behaviour and the way in which they analyse potential returns. These are:

- *Maximising behaviour.* Investors are assumed to be concerned with maximising a well-defined expected utility of their portfolio over a given period.
- *Information and knowledge.* Investors are able to form consistent beliefs about potential returns in the form of subjective probability distributions with the mean of the distribution being the measure of expected return and the variance indicating the respective risk. (One implicit assumption is that for the underlying 'objective' or 'true' probability distribution the first and second moments exist, too.)
- *Portfolio selection criteria.* With combinations of securities chosen accordingly, from the investor's view portfolios can be completely described by the mean and variance of expected returns.
- *Preferences.* Investors have utility functions which enable them to choose portfolios solely on the basis of estimated risks and expected returns and make them *risk averse*. The latter means that, at a given level of risk, investors prefer higher returns to lower, and at a given level of returns, they prefer lower risk to higher.

There are additional assumptions which are often made to facilitate the analysis such as the absence of transaction costs and taxes.

Volatility

In financial market analyses volatility is measured as the standard deviation of returns (σ) from a given mean (μ) – or its respective variance σ^2 – under the assumption that returns are normally distributed showing the following familiar bell-shaped curve:

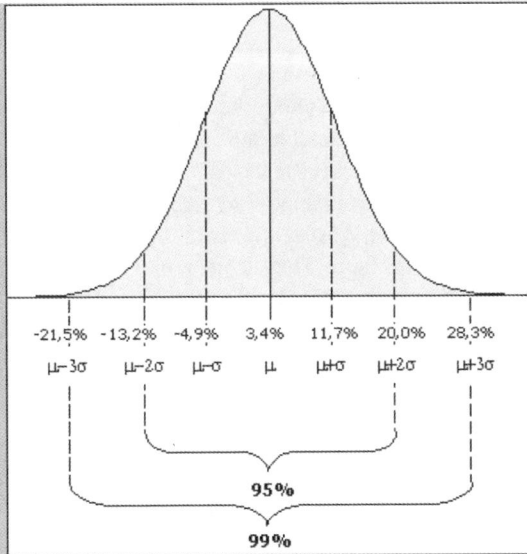

In financial markets, normal distribution plays a central role reflecting the law of large numbers. For example, individually, the outcomes of many financial transactions may be modelled by a binomial distribution with two realisations only, default or payment. However, in the limit, i.e. for many occurrences, the distribution of a sum of binomial variables converges to a normal distribution given that the outcomes are independent (for instance, in a recession where the likelihood of many simultaneous defaults increases, this assumption may be violated and the normal approximation invalidated).

Normal distribution is very convenient for analysing volatility. Since it is perfectly symmetric its mean is the same as its mode (the most likely point) and its median (which has a 50% probability of occurrence). The probability that a normally distributed return is contained between the values of $\mu - 2\sigma$ and $\mu + 2\sigma$ is about 95%, between $\mu - 3\sigma$ and $\mu + 3\sigma$ up to 99%.

The concept was extended in the 1960s by William Sharpe, John Lintner and Jan Mossin to what became known as the *capital asset pricing model (CAPM)*. The CAPM combines the mathematical model of portfolio theory with the *efficient market hypothesis (EMH)* in order to explain investors' behaviour in a general equilibrium framework that allows predictions of the relationship between the risk of an asset and its expected return, and of its deviation from a 'fair' return given its risk.

The EMH states in short that the prices of securities fully reflect available information. After digesting the information, and assessing the risks involved, demand and supply in the market are balanced at an *equilibrium price* with competition of a large number of market participants on both sides guaranteeing this to be a 'fair' price in the sense that there are no 'abnormal' returns given prevailing risks. There is a weak form, a strong and a semi-strong form of the hypothesis depending on the nature of information included. The *weak-form*

EMH asserts that securities prices reflect all information included in the history of past prices. According to the *semi-strong* form prices reflect all publicly available information. The *strong* form includes insider information as well.

The EMH makes implicit assumptions about the way in which knowledge about financial markets is built and information is processed and interpreted. In financial markets, so goes the argument, news spreads very quickly and is incorporated into the prices of securities almost without delay. As a result, price changes are independently and identically distributed. Investors are assumed to have *rational expectations* in the sense that they make efficient use of all the information available to them. They learn rapidly. In this framework, there is no room for *adaptive expectations* where people learn by experience, predictably but slowly. Further, there is no room for seeming 'irrationalities'. For example, this holds for *framing, preference reversal* and *anchoring* – phenomena known from behavioural psychology which were explored by Nobel prize winner Daniel Kahnemann and others – which, loosely speaking, all indicate that context matters for making judgements.

Studies have shown that risk aversion depends on the way a situation is *presented*, on whether the emphasis is on positive or negative aspects and whether the decision maker is made to feel a potential winner or loser. Usually, risk aversion tends to be greater under the promise of potential gains than under the threat of losses where people apparently become willing to take more risks – a phenomenon that is well known in financial markets.

In addition, experiments have demonstrated that people tend to search for points of reference to *anchor* expectations which, for example, helps explain why they often stick to the status quo, or why they put so much emphasis on average values or experts' opinions. More neglected phenomena are *social comparison effects* such as envy, although these, too, can be observed to markedly influence financial decisions and investors' attitudes. Still another seeming irrational behaviour that matters in financial markets is voluntary *precommitment* in the awareness of one's own weakness of will. Stop orders, i.e. market orders to automatically buy or sell a certain quantity of a security if a specified price is reached or passed, are one example.

The question is what insights could be gained from modifying the concept of rationality by a more realistic specification deriving conclusions about expectations of investors' choices from observed behaviour patterns rather than from an abstract model of market equilibrium? The answer depends on the extent to which *decisions reflect individual preferences*. There are various types of situations in which they do not. One example is *indecision*: a person who is not willing or able to choose between alternatives does not know her own preferences. In this case, an outside observer cannot know more or sensibly infer the intent from the appearance. Another example is *limits to information gathering and processing*. Given the complexity of the environment and the flood of news that investors face every day they may decide – deliberately or unconsciously – to refrain from 'optimising' and restrict themselves to 'satisficing', an approach which is at the centre of the concept of *bounded rationality*.

The difficulties mentioned are partly avoided when the concept of rational expectations is understood not as a behavioural approach but, as Thomas Sargent put it, as an equilibrium concept *focusing on outcomes*, as 'a powerful tool for making precise statements about complicated dynamic economic systems', modelling agents as economists whose behaviour is ruled by the same principles as that of the economists who model them. However, even in this case the problem remains that the EMH is *not directly testable empirically* since expectations, no matter how they are explained, are not observable. Each test on efficiency is also a test on the validity of an underlying model of market equilibrium with the additional difficulty that economic theory offers no commonly accepted 'true' model but a number of competing approaches and variants. Thus, *rejections* of the EMH may be caused either by market inefficiency or irrationality, or by an incorrect model of market equilibrium. One should also note that for prices determined by a wholly different kind of process – for example, for all those that are suspected to be determined 'far from equilibrium' (Appendix G) – the hypothesis entirely loses justification. Nevertheless, despite all criticism, it remains a common assumption made in financial literature underpinning the rationale for diversification.

If all relevant information is already discounted in the market, prices move only when new information becomes available. Markets are said to have *'no memory'* and price movements are often compared to a *random walk*. Present returns do not depend on past ones, which rules out the existence of successful trading systems based on available information. It apparently also rules out some other phenomena observed in practice. These include:

- *Bandwagon effects* and *herd behaviour*, where past reactions of investors as reflected in prices determine current decisions.
- A phenomenon known as *irrational exuberance* – initially a phrase used by Federal Reserve chairman Alan Greenspan in 1996 to describe a market he perceived as overvalued at the time.
- *Fads and fashions* where investors imitate one another leading to 'abnormal' wide swings in market prices.

Random Walk

One implication of the EMH is that returns are independent, and identically distributed (iid). Independent in this context means that returns are uncorrelated over successive time intervals. For identically distributed returns the expected value and variance are the same for each period of equal length. These are also characteristics of a random walk. The idea that speculative prices follow a random walk was first advanced by Louis Bachelier in 1900 in a paper presenting methods for analysing gambling in stocks, bonds and forward markets. Financial prices or gains and losses following a random walk are characterised by independent increments. The classic example of a random walk process is a drunk staggering blindly away from a lamp-post: he takes a series of small (!) steps either away from or towards the lamp-post with each step independent of the position he has already reached. Thus, even if he is 20 steps away from the lamp-post, he is just as likely to further step away from it than towards it. However, as only small steps are allowed, the position of the drunk at any instant is strongly correlated to his position in the previous instant.

According to the EMH future price changes cannot be inferred from past price changes and the best estimate of the future price would be the current one. The process is also said to follow a fair game or martingale. Loosely speaking, the difference between a martingale and a random walk concerns the independence condition. While the martingale rules out any dependence of the conditional expectation (i.e. the mean of the stochastic process) on information available in former time periods, the random walk also rules out dependence involving the higher conditional moments of the process. In order to see the implications, consider a financial series going through protracted quiet periods and protracted periods of turbulence. This behaviour could be modelled as a process characterised by successive positively autocorrelated conditional variances. Such a specification would be consistent with a martingale, but not with the more restrictive random walk.

In all these cases, successions of prices are not independent of one another. In addition, there are other 'anomalies' suggesting that markets are less than fully efficient. One is the *equity risk premium puzzle*. Studies of historical US data have found that common stocks produced seemingly 'abnormally' high returns compared to high-grade (low-risk) bonds. One conclusion was that in the 1930s and 1940s in the US stocks were strongly underpriced, however, this is not undisputed. Some scholars argue that the observed 'risk premiums' were largely the result of *unexpected* capital gains while others suggest that in the early 2000s the expected equity risk premium was irrationally low.

In this context, it needs to be emphasised that, in principle, the EMH does not rule out the existence of *outliers* and extreme events, it only limits the extent to which these can be expected to occur. Further, it does not rule out the temporary seeming emergence of *patterns*. It only excludes the possibility of *systematically exploiting* these phenomena. In principle, it can even be thought of as compatible with speculative manias and bubbles as long as each reaction in the chain is part of the effect of a new event coming as a surprise to market participants. Regarding the latter, modern finance theory distinguishes between *mean independence* and *variance independence* and, in assuming that the variance of returns is following a generalised autoregressive heteroscedastic (GARCH) process, attributes observed relationships in time to lags in stochastic disturbances overlapping the 'true' deterministic model structure.

Diversification does not stop at national borders. Financial services have always been the forerunners of globalisation and there have always been investors trying to benefit from spreading their activities across regions, markets and currencies. In principle, as long as international assets are not perfectly positively correlated with domestic ones an *international portfolio* allocated efficiently among domestic and foreign holdings may offer a higher return for a given risk – or a lower risk for a given return – than a purely domestic one. This can be seen in Figure 5.1 where the global efficient frontier represents the spectrum of international portfolios with different shares of domestic and foreign holdings that offer optimal combinations of risk and return. Point A shows a risk/return combination for an optimal purely domestically composed portfolio, point B the return for a respective international one with the same risk level.

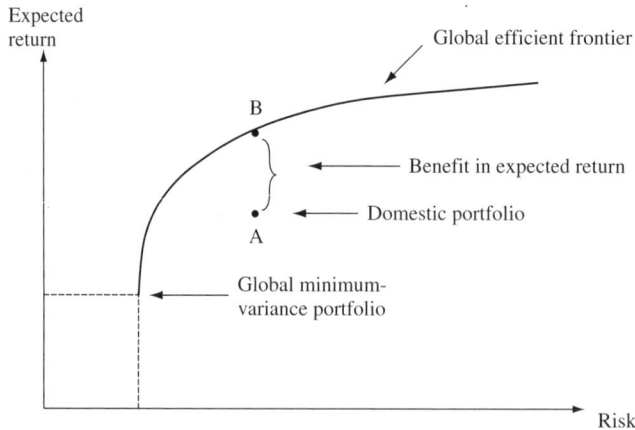

Figure 5.1   Benefits from international diversification

Garch

GARCH models assume that financial prices are stochastic functions of their own past. They have been widely applied to stock return, interest rate and foreign exchange data. The name stands for generalised autoregressive heteroscedastic models assuming that the variance of returns follows a predictable process. Autoregression means that historical data are used to predict future data, heteroscedasticity refers to a distribution characterised by a changing (non-constant) variance or standard deviation. In GARCH models, the conditional variance depends on the latest news but also on the previous conditional variance.

Assume a conditional variance defined as h_t using information up to time $t-1$ and denote the previous day's return with r_{t-1}. Then, the simplest model, a GARCH $(1,1)$ process, can be described as

$$h_t = \alpha_0 + \alpha_1 r^2_{t-1} + \beta h_{t-1}$$

GARCH models are consistent with the efficient market hypothesis. One of their properties is that they allow returns to be serially uncorrelated but not independent as they are related in a nonlinear way through variances.

Extending investment alternatives internationally allows benefit from divergences in economic development. For example, *business cycles* are rarely perfectly synchronised across countries and by investing internationally the fluctuation in a portfolio arising from the domestic business cycle may be reduced. Other reasons for low cross-border correlations include differences in natural resource endowments and government policies; *industries* concentrated in some countries may increase or reduce the vulnerability towards sector-specific risks. Another example is diversification across *regions*: investing in emerging markets may partly shelter portfolios from economic developments in industrial countries; investors holding assets from Latin America beside securities from Malaysia, Indonesia or the Philippines may benefit in a crisis emerging in Asian markets and vice versa.

One of the disadvantages of globalisation and regional economic and financial integration is that with growing convergence of markets the opportunities for diversification are reduced. As economies are increasingly exposed to the same sorts of shocks prices are more and more moving in tandem thereby narrowing the scope for risk-reducing combinations of assets.

5.1.2 Matching Positions

Diversification is one way to limit financial risks. Another is *hedging* which is the second important kind of activity driving markets and prices. In general, a hedging instrument is a contract, security or other instrument that can be used to partially or fully *offset* some type or element of financial risk. In chapter 3, some variants of hedging were mentioned: hedging with government bonds in order to avoid or limit losses in other markets; hedging with convertible bonds against movements in share prices; and hedging of interest-rate exposures with swaps. Hedging often involves partially or fully offsetting a long position in one security with a short, or short equivalent, position in a related security. Ideally, hedging allows the cancelling out or closing out of positions. One prerequisite is that the hedge instruments used are *fungible* with the initial ones. Fungibility refers to the standardisation and interchangeability of instruments requiring identical contract terms. Other prerequisites, as in the case of diversification, are transparency and that actors are able to move in and out of markets unhindered.

Although the concept is clear and easy to understand, in practice, hedging is fraught with *ambiguities*. The best example is an internationally operating firm trying to limit foreign exchange risk.

Traditionally, in this case, three *measures of exposure* are distinguished known as transaction exposure, translation exposure and economic exposure. The simplest case is *transaction exposure*: this is a measure of the firm's actual transactions that will foreseeably take place in foreign currency.

Transaction exposure always involves an *identifiable cash flow* with an exchange of currencies at maturity. For instance, this may result from a trade payment, a short-term investment in foreign currency, interest payments on foreign assets or dividend remittances from abroad. In these and other cases, there is a danger that the exchange rate moves against the firm's interest in the time to maturity. However, if the currency, amount and maturity of the exposure are known, full protection is possible by establishing a *matching position* in the same currency in the foreign exchange market of

$\Rightarrow$ opposite sign,
$\Rightarrow$ equal amount and
$\Rightarrow$ equal maturity

A Dutch exporter expecting to receive a payment in US dollars next month may sell the amount in advance in the forward foreign exchange market settling this transaction at maturity with the incoming dollars at the price agreed one month ago. In this way, the price in euro is 'locked in' and the position is no longer exposed to currency risk.

However, other forms of hedging do not involve this kind of *self-liquidating* transaction. Instead, an explicit decision is required not only about the extent to which a position should be hedged but whether, and in which way, it is to be seen exposed to currency risk at all. Take, for example, *translational hedging* which requires determining the *translation or accounting exposure* to currency changes. Translational hedging deals with the *valuation* of a firm's assets and liabilities in foreign currency and the resulting fear of losses on positions that are reflected in the balance sheet. Evaluating the motives and logic behind a hedge strategy in these cases is extremely difficult from the outside as the relation between the original position and the hedge may be a very loose one.

For example, is it hedging or the simple wish to reap the benefit from an expected change in the exchange rate when a firm decides to partly hedge the value of an inventory of goods which were produced and reported at historical costs but not yet sold, and wouldn't the firm at least need to know the final country of destination of these goods and the contract currency before making a decision? What if the company in question has a wide range of activities in many countries and assets and liabilities in more than one currency? Under which circumstances should the latter be regarded as (partly) offsetting one another? What if the currency earned with the sales is not intended to be changed into home currency but used to buy materials, or changed into a third currency for that purpose? Similar questions arise for other balance-sheet items, too.

Thus, translational hedging leaves much scope for interpretation. The picture becomes even more confusing when the third measure, a company's *economic exposure*, is included. This is the widest concept of all and roughly defined as the impact of an exchange-rate change on a firm's discounted cash flow or present value at a specified future date. In principle, this would include taking into account price and income elasticities in various markets, and the sensitivity of cost components to exchange-rate changes over long time periods, blurring even more the relationship between net exposure and hedge.

Problems similar to those in currency markets arise for other financial instruments that can be used either for speculative purposes or to shield a position from expected losses. Ambiguities also arise in cases where hybrid financial instruments with *embedded derivatives* are used. The latter are implicit or explicit elements in a contract that affect the outcome at settlement in a manner similar to a derivative. Is assuming a hedging intention justified in these cases? The attitude of the US Financial Accounting Standards Board (FSAB) is clear: although, in principle, an embedded derivative could qualify as a hedge this is regarded as highly unlikely and under its Statement 133 (*FAS 133*) embedded derivatives must be accounted for separately and recorded at fair value like all others.

The basic supposition of the FAS 133, which has been in effect since June 2000 in the US, is that a derivative is considered to be used for *speculation*, and bearing a respective risk, until the company proves that it has used it as a hedge. The same principle is found in the international accounting standard known as *IAS 39*, which applies to all of Europe's c.7 000 listed companies as of 1 January 2005. In principle, FAS 133 requires full disclosure of derivatives transactions which have to go through the profit and loss account. However, hedges only have to be reported on the balance sheet until a profit or loss is booked for the hedged position itself. In order to qualify for this treatment, the hedge must be shown to be highly effective – a criterion which is hotly debated. Although not prescribing a single method for assessing *hedge effectiveness* the FSAB suggests a *80/125 rule* which says that a hegde is effective if the ratio of the change in value of the derivative to that of the hedged item falls between 80% and 125%.

5.1.3   Exploiting Price Differences

Without knowing a firm's short- and long-term objectives and intentions it is impossible to tell the true motives behind a hedge strategy. In principle, the same holds for the third kind of activity driving financial markets, *arbitrage*.

In general, arbitrage is the *riskless* exploitation of price differences in different markets. Traditionally, in its narrow definition the term refers to prices for the same product in different locations: the more similarities between products the greater the scope for arbitrage. This explains why, for example, in short-term wholesale financial markets like those for money or foreign exchange the *law of one price* tends to hold while for tailor-made options in OTC trades nobody would expect it to do. Persisting price differences for similar products in different locations are usually the result of institutional barriers or other impediments to financial activities.

In the age of electronic communications and instantaneous execution pure arbitrage opportunities have become rare. In financial literature, a wider definition refers to the construction of a *zero investment portfolio yielding a sure profit*. In practice, yet another approach, sometimes called *risk arbitrage*, is to search for mispriced financial products in specific areas. A related strategy is *statistical arbitrage* which involves buying and selling equities as they deviate from historical trends; if the shares of one company are rising sharply statistical arbitrageurs would sell the stock short while at the same time buying peer companies of the same industry.

Another variant that received the attention of US regulators and the UK Financial Services Authority (FSA) is a practice known as *time-zone arbitrage*. This kind of arbitrage bets on the value of international securities in mutual funds. The funds are only priced once a day and, as a result, may end up holding securities that have not been traded for hours. Time-zone arbitrageurs try to exploit this pricing inefficiency by trading in and out quickly with large sums of money – a practice which may dilute the value of the fund for other investors.

As a rule, all these arbitrageurs rely on complex mathematical models that provide them with buy and sell signals. However, as these strategies are largely open to interpretation and in contrast to the traditional definition, positions may be exposed to price risks, here, too, the borderline between speculation and arbitrage is vague.

5.2   MARKET DYNAMICS AND THE ROLE OF EXPECTATIONS

Just like diversification, arbitrage tends to lead to a *realignment of markets* through the pressure it exerts on prices. Borrowing money at a low interest rate in one market in order to invest it at a higher rate in another market leads to a rising demand in the first, and a growing supply in the second, which – other things remaining equal – will exert an upward pressure on the interest rate in the first market and a downward pressure in the second. This is in contrast to the effects of hedging which, in general, tends to *reinforce price movements* in one market thereby widening existing differences. Selling a currency forward in order to hedge an existing long position in the expectation of a falling exchange rate may become self-fulfilling if it is not offset by other market activities.

As a rule, market prices can be broken up into several *components*. Changes may be observed:

- in nominal rates and prices;
- on a real, i.e. inflation-adjusted, basis;
- in risk premia or spreads, and
- in price expectations.

Each of these components and its determinants influence the decisions of actors in the markets whose interplay, in turn, determines market outcomes.

5.2.1   Nominal Comparisons

Nominal rates and prices usually play a role in short-term strategies and transactions where fears about a decline in value due to inflation are practically non-existent. For example, compared to the possibility of an hourly or daily decline of an exchange rate by several percent during a currency crisis an annual inflation rate of even 4% or more looks negligible. This explains why for short-term cross-border financial transactions, attention focuses on *nominal interest rate parity*.

Interest rate parity means that the discount or premium on a currency, which is the percentage difference between the spot and forward rates, is equal to the difference in interest rates between two currencies. There are two versions. The *covered* interest rate parity for the currencies of two countries, A and B, can be written as:

$$p=(F_A-S_A)/S_A=i_B-i_A$$

with p denoting the forward premium or discount, F_A the forward rate of the currency of country A, S_A the respective spot rate and i_A and i_B the interest rates in both countries. Whenever deviations from this relation occur, arbitrageurs have an incentive to borrow money at the lower – forward-premium or discount-adjusted – interest rate, convert it into the currency with the higher – forward-premium or discount-adjusted – rate and invest it in that currency covering the transaction with a forward contract thereby eliminating currency risk. As the foreign exchange premium is always paid to the holder of the currency with the lower interest rate, this also holds if the unadjusted interest rate is lower, but the forward premium exceeds the interest differential. In general, in currency markets, the presence of arbitrageurs ensures that covered interest rate parity holds continually.

It must be mentioned that there is a second relation, known as *uncovered* interest rate parity, which can be written as

$$p = (S_A^e - S_A)/S_A = i_B - i_A$$

with S_A^e denoting the *expected* exchange rate at maturity instead of the forward rate. This relation indicates a potential incentive to invest in a currency exploiting a difference in interest rates leaving the transaction uncovered, i.e. *exposed to currency risk*. However, in this case one would speak of speculation or position taking and not of arbitrage.

5.2.2   The Role of Prices

The longer the time horizon, the more important become real, i.e. inflation-adjusted, yields and rates. In comparing economies the concept of *purchasing power parity (PPP)* is widely applied, despite its many deficiencies. The idea is that for any two countries prices for the same good, or bundle of goods, adjusted for the exchange rate, should be the same. Any deviations, so the argument goes, would trigger an arbitrage process raising demand in the cheaper place, and supply in the more expensive one, until the law of one price would hold again. Adjustments of the exchange rate resulting from the increasing demand for the currency of the cheaper country and a declining demand for the other would contribute to this process.

There is an absolute and a relative version of PPP. In its *absolute form*, the relation is expressed as

$$P_A/P_B = S$$

with P_A and P_B denoting a price index for country A and country B and S the spot exchange rate as the price of one unit of the currency of country B expressed in the currency of country A.

As one author puts it, as a *theoretical* proposition PPP serves as a solid foundation for thinking about the conditions under which prices in international goods markets adjust to attain long-term equilibrium. However, *empirically* it has been a more elusive concept. There are many reasons given for observed changes in *real exchange rates* which indicate that PPP does not hold; these include trade barriers and other institutional impediments. Another explanation is that in an economy only some of the goods produced are internationally traded or tradable and that lags in the price adjustment between tradable and non-tradable goods in the economy may explain why general indices such as wholesale prices or consumer prices show deviations from PPP. Balassa and Samuelson explained deviations from PPP with the

Table 5.1   The hamburger standard[1]

Country	Price in local currency	Price in US dollars	Actual exchange rate (1 USD=)	Over (+)/Under (−) valuation[2]	Purchasing power price
United States	$2.65	2.65	1.00	–	–
Euro area	€2.75	3.316	0.8293	+24.2011	1.03
Britain	£1.99	3.6301	1.8242[3]	+36.8114	0.75
Hungary	Forint 492	2.3827	206.49	−9.923	186
Poland	Zloty 6.30	1.729	3.6438	−34.6836	2.38
Sweden	Skr 30.0	3.9328	7.6282	+48.3967	22.32
Switzerland	SFr 6.35	4.9769	1.2759	+88.1025	2.40

[1] Price of a Big Mac, based on 15 January 2003 data.
[2] Against the US dollar in percent.
[3] Dollars per pound.
Source: OANDA, http://oanda.com/products/bigmac/bigmac.shtml.

existence of differences in the productivity of non-traded goods across countries. Deviations may also occur because of taxes and transaction costs. Yet another explanation is the volatility of nominal exchange rates which drives exchange-rate adjusted prices away from what is often considered their long-term equilibrium path.

A popular measure of deviations from PPP is the *hamburger standard* that has been published by *The Economist* since 1986. McDonald's, which operates with more than 30,000 restaurants in 113 countries, claims its Big Mac is generally made according to the same recipe all over the world (exceptions include India, where no beef products are sold, and Islamic countries where the Big Mac is made with halal beef). This uniformity makes it an ideal candidate for purchasing power comparisons. For example, if a Big Mac costs €2.75 in the euro area and $2.65 in the US, the PPP exchange rate between the two currencies should be $2.75/2.65 = 1.0377$. The over- or undervaluation against the dollar in this case can be calculated as

$$\frac{\text{PPP} - \text{Exchange rate}}{\text{Exchange rate}} \times 100$$

As Table 5.1 demonstrates even in Europe the deviations are considerable – e.g. in the euro area where in January 2003 the overvaluation measured in this way was more than 24%.

The Balassa–Samuelson Effect

Bela Balassa and Paul Samuelson demonstrated how non-traded goods may systematically affect the deviations from PPP because of productivity differences across countries and sectors. A basic assumption they made is that in poor countries the labour force in the tradables sector is less productive than in rich countries, while international productivity differences in non-tradables are negligible.

For traded goods in all countries prices are assumed to be roughly the same. Then, higher labour productivity in the tradables sectors of rich countries implies higher wages than abroad *in all sectors* (wages are the same across industries in all countries because firms in both the traded and non-traded sectors compete for workers). As a consequence, production costs in non-tradables are higher, as is the price of non-tradables in these countries. In contrast, poor countries with lower labour productivity in the tradables sector will tend to have lower non-tradables prices, too, and a lower overall price level. Empirical studies suggest that many currency relationships of developing countries vis-à-vis the US dollar follow the Balassa–Samuelson theory. However the theory has been less successful in explaining differences across countries with more similar per capita incomes.

However, studies have shown that in relative terms there are indications of a *convergence* to Big Mac parity, which brings us to the alternative view of PPP: *relative PPP* refers to *changes* in prices and exchange rates and can be written as

$$s = p_A - p_B$$

with the small italics denoting percentage changes. Since the percentage change in the price level is the rate of inflation, the equation states that the percentage change in the exchange rate is equal to the inflation differential between two countries. Note that this is a *weaker concept* than absolute PPP. If the absolute version holds, the relative will too, but, if absolute PPP does not hold, relative PPP still may. One reason to compare changes in prices and exchange rates instead of levels is that, usually, national price level estimates are based on product baskets that differ in coverage and composition rendering direct international comparisons difficult.

In general, relative PPP, too, performs *poorly in empirical studies* even when taking into account that it is a long-term concept which is not expected to hold continuously. It was most successful in periods of fixed exchange rates when trade flows dominated international economic relationships and capital movements were strongly restricted. After the Second World War, it was found to hold between the 1960s and 1980s – albeit with wide departures over long subperiods – while thereafter it appeared of even more limited use in explaining international price and exchange-rate movements.

One reason for the loosening of international price relations is the rising importance of international capital flows and cross-border financial relationships for currency movements after the transition to floating exchange rates worldwide and the capital liberalisations in many countries in the 1970s and 1980s. However, although the overall validity of purchasing power parity can no longer be taken for granted, in international financial markets relative prices still matter in many respects. Often, calculations of yields and returns focus on real, i.e. inflation-adjusted rates. In addition, the law of one price is still valid in many individual markets for goods and services. This holds true for goods traded on international exchanges in particular, where there is one 'world market'; these include many commodities and the most important raw materials. Another aspect is that prices have a strong signalling function: although market participants are generally aware of the loose relation, international inflation differentials are an important 'anchor' for longer term exchange rate expectations.

5.2.3 Risk Premia and Spreads

Beside inflation adjustments, another important component of price determination in financial markets is *risk premia* or *spreads*. There are many sources of financial risk and one of the biggest problems for individuals, companies and financial institutions is to adequately price these risks and manage them. In financial literature, three main categories of risks are distinguished: one is *market risks*, which arise from changes in the prices of financial assets and liabilities, or in respective volatilities. A second category is *credit risks*, the danger that counterparties are unwilling or unable to meet their contractual obligations. Credit risks include the possibility of debtors being downgraded by rating agencies since this may trigger a fall in the market value of their obligations (Appendix D). It also includes sovereign risk which is not a debtor-but a *country-specific* category of risks. For example, this may occur when countries threaten to impose foreign-exchange controls making it impossible for counterparties to fulfil their contracts.

The third category is *liquidity risks* which, in general, take two forms. On the one hand, a transaction may not be conducted at prevailing market prices due to insufficient *market* activity. Experience has shown that in periods of financial turmoil in particular liquidity may dry up very suddenly when market makers stop answering telephones and quotes are no longer available. A spectacular case was the market for European currency options during the EMS crisis in September 1992, another was the reaction of world exchanges in August 1990 when Iraq invaded Kuwait: a comparison of US and Japanese exchanges during that month showed that the average daily time span for which futures on the Nikkei index were not available for trading was 60.2 minutes compared to 2.7 minutes for the S&P, which means that the Nikkei was untradable for an average of one hour for several days – in financial markets under stress an eternity.

The second type of liquidity risk arises from *firms'* inability to meet cash-flow obligations forcing early liquidation thereby transforming book losses into real ones. One example which triggered a long debate in financial literature is the case of *Metallgesellschaft* in 1994 which showed the pitfalls of a *rollover* of forward positions for hedging purposes. The company had large oil exposures as part of a strategy to hedge long-term delivery contracts with short-term futures contracts which were constantly renewed. In principle, in efficient markets, the decision whether a long-term position is hedged by one contract of equal maturity or divided into several transactions of smaller subperiods should make no difference as long as the hedge is not interrupted: for each contract period there is either a loss in the position to be hedged accompanied by a gain from the hedge contract or vice versa. In the end, gains and losses from hedges and the hedged position would cancel each other out, showing the same result with both alternatives. However, depending on the financial instrument used for hedging, under the rollover strategy margin calls from derivatives exchanges may pile up in the case of losses, or counterparties in the OTC market may demand collateral, and, as in the case of Metallgesellschaft, additional cash needs may force the firm to abandon the hedge prematurely and at high cost.

How these and other financial risks are met depends on both individual *preferences and attitudes* and on *circumstances*. One question in this context is how risks are perceived, another how they are measured. The most difficult category in this respect is liquidity risk as market liquidity may change rather dramatically in wholly unforeseen ways in periods of financial turmoil. In these cases, the line between *risk* and *uncertainty* becomes fuzzy.

Following the tradition of Frank H. Knight (1885–1972), some economists emphasise the importance of distinguishing between these two categories. In Knight's interpretation, *risk* refers to situations in which *mathematical probabilities* can be assigned to random events. By contrast, with *uncertainty* there is no scientific basis on which mathematical probabilities can be calculated. The latter may hold for unique and unprecedented situations where the alternatives are not really all known and understood – or where no alternatives exist at all.

One example brought to mind in this context is the occurrence of extreme events in financial markets such as the stock market crash of 1987, the EMS crisis in 1992 or the crisis of the Russian rouble in 1998. Modern statistic techniques try to deal with these sorts of situations in a field known as *extreme value theory (EVT)*. In general, extremes are defined as unusual or rare events which in classical data analysis are often treated as outliers or simply ignored. EVT focuses on the maxima or minima of iid random variables in successive periods modelling exceedances over a given threshold. However, in many respects the method is still in its infancy and fraught with large uncertainties.

Being able to assign probabilities to expected outcomes opens a wide spectrum of possibilities of measuring risks. There are no uniform, generally accepted means of risk measurement. Instead, current practices differ across markets and products reflecting the limits imposed by individual financial instruments and prevailing general uncertainties. There are numerous indicators of market and credit risks based on the calculation of probabilities, variances and correlations in order to estimate potential credit losses or the volatility of prices. In some markets, with growing technological facilities and methodological advances, special tools became increasingly popular, sometimes leading to the forgetting of related conceptual weaknesses. For example, *implied volatilities* play an increasing role, not only in options markets but as a general means of evaluating the riskiness of a company debt or – as in the case of indices such as the *VIX*, the CBOE Volatility Index of implied volatility of options on the S&P 500 – even the overall market. The implied volatility of options on a company's shares can be viewed as the *cost of insurance* against the worsening of prospects of the firm, measured by its share price. Many investment banks, as well as the big rating agencies, are increasingly using these kinds of signals from the stock markets as a guide to the riskiness of a company's debt thereby strengthening the tendency for risk spreads to widen with rising volatility. Implied volatilities are also used by analysts and other outside observers to learn about the 'moods' of markets. For example, together with the *term structure* of interest rates implied volatilities are taken as indicators of market uncertainty about future monetary policy.

A related measure that is increasingly used in foreign exchange markets is *risk reversal*. This indicator which is also derived from options markets is a combination of 'out of the money' call and put options with the volatility of the risk reversals given by the difference in volatilities of the included options. The instrument is intended to measure market expectations, in particular the *direction of uncertainty* regarding the future exchange rate. The direction in which the market expects the currency to move is reflected in the favoured contract: for example, if the risk reversal favours put over call options of a given currency market sentiment tends more towards expecting a decline of the exchange rate of that currency than a rise.

In credit markets a risk indicator of growing importance is *recovery ratings*. These tell investors the likely return if a bond or a loan defaults. Recovery ratings are issue-specific and thought to complement traditional corporate credit ratings which focus on the overall credit risk of a company not being able to meet its financial obligations. Recovery ratings refer exclusively to expected loss and recovery in the event of default with no relationship to the underlying default likelihood.

Risks and risk measurement determine *spreads* in the markets explaining differences in financial conditions for good and bad borrowers, small and big companies, blue chip and new technology firms, debtors from industrial countries and emerging market economies and many more. However, perceived dangers and uncertainties are not the only determinants of spreads. One important factor is *liquidity*: in general, other things left unchanged, spreads shrink in highly liquid markets and rise under tighter conditions thereby reflecting variations in borrowers' and investors' opportunities. Another important determinant is the *composition* of markets and the influence different *groups* of actors exert on market conditions. Their impact on the riskiness of markets is also determined by the way in which they form expectations and in which, in turn, their reactions then affect prices.

5.2.4 The Formation of Expectations

In contrast to economic theory, in financial markets information gathering and processing, knowledge acquisition, the formation of expectations and the resulting reactions may take many forms. Broadly, two different ways of seeing the markets can be distinguished. These are known as *fundamental* and *technical* analyses. The main difference between the two is that actors focusing on technical analyses, so-called chartists, get their information from studying the past history of prices. In contrast, fundamentalists search for economic developments and relationships which may cause price movements.

Fundamentalists are strongly influenced by economic theories; beside firm-specific data they study macroeconomic factors such as economic growth, prices, current accounts, productivity, investment and many other determinants of economic activity. They look at leading and lagging indicators of the business cycle, such as building permits and inventory changes or business spending and unemployment rates, in search of hints to future developments in overall markets as well as sector and industry prospects. The information and sources they rely on may differ widely. Being aware that economics does not offer a unanimous uncontested explanation of the economy they mostly follow a rather eclectic approach. In addition, they try to estimate the effects of non-economic influences on markets such as political events and natural disasters as well as all kinds of rumours reaching them in the course of the day.

Chartists, too, adopt many different strategies. The underlying assumption of their approach is that one need not bother about economic 'facts' since in immediately discounting any new developments prices themselves contain all relevant information available. Therefore, the history of prices is all that matters. Chartists try to identify systematic *patterns* in financial series which may be exploited for future trading.

Chart analysis has a *large subjective element*. There are hundreds of different indicators and the techniques applied range from visual inspection of a price series over technical trading rules to highly sophisticated combinations of different tools including statistical methods. Some are *trend-following* indicators such as the combination of *moving averages* of different length. Others signal when a market is to be considered 'overbought' or 'oversold' and showing signs of a coming 'correction'. Here, *filter rules* are an example: applying a filter aims to eliminate trades with a low probability of success. For example, an *x%* filter rule signals that a financial instrument should be bought if its price has risen *x%* from a recent low point and sold after a fall of *x%* from an earlier high point.

One of the most popular types of charts used in technical analysis is the *bar chart*. In a bar chart, each trading day is represented by a vertical line connecting the lowest and highest price of the day. In addition, the closing price is shown on the right side of the bar and the opening price on its left side (Figure 5.2.).

In studying bar charts investors try to detect recurring patterns, which they sometimes give characteristic names. For example, they search for *support and resistance levels* and analyse movements that indicate continuation such as *flags* and *pennants*. They consider *triangles*

Figure 5.2   The bar chart

hinting at periods of congestion within long-term trends and study top and bottom formations such as *head and shoulders* that indicate potential trend reversals (Figure 5.3).

In the Western world charts and other forms of technical analyses have their roots in commodities trading; they spread to financial markets with the emergence of financial futures and other exchange-traded derivatives in the 1970s. However, there is one widely used chart technique which was developed in Japan in the eighteenth century and first applied for analysing future contracts on the Dojima Rice Exchange in Osaka.

The *candlestick chart* resembles the bar chart in many respects (Figure 5.4). The line for each day consists of a thick part, the main body, which represents the range between the day's opening price and closing price with the colour of the body indicating which one was the higher. A black or red body indicates a higher opening price, a white or green body a higher closing price. In addition, there are thin lines showing the day's highest and lowest price. As with bar charts, investors using candlestick charts are studying formations looking for recurring patterns for which they have special names such as *hammer* or *hanging man*, or the top and bottom formations called *three Buddha patterns*. All in all, there are over 20 patterns used in candlestick charting.

Figure 5.5 gives an example of charts for daily values of the S&P 500 over six months from March to September 2004. Figure 5.5(a) is a visual example of a *candlestick chart*, while 5.5(b) shows the respective *bar chart*. Figure 5.5(c) combines the bar chart with so-called *Bollinger bands*. The latter is a rather sophisticated indicator allowing comparison of volatility and relative price levels over time. Bollinger bands measure volatility by placing trading bands around a moving average. In this example, the bands are two standard deviations away from a 20-day simple moving average (which is found adding up the closing prices from the past 20 days and dividing them by 20). Bands are blue for the lower, green for the average and red for the upper band. Since prices are constantly changing, the value of two standard deviations also changes and the bands are in a sense self-adjusting expanding when markets become more volatile and contracting during calmer periods.

In financial markets, both fundamental and technical approaches are frequently *applied side by side*. Their relative importance depends on factors such as actors' motives, technical capacities, flexibility and time horizon. For instance, great financial and technical strength

Price

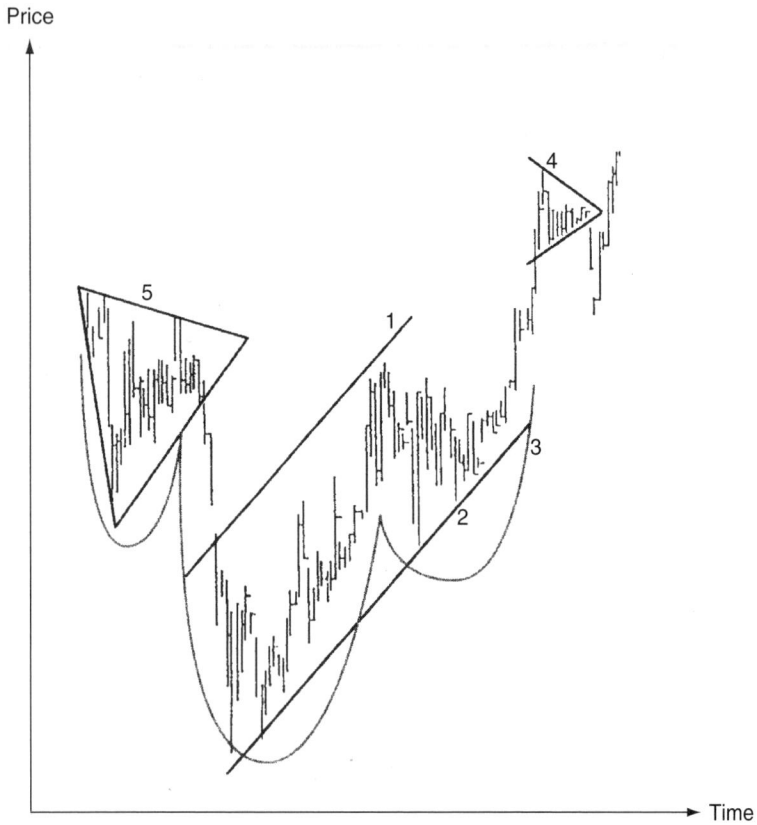

Figure 5.3   Price patterns. 1 Resistance line, 2 support line, 3 head and shoulders (reversed), 4 pennant, 5 triangle

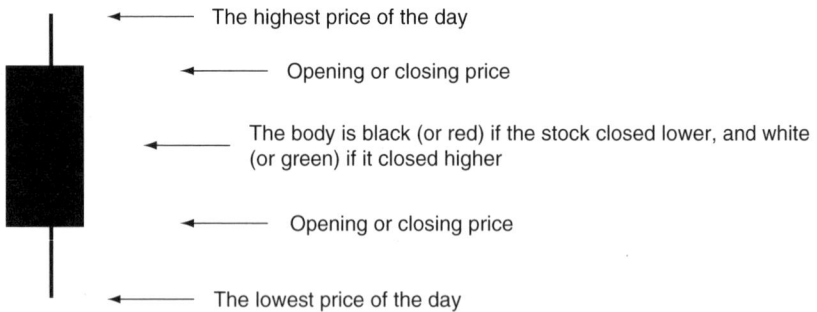

The highest price of the day

Opening or closing price

The body is black (or red) if the stock closed lower, and white (or green) if it closed higher

Opening or closing price

The lowest price of the day

Figure 5.4   Candlestick chart

enables market participants to invest in trading rooms and sophisticated computer programs, which allow them to exploit complex patterns and minor discrepancies in price movements that cannot be detected with the naked eye. Further, the shorter the time horizon, the greater the influence of technical analyses on trading decisions. The reason is that economic fundamentals change comparably slowly and require a relatively long time to get a clear picture.

(a) S&P 500 .. daily Candlestick chart

(b) S&P 500 .. daily OHLC plot

(c) S&P 500 .. daily OHLC plot

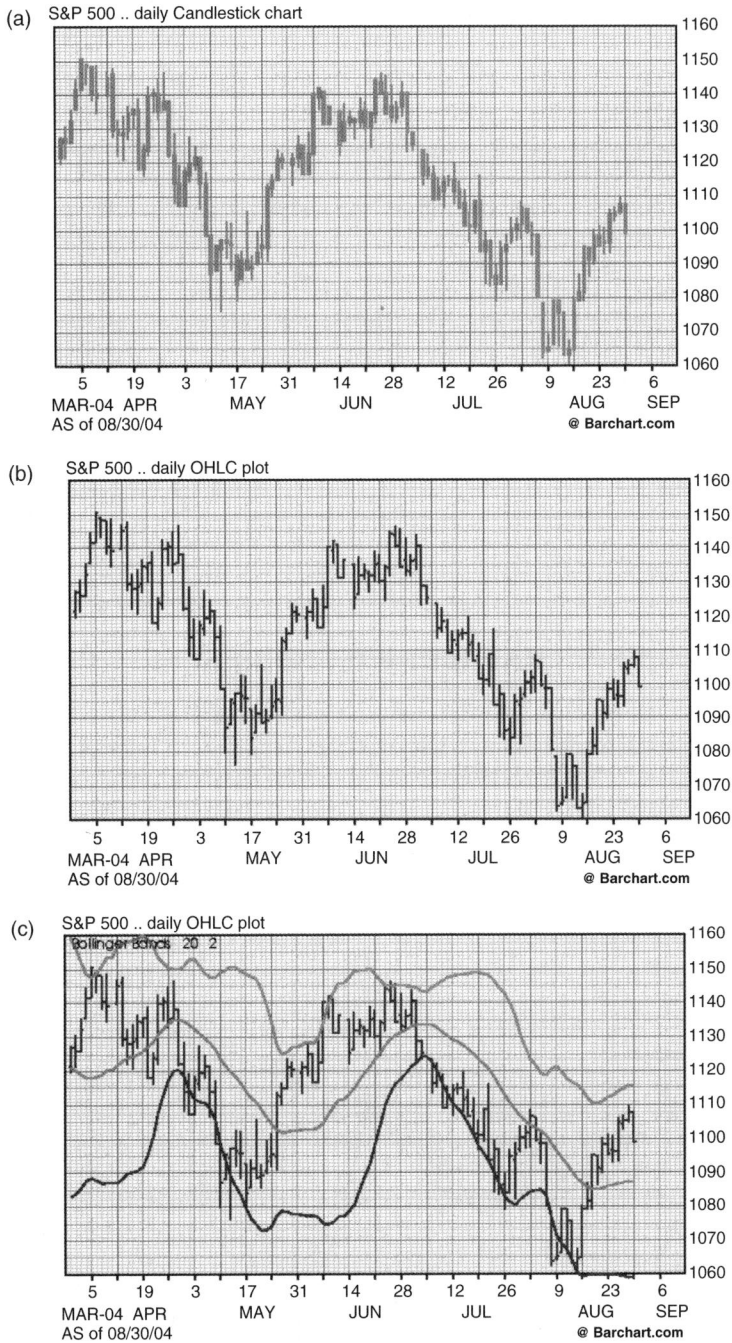

Figure 5.5   Charts

Market outcomes are determined by the interplay of different *groups of actors* and, as a consequence, are influenced by changes of their *relative weight* in the market. One example is the growing presence of institutional investors in equities markets which with their long-term orientation, strong emphasis of economic fundamentals and lack of exit options due to the high volume of their engagements provide an element of stability. Another example is the increasing role of hedge funds, which with their short-term view, their willingness to take high risks and their practice of moving in and out of markets very rapidly, are widely considered to contribute to market volatility.

However, group behaviour may affect the markets in many different ways. One example involves again institutional investors. Their decisions from time to time to switch between whole asset classes, such as from equity to fixed income and back, and to use derivatives to protect portfolios on a large scale, strongly increase the *interdependence* of markets thereby adding to the risks of *spreading volatility and contagion*. Another aspect is that each category of actors has its own *rhythm and dynamics* and the interaction of the many may result in wholly unexpected price movements. This may explain why, for example, at times, the causes of observed outliers are not clear at all – which does not mean that traders and market observers do not find an *ex post* explanation – while in other instances the relation between cause and effect appears wholly inadequate: on the one hand, small events sometimes seem to have too large an effect, and on the other hand truly dramatic developments may evaporate without leaving a trace.

5.3   PRICE PATTERNS

Depending on actors, motives, time horizons and technicalities, and also on the institutional environment, financial markets show a wide variety of *characteristic price patterns*. The aim of this section is not to find an explanation for the reasons behind various price movements but to present a broad picture taking a few examples in order to give an idea of the way in which markets differ. Most of these examples are gathered in a rather eclectic way from US markets which, as a result of their long history and variety of deep and liquid markets, seem particularly suited for making comparisons.

Looking first at *short-term rates*, Figure 5.6 shows how three US short-term interest rates developed since 1997. The *federal funds rate* line shows the interest rate at which depository

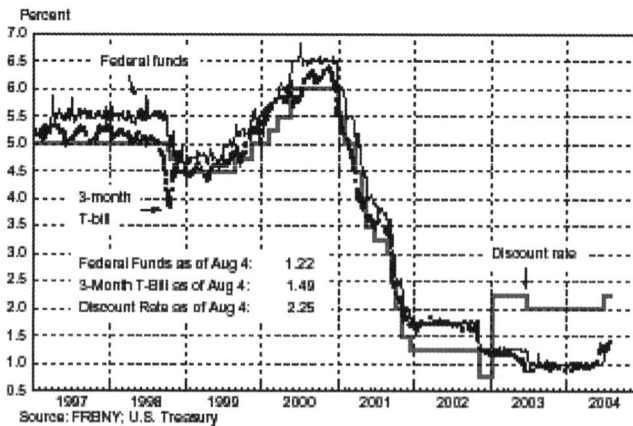

Figure 5.6   Short-term interest rates. *Source*: http://www.ny.frb.org/research/capital_markets/index. html

institutions in the US lend balances at the Federal Reserve to other depository institutions overnight. The rate of the *three-month Treasury bill*, a short-term government paper, is also shown in the figure. The *discount rate* is the rate charged by the US reserve banks for credit to depository institutions either through advances or through the discount of certain types of paper, including 90-day commercial paper. As a rule, until end of 2001 all three lines moved very much in tandem. Beside longer-term swings, which were followed by all three rates, the federal funds and Treasury bill rates showed remarkable short-term variations. In contrast, the discount rate as an institutional rate, an instrument set by monetary policy, changed only sporadically. Usually, the federal funds rate was above the Treasury bill rate indicating the higher borrowing costs of financial institutions compared to the government, while the discount rate mostly represented a kind of lower limit of the short-term market.

Figure 5.7 shows the development of some *long-term interest rates* for the same time period. It shows the rates for *high-quality corporate bonds* with an AAA rating and for a *10-year US government paper*. One remarkable feature is that both series follow roughly the same long-term movement as the short-term rates with a peak in the year 2000. However, while in the first years the short-term rates remained flat apparently clinging to the discount rate while long-term rates were clearly declining, in the second half of the period under consideration the development of the short-term rates was much more pronounced. Another feature is the difference between the two series, which demonstrates the line that separates even first-rate corporate borrowers from the benchmark. However, apparently this difference was changing over the years: it widened, at first slowly and then more clearly, until 2003 and then shrank again.

Figure 5.8 gives an impression of the relationship between *short-term and long-term interest rates in the very long run*, showing the development of US Treasury bond and Treasury bill rates over the last 80 years. Three observations can be made. The first is the much higher

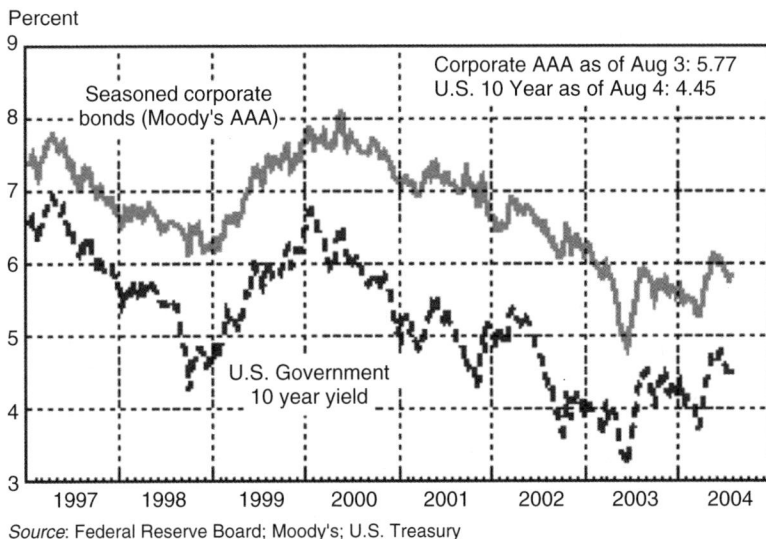

Figure 5.7   Long-term interest rates. *Source*: http://www.ny.frb.org/research/capital_markets/index. html

Figure 5.8   Short and long-term interest rates in the very long run. *Source*: http://www.cpcug.org/
user/invest/djb.gif

variations of short-term rates despite the fact that both series seem to follow the same long-term movement. Second, usually the short-term rate is below the long-term rate – although inverse yield curves seemed to occur with growing frequency in the 1970s – but during the 1930s and early 1940s, this difference was more pronounced than in later periods. Third, the US apparently went through a period of extraordinary high short-term and long-term rates in the late 1970s and early 1980s, accompanied by extraordinary strong variations in both rates.

Figure 5.9 allows a comparison of *bond and stock markets in the very long run* contrasting the Dow Jones bond average with the Dow Jones industrial average from 1920 to 2000. Two features are remarkable. The first is the much larger change of the stock market index clearly demonstrating why stocks are so much more attractive to investors in the long run. While the stock market shows a strong growth, it is difficult to detect a trend in the bond index at all. The second observation is that apparently if there is a trend in both series their relation seems rather an inverse one with rising stock prices accompanied by – albeit much smaller – falling bond prices. However, this relation seems to have broken down in recent years.

What can be said about *stock markets* in general? Are the differences in industrial values, technology stocks and the overall market as they are experienced by investors and reported in the media reflected in market indices? Figure 5.10 confirms this impression contrasting the development of two general indices – the Dow Jones industrial average and the S&P 500 – with the NASDAQ composite. Although, in the long run, all three go in the same direction, reaching their peaks and troughs roughly simultaneously, the movement appears much more pronounced for the technology values.

Another interesting relationship is between *stock and bonds markets*. Figure 5.11 shows different scenarios for the S&P 500 and US interest rates as they were represented in yield curves. The charts show the relationships between interest rates and stocks at different points in time. The lines in the figure on the right-hand side indicate the S&P closing value for a

(a)

(b)

Figure 5.9 Bond and stock markets in the very long run. (a) Dow Jones bond average; (b) Dow Jones industrial average. *Source*: http://www.cpcug.org/user/invest/djb.gif

given day, while the black line in the left figure is the yield curve on that date, the fading trails show where its position was the days running up to this. One apparent feature is the *looseness* of the relationship. In Figure 5.11(a) overall interest rates were comparably low with relatively high differences between short-term and long-term interest rates. At the same time, the stock market seemed to reach a local peak. Figure 5.11(b) shows the stock market in decline three years earlier. Short-term interest rates at that time were much higher and interest rate differentials much lower. Figure 5.11(c) goes back in time yet another couple of months, to when the stock market decline had just begun: bond markets showed a high overall level of interest rates and an inverse yield curve with long-term rates below short-term rates. When this was an indication of market investors expecting short-term interest rates to fall in the future, then obviously these expectations were to change fundamentally a few months later.

How about relationship of *stock markets in Europe and the US*? Do they move in parallel or are there apparent deviations indicating the influence of regional peculiarities? Figure 5.12 shows that the markets obviously follow a common trend and regional influences do not matter very much, as the Eurostoxx 50 and the Dow Jones are, at least at times, very close. However, as the development of the German DAX in the same figure shows national

DOW JONES INDUSTRIAL AVERAGE AND S&P 500 INDICES
Weekly

DJIA ... SP500

S&P 500 Index (right axis)

S&P 500 as of:
Aug 4 1,098.63

DJIA as of:
Aug 4 10,126.51

DJIA (left axis)

1994 1995 1996 1997 1998 1999 2000 2001 2002 2003 2004
Source: Federal Reserve Board

(a)

NASDAQ COMPOSITE INDEX
Weekly

NASDAQ as of:
Aug 4 1,855.06

1994 1995 1996 1997 1998 1999 2000 2001 2002 2003 2004
Source: Federal Reserve Board

(b)

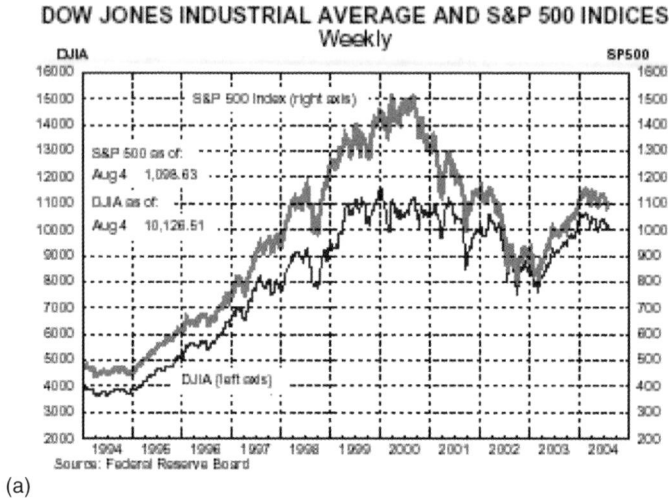

Figure 5.10 Comparison of stock market indices. *Source*: http://www.ny.frb.org/research/capital_markets/index.html

European indices may exhibit more pronounced deviations reflecting the low integration of individual stocks and markets.

Finally, *currencies*. Figure 5.13 presents the exemplary development of four exchange rates vis-à-vis the US dollar from March to July 2004. All appear highly volatile. The movements for two EU currencies, the euro and the British pound, look rather similar. The swings in the Japanese yen appear wider and, at least in the first three months, affected by different kinds of influences. On the other hand, the strong variations of the Hungarian forint demonstrate the struggle of the currency of a transition economy and new EU member under high market uncertainty.

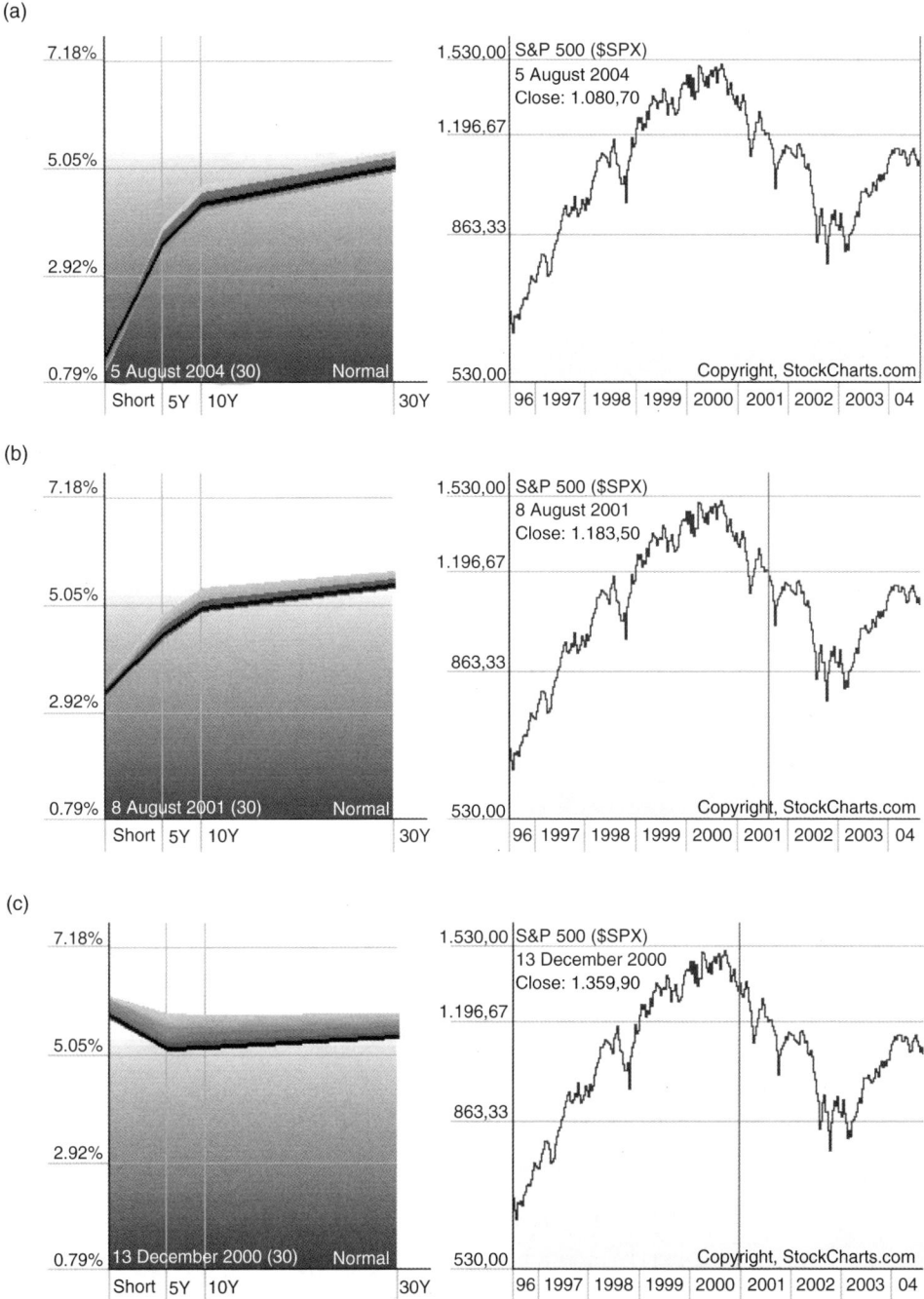

Figure 5.11   Stocks and yield curves. *Source*: http://stockcharts.com/charts/YieldCurve.html

```
Stoxx Ltd
  01-09-2004
  +20%


  +10%




    0%




  -10%
           Nov03      Jan04      Mrz04      Mai04      Jul04
Copyright 2003 Yahoo! Inc.                      http://de.finance.yahoo.com
```

Dow
^GDAXI
^STOXX50E

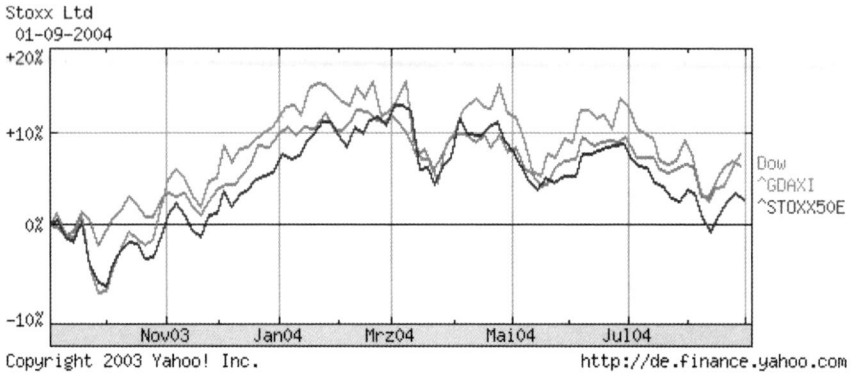

Figure 5.12   Stock market developments in Europe and the US

(a) Euros to 1 US dollar

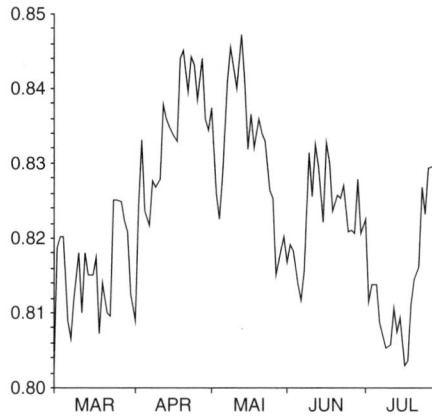

```
0.85


0.84



0.83




0.82



0.81



0.80
       MAR     APR     MAI     JUN     JUL
```

(b) British pounds to 1 US dollar

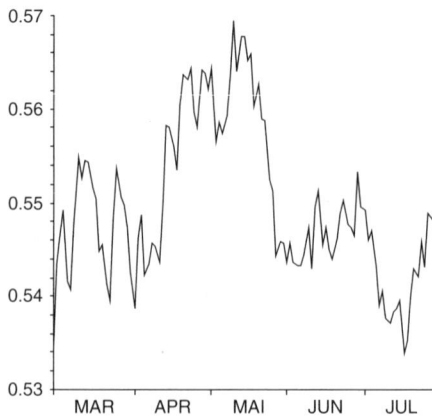

```
0.57



0.56



0.55



0.54



0.53
       MAR     APR     MAI     JUN     JUL
```

(c) Hungarian forints to 1 US dollar

(d) Japanese yen to 1 US dollar

Source: Thomson Financial, Datastream.

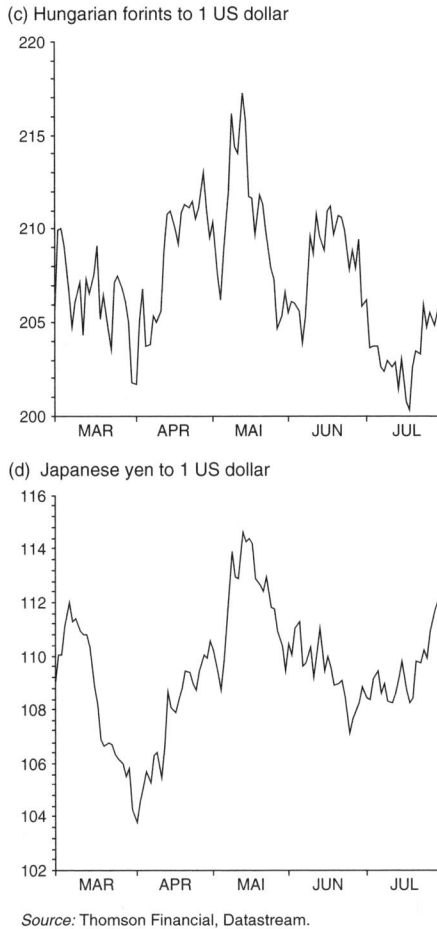

Figure 5.13   Exchange rates in 2004. *Source*: http://www.x-rates.com

This brief visual inspection of financial price series can only offer a momentary glimpse of markets. It cannot be – and is not intended to be – a substitute for thorough data analysis. It demonstrates the variety of patterns prevailing in the markets but also the similarities: today's financial markets are characterised by large and hardly foreseeable variations as well as high interdependencies both on a regional level and worldwide. Both pose considerable challenges to monetary authorities and financial regulators in Europe which will be analysed in the last chapter.

Summary

- Financial markets are dominated by three types of activities: diversification, hedging and arbitrage.
- Diversification has its roots in modern portfolio theory which emphasises that in order to maximise the return of a portfolio of assets for a given risk level it is important 'not to put all of one's eggs into one basket'.

142

- The capital asset pricing model (CAPM) combines portfolio theory with the efficient market hypothesis (EMH) explaining investors' behaviour in a general equilibrium framework.
- Hedging is an instrument to partially or fully offset some type or element of financial risk by establishing a matching position.
- In practice, the concept of hedging is fraught with ambiguities resulting from the definition of risk exposure.
- Arbitrage in the traditional meaning of the word is defined as the riskless exploitation of price differences for the same financial product in different markets.
- Traditional forms of arbitrage have become rare and are increasingly replaced by concepts such as risk arbitrage or statistical arbitrage, which involve risk elements.
- Market prices can be broken down into several components that determine investors' decisions and market outcomes in many ways.
- While nominal rates and prices dominate short-term decisions, inflation-adjusted yields and rates tend to play a role for longer periods of time.
- How financial risks are reflected in risk premia and spreads depends on individual judgements and preferences and on circumstances but also on market liquidity determining borrowers' and investors' opportunities.
- Expectation formation in financial markets can be broadly categorised according to the information used and distinguished into fundamental and technical analyses.
- A crude visual inspection of financial price series gives an impression of the variety of patterns prevailing and of existing relationships and interdependencies.

Exercises

1. Describe the rationale behind the advice to an investor 'not to put all eggs into one basket'. Relate this advice to the process of capital liberalisation and financial integration in Europe and discuss the inherent advantages and disadvantages of integrated markets in this context.
2. Discuss the main theoretical and empirical arguments against the efficient market hypothesis. Under which circumstances would you recommend sticking to the concept in analysing investors' behaviours and/or market performance?
3. Give an overview of concepts and ambiguities of hedges in international financial markets.
4. Discuss possible influences of diversification and hedging strategies on financial prices. Under which circumstances would you expect price fluctuations to be reinforced or dampened?
5. Describe the role of arbitrage in financial markets.
6. Evaluate the concept of purchasing power parity both as a theoretical proposition and an empirical relationship.
7. Describe the problems of measuring risks and uncertainties in international financial markets.
8. Describe the ways in which fundamentalists and chartists see financial developments and discuss the main advantages and disadvantages of both approaches.
9. Can you think of ways in which fundamental and technical analyses may lead to bandwagon effects and other forms of 'irrational' market behaviour?

Additional Links and References

The paper by Bachelier of 1900 on the nature of speculative prices is reprinted in:

Cootner, Paul H. (1964) *The Random Character of Stock Market Prices*, Cambridge, MA: MIT Press.

The classic contributions laying the foundations of modern portfolio theory and the capital asset pricing model are:

Lintner, John (1965) The valuation of risky assets and the selection of risky investments in stock portfolios and capital budgets, *Review of Economics and Statistics*, **47**, February, 13–37.
Markowitz, Harry M. (1952) Portfolio selection, *Journal of Finance*, **7**, March, 70–91.
Mossin, Jan (1966) Equilibrium in a capital asset market, *Econometrica*, **34**, October, 768–83.
Sharpe, William F. (1964) Capital asset prices: a theory of market equilibrium under conditions of risk, *Journal of Finance*, **19**, 425–42.

The development and popularity of the efficient market hypothesis owes much to the contributions of Eugene Fama:

Fama, Eugene F. (1965) The behavior of stock market prices, *Journal of Business*, **1**, 34–105.
Fama, Eugene F. (1970) Efficient capital markets: a review of theory and empirical work, *Journal of Finance*, **25**(2), 383–417.

The classic example of precommitment as a means of overcoming one's own weakness of will is Ulysses of whom we are told in the *Odyssey* that he had himself bound before setting out towards the Sirens. This, together with other forms of 'irrationality', is discussed in:

Elster, Jon (1984) *Ulysses and the Sirens – Studies in Rationality and Irrationality*, Cambridge: Cambridge University Press.

A highly readable general overview of the concept of rationality and its deficiencies is given in:

Dawes, Robyn M. (1988) *Rational Choice in an Uncertain World*, Orlando, FL: Harcourt Brace Jovanovich.

The question as to which extent decisions reflect preferences is discussed in:

Sen, Amartya (1982) Behaviour and the concept of preference, reprinted in Amartya Sen (ed.) *Choice, Welfare and Measurement*, Oxford: Oxford University Press, pp. 432–49.

Phenomena such as framing, anchoring and preference reversal are analysed in:

Grether, David M. and Charles R. Plott (1979) Economic theory of choice and the preference reversal phenomenon, *American Economic Review*, **69**(4), 623–38.
Hogarth, Robin M. and Melvin W. Reder (eds) (1987) *Rational Choice – The Contrast between Economics and Psychology*, Chicago: University of Chicago Press.
Machina, Mark J. (1987) Choice under uncertainty: problems solved and unsolved, *Journal of Economic Perspectives*, **1**(1), 121–54.
Machina, Mark J. (1989) Dynamic consistency and non-expected utility models of choice under uncertainty, *Journal of Economic Literature*, **27**(4), 1622–68.

See also Mark Machina's home page for his current research on decisions under uncertainty and related topics:

http://econ.ucsd.edu/~mmachina/

The view that the concept of rational expectations should focus on outcomes serving above all as a tool for econometricians is found in:

Sargent, Thomas J. (1995) *Bounded Rationality in Macroeconomics*, Oxford: Oxford University Press.

For the discussion of the equity risk premium puzzle see, for example:

Huh, Chan (1990) The equity-risk premium puzzle, *FRBSF Weekly Letter*, 13 April, http://www.frbsf.org/publications/economics/letter/1990/el90–15.pdf
Malkiel, Burton G. (2003) The efficient market hypothesis and its critics, *Journal of Economic Perspectives*, **17**(1), 59–82.

A short description of GARCH models and their applications can be found in:

Jorion, Philippe (1997) *Value at Risk: The New Benchmark for Controlling Market Risk*, Chicago: Irwin.

The technique of constructing a zero investment portfolio yielding a sure profit under the wider definition of arbitrage is described in:

Bodie, Zvi, Alex Kane and Alan J. Marcus (2002) *Investments*, New York: McGraw-Hill/Irwin.

The standard references for the Balassa–Samuelson theory are:

Balassa, Bela (1964) The purchasing-power parity doctrine: a reappraisal, *Journal of Political Economy*, **72**(6), 584–96.
Samuelson, Paul (1964) Theoretical notes on trade problems, *Review of Economics and Statistics*, **46**(2), 145–54.

For a detailed discussion of the strengths and weaknesses of the concept of purchasing power parity, and for the hamburger standard and other empirical evidence, see:

Krugman, Paul R. and Maurice Obstfeld (1997) *International Economics – Theory and Policy*, Reading, MA: Addison-Wesley.
Pakko, Michael R. and Patricia S. Pollard (2003) Burgernomics: A Big Mac guide to purchasing power parity, *Federal Reserve Bank of St. Louis Review*, December, http://research.stlouisfed.org/publications/review/03/11/pakko.pdf

International differences in hamburger prices may have to do with consumer preferences and perceptions. A highly readable collection of social studies emphasising this aspect and highlighting the role of McDonald's in Asia is:

Watson, James L. (ed.) (1997) *Golden Arches East – McDonald's in East Asia*, Stanford: Stanford University Press.

A brief overview of different risk categories in financial markets is given in

Jorion, Philippe (1997) *Value at Risk: The New Benchmark for Controlling Market Risk*, Chicago: Irwin.

Frank H. Knight's original contribution on risk and uncertainty in Part III, Chapter VII of his book, *Risk, Uncertainty and Profit* (Boston: Hart, Schaffner and Marx, Houghton Mifflin 1921) is available online at:

http://www.econlib.org/library/Knight/knRUP6.html#Pt.III, Ch.VII

An impression of the difficulties of applying extreme value theory (EVT) to financial data for risk measurement can be gained from:

Gilli, Manfred and Evis Kellezi (2003) An application of extreme value theory for measuring risk, Preprint, 8 February, http://www.unige.ch/ses/metri/gilli/evtrm/evtrm.pdf

Information on risk reversals and other types of foreign exchange option volatility is given by the British Bankers' Association at:

http://www.bba.org.uk/bba/jsp/polopoly.jsp?d = 129&a = 803

Historical price information including charts and latest news can be found at:

http://www.bloomberg.com/
http://finance.yahoo.com/

An overview of the methods and instruments of technical analysis is given in:

http://www.investopedia.com/university/technical/
http://www.stockcharts.com/education/
http://www.decisionpoint.com/TAcourse/TAcourseMenu.html

For an overview of the techniques of candlestick charts see:

Nison, Steve (1991) *Japanese Candlestick Charting Techniques*, New York: Simon & Schuster.

6
Policy Issues

Financial markets pose many kinds of *challenges* to policy makers and affect economic activity in many ways. In European countries well-functioning financial relationships are a prerequisite for the working of the economy. Financial market stability contributes to price and exchange-rate stability thereby strengthening trust in the currency. The soundness of the financial system enhances the overall credibility of financial institutions, while the design of the financial sector influences economic growth prospects in the long run.

However, the extent to which policy may affect market outcomes is clearly limited for at least three reasons:

- *Lack of information*: policy makers are not necessarily better informed than market actors and by interfering in the markets constantly risk doing more harm than good.
- *Lack of influence*: in some markets actors are beyond the authorities' reach, in other markets volumes are too high, or leeways to circumvent intended effects too numerous, for policy to exert a lasting influence.
- Market *openness* and, closely related, international policy *interdependence*: in the era of growing economic and financial integration and increasing globalisation the effectiveness of policy measures in one country depends on international developments and decisions made in other countries as well.

The ways in which the financial and the real side of the economy interact are still poorly understood. This aggravates the policy problem in two respects: the formulation of policy targets and the choice of appropriate instruments and strategies. In both respects, the European experience allows valuable insights into the underlying mechanisms.

6.1 POLICY TARGETS

Although often neglected in public debates financial systems, institutions and developments matter for economic policy making. On the one hand, they may threaten, or contribute to, economic stability. On the other, they influence the conditions and prospects of economic growth. Both are important targets of economic policy.

6.1.1 Stability

Monetary and financial stability are indispensable *prerequisites for economic development*, which has several aspects. It includes the calmness of markets and the foreseeability of price movements, the availability of low-risk finance and investment opportunities, the allocation of capital under sound conditions and the provision of a basis for the overall smooth functioning of the economy. As a rule, monetary and financial stability are closely *interrelated*. The effectiveness of a monetary strategy largely depends on the soundness of the financial sector and the functioning of the channels of the transmission mechanism of monetary policy.

On the other hand, people's overall trust in financial institutions depends on belief in the ability of the monetary authorities to maintain the value of the currency. This explains why policy making focuses on both issues: the *variability of prices* and the *riskiness of the financial sector*.

In Europe, responsibilities for the two are *divided*. While price stability generally comes under the responsibility of central banks, the stability of the financial system is often monitored by a separate institution. One example is the German BaFin (Bundesanstalt für Finanzdienst-leistungsaufsicht). As a consequence, while in wide parts of Europe monetary policy is decided centrally at a regional level, financial supervision is still largely a national matter requiring strong efforts of cooperation in order to achieve a level playing field across the region and prevent financial institutions from benefiting from '*regulatory arbitrage*'.

As a rule, the fight against price variability includes protecting both the *internal value* of a currency against inflationary pressures or loss of purchasing power and its *external value* against exchange-rate instability. In the euro zone the two targets are the responsibility of the European Central Bank (ECB). According to Article 2 of the ESCB Statute, which is an integral part of the Maastricht Treaty, price stability is the *primary objective* of monetary policy in the euro area. Article 107 of the treaty guarantees the *independence* of the ECB in pursuing this goal. This has two dimensions. On the one hand it means that monetary policy shall not be influenced by instructions from governments or other institutions. On the other, it shall be free to adopt a forward-looking, medium-term orientation, undisturbed by short-term developments and political considerations. Economies are constantly hit by *unforseeable shocks* that affect prices. At the same time, there are *significant time lags* in the influence of monetary policy on price developments making it impossible for a central bank to keep inflation at a specific point target all the time, or to bring it back to a desired level within a short period. With the *medium-term notion* the ECB retains some flexibility to respond in an appropriate manner to changing circumstances.

The medium-term orientation is also reflected in the way price stability is *defined* for the purposes of European monetary policy. It is a year-on-year increase in the harmonised index of consumer prices (*HICP*) for the euro area of below 2%, which is to be maintained over the medium term.

How can monetary policy achieve the target of price stability and in which way does it influence prices in the euro area? The main channel is by controlling the supply of the *monetary base* – the central bank is the sole issuer of banknotes and the sole provider of bank reserves – which, in turn, enables the ECB to influence *money market conditions* and *short-term interest rates*. In economic literature, the way in which monetary conditions affect the real economy and the overall price level is not undisputed. However, there is widespread agreement that in the long run, after all adjustments have taken place, changes in the money supply *are* reflected in changes in the general level of prices.

The ECB has outlined its view of the *transmission mechanism* of monetary policy, i.e. the various ways in which prices are influenced by official interest rates, in a diagram (Figure 6.1). According to this, the most immediate effects are on market interest rates and expectations with a direct link from the latter to wage and price-setting processes in the economy. Other channels are the supply and demand for money and credit, asset prices and the exchange rate. They all affect supply and demand in goods and labour markets in one way or the other and thereby domestic prices as well as import prices which, in turn, determine the overall price level.

How should monetary policy react to developments outside its control in order to preserve price stability? This depends on the *nature of shocks* which affect the euro area. The figure lists three examples: changes in the global economy, in fiscal policy and in commodity

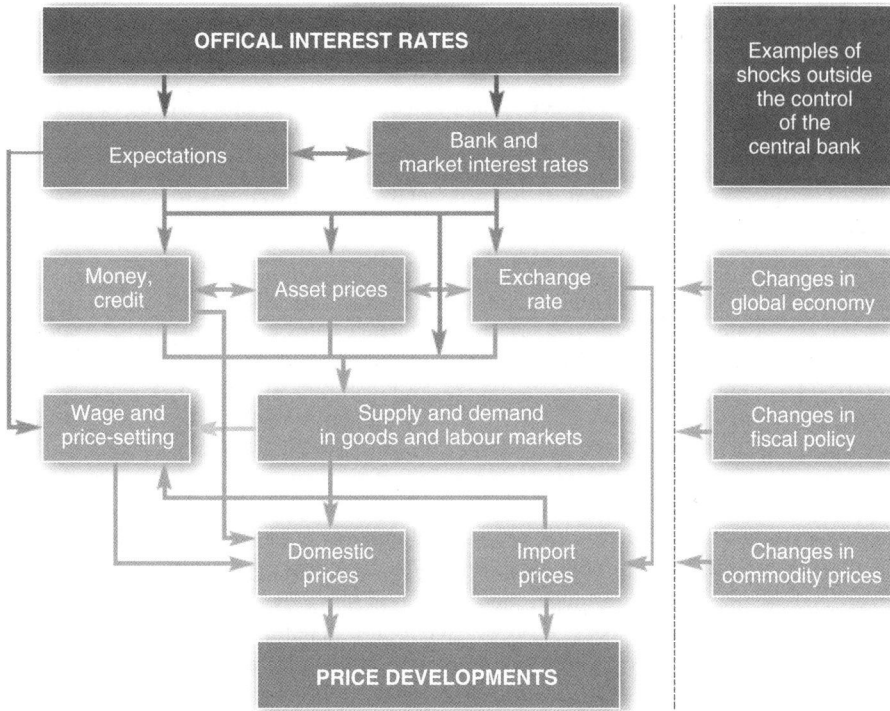

Figure 6.1 The transmission mechanism from interest rates to prices in the euro area. *Source*: European Central Bank (2004) *The Monetary Policy of the ECB 2004*, http://www.ecb.int/pub/pdf/other/monetarypolicy2004en.pdf, Chart 3.1

prices. Experience has shown that in the case of demand shocks, for example, output and prices often move in the same direction and a prompt reaction by monetary policy is not only appropriate in stabilising price development but, at the same time, may also help to stabilise real economic activity. There are other cases where output and prices move in opposite directions – one example is a rise in oil prices – and the reaction of monetary policy to the price changes risks increasing output and employment variability which, in turn, may even aggravate price instability in the longer run. In these cases, a cautious gradual response is usually considered the superior approach.

In principle, there are several monetary policy *strategies* available for a central bank. Those include:

- *Monetary targeting.* The central bank specifies a target rate of monetary growth and changes official interest rates in an attempt to speed up or slow down changes in the money supply. Two prerequisites must be met for this strategy to be successful: there must be a stable relationship between money and the price level and the money stock must be controllable by monetary policy even over short periods.
- *Direct inflation targeting.* Instead of monetary developments, this approach focuses on developments in inflation itself in relation to a published target with the central bank's inflation forecast placed at the centre of policy analysis and discussions. The main argument against this approach is that basing monetary policy decisions entirely on forecasted inflation

figures hinders the central bank in identifying the nature of threats to price stability in an encompassing and reliable framework and then in choosing the most appropriate policy response.

- *Exchange-rate targeting.* This strategy was pursued by several European countries prior to monetary union. It is considered an alternative for small, open economies where the production and consumption of internationally traded goods account for a large part of the economy and exchange-rate changes have a significant impact on the overall price level through import prices.
- A fourth alternative discussed recently is *asset price targeting.* The idea behind this proposal is that price developments cannot be controlled directly by central banks. Fluctuations in asset prices, such as equities, house prices or exchange rates are important determinants of inflation and asset price volatility threatens macroeconomic stability. As a consequence, central banks might respond with higher interest rates if, for example, stock markets climbed above a defined ceiling, or lower interest rates in reaction to a rising exchange rate. However, many economists think that this approach is likely to create more problems than it solves.

The ECB has adopted a *stability-oriented two-pillar strategy* based on two complementary perspectives on the determination of price developments (Table 6.1). One perspective is aimed at assessing the *short- and medium-term effects* of changes in real economic activity and financial conditions on prices under the assumption that over this time horizon supply and demand factors in markets for goods, services, labour and capital matter for price developments. The second perspective takes *a longer-term view* focusing on the link between money and prices. This serves mainly as a means of 'cross-checking' in order to guarantee consistency between short-, medium- and long-term monetary policy.

The policy of the ECB is based on the principles of *accountability and transparency.* For a new institution without a policy record it is crucial to establish a high degree of *credibility* from the beginning. As part of this policy the ECB announces a *reference value* for the growth of a broad monetary aggregate, *M3*, which is regarded as being consistent with the achievement of overall price stability. The reference value is expressed as a three-month moving average of 12-month M3 growth rates in order to smooth out monthly fluctuations, which can be rather volatile.

Among the available monetary aggregate candidates (Table 6.2) M3 has been chosen because it has shown a *stable money demand relationship* and *leading indicator properties*

Table 6.1   The two pillars of the ECB monetary policy strategy

Perspective	Time horizon	Focus	Assumptions
Perspective I	Short to medium term	Real economic activity, financial conditions	In the short and medium run prices are largely influenced by the interplay of supply and demand in the goods, services and factor markets
Perspective II: Monetary analysis	Longer term	Long-run link between money and prices	'Cross-checking' is needed to ensure that in the short- and medium-term view of the risks to price stability no relevant information is lost

Table 6.2   Definitions of euro area monetary aggregates

Liabilities	M1	M2	M3
Currency in circulation	x	x	x
Overnight deposits	x	x	x
Deposits with an agreed maturity of up to two years		x	x
Deposits redeemable at notice of up to three months		x	x
Repurchase agreements			x
Money market fund shares/units			x
Debt securities issued with a maturity of up to two years			x

Source: European Central Bank.

for future price developments. However, it is not regarded as an intermediate monetary target in order to avoid automatic policy reactions to money fluctuations due to factors other than inflationary pressures. Instead, the ECB uses a wide range of economic and financial indicator variables such as long-term interest rates, the yield curve, indicators of consumer and business confidence, output growth, wages and unit labour costs, import prices and the external value of the euro in assessing the risks for price stability.

The *determination of the reference value* for M3 is based on the relationship between changes in monetary growth (ΔM), inflation (ΔP), real economic growth (ΔYR) and the velocity of money circulation (ΔV) which can be written as:

$$\Delta M = \Delta YR + \Delta P - \Delta V$$

According to this identity – widely known as the *quantity equation* – the change in money in an economy in a given period equals the change in all nominal transaction in that period, which is approximated by the change in real GDP plus inflation, adjusted for the speed with which money is transferred between different holders determining how much money is actually needed to service a particular level of nominal transactions. The derivation of the reference value requires *assumptions* about the future development of potential output and the trend in the velocity of circulation of M3. For example, in 1998, the medium-term trend in real potential GDP growth for the euro area was estimated to be between 2–2.5% per annum while the M3 velocity was assumed to decline by a 0.5 to 1%. On the basis of these assumptions, the reference value was set at 4.5% per annum – and was kept constant over the following years. In May 2003, the ECB abandoned its approach to review the reference value for M3 on an annual basis arguing that according to its experience the underlying assumptions cannot be expected to change frequently.

The ECB has a range of *instruments* at its disposal for implementing monetary policy (Table 6.3). The most important group of operations is *open market operations* through which liquidity is provided to the banking system. Open market operations are conducted regularly and irregularly in the form of reverse transactions, outright transactions or foreign exchange swaps. In reverse transactions eligible assets are bought or sold by the Eurosystem – i.e. the national central banks on the initiative of the ECB – or credit operations are conducted against eligible assets provided as collateral. The second group of instruments consists of the *standing facilities*. The latter come in two variants, the marginal lending facility and the

Table 6.3   Monetary policy instruments of the Eurosystem

Operations	Liquidity-providing transactions	Liquidity-absorbing transactions	Maturity	Frequency
Open market operations				
Main refinancing operations	Reverse transactions	–	One week	Weekly
Longer-term refinancing operations	Reverse transactions	–	Three months	Monthly
Fine-tuning operations	Reverse transactions Foreign exchange swaps Outright purchases	Foreign exchange swaps Collection of fixed-term deposits Reverse transactions Outright sales	Non-standardised	Non-regular
Structural operations	Reverse transactions Outright purchases	Issuance of debt certificates Outright sales	Standardised/ non-standardised	Regular and non-regular Non-regular
Standing facilities				
Marginal lending facility	Reverse transactions	–	Overnight	Access at the discretion of counterparties
Deposit facility	–	Deposits	Overnight	Access at the discretion of counterparties

Source: European Central Bank.

deposit facility. They allow eligible financial institutions to invest daily liquidity surpluses or cover overnight liquidity needs. In addition, credit institutions are required to hold a *minimum amount of reserves* in their account with the national central banks of the Eurosystem.

The monetary policy strategy of the ECB stands for *a new generation of policy rules* characterised by greater flexibility and sophistication than former ones. While in debates in the 1970s and 1980s about *rules versus discretion* of monetary policy there was very little middleground with participants either favouring rules or dismissing them entirely, differences appear to have narrowed and despite acknowledging the overall advantages of rule-based systems there seems widespread agreement that even the best rules were, at most, a supplement to and not a substitute for individual *judgement*.

Rules versus judgement is one issue of monetary policy in the euro area, another is the *interdependence of policy instruments*. One requirement for the single monetary policy in Europe to be successful in stabilising prices is sound national *fiscal policies*. Under the *Stability and Growth Pact* all EU governments have committed themselves to maintaining a close to balance or surplus budgetary position under normal economic conditions. However, with increasing frequency of breaches the credibility of the pact suffered and there are growing demands to alter the rules in favour of a more 'pragmatic' approach.

Criticism of the Stability and Growth Pact has renewed interest in various *forms of fiscal and monetary policy coordination*. In general, coordination can be defined as any procedure aimed at ensuring that the choices made in one policy domain do not have unwanted repercussions in another. This can be

- unilateral or mutual;
- tacit, with each side deliberately adjusting to individually perceived or commonly defined needs, or explicit;
- based on strongly prescriptive rules or informality;
- statutory or voluntary.

Except for the cases of unilateral and tacit coordination the policy problem is aggravated by the requirement to define a *common policy target* and reach an agreement on both the state of the economy and the measures to be taken. This problem becomes even more complex in an international environment where a larger number of policy makers with different views and backgrounds is involved.

Price variability is one aspect of monetary and financial instability. Another is the *riskiness of financial systems* and the related challenges to financial supervision and regulation.

Historically, financial institutions have been regulated for several reasons. These include

- the provision of revenues and other benefits to the government;
- the prevention of negative externalities of bank activities;
- consumer protection;
- appeal to popularly elected legislators;
- protection of financial institutions from competition.

These days different views on the regulation of financial systems can be found in the economic literature. One calls for extensive rules arguing that banks fulfil a special economic role. Banks' liabilities are used as money and their '*moneyness*' is a public good satisfying the conditions of non-rivalry-in-consumption and non-excludability in exchange. In general, money has three *functions*. It serves as means of payment, store of value and, above all, unit of account and thus denominator of contracts. Given the special role of money and the 'moneyness' of bank liabilities in the economy, and the related uncertainty, the state is called to secure confidence in both the capacity of money to retain its value in order to fulfil the functions mentioned and the safety of financial institutions.

Another argument points to the *vulnerability* of banks and the danger of *bank runs* (Table 6.4). Maintaining low ratios of cash to assets and capital to assets relative to their high short-term debt banks appear inherently fragile. They face the constant danger of losing credibility at a sudden outbreak of crisis with the consequence that all depositors wish to withdraw their money at the same time. In addition, there is a risk of *contagion* if the difficulties of one bank

Table 6.4 The pros and cons of bank regulation

Pro regulation	Contra regulation
'Moneyness' of bank liabilities	Banks' incentives to limit risks
Bank vulnerability to loss of confidence, danger of bank runs	'Flight to quality' tendencies
Risk of contagion/systemic risk	Inefficiencies of market regulation, moral hazard
Market failure through asymmetric information	The transitory nature of information asymmetries

spread to others. A further reason for bank regulation is market failure as a result of *asymmetric information* between banks and customers. Under laissez-faire, so goes the argument, banks have an incentive to take high risks in search of short-term profits that may easily end in a process of ruinous competition. Customers cannot distinguish the 'good' from the 'bad' banks. They may recognise their mistake only when a bank fails and in this case it may be too late to switch to another institution if all the 'good' ones have already been driven out of the market.

There are, however, also *arguments against* extensive regulation. One argument is that in today's media society information asymmetries cannot be expected to last for long and banks themselves have an incentive to limit risks to maintain customers' confidence. In addition, banks may benefit from the failure of competitors that took excessive risks in winning over their customers and increasing their market share in the *'flight to quality'* in times of crisis. On the other hand, depending on the kind of rules and institutions bank regulation itself bears risks resulting from inefficiencies of the regulation process and from unforeseen and undesirable reactions of the regulated. In particular, there is the danger of *moral hazard*: aware of a government safety net and the willingness of the state or the central bank to act as lender of last resort, banks have an incentive to assume greater risks than otherwise with the costs borne either by more prudently run institutions or the taxpayer.

In the age of globalisation and 'allfinance', the discussion of the pros and cons of bank regulation can hardly deal with all aspects of the financial business. In practice, in recent years, there has been a tendency in European countries to consolidate the supervision of different kinds of financial activities such as banking, securities markets and the insurance business under one roof. In the UK, the self-regulatory system for the securities industry was abandoned in 1998 when the Financial Services Authority (FSA) took over the task of overseeing seven separate financial regulators – including the transfer from the Bank of England of responsibility for bank and money market supervision. Today the FSA oversees everything from consumer banking and home loans through building societies and financial advisers to stockbrokers and investment banks. In January 2001, the German government announced plans to amalgamate its three supervisory bodies, the BAKred, BAWe and BAV into a single independent institution, the BaFin, taking the UK as an example. The aim was twofold: to further strengthen the Finanzplatz Deutschland and to act as a catalyst for an intended Europe-wide regulatory system.

In general, the risks financial institutions face arise on different levels calling for a qualified response to each of them. On the level of the *individual firm* they can be divided into five categories:

- *credit risk*, which is the likelihood of counterparty default;
- *market risk*, i.e. the danger of losses from adverse movements in market prices such as stock prices, interest rates or exchange rates;
- *liquidity risk* arising from the cost or inconvenience involved in the unintended unwinding of a position;
- *legal risk*, which includes the danger that contracts may not be enforced;
- *operational risks*.

The latter include all kinds of risks related to running a business. In general, in this category, a distinction is made between operations risk and business-event risk. As a rule, *operations risk* is considered easier to model and evaluate than business-event risk. It includes transaction risks such as execution and booking errors, operational control risks such as rogue trading, fraud and other personnel risks, and systems risks such as programming errors and IT system failure.

Business-event risk covers a broad spectrum of other events that may happen in day-to-day operations including shifts in credit ratings, changes in reputation, regulatory changes, and even the occurrence of natural disasters and the collapse of markets.

For the *economy* as a whole, some of these risks matter more than others since they bear additional dangers. The biggest one is *systemic risk* or the risk of contagion with the failure of one institution triggering a chain reaction which threatens the stability of the whole financial system. A related risk is an overall loss of confidence in the banking system. Further, there is the constant danger of the emergence of financial bubbles, fads and fashions leading to large distortion of asset prices within the economy.

In an *international environment* these risks are amplified by reduced information and transparency of cross-border activities, the limits to political sovereignty, the difficulties in monitoring and controlling national financial markets and institutions from outside and the insufficiencies of payment and settlement systems and arrangements. Above all, as in the case of monetary policy, there is the danger that *counteracting* external developments or policy measures taken in other countries reduce the effectiveness of domestic policy efforts. As will be shown, although difficult to achieve, international policy cooperation may reduce this danger.

6.1.2   Finance and Growth

Beside monetary and financial stability, another policy target affected by financial conditions is economic growth. Financial markets and institutions determine how capital is *allocated* in an economy and how efficiently savings are channelled into productive investment. The *profitability* of production plans and opportunities for hedging and portfolio management strategies depend on the range of financial products and services available. In addition, financial sector growth itself may contribute considerably to overall economic growth. This in particular holds true for G7 countries where the share of financial services of GDP is higher than of many other industries.

In addition, there are *indirect effects* of the financial sector on economic growth. One is the influence its development has on the growth of a wider range of businesses it depends on. Examples for these so-called *producer services* are publishing, advertising, accounting, marketing, management consulting and legal and computer services. Strengthening a country's financial sector means creating a lasting additional demand and employment in these industries. For example, there are estimates that in New York each job in the securities industry alone generates about two additional jobs in the city with roughly 14% of total employment either directly or indirectly related to the industry.

A further often-neglected growth factor is the *shock absorption capacity* of the financial system. An economy where disturbances in real markets tend to be easily digested and partly offset in large, efficient financial systems has a lasting comparative advantage (Figure 6.2). Two key aspects in this context are transparency and the availability of risk management instruments and techniques. Financial market prices reflect information about the state of the economy, and the performance of individual actors, that helps reduce overall uncertainty and encourages investors and lenders to engage in long-term growth-stimulating activities. A high sophistication in financial affairs and the availability of a broad range of financial products for hedging and risk-taking purposes allow agents to cope with an uncertain environment and to react to emerging shocks and unforeseen events in a flexible and adequate manner. This increases their self-assurance in making long-term binding commitments and engaging in growth projects.

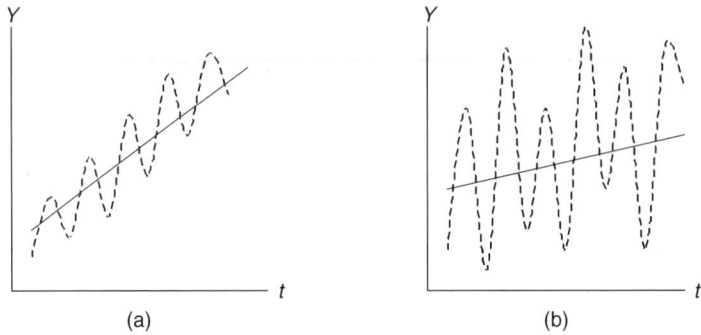

Figure 6.2   Volatility and growth. (a) High shock-absorbance capacity of the financial system. (b) Low shock-absorbance capacity of the financial system

On the other hand, the financial system itself is a constant potential source of major disruptions and its resilience in this respect, too, shapes the environment for economic growth. Deep and liquid financial markets reduce the risk of *financial disturbances* and the probability of sudden large price jumps and squeezes. A long-grown *market culture*, established formal and informal *rules and behaviour patterns* and effective *financial supervision* guarantee a sound environment for doing financial business thereby limiting the system's vulnerability to crises.

Another key factor influencing the relationship between financial development and growth is *openness*. Access to foreign capital markets may open up new sources of funding for domestic firms and individuals and increase competitive pressures on domestic financial institutions, as do activities of foreign financial institutions in domestic markets. On the other hand, a growing presence of domestic banks, securities firms and insurance companies in foreign markets may improve the overall performance of these institutions thereby strengthening the financial sector and respective growth prospects in their home country.

Just as openness adds to the variety of opportunities for financial institutions, consumers and investors, the *incompleteness* of domestic markets limits them thereby hampering economic activity. The absence or malfunctioning of markets for some instruments reduces the range of financial needs met by financial products with important consequences for saving, risk management and investment decisions. The effect is particularly damaging if markets such as bond markets, that would serve as a benchmark function, are non-existent. The case of '*missing markets*' is usually perceived as a problem in emerging economies at an early stage of financial development which are contrasted to the richness and sophistication of financial systems in advanced countries. However, experience demonstrates that developed economies are not spared from being hit by individual financial markets ceasing to function properly. One example is Japan, where since the late 1990s the financial system developed backwards in many respects and 'vanishing markets' for corporate finance severely hindered economic growth.

In economics, the linkages between finance and growth are not well understood. Traditionally, *growth theories* have very little to say about the role of finance on economic development. However, debates on the importance of financial systems often centre around their main findings. Many of the basic ideas in those theories date back to *classical economists* such as Adam Smith, David Ricardo and Thomas Malthus in the late eighteenth and early nineteenth centuries and Frank Ramsey, Allyn Young, Frank H. Knight and Joseph Schumpeter in the first half of the twentieth century. They developed the concepts of competitive behaviour, equilibrium dynamics and diminishing returns and explored the interplay of per capita income and population growth as well as the role of technological progress.

In general, approaches to explain economic growth seek to establish a relationship between an economy's development of aggregate output per capita and the main input factors required to produce this output. The foundations of *neoclassical growth models* were laid by Robert M. Solow in the 1950s. The Solow model establishes a production function which relates the total output (Y) produced in an economy in period t to three input factors: capital (K), labour (L) and a variable representing 'knowledge' or the 'effectiveness of labour' (A). The production function takes the form

$$Y_t = F(K_t, A_t L_t)$$

A is generally considered to represent the influence of an exogenously determined *technological progress*. In some model variants A is capital-augmenting rather than labour-augmenting or neutral in the sense that it affects both input factors equally (Hicks neutrality).

The economy grows – output per capita rises – only if the inputs into production rise. For given quantities of capital and labour, the amount of knowledge increase or technological progress plays a key role. Without technological progress, in the Solow model per capita growth must eventually cease.

The neoclassical production function assumes *constant returns to scale* and diminishing returns to each input. Doubling the quantities of all input factors doubles the amount produced. Increasing the quantity of one input lowers the average product of that input. The usual assumption is that the input factor capital can be accumulated while the factor labour grows with the exogenously given rate of population growth n. The model settles down to a general equilibrium or *steady state* over time in which the levels of Y and K grow at the same rate as the population while the per capita magnitudes remain unchanged.

The *simplicity* of the model is one reason why, despite much criticism, the approach has not lost its importance in modern macroeconomics. Whenever economists discuss practical issues of long-term growth they usually start with a simple neoclassical growth model. Another reason is the model's ability to yield substantive and seemingly reasonable *predictions*. Mankiw (1995) lists five of them in particular:

1. In the long run, the economy approaches a steady state independent of initial conditions. No matter whether countries are initially rich or poor, as long as all have the same steady state – which they do by assumption – the model predicts their *convergence*.
2. The steady-state level of income depends on the saving rate and population growth.
3. Steady-state growth per capita depends only on the *rate of technological progress*.
4. In the steady state, the stock of capital grows at the same rate as income leaving the capital–income ratio unchanged.
5. In the steady state, the marginal product of capital is constant. The marginal product of labour grows at the rate of technological progress.

The third prediction in particular has been widely criticised. In the neoclassical model, all steady-state growth is the result of advances in technology, but technological progress is taken as *exogenous*. Thus, in the end, no light is shed on the nature of economic growth. A second critique refers to the *wide spectrum of influences* that may affect the performance of the economy in the long run which are *disregarded*. Those include the economy's innovative capacity and changes in the quality of ideas and research over time or the influence of natural resources.

The Modigliani–Miller Theorem

Developed in the context of a general competitive equilibrium model of the Arrow–Debreu type the Modigliani–Miller theorem states the irrelevance of firms' financial decisions. In a perfectly functioning market system which enables every agent to exchange every good with every other agent without the need of intermediaries prices contain all information needed for agents to maximise utility and choices to be mutually compatible. The latter, in turn, allows markets to clear.

Modigliani and Miller demonstrated that in perfect capital markets, abstracting from transactions costs and taxes, the financial policies of firms become irrelevant because shareholders can recreate or undo them at any time. Financing decisions do not affect the value of a firm's production plan, which according to the law of one price is equal to the sum of claims on the firm. The intrinsic value of a firm's equity is the present value of net cash flows that can be produced by its existing assets plus the net present value of any investments to be made in the future. Given those existing and expected future investments, the firm's financial decisions will affect only the form in which shareholders receive future returns – either as dividends or capital gains – not their present value.

A further strongly debated issue is *convergence*. The neoclassical model fails to explain the persistent magnitude of inequality and poverty in the world where over 80% of income is owned by one-fifth of the population. Whether convergence is found empirically or not depends on the sample examined. There is evidence for convergence in samples of relatively homogenous economies such as OECD members or the states of the United States. However, the overall impression is that the cross-country distribution of world GDP has not shrunk since the 1960s and poor countries have not grown faster than rich ones.

Among the widely neglected aspects in neoclassical growth models is also the influence of the financial system. The *role of finance* in these models is a *strongly limited*, indirect one. Finance assists in the accumulation of capital, which is an important input factor, and contributes to the realisation of technological progress as far as it is embedded in the capital stock. In addition, the interest rate plays an important role in equilibrating savings and investment. However, the design of the financial sector is not of interest because under the assumption of perfect markets, and the validity of the *Modigliani–Miller theorem*, it has no influence on economic decisions. The presence of money as a transaction-facilitating medium of exchange does not affect steady-state optimality. Money is only a *veil* behind which real transactions take place.

The exogenous nature of the long-run per-capita growth rate in neoclassical approaches with the rate of technological progress entirely determined outside the model was widely considered unsatisfactory. *Models of endogenous growth* sought to overcome this weakness. They rely on the existence of externalities, increasing returns and the lack of inputs that cannot be accumulated. With capital broadly defined as including human capital, returns need not diminish in the long run.

The simplest endogenous growth model which has become a workhorse for many applications is the so-called *AK model*. Assuming one type of goods only, produced with capital as sole input factor, the production function for the output Y in period t can be written as a function of capital K multiplied by the capital productivity A:

$$Y_t = AK_t$$

In this model, *capital accumulation* in each period is equal to the part of Y that is invested, I, minus the depreciation of the existing stock of capital the rate of which is denoted as d:

$$\Delta K_t = I - dK_{t-1}$$

This is a closed economy, so investment is equal to the part of Y that is saved:

$$I_t = sY_t$$

with s being the saving rate.

However, the channelling of savings into investment comes at a cost which is denoted as δ, so that

$$I_t = \delta s Y_t$$

The idea is that δ represents the *cost of financial intermediation* influenced by the efficiency of the provision of financial services, a compensation for risks undertaken by the financial sector but also taxes raised by the government.

In this world, economic growth can be affected in three ways:

- by a rising capital productivity A;
- a growing capital stock K;
- or a rise in the efficiency of *transforming savings into investment* which would lower the cost of financial intermediation and free more savings for productive use.

Thus finance may affect growth via its influence on δ, A and s. The relationship between finance and the first two variables seems clear-cut. In economic literature, there are a number of channels by which financial activity may influence A, including the selection of investment projects, the provision of liquidity and the allocation of risks. In addition, the more efficient a financial system, and the more competitive the financial environment, the lower the fees to market organisations or financial institutions, the narrower the spreads between borrowing and lending rates and the lower the costs of transactions represented by δ. However, the effect of financial development on the third variable, *households' savings*, is ambiguous. A higher financial efficiency tends to result in more favourable risk-return combinations for savers, but this does not necessarily lead to a higher saving rate stimulating economic growth. On the contrary: the saving rate may decline under the prospects of higher returns since they allow the same future consumption to be realised with lower present savings and higher present spendings.

In principle, by emphasising the importance of externalities and increasing returns for economic development, models of endogenous growth open the opportunity for analysing long-run economic dynamics adopting an *evolutionary approach* to economic change.

Externalities include the whole spectrum of additional benefits from research and development investments, better education or more efficient institutions that are not easy to quantify but may exert considerable influence on long-term economic growth. These and other determinants of increased economic efficiency may lead to *scale economies* that may offset otherwise diminishing returns.

There is a wide variety of evolutionary theories, but most of them share several characteristics which, in a sense, constitute a kind of common basis:

- Evolutionary theories emphasise the *dynamics* of the economic process stressing the importance of history and *path dependence*. The economy is not expected to settle down in a steady state where nothing ever changes again.
- The theories are explicitly *microfounded*. As a rule, 'macrobehaviour' is sought to be explained by 'micromotives'.
- In contrast to traditional approaches, in a broad sense, *rationality is 'bounded'*: agents are assumed to have at best imperfect knowledge and understanding of their environment, learning is imperfect and dependent on agents' own history. As a consequence, there is *persistent heterogeneity* among them with their collective interactions determining economic outcome.

Evolutionary theories emphasise the importance of *institutions*. In financial relationships, the evolutionary approach paves the way for taking into account the role of *interactions* between different parts of the financial system, and between real and financial markets, for economic development that had previously been neglected. Constant exchange, the emergence of rules, norms and behaviour patterns, a development towards increasing complexity and the creation of an ever-more sophisticated financial market culture all shape the financial conditions for economic growth in the long run.

In mainstream economics, evolutionary growth theories never managed to receive the attention they deserve. One reason is the difficulty of incorporating their ideas into a formal mathematical framework. Another explanation is the prevailing desire to restrict theorising about economic growth to theorising about long-term equilibrium and not about processes. However, these approaches contributed to spreading the *awareness that institutions matter* for economic development and to the search for ways to measure their influence empirically.

Two main strands of *empirical research* can be distinguished. One draws attention to the *stage of financial system development*: under severe data constraints this focuses, above all, on the shares of bank lending and stock market capitalisation to GDP with the latter regarded as the superior form of finance. This approach must be considered highly unsatisfactory in that it paints a very crude picture of the nature of financial activities neglecting their many facets and the role those play in the growth process. In particular, what happens when the financial sector deepens and how this deepening affects investor and consumer behaviour and economic growth is not adequately explained.

The second strand of research emphasises the *role of governments* and the importance of *political systems*. The latter influence the financial environment of economic growth in many ways: they determine the extent of *official regulation* of financial markets and institutions, the scope for *direct state interventions*, and the degree of *informal interference* in the market mechanism.

In Europe, many examples can be found showing the importance of these factors, which include state bail-outs for failing industrial enterprises in Germany, France's insistence on state monopolies despite strong European pressures, or different attitudes towards financial regulation in European countries which range from largely informal practices in the UK to various degrees of formal rules and procedures on the Continent.

Path Dependence

When the long-term development of economic systems is influenced by their own history, they are said to be path-dependent. In these systems, small differences in initial conditions may lead to widely diverging processes. This is in strong contrast to traditional equilibrium models in economics where the effects of small deviations from the long-term steady state are assumed to cancel each other out over the course of time. Path dependence introduces a fundamental element of uncertainty to economics in limiting the knowledge agents may acquire depending on where they come from and on the institutional environment they face. Learning is gradual and cumulative in this environment and limited by former experience. In contrast to traditional equilibrium models as a consequence of the sensitivity to initial conditions long-term economic development is no longer predictable as the following example may illustrate:

Figure 1(a)   **Figure 1(b)**

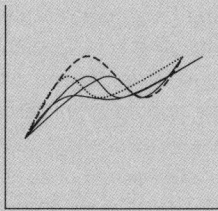   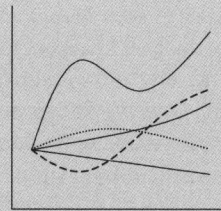

In the figure the developments of two systems under invisibly small differences in initial conditions are shown. Figure 1(a) demonstrates the system's evolution in a traditional environment. Although diverging the various paths appear sufficiently close to allow a long-term forecast – albeit with large tolerances. In Figure 1(b) the evolving patterns disperse considerably making meaningful predictions impossible.

Path dependence has interesting policy implications. It may offer additional scope for policy intervention in situations where under perfect foresight or rational expectations its measures would be counteracted immediately. Considering economic development, path dependence is one possible explanation why growth rates across countries do not converge in the long run imposing particular challenges to institutional design – which among others includes the design of the financial system.

Government influence is also manifest in the *legal system*, which sets the frame in which contracts are written and rights enforced. One early example is the bill of exchange which in the Middle Ages involved a risk of repudiation or non-payment since, unlike a bond or formalised contract, at least until the early sixteenth century, it lacked legal standing in most medieval courts. Another example is the fact that in the nineteenth century, when governments in acknowledging the need for pooling resources to finance industrial development provided for the protection of depositors, savings banks proliferated.

Legal systems worldwide originated from a small group of *legal traditions rooted in Europe*. Traditionally, a distinction is made between English common law and French, German or Scandinavian code law, with the former usually regarded as the superior with regard to the efficiency of financial standards. Due to the nations' colonial history the same legal traditions can be found in rich and poor countries in many parts of the world. In principle, laws in *code-law countries* set a minimum standard of behaviour expected with citizens obligated to comply with the letter of the law. In contrast, *common-law countries* have a 'non-legalistic' orientation. Their laws establish the limits beyond which it is illegal to venture and within which latitude and judgement are permitted and encouraged.

Code-law and common-law countries differ, among other things, in their approaches to *investor protection*: there are large variations in the legal rights of shareholders and creditors and in how effectively those rights are enforced across countries. The degree of investor protection affects the *availability of external finance* for firms and the risks for outsiders unable to directly influence management decisions. The supply of external finance, in turn, determines the *need for financial services* in an economy and thereby the size and development of the financial sector. Despite the wide variety of prevailing rules and practices, in general, common-law countries are regarded as more likely to protect investors' rights than code-law countries.

Another difference is seen in *accounting*. Accounting information is one of the pillars of a financial system: it enables investors to value a company, to form expectations about its future performance and to assess the quality of potential borrowers. In most code-law countries following a *legalistic approach* to accounting, accounting principles are national laws. Examples are, again, France and Germany. In these countries, accounting is not primarily oriented toward investors' needs but rather designed to satisfy government-imposed requirements in computing income taxes or to demonstrate compliance with overall macroeconomic principles.

In common-law countries such as the UK and the United States accounting practices are largely determined by accountants themselves rather than by national legislators and thus tend to be more *adaptive and innovative*. Those countries have large and developed capital markets, and the task of accounting is regarded, above all, as providing information for investors and creditors. Usually, education levels are high and users of financial accounting information are rather sophisticated.

There are no two countries with identical financial accounting practices. In Europe, beside national rules, there are *accounting directives* issued by the *European Commission* and incorporated into the national corporate legislation of member countries. Currently, reforms are under way in reaction to the *Enron debacle* and other financial scandals, one example of the growing *international dimension* of accounting.

Beside accounting rules there are other important legal concepts whose introduction facilitates financial activities thereby promoting economic growth. Those include the principle of limited liability, rules concerning the balance sheet structure, bankruptcy laws and seniority rules.

The concept of *limited liability* separates a firm's legal personality from that of its owners limiting the latter's liabilities to the size of their investment which allows a more efficient allocation of credit risks. Rules concerning firms' *balance-sheet structure* aim at minimising financial risks in matching assets and liabilities of equal maturity, currency and degree of liquidity and setting criteria for the relationship of short-term to long-term positions.

Seniority rules establish a hierarchy of claims in which, in general, debts have to be paid first and equity holders receive the residual. In addition, there are different levels of seniority for different forms of liability with debt owed to banks, or collateralised debt, having the highest priority, followed by ordinary bonds and subordinated debt. Seniority rules were a major step in the development of financial instruments with different risk and return characteristics, which are reflected in the pricing of these instruments.

Enron

In December 2001, Enron, a US power company that had turned itself into a trader in everything from energy to bandwidth filed for bankruptcy after reporting a $638 million third-quarter loss and the disclosure of a $1.2 billion reduction in shareholder equity partly related to partnerships run by its chief financial officer. The firm's bankruptcy raised questions about different financial services companies that facilitated its complex financial structure flattering its earnings and fostering the illusion of rapid growth. Among other things, Enron booked income immediately on contracts that would take up to 10 years to complete, used derivatives and hid speculative losses, buried debts and inflated asset values with complex financial instruments, employed an agressive tax avoidance strategy, and shifted debts into special-purpose vehicles it created, using them to manipulate its accounts. The case prompted a crisis of corporate accounting which with the downfall of Andersen, the Big Five professional services firm that was Enron's lead auditor, spread to European markets, too. European equity markets witnessed 'a flight from risk' with investors shunning stocks that faced accounting or financial concerns. They worried about the quality of corporate accounts fearing that heavily indebted companies would either collapse or be forced to raise large amounts of equity to restore the health of their balance sheets. Bond spreads widened for banks exposed to troubled companies. Rating agencies changed the way they assess corporate credits, issuing ratings actions faster and downgrading companies several notches at once, and credit-rating downgrades soared. As a consequence, credit markets became increasingly illiquid and market volatility rose.

In this context, the European Commission attacked the US GAAP (Generally Accepted Accounting Principles) hinting at the advantages of the more flexible International Accounting Standards (IAS) that Europe-based companies are required to use by 2005. In April 2002, EU finance ministers met to discuss the implication of the Enron collapse for European markets. In particular, they considered tightening rules on derivatives trading and the existing legislation on financial analysts, auditors and credit-rating agencies. They feared that complex derivatives instruments might escape proper supervision and aimed at preventing market abuse and manipulation, for example, by analysts' recommendations.

Bankruptcy laws protecting borrowers from their creditors and sheltering them from losing freedom, personal wealth and all future income in case they cannot service their debts increase willingness to fund investments with debt. In general, bankruptcy involves the *distribution of losses* between parties ranging from shareholders to employees. Ideally, the rules should make the allocation of risks predictable and transparent: debtors' assets should be equally distributed among creditors of equal rank, and the rules should aim at maximising the value of the debtors' assets for the benefit of all interested parties. Secure lenders, for example, should not be able to seize assets and get out if liquidation would raise less than the company was worth as a going concern. Finally, the rules should *provide for a fresh start* of entities emerging from bankruptcy. In practice, countries have widely varying bankruptcy laws seeking to balance between creditor and debtor rights: giving too much protection from creditors will make finance too expensive; offering too little protection risks stifling entrepreneurship.

Legal systems matter for economic growth, but their role must not be overrated. Critics hint at the inadequacy of the distinction between code-law countries and common-law countries in analysing the relationship between financial systems and economic development and stress the importance of *informal policy influence* as a sort of 'third way'. Recent history offers many examples: one is the *administrative guidance* that contributed to the economic success of Asian countries in the 1980s and early 1990s which at best had a very loose relationship to formal law and law traditions. For instance, administrative guidance developed both in civil-law countries like Japan and Korea and in countries with a common-law tradition such as Malaysia. On the other hand, all Latin American countries have a civil-law background, but growth records and the state of their financial systems are in few cases comparable to those of Asian civil-law countries.

History shows that, apparently, the role of legal systems differs in various *stages of economic development*. One argument says that a common-law tradition appears more appropriate for countries in an *early stage of industrial development*, in which the private sector is more active than the state in promoting economic growth, and in which a long time horizon allows judges to develop a legal tradition based on precedent on a case-by-case basis. By contrast, the civil-law tradition appears more suited to *late industrialisers* where the state becomes the driving force in the development process. A common argument in this context is that it took over a century and a half for the English common-law system to complete the limited liability form to its satisfaction, but only 10 years for the French civil code to emulate it.

In general, economic *backwardness* has the advantage that practices in other countries can be copied. As in technological development, backwardness in legal matters may generate a tendency for *leapfrogging*, with the followers in an initial state becoming the leaders that develop the superior system at some future time. However, some systems are easier to adopt than others: as a rule, writing a code authorising desired behaviour is easier than copying the theory and practice of a law tradition that evolved over centuries based on precedent. This may help explain why, for instance, the Meiji constitution in Japan in the nineteenth century was modelled after the Prussian example and not after a common-law framework which could not as easily be imitated.

Beside legal systems and informal mechanism there are many other ways in which governments and policy systems shape the financial environment for economic growth. Historically, one of the biggest influences of the state was the relationship between financial market development and *public finance*. The latter affects the financial system in several ways, one of which is *taxes*. These influence business prospects and returns and the overall attractiveness of financial places – an argument that plays an increasing role in the *competition of financial centres* in Europe and worldwide. For instance, in Germany, up to 1991, there was a turnover tax on securities transactions requiring purchasers to pay between 0.1 and 0.25% of the value of securities changing hands. Another example is that stakes on the books of German banks are often at low historical values, and until 2002 the gains from selling them at higher market values were taxed at more than 50% – hindering large-scale consolidation and the development of the Finanzplatz Frankfurt.

Taxes and other financial burdens may severely damage a place's competitiveness thereby reducing its growth prospects. In contrast, *governments' constant needs* to finance infrastructure projects, social and military expenditures and debt service which make them become *major borrowers* in the capital markets may increase a place's competitiveness. There is a long history of how financial systems, instruments and innovations in Europe were enhanced by rulers' financial demands thereby contributing to the rise of European cities.

The most ambitious government project in Europe for stimulating long-term economic growth in recent years has been *regional monetary integration*. The introduction of a common currency was expected to enhance economic development in two ways. First, reducing transaction costs and eliminating foreign exchange risk was expected to stimulate intra-regional trade in goods and services thereby leading to further *convergence*. At the same time, the transition from 12 currencies to one was considered an important step on the way to a *single European market for financial services* creating large and liquid financial markets, and stimulating competition between financial institutions, which, in turn, was hoped to result in more favourable conditions for both savers and investors. However, early experience has shown that the growth effects of the common currency are at best limited. Apparently, EMU membership is compatible with *significant and sustained differences* in national real growth performance.

Summary

- Financial markets and relationships affect the economy in many ways and pose many challenges to policy making.
- Monetary and financial stability are indispensable prerequisites for economic development.
- Financial systems and institutions influence the conditions and prospects of long-term economic growth.
- In Europe, responsibilities for monetary and financial stability are divided between central banks and financial regulators.
- Price stability refers to the internal and external value of a currency. For the euro both come under the responsibility of the European Central Bank (ECB).
- Arguments for and against regulation of financial institutions to reduce the riskiness of financial systems can be found in economic literature.
- In contrast to monetary stability, financial stability in Europe is largely the responsibility of national supervisors requiring much effort to create a level playing field for financial institutions within the region.
- The relationship between finance and growth is still largely unexplored with traditional models of economic growth neglecting the role that financial systems and institutions play in the growth process.
- Evolutionary approaches to economic growth emphasise the role of institutions in general thereby paving the way for studying the importance of financial institutions as well.
- Recent empirical research found evidence for the role of governments and political and legal systems in the growth process.
- There is a danger of overrating the importance of the distinction between code-law and common-law countries as experiences in other parts of the world demonstrate.

Exercises

1. Describe the main instruments by which the European Central Bank may influence money market conditions and interest rates in the euro area.
2. Discuss the limits of monetary policy in influencing:

   – wage and price setting processes
   – the overall price level in the euro area.

3. Discuss the role of:

   – fiscal policy
   – external shocks

   on monetary policy in Europe.
4. What are the incentives

   – for governments to regulate banks?
   – for banks to adopt an approach of self-regulation?

5. Describe the main risks to financial stability; give examples.
6. In which respects are financial risks amplified by international operations of financial institutions? Can you imagine cases in which risks are diminished by international financial activities?
7. Describe the dynamics of systemic risk.
8. Describe the role of finance in theories of economic growth and discuss the ways in which financial markets and institutions may influence the growth process in practice.
9. Discuss the influence of governments on the development of financial systems and economic growth.
10. Explain the phenomenon of leapfrogging and discuss its relevance in the relationship between finance and growth.

Additional Links and References

A detailed survey of the monetary policy of the ECB is provided at:

http://www.ecb.int/pub/pdf/other/monetarypolicy2004en.pdf

For the discussion of the pros and cons of asset price targeting of monetary policy see:

Bean, Charles (2003) Asset prices, financial imbalances and monetary policy: are inflation targets enough? BIS Working Paper No. 140, September, http://www.bis.org/publ/work140.pdf.
Bernanke, Ben S. and Mark Gertler (2001) Should central banks respond to movements in asset prices? www.princeton. edu/~bernanke/asset.doc.

A detailed overview of the pros and cons of financial regulation in general can be found in the following contributions to a controversy in the *Economic Journal* of May 1996:

Benston, George J. and George G. Kaufman (1996) The appropriate role of bank regulation, *Economic Journal*, **106**, 688–97.
Dow, Sheila C. (1996) Why the banking system should be regulated, *Economic Journal*, **106**, 698–707.
Dowd, Kevin (1996) The case for financial laissez-faire, *Economic Journal*, **106**, 679–687.

Classic early contributions to the basic ideas of economic growth theory include:

Knight, Frank H. (1944) Diminishing returns from investment, *Journal of Political Economy*, **52**, 26–47.

Malthus, Thomas (1798) *An Essay on the Principle of Population: A View of its Past and Present Effects on Human Happiness; with an Inquiry into Our Prospects Respecting the Future Removal or Mitigation of the Evils which It Occasions*, published: London: John Murray, 1826. Sixth edition. http://www.econlib.org/library/Malthus/malPlong.html

Ramsey, Frank (1928) A mathematical theory of saving, *Economic Journal*, **38**, 543–59.

Ricardo, David (1817) *On the Principles of Political Economy and Taxation*, published: London: John Murray, 1821. Third edition. http://www.econlib.org/library/Ricardo/ricP.html

Schumpeter, Joseph (1934) *The Theory of Economic Development*, Cambridge MA: Harvard University Press.

Smith, Adam (1776) *An Inquiry into the Nature and Causes of the Wealth of Nations*, published: London: Methuen and Co., Ltd., ed. Edwin Cannan, 1904. Fifth edition. http://www.econlib.org/library/Smith/smWN.html

Young, Allyn (1928) Increasing returns and economic progress, *Economic Journal*, **38**, 527–42.

A standard textbook of growth theory is:

Barro, Robert J. and Xavier Sala-i-Martin (2003) *Economic Growth*, Cambridge, MA: MIT Press.

See also the very stimulating home page of Sala-i-Martin:

http://www.columbia.edu/~xs23/home.html

A lucid discussion of theoretical and empirical aspects of economic growth in defence of the neoclassical approach is provided by:

Mankiw, N. Gregory (1995) The growth of nations, *Brookings Papers on Economic Activity*, 1, 275–310.

For the evolutionary approach to economic change see:

Arthur, W. Brian (1994) Self-inforcing mechanisms in economics, in W. Brian Arthur (ed.) *Increasing Returns and Path Dependence in the Economy*, Ann Arbor, pp. 111–32.

Dosi, Giovanni (1997) Opportunities, incentives and the collective patterns of technological change, *Economic Journal*, **107**, 1530–47.

The relationship between micromotives and macrobehaviour is the topic of a widely regarded book with the same title:

Schelling, Thomas (1978) *Micromotives and Macrobehaviour*, New York: W.W. Norton & Company.

A brief survey of the relationship between finance and growth in economic theory is provided in:

Thiel, Michael (2001) Finance and economic growth – A review of theory and the available evidence, European Commission, Directorate-General for Economic and Financial Affairs, Economic Paper No. 158, July.

For a discussion of the applicability of evolutionary theories to financial systems see:

Reszat, Beate (1998) Emerging financial centres, HWWA Discussion Paper No. 52, http://www.hwwa.de/Publikationen/Discussion_Paper/1998/52.pdf

The implications of 'missing markets' are discussed in detail for bond markets in:

Herring, Richard and Nathporn Chatusripitak (2001) The case of the missing market: the bond market and why it matters for financial development, Wharton Financial Institutions Center Working Paper 01–08, http://fic.wharton.upenn.edu/fic/papers/01/0108.pdf

There are some additional useful websites on economic growth such as the growth project page of the World Bank:

http://www.worldbank.org/research/growth/

See also Harvard's Center for International Development:

http://www2.cid.harvard.edu/ciddata/

and Jonathan Temple's site with economic growth resources:

http://www.bris.ac.uk/Depts/Economics/Growth/index.htm

6.2   POLICY COOPERATION

Policies directed at monetary and financial targets in order to stimulate economic growth and cope with instabilities and other market imperfections are particularly vulnerable to external influences and disturbances. This has two reasons: one is the *limits to sovereignty* as a consequence of globalisation of financial markets and activities. The other is the *interdependence of policy targets and strategies* which is largely the result of regional and worldwide economic, monetary and financial integration. Both provide a rationale for regional and international policy cooperation.

6.2.1   Limits to Sovereignty

Financial markets were the forerunners of globalisation. The financial industry was one of the first making the transition from *internationalisation* – i.e. the central operation and control of worldwide activities – to the *dispersion of central functions* to all major nodes of the world economy and constant interaction within large *networks*. It is perhaps the most oft-cited example of how the sovereignty of national governments is challenged by global phenomena.

   Figure 6.3 demonstrates the *stages* from bilateral economic relations between countries over internationalisation to globalisation: the three countries in Figure 6.3(a) have traditional trade relationships with one another. In Figure 6.3(b) the firms of countries A, C and E have wider foreign activities not only focusing on few reciprocal relationships but also trading with, or operating in, third countries in the course of growing internationalisation. In Figure 6.3(c) the distinction between home countries of individual firms has been abandoned. Firms have become truly global with regional centres in all major places in the world, as well as some smaller ones.

   Globalisation is widely regarded as the result of a fundamental *structural change* in the world economy since the mid-1980s which above all was characterised by a shift from manufacturing to services industries. The main driving forces behind this development were:

- the *deregulation* of markets, in particular of financial markets, in many parts of the world;
- *technological developments* and progresses made in microelectronics and telecommunications;
- strong *imbalances* in international trade requiring large capital transfers.

   In public discussions, globalisation is often used as a synonym for interdependence, but the two differ fundamentally. In economic literature, *interdependence* stands for a *strategic*

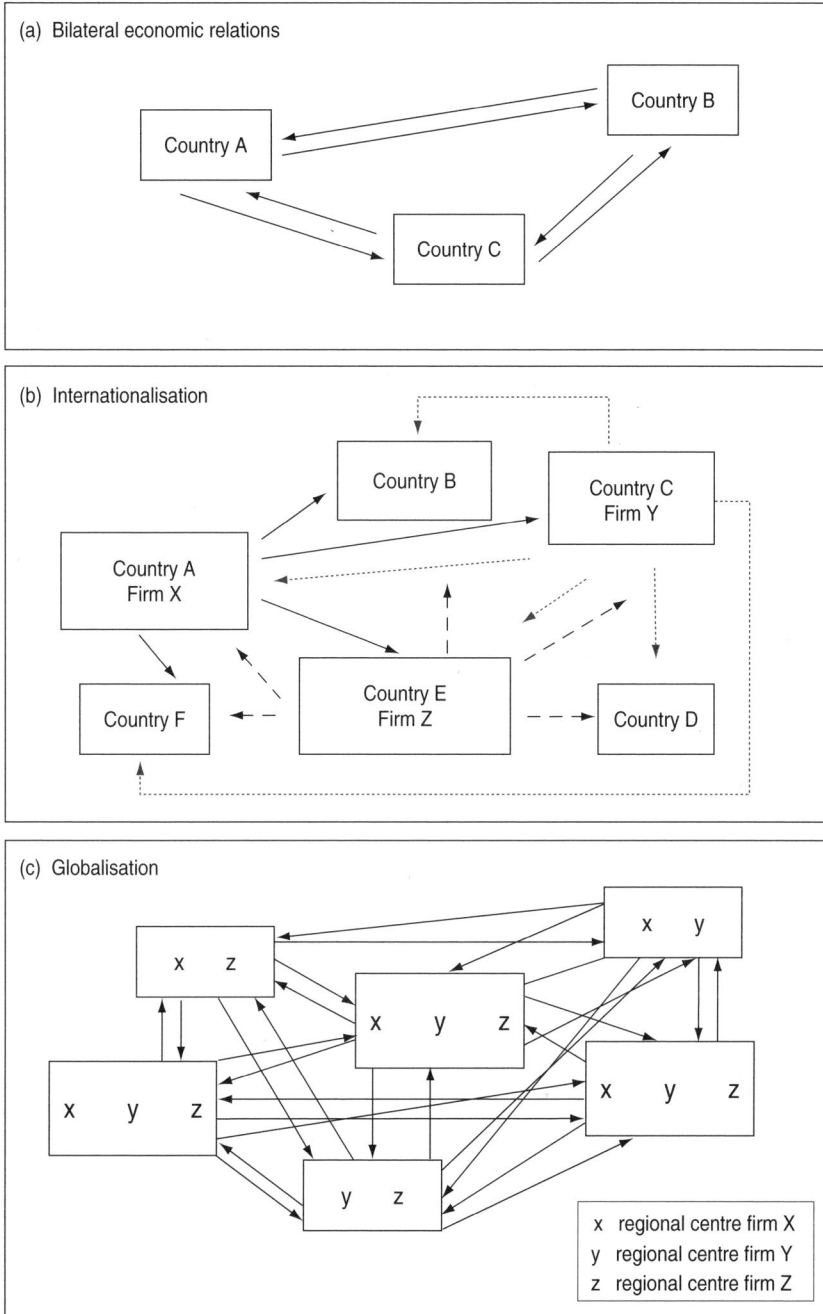

Figure 6.3   From bilateral relationships to globalisation

Table 6.5   Globalisation and interdependence

	Globalisation	Interdependence
Nature	Microeconomic process	Macroeconomic phenomenon
Characteristics	Integrated cross-border corporate networks A global web of interconnected nodes in which value and wealth are generated and distributed	Mutual influence on economic developments and economic policy targets and instruments
Spatial effect	Decoupling the spatial structure and dynamics of private-sector economic activities from the territorial structure causing a 'mismatch' between political and economic geography Exclusion of countries and regions from growth dynamics	Narrowing the distance between sovereign nations and regions requiring closer economic policy cooperation
Policy effects	Weakening of state sovereignty	Weakening the effectiveness of economic policy
Nature of the policy problem	Economic policy as global-governance problem	Economic policy as strategic problem

relationship between states or policy makers whose decisions exert a mutual influence on each other which has to be taken into account in choosing a policy strategy. In this sense interdependence is a *macroeconomic* phenomenon. By contrast, globalisation refers to the activities of *firms* in the world economy and is, in principle, of *microeconomic* nature (Table 6.5).

Globalisation is a form of *spatial organisation* of international activities which bears no resemblance to traditional foreign trade and investment relationships (Table 6.6). As part of wide industrial and financial networks global companies are characterised by a high degree of flexibility. As a rule, they strongly rely on *intra-firm trade*, i.e. on trade between operations of the same company in different countries. A further practice is the *international sourcing* of intermediate inputs, highly effectively exploring comparative advantages of countries in shifting individual parts of the production process to the most favourable locations. In addition, global companies tend to form international *strategic alliances*, and in particular their producer–supplier relationships are often characterised by a very flexible *collaborative* nature. Instead of cost considerations or the transfer of resources that were the motives for traditional direct investments, their acquisitions in foreign countries are mainly driven by *market access considerations* and the desire to maintain some form of presence in a number of countries.

The same principles that rule activities of multinational firms in manufacturing and services industries in general can be observed in the financial industry. Global financial institutions, too, operate and are part of worldwide networks and circumvent markets by internal trades. They are also highly flexible in their choice of strategies and locations. For example, global financial institutions react to a changing environment:

- by shifting between financial assets;
- relocating activities between time zones or from one place to another, to offshore centres or virtual market places;
- moving positions to related institutions such as special-purpose vehicles and hedge funds.

Table 6.6 Traditional foreign and global economic operations

	Global firms' operations	Traditional activities
Trade	*Intra-firm trade*: • trade between operations of the same company in different countries • internal transactions circumventing markets • transactions at notional transfer prices • highly flexible factors of production	*Traditional foreign trade*: • exchange between unrelated parties (arm's length trade) • market transactions • transactions at market prices • country-specific specialisation, immobile factors of production
Production	*International sourcing*: • disaggregation of the production process into a number of stages along the value chain • production spread across countries exploiting comparative advantages • numerous trade transactions taking place before the goods are finished	*Traditional production of export goods*: • uniform production processes • production concentrated in one location • a single export transaction is needed to transfer the finished good to the foreign market
Producer relationships	*Strategic alliances*: • under circumvention of markets • high flexibility • collaborative, non-price-regulated relationships between suppliers and producers, long-term commitments, mutual feedback of information	*Traditional relationships between suppliers, producers and consumers*: • market-based • low flexibility • outcomes negotiated in the market place, working of the price mechanism
Direct investments	*International mergers and acquisitions*: • market access considerations • frequently changing ownership, reorganisations involving selling off assets	*Traditional foreign direct investments*: • cost and profit considerations • transfer of resources

While interdependence is narrowing the distance between national and regional economies creating a strategic need for policy cooperation, globalisation is *decoupling* the spatial structure and dynamics of private-sector economic activities from the territorial structure calling for a different kind of policy response. Under globalisation policies to influence financial markets and institutions a *global governance problem* emerges, that is, the problem of restoring the ability of governments to exercise public policy in a globalised environment, with a special emphasis on the regulatory and supervisory dimension.

The consequence of globalisation is a *'mismatch'* between the economic and the political realm which is a constant challenge to the sovereignty of governments. In general, there are three kinds of policy options to meet this challenge (Table 6.7).

The first is *defensive intervention*. Policy makers may try to maintain or resurrect barriers to global activities through protectionism or other regulative measures. Examples are *capital controls* or the hotly debated *Tobin tax*, a proposal to levy a tax on foreign exchange transactions in order to fight currency speculation (Appendix D). Defensive intervention may

Table 6.7   Policy options under globalisation

Strategy	Examples		Disadvantage
	in industry	in international finance	
Defensive intervention	Protectionism Trade barriers	Capital controls Tobin tax	Counteracting liberalisation and integration efforts
Offensive intervention	States competing for foreign investments States competing for export orders	Cities competing as financial centres National authorities favouring regulatory arbitrage	Danger of ruinous competition between states
Global public policy	Arrangements to fight international money laundering	Basel Accord for internationally operating banks	Legally nonbinding rules, limits to enforceability

temporarily ease pressures for individual countries. However, it is no solution for the world financial system for which it means a clear backlash *jeopardising the achievements* of liberalisation and integration reached so far.

A second policy option is *offensive intervention*. Here countries themselves become global competitors either searching to provide an attractive environment for global companies within their own territorial boundaries or lobbying other countries on behalf of the worldwide activities of their domestic corporations. In international finance, examples can be found for both strategies. On the one hand, financial centres such as London, Frankfurt and Paris try hard to create favourable conditions to attract foreign financial institutions, on the other, countries' politicians and financial authorities deliberately search to influence international negotiations and regulations in a direction that would benefit the international activities of their domestic banks at the expense of others. The drawback here is that offensive intervention easily ends up as a kind of *ruinous competition* between states leaving all worse off.

A third option to cope with the challenges of globalisation is known as *global public policy*. This concept was developed as a direct reaction to the observation that the activities of multinational firms are not restricted to national boundaries but extend to a much broader and more fluid geographic space. Global public policy aims at realigning political with economic geography. Under this concept states' sovereignty is no longer defined by territoriality but on a *functional or sectoral* basis. This requires a *qualitatively new form of cooperation* among countries corresponding to the structure of global corporate networks. Global public policy does not intend to establish a global government, there is no attempt to create a new Bretton Woods system or any other form of institution or rule governing financial markets from above, which in all its inflexibility would be considered unsustainable. Rather the concept adheres to the idea *of global governance* addressing the operational and not the formal dimension of state sovereignty.

Global public policy is structured around *legally nonbinding* international arrangements. Possible applications are in the domains of international crime, where the fight against money laundering may serve as an example, and dual-use goods and technologies. Again, international financial relationships are in the forefront. Despite all the criticism, the most often-cited example of a successful global public policy approach is the capital-adequacy rules of the *Basel Accord*.

> **Bank of Credit and Commerce International (BCCI)**
>
> BCCI was a major international bank which was at the centre of the world's worst finan-
> cial scandal in 1991. The bank was made up of multiple layers of entities, related to one
> another through an impenetrable series of holding companies, affiliates, subsidiaries and
> banks-within-banks aimed at avoiding centralised regulatory review with the objective of
> keeping its affairs secret and committing fraud on a massive scale. Its corporate structure
> was based on a non-bank holding company in Luxembourg which owned two separate
> banking networks incorporated in Luxembourg and the Cayman Islands. The holding
> company was unregulated. BCCI was involved in money laundering, bribery, support of
> terrorism, arms trafficking and the sale of nuclear technologies, the commission and facil-
> itation of income tax evasion, smuggling, illegal immigration and illicit purchases of banks
> and real estate. The majority of its assets were initially from Abu Dhabi. At its peak, the
> bank operated in 78 countries and had over 400 branches claiming assets of $25 billion.
> BCCI had an uncommon auditing system – Price Waterhouse were the accountants for
> BCCI Overseas while Ernst & Young audited BCCI and BCCI Holdings in London and
> Luxembourg. When, in July 1991, the Bank of England shut BCCI around a million
> investors were affected. The liquidators, Deloitte & Touche, filed a lawsuit against its
> auditors which was settled for $175 million in 1998. A further lawsuit against the Sheikh of
> Abu Dhabi was launched in 1999 for around $400 million. BCCI creditors also instituted
> a $1 billion suit against the Bank of England. After a nine-year struggle due to the Bank's
> statutory immunity the suit was accepted and went to trial in January 2004. The affair
> showed the limits of international official collaboration. The Basel Committee responded
> to it by issuing a set of minimum standards for the supervision of international banks.

6.2.2 Financial Supervision

The beginnings of international rules for financial supervision date back to the 1970s
(Table 6.8). The emergence of the Euromarkets in the 1960s and early 1970s first raised the
question of how to monitor and regulate the growing activities of *internationally operating
banks*.

The traditional approach to financial regulation had been *surveillance* on a *territorial*
basis. The country in which deposits were held imposed reserve requirements on domestic
banks and on branches and subsidiaries of foreign banks. Its authorities monitored bank
activities and set the rules for bank business, and in case of emergency were prepared to act
as lender-of-last resort rescuing banks from illiquidity. However, this approach does not
work in the case of *external markets* such as the Euromarkets. Absence of reserve requirements on deposits denies policymakers direct monetary control of these markets, and given
the apparently footloose nature of offshore banking territorial surveillance of banks is only
effective if agreement is reached among all countries where offshore activities might take
place.

With operations of banks and other financial institutions spreading across a *large number
of countries and jurisdictions*, problems in a financial institution located in one place can be
transferred very quickly to markets elsewhere. A bank with a subsidiary in an offshore centre
that does not properly regulate and supervise its activities has an incentive to take higher risks
than the authorities in the home country – or most other countries – would accept. If the bank

Table 6.8   Chronology of European and international bank supervision

Year	Event	Remarks
1974	Basel Concordat	Principles of surveillance, lender-of-last resort responsibilities
1975	Establishment of the Basel Committee on Banking Supervision by the G-10 central bank governors	Senior representatives of central banks and supervisory authorities from G-10 countries with a permanent secretariat at the BIS in Basel
1980	Basel Concordat complemented	Consolidation of commercial banks' worldwide accounts
1985	'Europe 1992' plan drafted by the European Commission	Abolishment of capital controls in EMS member states by 1990, minimal amount of regulation shared by all EC countries, complete freedom of financial services based on mutual recognition, home country control
1988	Publication of the Basel Capital Accord (Basel I)	
1989	Solvency Ratio Directive and Own Funds Directive in Europe	Implementation of the rules of the Basel Accord in Europe
1992	Implementation of Basel I	
1993	Capital Adequacy Directive (CAD) in Europe	Harmonising capital requirements for financial institutions in different systems in Europe regulating functions instead of institutions
1996	Amendment to Basel I leading to CAD II in Europe	Introduction of trading-book requirements to account for market risks
1999	First consultative paper on Basel II	
2004	Publication of the EC proposals for CAD III	
2006	Envisaged implementation of Basel II	

manages a substantial part of its risks offshore, its viability could be jeopardised thereby threatening the stability of the home country's markets or even the financial systems of entire regions or worldwide.

The only way to cope with these kinds of dangers is *consolidated supervision* of the total operations of the bank by the home country authorities and the development of adequate regulatory and supervisory standards in places with offshore activities. Consolidated supervision requires home supervisors *access to information* on the worldwide operations of banks. With the continuous growth of financial conglomerates, and the involvement of financial institutions in many different areas, this may become a rather complex task, as the example of the Bank of Credit and Commerce International (BCCI) demonstrates.

The foundations for consolidated worldwide supervision were laid in the Basel Concordat of 1974. Under the auspices of the Bank for International Settlements (BIS) the financial authorities of major industrial countries chose the *domiciliary* concept as an alternative to the territorial approach to surveillance. They agreed that each country would assume lender-of-last-resort responsibility for its offshore banks with the country in which a bank's headquarters is domiciled imposing consistent regulation across all its offshore branches and subsidiaries. In 1980, this agreement was complemented by rules requiring banks to *consolidate worldwide accounts* enabling bank supervisors to monitor and regulate offshore and onshore operations on a consistent basis.

During the 1980s, the growth of international bank activities led to mounting concerns about the *safety* of financial institutions. The UK and the US were the first countries to come up with the idea of global harmonised *capital standards* in order to limit *credit risks*. In London, extensive financial deregulation under the 'Big Bang' had created a need to redefine the rules of the game for both domestic and foreign institutions. At the same time, in the US, the Federal Reserve Bank sought to contain the increasing dangers resulting from global economic imbalances, the Latin American debt crisis and a growing overall fragility of the banking system. A further need for a harmonised strengthening of regulation arose from the rising presence in international markets of Japanese banks, which had considerable competitive advantages as a result of the lax rules they faced at home.

In 1988, an agreement was reached which became known as the *Basel Accord*. The framework consists of *four elements*:

1. the definition of capital;
2. the determination of risk-weighted assets;
3. the required ratio of capital to risk-weighted assets;
4. the conversion of off-balance sheet instruments into risk-weighted assets.

The Basel Accord calls for *minimum capital* at internationally active banks of 8% of risk-weighted assets, measured at book value and not at market value. *Risk-weights* range from zero over 20 and 50 to 100% depending on the type of borrower or collateral. A distinction is made between:

- sovereigns, split into OECD and non-OECD;
- banks (OECD and non-OECD, with the latter divided into less than one year and more than one year);
- retail mortgages;
- other private-sector exposures (Table 6.9).

Under the agreement capital is grouped into two tiers: *Tier I or Core Capital* is defined as equity capital and disclosed reserves from post-tax earnings; Tier I Capital must be at least 4% of the total. *Tier II or Supplementary Capital* includes all other capital elements such as undisclosed reserves from post-tax earnings, general provisions or loan-loss reserves, hybrid capital that combines characteristics of both debt and equity, and subordinated debt – unsecured debt of fixed maturity that is subordinated to all other claims. There are special restrictions: Tier II Capital is limited to 100% of Tier I Capital, subordinated debt is limited to a maximum of 50% of Tier I Capital, and general loan-loss reserves must not exceed 25% of Tier II Capital.

Off-balance sheet exposures are converted to *credit-risk equivalents* by multiplying the respective nominal principal amounts by a conversion factor and then weighting the result according to the nature of the counterparty. *Conversion factors* range from 100% for instruments that substitute for loans such as standby letters of credit, over 50% for transaction-related contingencies to 20% for short-term, self-liquidating liabilities related to trade such as commercial letters of credit.

In the *European Community*, the rules of the Basel Accord were implemented by two directives, the *Solvency Ratio Directive* and the *Own Funds Directive* that defined bank capital. There had been a long struggle coping with the differences in the Continental model of

Table 6.9   Risk-weight categories under the Basel Accord

Percentage	Categories
Zero	Cash
	Claims on central governments and central banks denominated and funded in national currency
	Other claims on OECD central governments and central banks
	Claims collateralised by cash of OECD central-government securities or guaranteed by OECD central governments
20	Claims on multilateral development banks or guaranteed or collateralised by securities issued by such banks
	Claims on or guaranteed by OECD banks
	On OECD securities firms subject to comparable supervision and regulation
	On banks outside the OECD, or guaranteed by those banks, with a residual maturity of up to one year
	On nondomestic OECD public-sector entities or guaranteed by or collateralised by securities issued by those entities
	Cash items in the process of collection
50	Loans fully secured by mortgage on residential property that is or will be occupied by the borrower or is rented
100	Claims on the private sector
	On banks outside the OECD with a residual maturity of over one year
	On central governments outside the OECD
	On commercial companies owned by the public sector
	Premises, plant and equipment and other fixed assets
	Real estate and other investments
	Capital instruments issued by other banks
	All other assets

Source: Bank for International Settlements.

universal banking and the Anglo-Saxon distinction between banking and securities activities. While, for example, under the German model of universal banking securities firms were banks with a single regulatory authority overseeing them, in the UK separate regulatory functions had been established with the 1986 Financial Services Act for both groups with banks supervised by the Bank of England and securities markets remaining self-regulated.

In the 1993 *Capital Adequacy Directive (CAD)* agreement was reached to regulate *functions instead of institutions* in Europe. Uniform capital requirements were established applicable to both the securities operations of universal banks and non-bank securities firms. Accordingly, a universal bank would identify part of its balance sheet as '*trading book*' for which capital would be held in accordance with the CAD while capital requirements for the remainder of the bank's balance sheet would be determined in accordance with the Basel rules.

In 1996, the Basle Accord was amended in order to account for *market risk* (i.e. the danger of losses in banks' trading books due to price fluctuations) and the Capital Adequacy Directive became CAD II respectively. For the first time, banks became allowed to use their own *internal VAR models* to calculate risks after regulators' approval.

Today the Basel Accord has been adopted by *more than 100 countries*. Initially directed at internationally operating banks only it has become the globally recognised standard for banks in general. Its categories largely reflect the state of bank business in the 1980s.

However, in the meantime, financial institutions have begun to develop sophisticated systems to differentiate between the riskiness of assets and counterparties that call for modification. In addition, the flaws of the approach have become more and more visible: the concept of the Basel Accord has been criticised as *arbitrary* with its risk classification scheme making the international financial system less stable, not more. For example, the division into OECD and non-OECD countries makes Turkish bonds appear less risky than those of Hong Kong or Singapore – to name only one example. No distinction has been drawn between the amount of capital a bank needs to allocate for different types of corporate loans, regardless of risk level. General Electric is considered as risky as any start-up company. As a result, banks were *encouraged to make more risky loans* carrying better terms to compensate them for the greater probability of default with the consequence that the overall quality of loan portfolios worsened.

In addition, the *risk assessment methodology* of the accord appears flawed today in assuming that a portfolio's total risk is the sum of the risks of its parts and not taking into account risk-reducing management strategies and the overall influence of portfolio size on riskiness. Further, in giving preferential treatment to *government securities* which are considered as risk-free the approach neglects the possibility of sovereign debt defaults such as those of Russia in 1998 and Argentina in 2002.

The ways banks managed to circumvent the rules hint at further weaknesses of the approach. The accord has contributed substantially to the shift towards *asset securitisation* worldwide. Banks started to transform illiquid financial assets into marketable instruments, which enabled them to maintain their capital levels unchanged while increasing their economic risks. Another criticism concerns the treatment of *short-term loans to banks*. Assigning to them a 20% weight, compared to the 100% weight for lending to private non-bank companies, for instance, increased the incentive to lend to Asian banks in the 1990s thereby contributing to the Asian crisis of 1997/98.

Initiatives to develop new rules governing bank capital, known as *Basel II*, date back to June 1999 when the Basel Committee on Banking Supervision circulated a first consultative paper on the issue. A second paper followed in January 2001, a third and final one in May 2003.

Under Basel II banks will be able to *fine-tune* the amount of capital applied to individual loans matching the risks more closely. Compared to the former accord which dealt almost exclusively with capital standards, the new approach will be based on *three* pillars: minimum capital requirements; supervision by dialogue; and disclosure (Table 6.10).

Basel II leaves the definition of regulatory capital, the division into Tier I and Tier II Capital, and the rules limiting its composition, unchanged. The same holds for the 8% ratio. One crucial difference lies in the *types of risks* included. There is a new capital charge for *operational risk*, in addition to charges for credit and market risks that already exist. In addition, the concept takes into account *concentration risk*: banks with a high degree of credit-risk concentration to a single borrower or sector will have a larger capital charge than those with a well-diversified portfolio.

Another change concerns the *measurement of credit risk* which will allow banks to choose between *three methods* of increasing technical sophistication: a standardised approach which is essentially a revision of Basel I assigning risk weights to different assets, and an *internal*

Table 6.10   Elements of the three pillars of Basel II

Minimum capital requirements	Supervision by dialogue	Disclosure
Credit risk	Banks are required to have an internal process for assessing their capital requirements in relation to their individual risk profile	Consolidation
Operational risk	The process will be evaluated by supervisors who will take action if they consider it unsatisfactory	Capital
Total minimum capital	Banks are expected to operate with capital above the Pillar 1 minimum both to provide a cushion and to reflect their specific risk profile	Risk exposure and assessment
	Supervisors should intervene at an early stage to prevent capital from falling below a level considered adequate	Capital adequacy

ratings based (IRB) approach which allows banks to use their own internal models for risk assessment. The latter is further divided into two frameworks which differ by the extent to which banks and supervisors contribute to the assessment of borrowers' creditworthiness (Table 6.11).

In contrast to Basel I, the new approach will no longer focus solely on credit risk but on the banks' *overall risk profile*. Accordingly, risk measurement will be closer to market practices and instead of relying exclusively on capital ratios the aim will be to influence overall risk management and *attitudes* towards risk. This is reflected in the importance of the *second pillar* which consists of a system for *dialogue* between banks and supervisors. The idea is that even the most elaborate rules for capital requirements cannot deal with the peculiarities of each individual institution.

Further, by establishing new disclosure rules as *third pillar* there will be an additional reliance on disciplinary market forces enabling investors, depositors and supervisors to get a more accurate picture of banks' performance. There is an expectation that informed market participants will acknowledge risk consciousness and sound risk management and sanction respective failures. Disclosure will include four key areas:

Table 6.11   Two approaches to internal risk assessment

Information	Foundation IRB approach	Advanced IRB approach
Probability of default (PD)	Provided by banks based on internal ratings	Provided by banks based on internal ratings
Loss given default (LGD)[1]	Specified by supervisors	Provided by banks based on internal estimates
Exposure at default (EAD)[2]	Specified by supervisors	Provided by banks based on internal estimates
Maturity (M)[3]	Specified by supervisors	Specified by supervisors

[1] Expected loss at the time of default taking into account proceeds from payments made by the borrower and from utilisation of collateral and guarantees.

[2] LGD as percentage of the expected exposure to the borrower at the time of default.

[3] Residual maturity of the loan or effective maturity.

- the scope of application of the Basel rules to entities within a banking company;
- the composition of capital and the accounting policies for the valuation of assets and liabilities;
- exposure assessment and management processes; and
- capital adequacy for different types of risks and the total.

As banks may use their own internal rating methods after regulators' approval, risk assessment techniques will be *more sophisticated* under Basel II. Since the amendment of the accord in 1996 to set requirements for tradings books banks have been allowed to use their own value at risk (VAR) models to calculate market risks. The new approach paves the way for the use of respective *credit risk models*, too, although there is an ongoing debate about the accuracy of these models.

Greater sophistication is one reason why, in the beginning, Basel II will impose big *challenges* on the international banking industry, in particular in information technology. The modelling of multiple financial risks is *mathematically complex*. In addition, banks will have to ensure that they have *historical* financial and customer data going back a minimum of two years. And, given that a large global bank will have hundreds of *different systems*, using different technologies and being based around different business processes implementation costs will be high. However, in the longer run, especially for large institutions, the expected *cost savings* from system improvements and the advantages of needing less capital to cover risks may be substantial, too. The latter depends on the various bank businesses and their riskiness. For example, banks with a large share of residential mortgages may need less capital under the new rules while those with strong capital market activities and industrial shareholdings may have to increase their capital.

Value at Risk

In the 1990s, value at risk (VAR) models became the standard for risk management of big internationally operating banks (Appendix H). Since 1996 under an amendment of the Basel Accord they have been allowed to determine market risks related to trading books. The value at risk is a number which is computed to answer the question of how much capital should be kept aside to cover potential losses from trading activities. It is denominated in currency units and expressed in terms of some confidence interval referring to the loss which is not exceeded but in a small percentage – usually 5% or 1% – of occurrences. The Basel Committee has chosen a confidence level of 99%, but some banks use lower levels as well. In recent years, some banks have started to develop credit risk models on a similar basis in order to establish the VAR of loan portfolios. These impose additional challenges on the banks. In particular, data on credit risk are much more limited compared to the long series of returns data available for trading-book VAR calculations.

One fear related to the introduction of the new rules is that they might *distort competition* between banks under different regulatory regimes opening new ways to regulatory arbitrage. Already, the US authorities annnounced that the new rules in their most complex form will apply only to about 10 US banks with another 10 or so expected to adopt the standard voluntarily. In general, Basel II allows considerable flexibility leaving much of the implementation to national regulators: observers have counted 44 areas of *national discretion*. Experience has shown that supervisors in different countries tend to apply very different standards which threatens to *undermine the rules' universality*. In addition, given the complexity of the approach and the large number of countries involved there are fears that there will not even be enough regulators for the task.

In Europe, the Basel II rules will become law under a new *Capital Adequacy Directive (CAD III)*. This will apply to banks and investment firms in all EU member states, but, there are intense pressures to soften the rules for small banks and investment firms so that the final outcome of the legislation process is still uncertain.

Another open issue is *how* financial regulation in Europe will be *implemented* in the future. Under the current EU regulatory system different committees of national authorities draw up the fine print of financial regulation. There is no clear home countries' responsibility for monitoring the various subsidiaries of financial groups. Rather, banks and financial institutions are subjected to the scrutiny of a range of authorities with supervisory practices and reporting and control standards differing widely across countries.

6.2.3   Monetary Policy Cooperation

For financial supervision globalisation of financial markets and activities is the main rationale for policy cooperation. For monetary policy it is the international *interdependence* of targets and strategies and the resulting *conflicts of interest* between the world's major economies. For example, a tightening of monetary policy in the euro zone in order to fight inflation triggering a rise in euro interest rates will – other things remaining equal – almost inevitably attract capital from other major currencies such as the US dollar resulting in the initial impact of the policy measure being weakened in Europe by the inflow of liquidity (although the effect, in turn, may be dampened by the resulting rise in the euro exchange rate lowering import prices and the overall price level). In the US an effect would probably be felt, too, although the outcome may be uncertain. The concomitant liquidity shortage may raise interest rates exerting a deflationary influence while the devaluation of the currency may have an inflationary impact (Figure 6.4).

In this example, policy targets in both currency areas may be in conflict and policy cooperation agreeing on a coordination of monetary or exchange-rate strategies may be difficult to achieve. Another example is the fight against *exchange-rate volatility*. In this case, policy-makers in both regions may agree on the target and given the huge volume of daily foreign exchange trading that makes a success of unilateral currency interventions highly improbable the incentives to cooperate are high.

While policy debates centre around international coordination of *dollar, yen and euro monetary policy*, in economic theory the issue is traditionally discussed in a simplified world of two countries with identical economic structures and policy instruments and symmetric policy targets. The countries' situation is compared to a *prisoners' dilemma*. This is a classical paradox often used in game theory to illustrate a conflict between individual and collective rationality (Table 6.12).

Two persons have been arrested under the suspicion of having committed a crime together and are interrogated separately. The police do not have sufficient evidence for a conviction and offer each of them the same deal. If one confesses and the other remains silent, the one who talked will get parole while the other will get a life sentence. Each knows that if neither of them confesses, the case against them is weak and they will both end up with one year in prison on lesser charges. However, if both confess, each will get 20 years in prison.

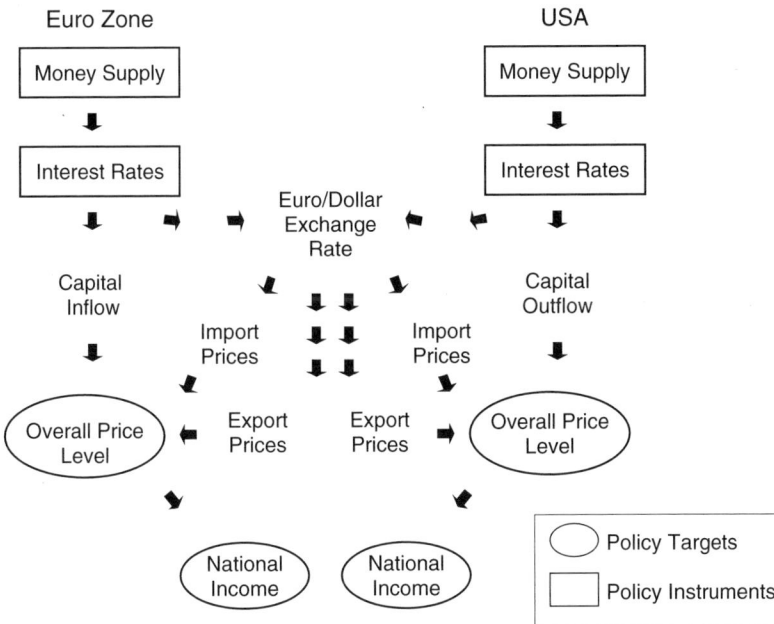

Figure 6.4   Monetary policy effects under interdependence

Table 6.12   The prisoners' dilemma

		Prisoner B's strategies			
Prisoner A's strategies		Not confess		Confess	
	Not confess	1 year	1 year	Life	Parole
	Confess	Parole	Life	20 years	20 years

In this situation, under the assumptions of *game theory* confessing is the *dominant strategy* for both. Given the other 'player's' choice each can always reduce the own sentence by confessing. As a consequence, both confess and get heavy jail sentences. This is the core of the dilemma.

From the perspective of the optimal interest of the '*group*' (consisting of both players) the correct outcome would be for both to cooperate and remain silent, as this would minimise the total time both would spend in jail. However, given the impossibility of communicating this would require them to trust each other; instead, they follow selfish interest and lose.

Whether international monetary policy 'games' are characterised by a similar situation is not undisputed. One argument is that the prisoners' dilemma is the result of very special *assumptions*. Allowing for a *different behaviour*, for example as the result of education or established rules, fear and beliefs – only think of the *esprit de corps* or feeling of loyalty, often found in gangs – or *permitting communication* between players, would fundamentally alter the game since in these cases they could tacitly agree or negotiate a different outcome. The same holds if the game might be *repeated* and the participants were able to remember each other's behaviour in previous rounds – as they do in political negotiations. This would pave the way for credible threats and sanctioning of uncooperative behaviour but also for learning and forgiveness. The scenario would also be different with a *larger number* of players allowing them to form coalitions thereby destroying the game's symmetry.

In practice, there are many *options for monetary policy* to cooperate:

- Central banks may decide to *directly intervene* in the foreign exchange markets and coordinate their strategies accordingly.
- Which may be done either *sporadically* or following *fixed rules*.
- They may choose to *sterilise* the effects of currency interventions on the domestic money supply which, however, risks lowering their effectiveness.
- Alternatively, they may decide to steer the money supply under their sphere of influence or the exchange rate by *coordinated interest rate changes*.

In each case they need to reach *agreement* about targets and the setting of instruments which includes having an idea of the relationships governing economic activity, the determinants of currency relations and/or money demand and supply, and the effects of interest-rate policy – no easy task given that there are competing economic models with widely differing policy implications. The decision problem becomes more complex the more 'players' are involved. This particularly holds true if monetary and fiscal policies need to be coordinated within countries as well. In these cases, actors may prefer rules over discretion if only for the sake of simplicity or for being able to defend their strategy at home.

Focusing on the exchange rate, in principle, policy may choose between different *currency regimes* (Table 6.13). The two extremes are a clean float and a monetary union. In a *clean float* governments abstain completely from directly or indirectly influencing currency relations. However, this is an ideal case. There are serious doubts whether such a system ever existed. *Monetary union*, the deliberate decision of a group of countries to abandon their national currencies in favour of a new common one, is a unique experiment in history conducted by the euro-zone countries.

In between, there are several systems of varying binding force. The most widely spread is a *managed float* where governments try to influence the exchange rate in a discretionary way. Examples are the at times coordinated at times single-handed currency interventions of the central banks of the US, Western Europe and Japan in the US dollar market. A more stringent approach is a *currency peg* fixing the price of a currency to another one or to a *currency basket* with the weight of each currency usually reflecting its relative importance for the country in question. These options are often chosen by developing countries or economies in transition. The most binding form of currency arrangement behind monetary union is a system of *multiple fixed exchange rates*, either against one another or in relationship to a third currency. An example of the latter is the Bretton Woods system of fixed dollar exchange rates which prevailed worldwide until the early 1970s.

Recent experience with monetary cooperation in Europe has reopened the debate on the prospects for a more coordinated approach in *other regions* in the longer run and about a worldwide system of *trilateral monetary policy coordination* between the US, Europe and Japan. There would be undeniable benefits. Economies in Asia and Latin America have been severely hit by currency crises in the past, and in the relation between dollar, euro and yen instability is widely considered as a constant threat to economic growth – not only in their home countries but also in those countries whose imports or foreign debt are to a large extent denominated in these currencies.

Table 6.13 Currency regimes

Regime	Characteristics	Remarks
Single currency arrangements		
Clean float	Governments do not influence exchange rates at all	Ideal case, no realistic option
Managed float	Discretionary official influence on the exchange rate	Common practice under nominally flexible exchange rates, preferred by industrial countries vis-à-vis the US dollar
Unilateral peg to one currency	Fixed bilateral exchange rates	The chosen currency is typically the leading reserve currency in a region or worldwide and/or the invoice currency of the main trading partners
Unilateral peg to a basket	Weighted fixed exchange rate to a group of currencies	The currencies included typically reflect the trade structure of the country
Crawling peg	Weighted fixed exchange rate to a group of currencies with regular or irregular adjustments	The crawl may be rule-bound or discretionary, following the development of certain indicators or policymakers' judgement
Groups of currencies		
System of fixed but adjustable exchange rates	Fixed multilateral exchange rates either vis-à-vis one another or a third currency	Examples: Bretton Woods system, European 'snake in the tunnel', EMS. Adjustments usually take place as reaction to currency crises. There is an element of flexibility through fluctuation margins around the parities
Monetary union	Common currency	Unique experiment in history

However, there are also serious opponents, at least to trilateral cooperation. They argue, for example, that the *current practice* of G7 central banks to regularly exchange information, macroeconomic assessment, analysis and policy ideas is enough and further cooperation to jointly determine monetary targets and strategies for the three major currencies would not be worth the risks and costs.

Trilateral monetary coordination would be *fraught with many uncertainties*. One reason is that the policy of the major central banks in the world is not only a matter of agreeing on the transmission mechanism of a monetary strategy. For example, how would the ECB and the Federal Reserve have reacted to the Japanese economic and financial crisis of the last decade? What would the ECB and the Bank of Japan have done in the LTCM debacle? Would they have shown the same attitude and flexibility as the Federal Reserve or would they have risked the international financial system to go bust? How would they have dealt with the Asian crisis or September 11 and how long would it have taken them to react? Would the three together actually have enough discretion left under a rule-bound coordinated policy in similar cases to ward off the dangers for the world financial system?

Apparently, what works well on a regional level might easily be doomed to fail internationally. Public debates of these issues, in particular in other world regions, often neglect that monetary integration in Europe benefits from two factors: on the one hand, policy coordination in a comparably homogeneous, highly integrated economic environment apparently is – despite all challenges – a manageable task. On the other hand, the European experiment with a common currency rests on a long tradition of maturing mutual understanding. The process of monetary integration in Europe was *a long-lasting gradual one*, favoured by many circumstances, and the currency regime has always been a small, albeit important, item in a long list of integration projects.

European monetary integration is only one element in the process of economic and financial integration and the – preliminary – last step in the development of a common monetary and financial culture that is *deeply rooted in history*. There is a direct line from the Italian merchant banks at the Champagne fairs in France in the thirteenth century via the establishment of the Amsterdam Bourse as Europe's leading securities market in the seventeenth century to the more recent role of London as hub of international foreign exchange and bond trading. This created a *tradition of openness* in the region facilitating the development of institutions that found its latest expression in recent efforts to formally establish and complete a common legislative framework for investors and consumers of financial services under the *Single Market programme*.

The beginnings of this development in the 1950s looked rather modest. The end of World War II had left Europe as *a scattered landscape* both in real and financial terms. The European capital markets were virtually nonexistent. London's supremacy was broken and New York had become the most important financial centre in the world. Finances were in disarray. In many parts of the region, banks' functions were widely reduced compared to pre-war conditions and many international financial relationships had broken down. With the exception of the Swiss franc currencies were not convertible and no markets for foreign exchange existed. Cross-border payments were settled through the *European Payments Union*, an intra-European clearing mechanism that was established in 1950 and lasted until restoration of convertibility for major European currencies in 1958.

European and international economic policy making in those years focused on *reconstructing* European economies. European economic integration started with the European Coal and Steel Community in 1951 which was succeeded by the European Economic Community (EEC) established by the *Treaty of Rome in 1957*. Monetary and financial integration was no explicit aim in these first post-war initiatives. After the creation of the *Bretton Woods system* European currencies were embedded in the worldwide system of fixed exchange rates with little incentives for their own active exchange-rate policy; cross-border capital mobility remained widely restricted. However, in the 1960s the first signs of rising cross-border financial activities began to show with the first *Euromarkets* for currencies and bonds emerging.

The rise of the Euromarkets and the concomitant growth of international business in London from the 1960s onwards compensated the City for a loss of home business as a result of the decline of the British economy after the war. However, above all, it served to *reestablish its leading role* in the world of finance. While before 1914, 30 foreign banks had been established in London, and another 19 came between the wars, in 1969, 87 more arrived. In the 1970s, 183 institutions followed, and still another 115 in the first half of the 1980s, so that all in all, between 1914 and 1985 the number of foreign financial firms in the City grew more than fourteen-fold. Despite this revival, during these years, the place remained a *remarkably conservative* one rarely inclined to financial and technological innovation. European banks dominated the scene. To cite one observer:

Prior to 1983 the American commercial and investment banks had paid little attention to London, regarding it as the 'Siberia of investment banking, a place to banish those the firm wished to forget.' There was hardly any need to be in London. Cross-border business in equities and corporate finance was limited and entry to the Stock Exchange was barred. The Eurobond market had moved from New York to London in the 1960s but the participants formed their own tight community and for many years the investment banks did not seek to build more rounded businesses on top of them'. (Augar 2000: 70)

With the establishment of the Euromarkets came *the first pan-European financial institutions*. The emergence of an international bond market led to the creation of two international clearers, Euroclear and Cedel, and for interbank transactions the SWIFT network was established.

The Euromarkets can be regarded as the first step towards concentration and integration of financial activities in the European region that goes beyond the traditional foreign funding of domestic financial needs known in European trade since at least the Middle Ages. This process was *entirely market-driven*; monetary authorities rather distrusted the markets as a potential source of instability and a source of financial liquidity outside their control. In their reliance on *special techniqu*es of risk sharing and risk reduction the Euromarkets showed financial institutions the way to act in an unfamiliar international environment *coping with different systems and standards* and, at the same time, made them become aware of the *benefits* of a market without borders. In this they created a climate in which future ideas of a convergence of rules and regulations, and the establishment of common institutions, would thrive.

Another influence contributing to this climate of building common markets and institutions in the realm of European finance was *exchange-rate policy*. Since its early beginnings the EEC members had defended the exchange rates of their currencies vis-à-vis the US dollar within the Bretton Woods system within margins of ±0.75%, a rule that was abandoned only with the worldwide agreement to widen bands in 1971.

With the breakdown of the Bretton Woods system the need for a common European approach to fixed exchange rates became more urgent. Since 1969 there had been plans for a stepwise reduction of fluctuation margins in Europe (*Werner Plan*), and in 1972 six European countries – the Benelux countries, France, Germany and Italy – agreed to establish the '*snake in the tunnel*', a system of narrow fluctuation limits within the wider bands of the still existing Bretton Woods system. They were followed by Denmark, Ireland and the UK within a couple of months. In 1973, when the Bretton Woods system collapsed, the European countries decided to stick to the 'snake' but their success was not a lasting one. Of the system's initial eight members only five were left in the so-called '*mini snake*' consisting of the Benelux countries, Denmark and Germany when it was replaced by the newly established *European Monetary System (EMS)* in 1979 (Table 6.14).

The new system differed fundamentally from its predecessor. The *intervention mechanism* was much more complex consisting of two components: one was a bilateral grid of parities for the member currencies specifying central rates for each exchange rate as well as the maximum range of fluctuations. The other was *a basket of member currencies, the ECU*, which served as a unit of account and parallel currency to the system and was intended to become a single currency substituting for the national monies of the European Community later on.

The EMS in its initial form did not last either. It *disintegrated in two stages* after the details of full European monetary union were decided in the *Maastricht Treaty* in December 1991 inviting currency traders to test the new agreement in several *waves of speculation*. The first wave came in the summer and autumn of 1992 with the result that Britain and Italy left the

Table 6.14   Chronology of exchange-rate arrangements in Europe

Year	Event	Details
1972	Begin of the 'snake in the tunnel'	Fluctuation margins of 2.25% between member currencies and 4.5% against the US dollar
1979	EMS start	Establishment of the ECU
1990	EMU: start of the first stage	Removal of capital controls
1993		Widening of fluctuation margins to 15%
1994	Start of the second stage	Establishment of the European Monetary Institute (EMI), predecessor of the European Central Bank
1998		Fixing of irreversible bilateral exchange rates Establishment of the ECB
1999	Start of the third stage	Introduction of the euro
2002		National coins and notes are no longer legal tender
2004	New entrants' participation in EMS II	The newcomers are Cyprus, Czech Republic, Estonia, Hungary, Latvia, Lithuania, Malta, Poland, Slovakia and Slovenia
And for the future:		
2006	Ecofin to examine Maastricht criteria of the new member states	
2007	Earliest possible introduction of the euro as unit of account in new member states	
2008	Issue of euro coins and notes in new member states	

system. The second wave occurred in the following year with devastating attacks on the French franc. After this, the EMS was formally preserved in *a wide-band version of ±15%* until the start of monetary union in 1999.

Like the Euromarkets European exchange rate policy became one of the building blocks of a common monetary and financial culture in Europe that paved the way for further integration and harmonisation. It was *the first policy-driven effort*, and the currency crises on its way demonstrated that the markets did not always agree with, or believe in, the results.

Over the years, there was a growing understanding that, given transaction volumes and the capacities to find leeways and leakages for circumvention, in order to be efficient, rules governing financial markets must either *completely rule out market interference* or leave a *wide degree of flexibility* and scope for market forces to find their own way. In Europe, in the realm of monetary policy, with the introduction of the common currency the first approach was chosen. In *financial market development*, for a long while the second one appeared more promising with the pendulum swinging back in the other direction only recently.

Liberalisation of European financial markets started with deregulation in Britain in the early 1980s as a by-product of a series of economic reforms aimed at reducing state influence. In 1983, *the London Stock Exchange (LSE)* abolished membership restrictions and opened itself to competition abandoning the separation between *jobbers* (dealing in stocks held on their own books) and *brokers* (buying and selling stocks solely on clients' orders), and removing the system of *fixed commissions*. The consequences were far-reaching and in their dimensions hardly foreseen by anyone involved in the process.

Table 6.15   Big Bang acquisitions

Brokers and jobbers	Acquiring firm
Laing & Cruickshank	Credit Lyonnais
Grievson Grant	Kleinwort Benson
de Zoete & Bevan	Barclays
Wedd Durlacher Mordaunt*	Barclays
Pinchin Denny*	Morgan Grenfell
Pember & Boyle	Morgan Grenfell
Philips & Drew	Union Bank of Switzerland
Moulsdale*	Union Bank of Switzerland
Smith Brothers*	Smith New Court
Scott Goff, Layton & Co	Smith New Court
Giles & Cresswell*	Smith New Court
Savory Milln	Swiss Bank Corporation
Rowe & Pitman	S.G. Warburg & Co
Akroyd & Smithers*	S.G. Warburg & Co
Mullens	S.G. Warburg & Co
L. Messel	Shearson Lehman
Vickers da Costa	Citicorp
Scrimgeour Kemp Gee	Citicorp
Fielding Newson Smith	National Westminster Bank
County Bisgood*	National Westminster Bank
Wood Mackenzie	National Westminster Bank
W. Greenwell	Midland Bank/Samuel Montagu
James Capel	Hongkong and Shanghai Bank
Hoare Govett	Security Pacific
Henderson Crosthwaite (Far East)	Barings

* Jobber.
Source: Financial Times.

In preparation for the '*Big Bang*', which came into force in October 1986, mainland European and, in particular, *American and Japanese* financial institutions strongly expanded their *presence in London*. This put considerable competitive pressures on the 225 broking and jobbing firms belonging to the LSE in 1986 and led to a wave of mergers and acquisitions. Very few survived (Table 6.15). Within a year of the Big Bang announcement 18 of the top 20 brokers and all the major jobbers had made a merger.

The Big Bang changed *the face of the City*. Before, the total number of people in stockbroking was around 10,000 and individual firms in London comprised 200 or 300 people at most; with a staff of 1300 James Capel was by far the largest of them. As a result of *mergers*, broking firms increased to 600 or 700 and became part of large organisations employing thousands of staff. All invested heavily in *office space*. One of the most disputed outcomes of this development was the transformation of the *Docklands*; the City, which over centuries had been the '*square mile*' was losing shape. Between 1985 and 1989 alone 2.6 million square feet of office space were completed in the Docklands and another 16.5 million square feet in the City itself.

Market culture changed as well. American ways of doing business gradually took over ringing in the slow 'death of gentlemanly capitalism' (Augar 2000). Until the Big Bang the

City had been a *highly stratified system* characterised by dense social networks and recruitment of 'old boys' from private schools and Oxbridge. With the arrival of a growing number of foreign financial institutions market culture became a mixture of old English and new, largely American rites. The more *'cut-throat' habits* prevailing in New York dealing rooms now began to show up in London as well and traders were more and more explicitly encouraged to demonstrate their willingness to take risks and 'move for the kill' (Crang 1998). At the same time, the market became *more innovative* and ready to compete with others on an *international level*.

Soon *other European markets* began to sense the winds of change too: state intervention became widely discredited. *Extensive reforms* were undertaken in France, Germany, Italy and Switzerland. In *Germany*, the first of several successive Financial Market Promotion Laws was launched. However, the outstanding example is *France*, a country where government traditionally played a much larger role than elsewhere through direct state ownership of financial institutions. Between 1984 and 1986, in France an *entirely new market culture* developed: controls were lifted, new financial instruments created and new markets, in particular for futures trading, established.

The Big Bang was only the beginning of a *Europe-wide financial consolidation* – a process that is still going on. However, while in the UK reform largely concentrated on the stock market, on the Continent the focus was more on banking systems. It was a *stepwise process*. When the Second Banking Directive, aimed at creating a single market for banking services in the EU, was implemented in 1993, the first big wave of mergers and acquisitions in European banking was already completed (Table 6.16).

The process changed the *composition of actors* in European markets opening up *a new international dimension*: for the first time in the financial history of Europe, institutions from

Table 6.16 Mergers and acquisitions in European banking[1]

Countries	1989–90		1991–92		1993–94		1995–96[2]	
	Number	Value	Number	Value	Number	Value	Number	Value
Belgium	11	0.0	22	1.0	18	0.6	12	0.4
Finland	6	0.4	51	0.9	16	1.0	4	0.8
France	52	2.7	133	2.4	71	0.5	43	3.2
Germany	19	1.1	71	3.5	83	1.9	27	0.7
Italy	41	8.2	122	5.3	105	6.1	65	3.0
Netherlands	12	10.9	20	0.1	13	0.1	7	0.8
Norway	12	0.4	23	0.1	24	0.2	2	0.4
Spain	30	4.0	76	4.3	44	4.5	26	2.1
Sweden	10	2.0	38	1.1	23	0.4	8	0.1
Switzerland	31	0.5	47	0.4	59	3.9	14	0.7
United Kingdom	86	6.4	71	7.5	40	3.3	28	21.7
By comparison:								
Japan	8	31.2	22	0.0	8	2.2	17	33.8
United States	1 501	37.8	1 354	56.8	1 477	55.3	1 176	82.5

[1] Value in billions of US dollars.
[2] As of 4 April 1996.
Source: Folkerts-Landau, David *et al.* (1997) *International Capital Markets – Developments, Prospects, and Key Policy Issues*, Washington, DC: International Monetary Fund, Table 59.

other world regions began to compete with European ones *in their domestic field* on a large scale and on an equal footing. In addition, there was a rising awareness of the financial services sector as *motor of economic growth* and *source of income and employment* at a time when traditional industries in manufacturing were in decline. The biggest consequence was the plan to create *a Europe-wide single market* for financial services.

There had been official European integration efforts before. For example, the internal market in banking had been established with *the first banking directive* of 1977 which enabled banks in the European Community to establish branches or subsidiaries in member countries. However, after the *Single Market Act* of 1985, there was widespread agreement that more progress was needed. A borderless market with unrestricted movement of people, goods and services in Europe would require further liberalisation of financial flows and payments and the convergence of financial market legislation to fully exploit the benefits of integration. The aim was to make both individuals and firms *take advantage of*:

- deeper and more liquid financial markets;
- a wider range of financial instruments available for risk management and portfolio diversification;
- more intense competition between financial institutions ensuring better prices and higher efficiency;
- the scale economies banks, securities firms and other financial intermediaries were expected to realise from rising opportunities.

Full liberalisation of capital flows in the EU was reached in mid-1990. The integration process that followed was based on *four principles*:

- the harmonisation of standards;
- home-country control and supervision;
- the provision of a single European passport for financial institutions; and
- mutual recognition.

In the Single Market framework financial services are *divided along functional lines* focusing on the banking, securities, brokerage and insurance sectors. Several key directives set the rules for EU-wide harmonisation in these sectors:

- The second banking directive of December 1989 that came into force in 1993 introduced the *single EU banking licence* allowing credit institutions authorised to do business in one member state full access to other EU markets.
- The investment services directive of 1993 defines the modalities for the free provision of services by *brokers and securities markets.*
- The third life and non-life directives of 1992 were established to coordinate laws, regulations and administrative provisions relating to the various parts of the *insurance industry* and set minimum rules for the qualitative and quantitative investment of assets.

In 1998, the EU launched its most ambitious programme, the *Financial Services Action Plan (FSAP).* This includes over 40 new laws establishing a unified set of rules for investors and consumers under a strict timetable. The aim was to complete the legislative framework for the internal market in financial services and to eliminate remaining deficits in the substance of EU legislation.

The various components of the FSAP can be divided into *four broad areas* (Table 6.17). The first is the creation of a single European *wholesale* market for financial products and

Table 6.17   FSAP components

Objective	Main subject areas
1. Single wholesale market	EU-wide capital raising
	Common legal framework for integrated securities and derivatives markets
	Uniform financial statements for listed companies
	Containing systemic risk in securities settlement
	Cross-border corporate restructuring
	Single market for investors
2. Open and secure retail markets	Distance selling of financial services
	Financial service providers' duty of information towards purchasers
	Cross-border payments
	E-commerce policy for financial services
3. Prudential rules and supervision	Reorganisation and winding-up of insurance undertakings and banks
	Disclosure of financial instruments
	Supervision of financial conglomerates
4. Wider conditions for an optimal single financial market	Harmonisation of tax regulations
	Creation of an efficient and transparent legal system of corporate governance

services. This includes the issues of EU-wide capital raising, of stock market listings and prospectuses, and regular reporting. Other measures in this group are the establishment of a common legal framework for integrated securities and derivatives markets and of a single set of financial statements for listed companies, the containment of systemic risk in securities, the creation of a secure and transparent environment for cross-border restructuring, including takeovers, and of a single market for investors. There is also a pension funds directive and a new UCITS directive replacing the one that was established in 1985 setting minimum standards for a single licence for unit trusts throughout the community.

The second group of components aims at creating open and secure *retail* markets. This consists of nine measures such as those on the distant selling of financial services, on clear and comprehensible information for purchasers, on insurance intermediaries, a single market for payments, and e-commerce policy for financial services. The third area deals with *prudential rules and supervision* including the re-organisation and winding up of insurance undertakings and banks, the disclosure of financial instruments and the supervision of financial conglomerates. The last group contains issues of *wider conditions* for an optimal single financial market such as harmonisation of tax regulations or the creation of an efficient and transparent legal system of corporate governance.

The FSAP is intended to be implemented in 2005 and most measures have been completed in advance. As a result, EU financial markets and cross-border transactions have grown in size and improved in efficiency. However, there is a widespread impression that while a great deal of progress has been made there are still many impediments to financial integration. Markets and systems are still fragmented, institutional barriers still exist and commitment to financial reform and integration in EU countries at the level where individual measures are adopted is often lacking. In addition, the influence of the common currency which was expected to be a catalyst for integration complementing the FSAP has fallen behind expectations.

Summary

- Monetary and financial policies are vulnerable to external disturbances. The reasons are limits to sovereignty and interdependence of policy targets and instruments across countries.
- Globalisation differs from interdependence – and differs substantially from traditional foreign trade and investment relationships.
- There are three policy options to cope with the undesirable effects of globalisation: defensive intervention, offensive intervention and global public policy.
- The Basel Accord is widely regarded as successful example of the global public policy approach.
- In the EU, the rules of the Basel Accord have been implemented in various directives.
- From 2006 onwards, there will be a new framework for regional and international financial supervision known as Basel II, which will be based on three pillars: minimum capital requirements, supervision by dialogue and disclosure.
- While globalisation is the main rationale for policy cooperation in financial supervision for monetary policy cooperation interdependence is the main driving force.
- There are several kinds of currency regimes. A common requirement for each form of coordinated monetary policy is agreement on targets and the effects of instrument settings.
- European Monetary Union is the preliminary last step in a process that started in the 1950s as one component of European economic integration.
- European exchange-rate policy presented one of the building blocks of a common monetary and financial culture. Others were the emergence of the Euromarkets in the 1960s, the process of Europe-wide financial liberalisation that followed the UK Big Bang in the mid-1980s and the Single Market programme with the Financial Services Action Plan (FSAP).

Exercises

1. Compare the activities of globally operating firms with traditional foreign trade and investment relationships.
2. Describe in which respects globalisation differs from interdependence.
3. How do international activities of financial institutions weaken state sovereignty? Find examples.
4. Describe the policy problem and discuss the pros and cons of policy options under globalisation.
5. Describe the principles of territorial and domiciliary approaches to financial regulation, their advantages and limits under globalisation.
6. Compare Basel I and II. Which problems will be solved under the new regime? Which ones, do you think, will remain unsolved and which additional ones may emerge?
7. Describe the dilemma of monetary policy in interdependent nations and discuss possible solutions.

8. In which way did

   – the rise of the Euromarkets
   – the process of financial liberalisation in the UK
   – European exchange rate policy

   contribute to laying the foundations for EMU?
9. Discuss the role of the FSAP in the process of economic integration in Europe.

Additional Links and References

There are many excellent publications on the phenomenon of globalisation. Here are some examples:

Castells, Manuel (1996) *The Rise of the Network Society*, Oxford: Blackwell.
Daniels, Peter and William F. Lever (eds) (1996) *The Global Economy in Transition*, Essex: Addison Wesley Longman.
Dicken, Peter (2003) *Global Shift*, New York: Guilford Press.
Held, David *et al*. (1999) *Global Transformations*, Stanford: Stanford University Press.

Globalisation is usually regarded as inevitable. However, one publication demonstrates how an earlier period of globalisation in the late nineteenth century was eventually reversed, arguing that this might happen again. See:

O'Rourke, Kevin H. and Jeffrey G. Williamson (1999) *Globalization and History – The Evolution of a Nineteenth-Century Atlantic Economy*, Cambridge, MA: MIT Press.

For a detailed discussion of the globalisation phenomenon and its implications for state sovereignty, and in particular for the concept of global public policy see:

Reinicke, Wolfgang H. (1998) *Global Public Policy – Governing without Government?* Washington, DC: Brookings.

There are many publications and working papers on Basel II and its predecessors. Here is a small selection:

Basel Committee (1988) International convergence of capital measurement and capital standards, http://www.bis.org/publ/bcbs04A.pdf
Basel Committee (1996) Amendment to the capital accord to incorporate market risks, http://www.bis.org/publ/bcbs24.pdf
Basel Committee (2001): The new Basel Accord, press release, 16 January, www.bis.org/press/p010116.htm.
Deutsche Bundesbank (2001) The New Basel Capital Accord (Basel II), in *Deutsche Bundesbank: Monthly Report*, April, pp. 15–41, http://www.bundesbank.de/vo/download/mba/2001/04/200104mba_art01_baselaccord.pdf
Jackson, Patricia (2001) Bank capital standards: the new Basel accord, *Bank of England Quarterly Bulletin*, Spring, 55–63, http://www.bankofengland.co.uk/qb/qb010101.pdf
Rodriguez, L. Jacobo (2002) International banking regulation – Where's the market discipline in Basel II? *Policy Analysis*, No. 455, 15 October, http://www.cato.org/pubs/pas/pa-455es.html

The BIS consultative papers on the new Basel Accord can be found here:

http://www.bis.org/bcbs/bcbscp3.htm

There is a flood of books, articles and websites on the prisoners' dilemma. One which shows the solutions offered by repetitions of the game is:

Axelrod, Robert (1984) *The Evolution of Cooperation*, New York: Basic Books.

For the analogy between the prisoners' dilemma and monetary policy cooperation and for an in-depth analysis of the latter see:

Krugman, Paul R. and Maurice Obstfeld (1997) *International Economics – Theory and Policy*, Reading, MA: Addison-Wesley.

Arguments against an institutionalised monetary policy coordination for the dollar, yen and euro are found in:

Rogoff, Kenneth (2003) A vote against grandiose schemes, *Finance & Development*, **40**(1), http://www.imf.org/external/pubs/ft/fandd/2003/03/rogo.htm

The development of the City of London after World War II is described in:

Augar, Philip (2001) *The Death of Gentlemanly Capitalism*, London: Penguin Books.
Hall, Peter (1998) *Cities in Civilization*, London: Weidenfeld & Nicolson.
Hamilton, Adrian (1986) *The Financial Revolution*, Harmondsworth: Penguin.

For the financial market reforms in Continental Europe since the 1980s see:

Allen, Franklin and Douglas Gale (2001) *Comparing Financial Systems*, Cambridge, MA: MIT Press.
Gros, Daniel and Karel Lannoo (2000) *The Euro Capital Market*, New York: John Wiley & Sons, Inc.

For an overview of the Financial Services Action Plan (FSAP) see

Deutsche Bank Research (2002) EU financial market special, *Frankfurt Voice*, June, http://www.dbresearch.com.
HM Treasury, Financial Services Authority (FSA), Bank of England (2003) *The EU Financial Services Action Plan: A Guide*, http://www.bankofengland.co.uk/publications/FSAP-guide.pdf

6.3   EMU AND FINANCIAL INTEGRATION

According to a study for the European Commission, a single financial market would add 1.1% to EU growth over the next decade and lower the cost of capital for companies by up to 0.5%. One important element in this and other scenarios is the impact of the common currency on EU markets. However, so far the introduction of the euro has contributed much less to European financial integration than expected.

Many of the reasons for this failure have become apparent in earlier chapters. In this section they will be summarised and put into context. The most important conclusions that can be drawn from studying the developments so far are:

- Monetary integration is one important element of the integration process, but not by far the only one. Financial integration does not require monetary integration.
- The contribution of monetary integration to European financial integration differs across markets.
- A common currency is no substitute for the removal of institutional barriers and other impediments to financial integration.

Let us first look at *markets*. Before the launch of the common currency, the most obvious and immediate effect observers expected was on foreign exchange markets. In January 1999, *foreign exchange trading* in euro replaced that in 12 national currencies and there was widespread agreement that this would considerably reduce market volumes. However, there were also voices expecting rather a constant or even rising foreign exchange turnover. They pointed to the inevitable shifts in international portfolios whose direct and indirect effects would induce further trading and stimulate market activity, and to the uncertainties among dealers and financial institutions facing this unique historic experiment which would result in ever new rounds of search, learning and adjustment processes.

According to the Triennial Central Bank Survey conducted under the auspices of the Bank for International Settlements daily estimated foreign exchange turnover worldwide declined from $1.49 trillion in 1998 to $1.21 trillion in 2001. However, the next survey in 2004 showed a large increase in activity with daily turnover between 2001 and 2004 *rising by 57%* to about $1.9 trillion; growth was observed in all market segments and driven by all types of counterparties. These include investors disappointed by poor equity returns and low bond yields in search of new forms of investment which regard currencies increasingly as an asset class, asset managers more actively managing currency risk and macro hedge funds specialising in big currency bets. An additional influence triggered by the strong dollar exchange rate was the emergence of new dealers in currencies contributing to investment banks' rise in trading profits.

The euro played a rather modest role in this development. Although still being the second most actively traded currency worldwide being involved in 37% of foreign exchange transactions its importance has slightly decreased. This is generally regarded as a sign that *stabilisation* has taken place after the initial sharp decline attributable to the elimination of trading in the legal currencies of the euro. Stabilisation is also reflected in the declining importance of the euro/dollar currency pair which – although remaining the most actively traded currency pair – accounted for 28% of turnover compared to 30% in 2001. Another remarkable development is the rise of sterling, the fourth most-used currency worldwide behind the Japanese yen which in 2004 was involved in 17% of transactions compared to 13% in 2001.

As well as the foreign exchange market, the biggest and most immediate integration impact of the euro was on *wholesale money markets* (Figure 6.5). The launch of the euro saw a marked decline in the share of currency swaps as the result of the switch from 12 currencies to one. At first glance, somewhat surprisingly, integration advanced most rapidly in the riskiest market segment, the *unsecured deposit market*: its share rose from 48 to 53%. However, on closer inspection it turns out that most of this change occurred in the *overnight market*. For longer maturities, the share of repos rose while that of deposits declined. For longer maturities repos and swaps have a greater importance as they provide greater security; nevertheless,

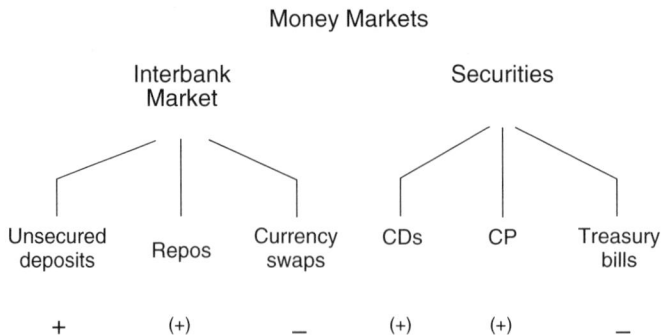

Figure 6.5   Effects of EMU – money markets

participants agreed that the repo market did not become as integrated as the unsecured market. Conditions for repos still show a diverging pattern across euro area countries. One reason is the *costs of managing the collateral* involved; there are differences with respect to the reduction of risk achieved by the cash lender, the opportunity cost incurred by the collateral lender (i.e. the cash borrower) and the cost of cross-border management of the collateral borne by both parties such as settlement, marking to market, coupon treatments or legal arrangements. Other factors leading to an ongoing preference for deals in domestic assets include *national investment guidelines* limiting holdings of foreign securities, differences in tax treatments of bonds and an uneven distribution of collateral throughout the euro area.

Short-term securities markets showed different integration patterns after the introduction of the common currency. The market for treasury bills declined under governments' efforts to meet the requirements of the Stability and Growth Pact. In the markets for commercial paper (CP) issued by corporations, and bank certificates of deposits (CDs) adjustment to more integration was visible but comparatively slow, retaining a strong domestic orientation. One explanation is the *traditional focus of money market funds* on domestic retail markets. Another is *lack of infrastructure* and a harmonised trading environment which is reflected in the segmentation of clearing and settlement systems, differences in fiscal treatment and a lack of uniform legal documentation.

At the other end of the maturity spectrum (Figure 6.6), the most remarkable development in bond markets was the development of non-government bonds in Europe. The arrival of the euro opened up new opportunities to corporations, financial institutions and other non-government borrowers (Table 6.18). Typically, the market in non-sterling European currencies was dominated by banks – in particular German banks – which remained the largest issuers after the launch of the common currency. However, non-bank corporations showed the highest dynamism more than doubling their share of oustanding euro-denominated securities between 1995 and 2000.

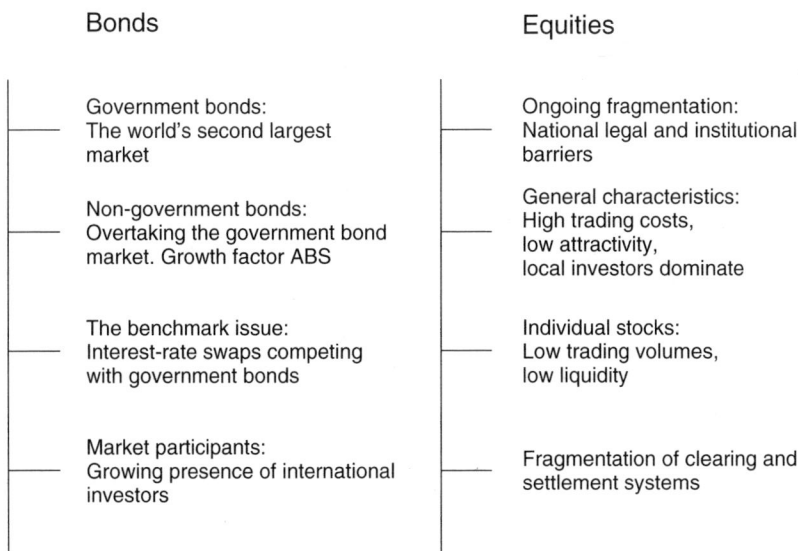

Bonds

Government bonds:
The world's second largest market

Non-government bonds:
Overtaking the government bond market. Growth factor ABS

The benchmark issue:
Interest-rate swaps competing with government bonds

Market participants:
Growing presence of international investors

Equities

Ongoing fragmentation:
National legal and institutional barriers

General characteristics:
High trading costs,
low attractivity,
local investors dominate

Individual stocks:
Low trading volumes,
low liquidity

Fragmentation of clearing and settlement systems

Figure 6.6   Effects of EMU – bond and equity markets

Table 6.18   Shifts in Euro non-government securities markets[1]

Instruments/institutions	1995	2000
Corporations	8.2	17.7
Financial institutions	57.0	53.6
Commercial banks	49.6	44.7
Other	7.4	8.9
Collateralised debt		
ABS	–	–
Pfandbriefe	18.6	19.6
of which: Jumbos	1.2	8.8
Government-sponsored enterprises	11.8	5.8
Supranationals	4.5	3.4
Total (in trillions of US dollars)	3.4	4.0

[1] Percentage of outstanding non-government securities, end of period.
Source: Study Group on Fixed Income Markets (2001) The changing shape of fixed income markets, BIS Paper No. 5, October, Table 2, http://www. bis.org.

The replacement of national currencies opened up new opportunities on the demand side, too. Institutional investors such as pension funds and insurance companies, and other financial institutions facing restrictions on their investments in foreign currency instruments, suddenly had a much wider choice of assets available. French and German institutional investors in particular became a driving force in the market with German institutions already strongly increasing their purchases of euro-denominated securities in 1998, ahead of the formal introduction of the euro. Their presence is not only adding considerably to market liquidity but, due to the peculiarities in investor behaviour, also contributing to market stability.

While bond trading showed notable integration tendencies since the late 1990s, other markets seemed less affected by the launch of the euro. This in particular holds true for *equities*. The contribution of the common currency to the process of consolidation that undeniably is under way among European stock exchanges appears a rather modest one. Fragmentation across national lines remains high; each country still has its own *legal and regulatory apparatus* although the number of cross-country alliances is rising. Trades are still mainly conducted among *local investors*, and trading volumes and liquidity for individual stocks are low. *Trade execution fees* are still higher than, for example, in the US thereby reducing the ability of European exchanges to attract listings from other parts of the world.

In reaction to the euro there were major *changes in the way shares are traded*. Months before the introduction of the common currency, institutional investors, investment banks and asset managers started to *disband country desks* and reorganised their equity and trading operations on an area-wide basis focusing on industrial sectors instead. The idea was that in eliminating currency risk the euro would further accelerate the process of European economic integration which – together with the unified monetary policy stance through the creation of the Eurosystem and an increasing cohesion of fiscal policies through the provisions of the Maastricht Treaty – would make economic conditions become *more synchronised* across countries thereby diminishing the relative importance of country-specific influences on share prices.

In a sense, there is a tendency for those expectations to more and more become *self-fulfilling*. As cross-border equity trading grows, trading infrastructures within Europe become increasingly linked, and the results of *analyst reports and high-quality securities research* are more widely circulated, pricing mechanisms are converging. Of growing importance in this process are practices such as block trading and portfolio insurance. *Block trading* was introduced in the UK after the Big Bang in order to accommodate institutional investors that sought to build up large positions in European stocks without causing market prices to rise, and spread to other European markets. In recent years, a special variant emerged that further sped up price convergence: *accelerated trades*. These are coordinated actions of hundreds of traders of big brokerages designed to build momentum selling millions of shares within hours to large numbers of international institutional investors.

Even before the introduction of the euro, there was a heightened overall awareness of the opportunities of cross-border trading in the region giving stock exchanges greater incentive to expand across national boundaries thereby contributing to the first signs of *emergence of an equity culture* across Europe. However, *impediments* remain high: one is legal and regulatory differences. These include listing requirements, accounting rules and tax treatment with the latter not only refering to different taxes but also to mechanisms for tax collection and double-taxation treaties. Another is the *home-country bias* investors show due to information costs associated with international trading. Cultural differences and language barriers still make it difficult and expensive to obtain information about foreign companies and developments and, although its introduction eliminated some intra-European currency risk and simplified cross-country comparisons of corporate data, the euro is but one factor in a vast variety of influences determining supply and demand in stock markets. A further impediment is the fragmentation of clearing and settlement systems.

One apparent conclusion to be drawn from the development of different markets and market segments since the launch of the euro is that its contribution to European financial integration *differs across markets*. Its role as a catalyst has been stronger the more national markets have in common and the greater the importance of currency risk as a discriminating factor. It has been *most successful* in the interbank market for very short-term unsecured deposits and in markets for bonds where standardisation is comparatively high. It played a *lesser role* for collateralised instruments and equities where differences in institutions and systems as well as cultural aspects impose additional barriers and limit comparability.

In general, impediments to the integration of financial markets under a common currency can be grouped into five categories:

- Maturities. The longer the *investment horizon*, the greater the probability that country- or instrument-specific influences become felt making prices for seemingly similar products of different origin move apart. For example, over short time periods the risk of widening spreads for certain government and non-government securities is low so that the one can be used as *hedging vehicle* for the other. However, over longer periods both tend to move less closely, in particular in times of turmoil.
- Liquidity. Prices for seemingly similar financial instruments may get out of sync even with other influences unchanged when *squeezes* in some markets occur and liquidity dries up while others remain unaffected. For instance, this was an occasional problem of German government futures contracts after the launch of the euro.
- Standardisation and transparency. In highly *standardised and transparent markets* currency risk is often the only or most important element hindering integration. Markets for foreign exchange and exchange-traded derivatives are the best examples.
- Third-market dependence. This bears the risk that prices for seemingly similar instruments drift apart because some of them are influenced by developments in another market they

are closely related to. One example is the link between different cash instruments and the relations to their derivatives.

• Institutional differences. Beside the influences described in the various sections these include *different stages of market development*, an aspect that, for example, may become important for the new EU member countries from Central and Eastern Europe.

The higher developed, more standardised and more liquid comparable financial instruments of different origin are, and the greater the degree of financial integration reached before, the stronger the effects of monetary integration and the introduction of a common currency. By contrast, imposing a single currency on immature, strongly specialised or highly fragmented markets may not only lower its effectiveness but increase the *likelihood of additional frictions*.

Another sector where the influence of the euro has only modestly been felt so far is *banking*. In the beginning, aspirations were high (Figure 6.7); with the advent of the common currency, the banking sector was expected to become far more efficient. Monetary integration would allow financial institutions to exploit *economies of scale* from at least two sources: one is *geographic widening* of business across Europe, the other is growth through mergers and acquisitions. Both were expected to bring bank profitability closer to the levels prevailing in the US. However, both did not materialise in the expected way.

Traditionally, *cross-border activities* of banks depend, above all, on country size and economic relevance. In preparation for, and with the advent of, the euro the number of banks with cross-country operations increased markedly as the data for the five countries with the biggest numbers of banks demonstrate (Table 6.19). *Target countries* were above all those that already had a larger number of foreign banks such as Belgium, France, Italy, the Netherlands and Spain. The exception is Luxembourg which saw a decline in foreign bank presence from many countries. Above all, banks tended to strengthen their presence in *neighbouring countries*. However, cross-penetration was not restricted to the euro area. Even before EMU banks from

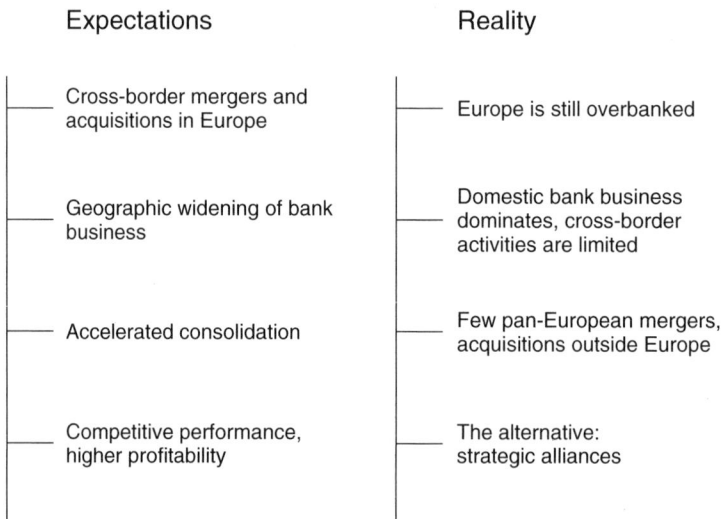

Expectations	Reality
Cross-border mergers and acquisitions in Europe	Europe is still overbanked
Geographic widening of bank business	Domestic bank business dominates, cross-border activities are limited
Accelerated consolidation	Few pan-European mergers, acquisitions outside Europe
Competitive performance, higher profitability	The alternative: strategic alliances

Figure 6.7   Effects of EMU – banks

Table 6.19 Examples of cross-border penetration of banks in the euro area

Country of origin	France		Germany		Italy		Netherlands		Spain	
Host country	1998	2001	1998	2001	1998	2001	1998	2001	1998	2001
Belgium	7	10	6	7	1		6	8	3	2
Finland	1	1		2						
France			10	14	5	6	3	4	9	7
Germany	10	17			5	5	7	8	2	1
Greece	4	4	2	2	1	1	2	2		
Ireland	2	5	1	3			3	4	2	2
Italy	10	13	11	12			5	7	4	3
Luxembourg	7	6	36	30	9	7				1
Netherlands	3	4	4	8	1	1				
Austria	1	1	3	6	1	1	2	3		
Portugal	5	5		3			1	1	6	7
Spain	10	16	4	7	5	4	3	4		

Source: Bundesverband deutscher Banken (2002): Übersicht über das Bankgewerbe im Euro-Währungsgebiet, http://www.bdb.de.

Table 6.20 Examples of cross-border penetration of banks from outside the euro area

Country of origin	Denmark		Sweden		UK	
Host country	1998	2001	1998	2001	1998	2001
Belgium					2	6
Finland	2	1	2	12	1	2
France			1	2	15	17
Germany	5	4	1	1	8	10
Greece					5	3
Ireland					9	12
Italy					8	9
Luxembourg			2	2	5	4
Netherlands					4	6
Austria				1	2	3
Portugal					2	3
Spain	1	1			7	9
Denmark			3	3	2	2
Sweden	2				6	6
UK	3		3	3		

Source: Bundesverband deutscher Banken (2002): Übersicht über das Bankgewerbe im Euro-Währungsgebiet, http://www.bdb.de.

non-member countries operated in other European countries and, as a group, further increased their presence in reaction to the euro and other developments (Table 6.20). This in particular holds true for British banks that are competing with other European ones on their home territories.

Despite the increase of cross-border activities, Europe remains largely divided by *national barriers*. Even the big banks still derive 50 to 75% of their profits from domestic markets.

This is true not only for the interbank market but in particular for *retail business*. Except for Ireland and the Benelux countries, the share of loans from banks in the euro area to non-banks in other member countries is traditionally less than 2.5%, and this has not changed with the euro.

What *has* happened is an adjustment of systems. One concomitant of the restructuring process in the banking industry in recent years is a shift in Continental Europe *from traditional bank lending to investment banking*, with the consequence that the dichotomy between bank-based and market-based systems is eroding steadily. Competition in the market for investment services increased as the convergence of underwriting fees indicates. These days, for banks it is often a matter of survival to adapt to a changing environment by becoming engaged in bond underwriting, selling capital market products to households and securitising bank loans in bundling them into packages to be sold in the market.

However, this process owes less to the introduction of the euro and is more a reflection of an overall international trend. The same is true for *mergers and acquisitions* in the banking industry. The wave of pan-European mergers that was supposed to follow the introduction of the euro did not happen. There have been some spectacular cases such as HSCB's acquisition of Crédit Commercial de France and HVB's purchase of Bank Austria in 2000, but consolidation has mostly taken place *within countries*, and after the first experiences with foreign takeovers states have become more, rather than less, protective towards outsiders. Most 'mega-mergers' since the late 1990s in Europe have taken place domestically. In Switzerland, Swiss Bank Corporation and Union Bank of Switzerland formed UBS with combined assets of $749 billion. In France, BNP took over Paribas. In Spain, Banco Santander and Banco Central Hispanoamericano formed BSCH and then the latter took over Banesto. In Britain, there were the takeovers of NatWest by Royal Bank of Scotland and Halifax by Bank of Scotland. In Germany, examples are the merger of Bayerische Vereinsbank and Bayerische Hypotheken- und Wechselbank to become Bayerische Hypo- & Vereinsbank and Dresdner's acquisition by Allianz that kept the bank 'in the family'.

Instead of cross-border consolidation within Europe, banks have turned to the US. HSBC's acquisition of the US lender Household International at the end of 2002 is but one example. Others are BNP Paribas, ABN Amro, Royal Bank of Scotland and Société Générale. The case of BNP Paribas may serve to demonstrate the difficulties European financial institutions faced in their search to become more competitive through mergers and cross-stakes before the arrival of the euro. For the French bank cross-border expansion turned to be ruled out by the defensive nature of banking sectors in other EU member states. On the other hand, foreign entry into France was permitted solely under the condition that the centre of decision making of the new entity remained inside the country. In its frustration at the prospects of a deal in Europe the bank eventually shifted focus to the US acquiring assets in Honolulu and California where it became the fourth-largest bank.

Banks' efforts towards international consolidation and increase of competitiveness outside Europe are not restricted to activities in the US. One example is ING; the Dutch group is constantly building up strategic alliances in other parts of the world. For instance, its stake in Kookmin Bank, South Korea's largest bank, serves to deepen a relation that allows it to offer ING-branded financial services to Korean retail customers thereby strengthening its presence in one of Asia's fastest-growing markets. Similar alliances exist with ANZ Bank in Australia and Vysya Bank in India.

One alternative to cross-border mergers and acquisitions are *strategic alliances*. These have gained more and more attraction with the concerns raised about the efficiency of ever bigger financial institutions in recent years. In contrast to a view widely held in the industry and outside, little empirical evidence has been found so far of scale economies for large banks, and no evidence whatsoever for the largest ones. The same appears to hold for insurance companies and brokerages. In addition, there is a growing awareness of the danger that the tendency towards all-finance conglomerates might magnify operational risks as the result of incompatible systems and an unforeseen rise of exposures in merged credit portfolios. For Europe, these findings are of particular importance since, on average, the top European financial institutions are already much larger than, for instance, those in the US – a fact that apparently did not help improve their performance in the past.

Despite the FSAP there are still many institutional barriers to financial integration in Europe which could not be compensated by the introduction of a common currency. One is tax systems: *taxation of income and capital* is an area in which differences across countries are still high. In the 'old member' EU, 15 different company tax systems apply. Countries' tax systems still favour domestic investments which might help explain the observed home bias in international portfolios. Dividends are subject to double taxation, and in some member countries the tax credit granted to resident shareholders for the tax paid at company level is not available to non-residents. Considerable differences exist in the effective tax burden: for a subsidiary of a parent company this can reach more than 30 percentage points depending on the location of both. As a consequence, investments may not take place in the lowest cost locations but where the lowest taxes are paid. Differences in tax systems help explain why, for example, in the middle of the process of financial integration and convergence of systems in Europe Ireland managed to establish itself as an outstanding international banking centre.

Deposit insurance is another example of institutional barriers. These days, banks in Europe are increasingly competing for an international clientele, and deposit insurance is one important element of this competition. EU standards regulate little beyond the minimum insured amount of €20,000 prescribed in the EU deposit insurance directive. Schemes in member countries differ widely in premiums, coverage limits, sources of funding, whether they also insure deposits in foreign currency, whether the administration of the scheme is official, private, or joint, and whether bank membership is voluntary or compulsory.

One open issue so far is the impact the euro will have on *Europe's financial landscape* in the longer run (Figure 6.8). Traditionally, *London* is the place with the most advantages. The high concentration of financial institutions in the City allows them to realise considerable scale economies. Further, they benefit from the existence of high quality professional and support services such as accounting, actuarial and legal services and IT, and from an efficient infrastructure including office accommodation and telecommunications. In addition, there is the use of the English language. These days, these advantages are often contrasted with the disadvantage resulting from the fact that Britain is not a member of the euro area. However, this argument is rather used outside the City. In London itself, the euro is widely regarded as *one stress factor among others*. Expensive property rates and a worsening of infrastructure are considered at least as threatening to the City's long-term attractiveness.

Similar modifications must be made concerning the role of *Frankfurt* which was expected to benefit the most among European financial places from EMU because of the size of the German economy, the former importance of the D-mark, the dominance of German banks in the euro area and the location of the European Central Bank. Although the presence of foreign institutions has clearly risen after the launch of the euro, anecdotal evidence gives the impression that Frankfurt's relative position has not improved markedly. For example, when DePfa, one of Germany's biggest financial institutions and a specialist in public-sector finance, relocated from Wiesbaden to Dublin, the head of the bank moved from Frankfurt to London. Big

London	Frankfurt
Concentration of financial services; scale economies and lock in	Size of the German economy
Producer services	Former role of the D-mark
Infrastructure	Dominance of German banks
Legal system	Location of the ECB
English language	

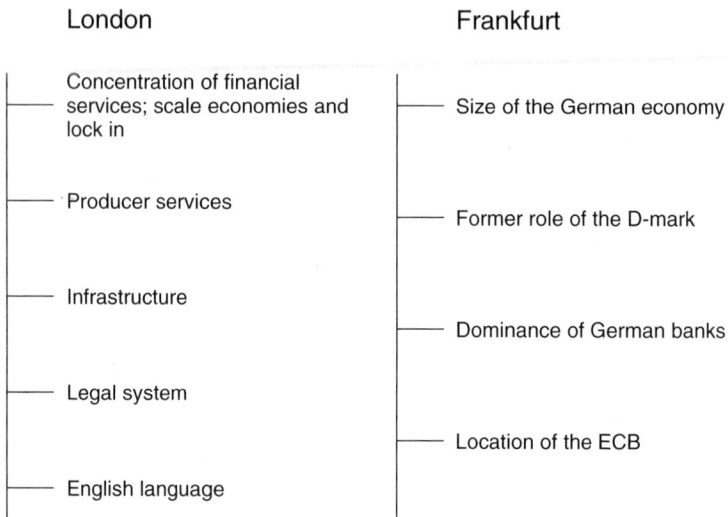

Figure 6.8   Effects of EMU – financial centres

German banks have long shifted major activities such as foreign exchange and investment banking to the UK and there were even rumours that Deutsche Bank, the symbol of German financial power, was harbouring plans to abandon Frankfurt in favour of London. In general, in the financial industry identification with Frankfurt is low. Employees commute between Frankfurt and London or other places for the weekends, and many traders are not even located in Frankfurt but use its trading infrastructure and new technologies for doing business from afar.

So far, the advent of the common currency has not prompted business to shift from London to locations in the euro area on a massive scale. On the contrary, the spatial closeness of one of the world's leading financial centres to the euro zone countries tended to further increase the city's attractiveness to financial institutions both in and outside Europe. On the other hand, London's rivals in Frankfurt, Paris and other places are constantly coming up with new challenges. The debate on the hierarchy of financial locations in the region will gain new impetus if and when Britain decides to join the euro.

There is a growing role of locations outside Europe in shaping the European financial landscape with competition between European financial places and institutions increasingly taking place outside the region. Recent moves of Eurex and Euronext-liffe to enter the US markets are but one example. The growing presence of European banks in other parts of the world is another one. This expansion is not free of risks. Poorly performing foreign investments and acquisitions threaten to worsen earnings quality and increase banks' overall risk profile. In particular, the establishment in emerging economies makes the banks highly vulnerable to systemic risk during financial crises which, in turn, may have repercussions on home markets. One example is the expansion of Spanish banks in Latin America which, at first, was considered one of the most important elements of bank internationalisation in recent years and later became one of its most fatal examples as crisis struck in Argentina.

What are the *lessons to be learned* from the experience with the common currency so far? Does financial integration require monetary integration? No matter what overall economic benefits the euro has, the answer is certainly: no. In international financial markets the currency is but one discriminating factor, and this can be hedged or diversified away, and a common currency is no substitute for the removal of institutional barriers and other impediments to financial integration.

However, there are still other lessons to be learned from the European experiment. It turned out that for *less developed financial systems* the introduction of a common currency may be instrumental in speeding up adjustment and financial integration. However, this comes at a cost in the form of additional risks and uncertainties that are reflected in pricing problems.

For *highly developed systems* the benefits may be even greater and associated with lower risks. In these cases, scale economies and access to a larger number of markets for financial institutions and their customers matter. The disadvantages are that closer integration and the reduction of the number of currencies reduces the opportunities for diversification and risk management. One consequence that could be observed in recent years is the increasing attractiveness of emerging markets outside Europe to international investors – with sometimes doubtful implications for the financial stability of these regions.

The effects of the euro on the *role of financial centres* are less clear than many observers expected. Apparently, for a financial centre to benefit from monetary and financial integration access to the Single Market for financial services in Europe is more important than participation of the home country in the common currency or the location of the European Central Bank.

Summary

- Monetary integration is one important element of the integration process, but by far not the only one. Financial integration does not require monetary integration.
- The contribution of monetary integration to European financial integration differs across markets.
- The longer the *investment horizon*, the greater the probability that country- or instrument-specific influences become felt making prices for seemingly similar products of different origin move apart.
- Prices for seemingly similar financial instruments may get out of sync even with other influences unchanged when *squeezes* in some markets occur and liquidity dries up while others remain unaffected.
- In highly *standardised and transparent markets* currency risk is often the only or most important element hindering integration. Markets for foreign exchange and exchange-traded derivatives are the best examples.
- Concerning the role of financial centres in the process of monetary and financial integration, access to the Single Market is more important than the currency.
- A common currency is no substitute for the removal of institutional barriers and other impediments to financial integration.

Exercises

1. Discuss the observed parallels and differences in the integration of money markets and markets for long-term securities after the launch of the euro.
2. Describe the barriers to integration in European banking under EMU.

3. Where do you see the main adavantages and disadvantages of the common currency

 – for highly developed financial systems;
 – for less developed systems?

4. Discuss the reasons from the point of view of a financial institution for a presence

 – in London
 – in Frankfurt
 – in Dublin

 under EMU.

Additional Links and References

The figures showing the potential benefits of an integrated European financial market are from:

London Economics (2002) Quantification of the macro-economic impact of integration of EU financial markets, final report to the European Commission – Directorate General for the internal market, in association with Price-waterhouseCoopers and Oxford Economic Forecasting, November, http://europa.eu.int/comm/internal_market/securities/overview_en.htm

For the impact of the euro on European financial markets and financial integration see:

Galati, Gabriele and Kostas Tsatsaronis (2001) The impact of the euro on Europe's financial markets, BIS Working Paper No. 100, July, http://www.bis.org/publ/work100.pdf
Santillán, Javier, Marc Bayle and Christian Thygesen (2000) The impact of the euro on money and bond markets, European Central Bank Occasional Paper No. 1, July, http://www.ecb.int/pub/pdf/scpops/ecbocp1.pdf

The latest results of the BIS Triennial Central Bank Survey of Foreign Exchange and Derivative Market Activity from April 2004 are available at:

http://www.bis.org

The impediments to stock market integration in Europe are described in:

McAndrews, James and Chris Stefanadis (2002) The consolidation of European stock exchanges, *Federal Reserve Bank of New York: Current Issues*, **8**(6), http://www.newyorkfed.org/research/current_issues/ci8–6.pdf

For the discussion of the relation between bank performance and size see, for example:

Walter, Ingo and Roy Smith (2000) *High Finance in the €uro Zone – Competing in the New European Capital Market*, London: Prentice Hall.

Differences in tax systems within Europe are discussed in:

Adam, Klaus, Tullio Jappelli, Annamaria Menchini, Mario Padula and Marco Pagano (2002) Analyse, compare, and apply alternative indicators and monitoring methodologies to measure the evolution of capital market integration in the European Union, CESF, University of Salerno, 28 January, http://europa.eu.int/comm/internal_market/en/update/economicreform/020128_cap_mark_int_en.pdf

For the differences in deposit insurance systems in Europe and their implications see:

Huizinga, Harry and Gaetan Nicodème (2002) Deposit insurance and international bank deposits, European
    Commission, Directorate General for Economic and Financial Affairs, Economic Papers, No. 164, February,
    http://europa.eu.int/comm/economy_finance/publications/economic_papers/2002/ecp164en.pdf

The Centre for the Study of Financial Innovation (CSFI), a London-based think tank,
publishes an annual survey of the risks banks face asking financial practitioners, regulators and
analysts about their concerns:

CSFI (2002): Banana Skins 2002, http://www.csfi.org.uk

7
Conclusions

One lesson to be learned from the preceding policy chapter is that the balance between national interests and international necessities, between individual and collective 'rationality', is apparently easier to reach at a regional level than worldwide. In particular, it seems easier to achieve among European countries with their common history of financial markets and institutions and common experiences, traditions, beliefs and behaviour patterns that developed over the centuries to a kind of market 'culture' that differs from those in other parts of the world.

As the third and fourth chapters demonstrated European financial markets are special in many respects. On the one hand, participants are more old-fashioned, and structures more encrusted, than elsewhere. On the other hand, in the past, the variety of systems and institutions in the region has always been – and still is – a driving force of ideas and innovations, which then spread around the world. Early examples are the ways in which European financial actors and institutions reacted to the risks and challenges of rising merchant empires (in the Middle Ages and later on), their eagerness to exploit new technologies to increase the efficiency of financial trading and bridge distances, and their flexibility in developing special techniques of risk sharing and risk reduction enabling them to survive, and, on average, perform well, in an ever-more complex global environment.

Recent experience indicates that some of these differences will survive even under growing worldwide integration. They will be reinforced by the region's latest historic experiment: the creation of a European single market for financial services including a common currency. While gradually closing the gaps between regional financial systems it will almost certainly make the differences to other parts of the world become more pronounced – establishing an ongoing need for explicitly studying European financial systems in the global economy.

Appendix A
Bill of Exchange as Medieval Credit Instrument

EXAMPLE: EXCHANGE AND RE-EXCHANGE BETWEEN LONDON AND ANTWERP

The example includes a purchase in London of a bill on Antwerp and the return of the proceeds thereof from Antwerp to London by re-exchange, which is profitable as long as the exchange rate in Antwerp is below the London rate. The exchange rates used are those mentioned in a report of 1564.

A is a deliverer or banker in London who decides to take £100 st. and buy a bill on Antwerp at a prevailing rate of 22 s. 6 d. gr. (The Flemish pound in Antwerp is divided into 20 shillings of 12 deniers groat.) B is the taker who is expecting a sum in Antwerp, but is in need of the money in London.

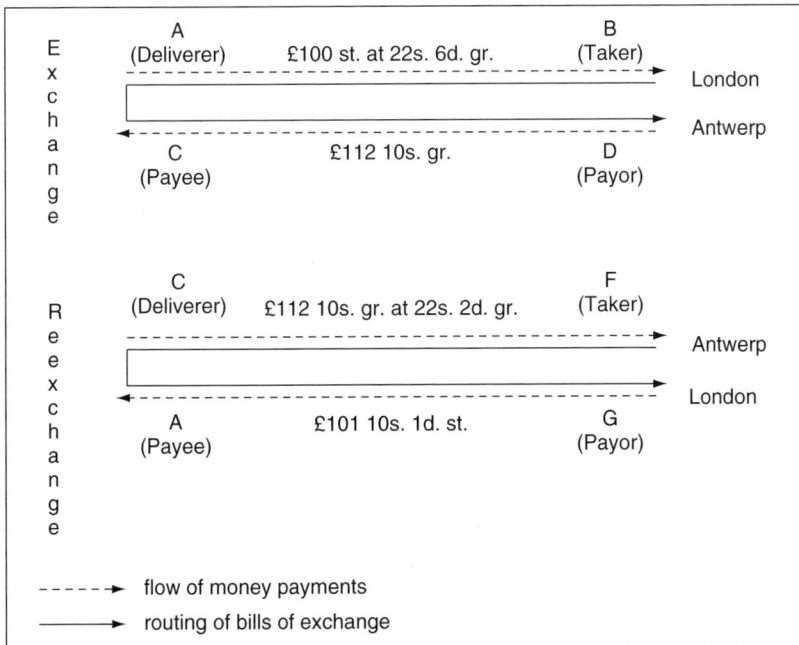

Figure A.1 Exchange and re-exchange between London and Antwerp. *Source*: De Roover, Raymond (1974) What is dry exchange? A contribution to the study of English mercantilism, in Julius Kirshner (ed.) *Business, Banking, and Economic Thought in Late Medieval and Early Modern Europe – Selected Studies of Raymond de Roover*, Chicago: University of Chicago Press

In return for a loan from A, B is making out a bill, payable at usance in Antwerp by his Agent, D, in favour of A's agent C. The bill matures at the end of one month. At that time, C collects the sum of £112 10 s. gr. – which is the equivalent of £100 st. at 22 s 6 d. gr. – from D. Now, instead of keeping this sum idle, A instructs his agent C to find a new taker, F, and to remit the sum of £112 10 s. gr. to London by exchange. C buys from F a usance bill on London at 22 s 2 d. gr. per pound sterling maturing after another month and sends it for collection to A in London where A gets £101 10 s. 1 d. st. or the equivalent of £112 10 s. gr. at 22 s 2 d. gr. per pound sterling. A's profit of £1 10 s. 1 d. st. on £100 st. in two months comes not from an interest rate – which might be considered as usury – but from the difference in the exchange rate between Antwerp and London.

In Europe, after France's lead in adopting a law supporting the Tobin tax, and under pressures from NGOs (such as Attac or War on Want, the London-based development campaign) on other governments to follow, debates on the pros and cons of the tax heightened. Two questions arise: is the plan desirable? Is it feasible?

Initially, the proposal made by Nobel-laureate James Tobin in the 1970s intended to slow foreign currency speculation by imposing a small tax on foreign-exchange transactions. Today, its proponents usually add a second element: to use the proceeds to reduce poverty in the world. Estimates by the European Commission indicate that a turnover tax of 0.01% to 0.1% would generate between $20 billion and $200 billion a year. By comparison, in 2000, official development finance was $66 billion.

Start, then, with desirability. The massive attacks on currency speculation by those who favour the proposal are reminiscent of earlier heated debates on the advantages and disadvantages of free, unregulated markets. Still, the result of all these debates is the markets we have today. These days, there is widespread agreement that in facilitating the price discovery process and adding the liquidity needed to guarantee smooth continuous trading without large disruptions and price variations, speculation is essential to efficient markets. However, there is equal unanimity that the rising severity and frequency of international financial crises, and especially the group of countries concerned, in recent years present a particular problem.

Typically, in contrast to earlier currency crises, the more recent crises are not rooted in, and widely limited to, industrial countries but, above all, concern developing countries and emerging economies for which the consequences are much harder to bear. In former crises good reasons could be found for policy not to interfere and to leave the markets alone. Highly advanced industrial countries can be expected to cope with the consequences; their markets are efficient and sophisticated and able to weather a storm, and when they are hit by a crisis this can be considered as a kind of natural selection process in which the fittest survive to the benefit of the whole system.

However, the spread to developing countries and emerging economies poses new policy challenges. One is contagion: as the Asian crisis of the late 1990s demonstrated, once crisis strikes it is not contained to regions and markets. A second is official commitment: in contrast to former times when the burden to sort out the problem was left to governments and national monetary authorities of the countries concerned, today international lenders of last resort such as the IMF, the World Bank and others step in with huge amounts of taxpayers' money (Table B.1). Other challenges are the possible political instability and the waste of development aid.

Table B.1 Official commitment during the Asian crisis[1]

Country	IMF[2]	IBRD	ADB
Thailand	3.9 (505)	1.9	2.2
Indonesia	10.1 (490)	4.5	3.5
Korea	21.0 (1939)	10.0	4.0

[1] In billions of US dollars.
[2] In parantheses in percent of quota.
Source: Bank for International Settlements (1998) *Annual Report*, Basle, Table VII.9.

Thus, the severity of the problem is widely recognised and the question is how to solve it. A tax on foreign-exchange transactions, to put it bluntly, is not the right way. In order to see why we have to ask what is known about these trades and about the alleged market volumes on which calculations of tax incomes are based.

There are two aspects: the first is availability of data. The only coherent source of information on market volumes is a survey conducted every three years by central banks and monetary authorities of countries with large and medium-sized foreign-exchange markets under the auspices of the Bank for International Settlements. However, these represent only a small fraction of total foreign-exchange business worldwide and allow a momentary glimpse of a market which is permanently in motion and where actors, amounts and types of transactions can vary considerably from month to month. While participants were formerly asked to report all arm's-length trades – which meant trades in which the dealer is indifferent as to the counterparty – in the latest 2004 survey they included trades with their own branches and subsidiaries and between affiliated firms. Excluded again are back-to-back deals and trades to facilitate internal bookkeeping and internal risk management within a given institution, as well as trades between desks and offices of the reported dealer located in the same country. Deals of large globally operating firms within private corporate networks bypassing banks are also excluded.

The second aspect concerns tracking. An earlier argument against the Tobin tax was that it would be impossible to implement the tax without the agreement of almost every conceivable jurisdiction in the world. However, a recent view of the proponents of the tax is that with growing use of real-time-gross-settlement (RTGS) payment systems involving a limited number of money-centre banks worldwide this seems no longer valid. The latter, however, unveils a fundamental ignorance of the mechanics of foreign-exchange trading: it is not the amounts settled via a payment system that matter in this context, but the deals behind that influence market conditions – and the two are not the same.

The foreign-exchange market is largely an interbank market (Table B.2). In 2004, reported interbank trades with dealers accounted for an estimated 53% of total turnover and trades with other financial institutions for another 33%. Most of those trades are short-term spot transactions and swaps (Table B.3). In addition, as the UK data for London, the world's biggest centre of foreign-exchange trading show, most of the forward-looking trades, i.e. forwards and swaps, are very short term by nature (Table B.4).

A spot transaction is an exchange of two currencies for settlement within two business days. Due to established customs, when a currency is bought or sold spot in the interbank market, no accounts are debited or credited, that is no money actually changes hands, until maturity, and it is only the *difference*, i.e. the gain or loss, that has to be paid and settled – via RTGS or any other method.

A swap is an exchange of two currencies for a specific period and a reversal of that exchange at the end of the period consisting either of a combination of a spot and a forward leg or of two forward trades with different maturities.

For example, in a euro/dollar spot against forward swap transaction the euro is bought (sold) for two days at an agreed spot rate and *simultaneously* sold (bought) back at a later date. Swaps give the dealer

Table B.2   Reported foreign exchange turnover by counterparty[1]

Counterparty	1995	1998	2001	2004
With reporting dealers	728 (64)	908 (64)	689 (59)	936 (53)
With other financial institutions	230 (20)	279 (20)	329 (28)	585 (33)
With non-financial customers	179 (16)	242 (17)	156 (13)	252 (14)
Total[2]	1 137 (100)	1 430 (100)	1 174 (100)	1 773 (100)
Estimated gaps in reporting	53	60	26	107

[1] Daily averages in April, in billions of US dollars, in parentheses percentage shares.
[2] Excluding estimated gaps in reporting.
Source: Bank for International Settlements (2004) Triennial central bank survey of foreign exchange and derivatives market activity – preliminary global results, Basle, September, Table 2.

Table B.3   Reported foreign exchange turnover by instrument[1]

Instrument	1995	1998	2001	2004
Spot	494 (43)	568 (40)	387 (33)	621 (35)
Outright forwards	97 (9)	128 (9)	131 (11)	208 (12)
Foreign exchange swaps	546 (48)	734 (51)	565 (56)	944 (53)
Total[2]	1 137 (100)	1 430 (100)	1 174 (100)	1 773 (100)

[1] Daily averages in April, in billions of US dollars, in parentheses percentage shares.
[2] Excluding estimated gaps in reporting (see Table B.2).
Source: Bank for International Settlements (2004) Triennial central bank survey of foreign exchange and derivatives market activity – preliminary global results, Basle, September, Table 2.

Table B.4   Maturities of forwards and swaps in the London market[1]

Instrument	1995	1998	2001	2004
Up to seven days	72	78	69	72
Over seven days and up to one year	28	21	30	27
Over one year	0.01	0.01	0.01	1

[1] Daily averages in April, in percent.
Source: Bank of England (2004) The UK Foreign Exchange Market and Over-the-counter Derivatives Market in April 2004, 28 September, Table 2.

a high degree of flexibility, which is one reason why their volume has risen so much in recent years and even replaced the spot market as the biggest foreign-exchange market segment.

Expecting a rise (fall) in the exchange rate a dealer may buy (sell) a currency spot and then, if expectations are not fulfilled in time or prospects continue to look favourable, prolong the position by a swap. The initial spot position is closed with the spot leg of the swap – and immediately reopened with the forward leg. The process can be repeated again and again. Each time, the forward position from one swap is closed with the spot leg of the next one and, again, reopened immediately with the forward leg, and so on. In all these cases, accounts are only credited or debited with the *difference*, i.e. the gain or loss occurring once a position is closed.

The policy lessons from these market technicalities are twofold.

First, the lack of information and transparency in the market calls for a modest approach, preferably involving the banks themselves in appealing to their overall responsibility. In the realm of international finance, in particular, there are many cases of voluntary self-restraint that may serve as a template. Examples are:

- the Model Code of the international association of foreign exchange dealers (the ACI or Association Cambiste Internationale) or, more recently;
- the Wolfsberg Principles, guidelines concerning anti-money laundering established by 12 international banks;
- the sound practices for banks' interactions with highly leveraged institutions issued by the Basle Committee on Banking Supervision in 1999, or;
- the Trading Principles concerning customer relations in foreign-exchange trading that leading financial intermediaries agreed on in February 2001 in reaction to mounting public worries.

Second, in order to contain currency crises in emerging markets a clear definition of policy goals is needed. In the current system there is no possibility – and, given the overall efficiency of the market, not much need – to control foreign-exchange trading at large. Instead, efforts should concentrate on emerging market currencies and the small group of international banks under the sphere of influence of the G7 countries dominating this market segment. Further, mixing poverty reduction or other goals with the aim of stabilising markets only risks rousing desires and sending the wrong signals thereby shifting attention from perhaps more feasible, but less profitable, solutions than the Tobin tax to this popular but highly ineffective, and probably even harmful, approach.

Additional Links and References

A summary of the debate on the Tobin tax is given in:

Wolf, Martin (2002) Misplaced hopes in Tobin's tax, *The Financial Times*, 20 March. http://globalarchive.ft.com/globalarchive/article.html?id = 020320002356&query = Misplaced + hopes + in + Tobin%27s + tax.

There is a Tobin tax initiative on the web where the main arguments and links to further groups supporting the plan such as Attac or War on Want can be found:

http://www.ceedweb.org/iirp/projdir.htm

For the latest global results on foreign-exchange market turnover and amounts outstanding published by the BIS see:

http://www.bis.org/

and for respective UK data:

http://www.bankofengland.co.uk

The paper mentioned stressing the role of settlement systems for the feasibility of the tax is:

Schmidt, Rodney (1999) A feasible foreign exchange transaction tax, The North-South Institute, Ottawa, http://www.currencytax.org/files/research_items/schmidt1999.pdf

Examples of estimates of tax revenues can be found in:

Wahl, Peter and Peter Waldow (2001) Currency transaction tax – a concept with a future, WEED Working Paper, World Economy, Ecology & Development Association (WEED), Bonn.

For information on the mentioned documents see:
For the Wolfsberg Principles

http://www.wolfsberg-principles.com/

Concerning the advantages and disadvantages of the Wolfsberg Principles and related approaches to international money laundering see also:

Winer, Jonathan M. (2002) Illicit Finance and Global Conflict, http://www.fafo.no/pub/rapp/380/380.pdf

For the Model Code of the ACI – the Financial Markets Association of foreign exchange dealers see:

http://www.aciforex.com/mktpractice/model_code.htm

For the Sound Practices for banks' interactions with highly leveraged institutions issued by the Basle Committee on Banking Supervision see:

Basle Committee on Banking Supervision (1999) Sound practices for banks' interactions with highly leveraged institutions, Basel Committee Publications No. 46. http://www.bis.org/publ/bcbs46.htm#pgtop

The principles concerning customer relations in foreign-exchange trading of leading banks are reprinted in:

Progress in implementing the recommendations of the working group on highly leveraged institutions (HLIs), note to the FSF by the chairman of the HLI Working Group, March 2001, http://www.fsforum.org/publications/publication_21_24.html

The monetary arrangement in the CFA franc zone in Africa is a colonial heritage. When the CFA was established in December 1945 the term originally stood for *Colonies françaises d'Afrique* (French colonies of Africa). In 1958, it changed to *Communauté française d'Afrique* (French Community of Africa) and today it is known as *Communauté Financière Africaine* (African Financial Community).

There are two regions with currencies called CFA franc with the same fixed value guaranteed by France and two institutions issuing CFA franc which are located in Dakar (Senegal) and Yaoundé (Cameroon). These are:

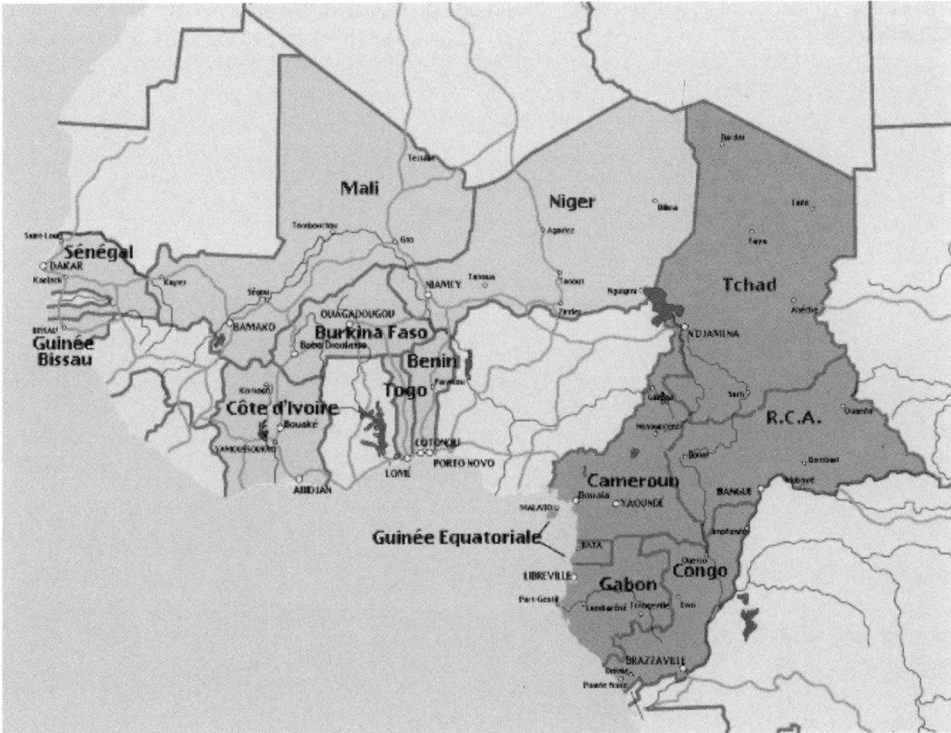

Figure C.1   CFA franc zone. *Source*: http://www.izf.net/izf/Documentation/Cartes/Zone.htm

- The eight countries of the West African Economic and Monetary Union (UEMOA): Benin, Burkina Faso, Côte d'Ivoire, Guinea-Bissau, Mali, Niger, Senegal and Togo. Their currency is the *Communauté Financière en Afrique centrale franc BCEAO* (Central Bank of West African States).
- The six countries of the Central African Economic and Monetary Community (CEMAC) with the *Coopération financière en Afrique centrale franc BEAC* (Central Bank of Central African States): Cameroon, Central African Republic, Chad, Republic of the Congo, Equatorial Guinea and Gabon.

Since January 1994, the value of the CFA franc has been fixed to 0.01 French franc, which means that since the launch of the common currency in Europe in January 1999 it has been worth 0.00152449 euro. At this rate, the French Treasury guarantees unlimited liquidity in euro.

The prospective shift of the peg of the CFA franc from the French franc to the euro raised a couple of questions concerning the nature of the monetary relation between France and the African nations and the role of other EMU members. The general view is that while the Maastricht Treaty left some room for interpretation in this matter the free convertibility of CFA francs into euros by France must be regarded as a budgetary arrangement between the French Treasury and the central banks of the CFA franc zone and not as an exchange rate arrangement affecting all EMU countries.

The relationship between Europe and the CFA franc zone is a very unequal one. While economic relations with Europe are important for the African countries, the aggregated GDP of members of the CFA franc zone is only 0.5% of the GDP of the euro area.

Recently, there have been discussions about whether the CFA franc zone could be a model for monetary coordination in other regions. However, member countries are extremely diverse, economic interdependence between them is low (which is partly explained by the lack of infrastructure hindering trade), they are heavily indebted and highly dependent on exports of very different primary goods, foreign investment other than of companies exploiting natural resources is of minor importance and there exist strong market imperfections. All this makes them improbable candidates of an optimal currency area or model for others.

Appendix D
Rating Agencies

There are 130 to 150 credit rating agencies in the world, but only three are recognised worldwide: Standard & Poor's, Moody's Investor Service and Fitch Ratings. These three are present in most countries and have a universal rating scale and their market share of revenues is over 90% (Table D.1).

Rating agencies evaluate a debtor or debt instrument and assign a grade that is intended to reflect the relative creditworthiness, i.e. the relative probability of default, compared to other debtors or debt instruments. There is a long history of credit rating which started in the nineteenth century in the United States when the railroad industry began to expand across the continent and into undeveloped territories and raised capital through the bond market.

Standard & Poor's is the oldest agency. Poor's Publishing was established in 1860 by Henry Varnum Poor, who in 1868 published the *Manual of the Railroads in the United States* containing operating and financial statistics and other information on the business conditions of the newly emerging borrowers. In 1941, the firm merged with Standard Statistics, which was founded in 1906, and since 1916 assigned debt ratings to corporate bonds and sovereign debt.

Moody's Investor Services was established in New York in 1900. In 1909, the firm became the first to issue credit ratings in the United States. By 1924, Moody's ratings covered almost 100% of the US bond market and continued to publish and monitor ratings even during the Great Depression.

Fitch Publishing Company was founded in 1913, again in New York. It began as a publisher of financial statistics. In 1924, Fitch introduced the now familiar rating scale from AAA to D. In 1997, Fitch merged with IBCA, London, increasing its worldwide presence in banking, financial institutions and sovereigns. Today the firm is owned by a holding company, FIMALAC, Paris, and has dual headquarters in New York and London.

The ratings of the Big Three follow largely the same scheme although they differ slightly in interpretation (Table D.2). Ratings range from AAA which is the highest quality to D standing for payment default. The list in the table is not exhaustive with further categories existing between the classes shown here. Debt rated BB or lower is regarded as having significant speculative characteristics and is often refered to as 'high yield', 'speculative grade' or 'junk' in contrast to 'investment grade' debt with a higher rating. The investment grade distinction is important for investors following a conservative strategy, either deliberately or in complying to official regulation.

Issue credit ratings can be either long term or short term with the latter generally assigned to obligations considered short term in the relevant market. There are corporate ratings and sovereign ratings.

Table D.1 Revenues in the global rating industry 2001

Company	Revenues[1]	Market share of revenues[2]
Standard & Poor's	870	41
Moody's	797	38
Fitch	302	14
Others	132	6

[1] In billions of US dollars.
[2] In percent.
Source: Financial Times.

Table D.2 Standard & Poor's, Moody's and Fitch notation

Standard & Poor's	Moody's	Fitch	Description[1]
AAA	Aaa	AAA	Highest quality
AA	Aa	AA	High quality
A	A	A	Still strong
BBB	Baa	BBB	Medium grade
BB	Ba	BB	Slightly speculative
B	B	B	Poor, but still capacity
CCC	Caa	CCC	Capacity depending upon favourable circumstances

[1] Similar ratings across agencies have slightly different meanings. This one is the author's interpretation following Standard & Poor's.

Part of the analysis of any issuer or issue are considerations about country-risk and the currency of repayment taking into account that a debtor's capacity to repay foreign currency debt may be lower than the ability to repay local currency debt.

Rating agencies use a combination of quantitative and qualitative factors. Studies have shown that differences in ratings assigned to sovereign borrowers can be mostly attributed to a few determinants. These include per capita income, GDP growth, external debt burden, inflation experience and default history. Fitch has drawn some criticism for using sophisticated econometrics and neural networks in cases of limited samples of sovereign nations and sovereign defaults despite the known limitations of this approach.

Corporate ratings help companies and governments to get access to markets and improve their costs of funding. However, their use differs across regions. While in the US corporate sector ratings are so integrated into investors' thinking that there is a direct correlation between a rating and the cost of finance, Europe is still lagging behind. Europeans see the role of the rating agencies rather with suspicion. In February 2004, the European Parliament rejected a proposal to create a European registration authority to supervise rating agencies, but it asked the European Commission to review this issue and present its conclusions by July 2005.

During the last decade, rating agencies have been criticised for becoming increasingly influential in market behaviour. In some cases, their decisions to downgrade sovereign debt accelerated capital outflows from crisis-prone countries making an already bad situation worse. One often cited example is their treatment of South Korea during the Asian crisis. The country, which in October 1997 was still rated at the same level as Sweden and Italy, found itself downgraded to junk status a few months later. The agencies were also criticised for their role in corporate crises such as the decline of the energy trading sector in the US after the Enron collapse. In continuing to downgrade energy traders during the crisis they made it ever more expensive for the firms to obtain financing and continue operations.

These and other examples show the crucial role that ratings play in today's financial markets giving the agencies a tremendous responsibility. They also illustrate the constant dilemma of the industry. Often accused in the past for failing to spot a crisis and making rating changes too late, the rating agencies themselves may become a risk to the markets when frequent downgradings are raising overall credit risks.

The agencies' role and responsibility will even grow under Basel II. The new rules make it near mandatory for banks to use the credit ratings of the Big Three when calculating how much capital to set aside against bonds and loans. Under the standardised approach of Basel II external ratings will serve to measure the risk sensitivity of corporate, sovereign and interbank exposures. Banks will distinguish between unrated exposures and those rated by a recognised rating agency. For rated corporate and sovereign exposures the weight will depend on the rating while for the unrated it will be 100% (Table D.3).

Table D.3   Percentage risk weights under Basel II

Exposure to	AAA to AA−	A+ to A−	BBB+ to BBB−	BB+ to BB−	B+ to B−	Below B and defaulted	Unrated
Sovereigns	0	20	50	100	100	150	100
Banks 1	20	50	100	100	100	150	100
Banks 2 < 3 months	20	20	20	50	50	150	20
>3 months	20	50	50	100	100	150	50
Corporates	20	50	100	100	150	150	100

Source: Jackson, Patricia (2002) Bank capital: Basel II developments, in *Bank of England: Financial Stability Review*, December, Table A, http://www.bankofengland.co.uk/fsr/fsr1art3.pdf

For interbank exposures there are two options. Under the first one (Bank 1 in the table) risk weighting will be based on the weighting of the sovereign of the country in which the bank is incorporated. Under the second option (Bank 2) it will be based on assessment of the individual bank. For the latter approach exposures of less than three-month maturity will receive preferential treatment.

Additional Links and References

For the determinants of sovereign ratings and their impact on market volatility see, for example:

Cantor, Richard and Frank Packer (1996) Determinants and impact of sovereign credit ratings, *Federal Reserve Bank of New York Economic Policy Review*, October, 37–53, http://www.newyorkfed.org/research/epr/96v02n2/9610cant.pdf

Reisen, Helmut and Julia von Maltzan (1998) Sovereign credit ratings, emerging market risk and financial market volatility, HWWA Discussion Paper No. 55, http://www.hwwa.de/Publikationen/Discussion_Paper/1998/55.pdf

Setty, Gautam and Randall Dodd (2003) Credit rating agencies: their impact on capital flows to developing countries, Financial Policy Forum, Derivatives Study Center, Special Policy Report No. 6, http://www.financialpolicy.org/FPFSPR6.pdf

Nouriel Roubini's Global Macroeconomic and Financial Policy Site at the Stern School of Business, New York University includes a very detailed site on rating agencies:

http://www.stern.nyu.edu/globalmacro/Sovereign_debt/credit_rating_agencies.htm

For further information see also the sites of the Big Three:

http://www.moodys.com/cust/default_alt.asp
http://www.fitchratings.com/corporate/index.cfm
http://www2.standardandpoors.com/NASApp/cs/ContentServer?pagename = sp/Page/HomePg&r = 1&l = EN

The theory of optimum currency areas, which dates back to the early 1960s and 1970s, tries to answer the question under which conditions a country should join a fixed exchange rate area. The concept was developed in the Bretton Woods era when major Western currencies were fixed to the US dollar. When the Bretton Woods system was abandoned in the early 1970s, interest in the theory waned, but with plans to introduce a common currency in Europe at the beginning of the 1990s, and again with the EU accession of countries from Central and Eastern Europe, it experienced a kind of renaissance. The revival of the theory was also reflected in the 1999 award of the Nobel prize to Robert Mundell, one of its founding fathers.

The basic idea is that a floating exchange rate may cushion an economy from the effects of external disturbances but also has disadvantages. For instance, relative prices become less predictable and governments' efforts to fight inflation may be less effective than under fixed exchange rates. However, joining a group with mutually fixed exchange rates has advantages and disadvantages, too, and the theory of optimum currency areas provides the tools for analysing its prospects.

The costs and benefits for a country of joining a fixed exchange rate area are illustrated in Figure E.1. The benefits are represented by the GG schedule. Above all, these are gains in monetary efficiency as a fixed exchange rate reduces the uncertainties and transaction costs associated with a floating rate. They are supposed to rise with increasing economic integration between the joining country and the exchange rate area. The costs of joining are represented by the downward sloping LL schedule. It consists mainly of the loss of an instrument of economic policy – the exchange rate or the money supply – for stabilising domestic output and employment. This cost is reduced with increasing economic integration since the latter is assumed to reduce economic instability and thereby the loss from the inavailability of the exchange rate instrument.

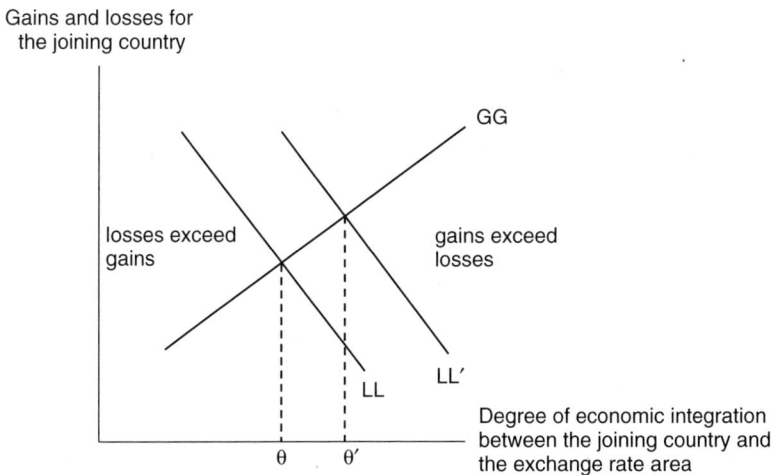

Figure E.1 The costs and benefits for a country of joining a fixed exchange rate area

The conclusion drawn from these considerations is that the country should join the fixed exchange rate area as soon as the economic benefits exceed the cost, with the critical level determined by the intersection of GG and LL.

Now consider what happens if the cost is rising, for example, because the size and frequency of country-specific disturbances to the joining country's product markets are increasing. This shifts the LL schedule upward to LL': for a given level of economic integration with the fixed exchange rate area the country's cost for not being able to use the exchange rate instrument to fight the disturbances rises. As a consequence, the critical level for joining shifts from θ to θ' – the degree of economic integration must be higher for offering an incentive for the country to join.

What characterises an optimum currency area in this framework? Optimum currency areas are groups of countries or regions with economies closely linked by trade relations and factor mobility because in these cases the gains from joining a fixed exchange rate area for a country are high and likely to exceed the related cost.

Is the EU an optimum currency area? Looking at trade figures this can be doubted. On average, intra-European trade is low and the factor labour in the region is still highly immobile. On the other hand, integration in both goods and labour markets is much higher between European countries than with other regions which, for example, makes the prospect for coming to a trilateral exchange rate arrangement with the United States and Japan, as discussed in economic literature, even less promising.

However, the definition of optimality in the present framework is vague and depends on the factors included. For example, one argument for a trilateral worldwide monetary cooperation is not trade or labour mobility but the mobility of capital and the high degree of substitutability between assets denominated in US dollar, yen and euro.

One pitfall of the theory is its emphasis on current circumstances. One of the aims of EMU is to promote economic integration in Europe in the long run and in this case the initial conditions at joining matter less than the expected future gains from fixed exchange rates. In particular, this argument holds for the new member states from Central and Eastern Europe which hope to become closer – and more rapidly – integrated by joining the common currency gradually more and more fulfilling the conditions of an optimum currency area.

Additional Links and References

For a brief description of the theory of optimum currency areas see

Krugman, Paul R. and Maurice Obstfeld (1997) *International Economics – Theory and Policy*, Reading, MA: Addison-Wesley.

The classic studies on optimum currency areas are:

Kenen, Peter (1969) The theory of optimum currency areas: an eclectic view, in Robert A. Mundell and Alexander K. Swoboda (eds) *Monetary Problems of the International Economy*, Chicago: University of Chicago Press, pp. 41–60.

McKinnon, Ronald (1963) Optimum currency areas, *American Economic Review*, **53**, 717–25.

Mundell, Robert A. (1961) A theory of optimum currency areas, *American Economic Review*, **51**, 657–65.

For further information on the person and the theory see also the home page of Robert Mundell:

http://www.columbia.edu/~ram15/

A detailed overview of the theoretical and empirical literature on optimum currency areas is given in:

Horvath, Julius (2003) Optimum currency area theory: a selective review, Bank of Finland, Institute for Economies in Transition (BOFIT) Discussion Paper No. 15, http://www.bof.fi/bofit/fin/6dp/03abs/pdf/dp1503.pdf

Appendix F
Luxembourg

Luxembourg's beginnings as an international financial centre date back to the 1960s. The same US tax on borrowing that brought the international bond market to London helped Luxembourg become a centre of syndicated loans. In summer 2002, there were 185 banks in the Grand Duchy, with a total of about €720 billion of assets and 24,000 employees. The banking sector is the country's most important industry accounting for one-quarter of its GDP.

In the past, Luxembourg's biggest competitive advantage was its success in attracting investors seeking to avoid paying taxes in other countries. Its financial business is largely dominated by German banks which got a boost in the 1980s when German savers moved their money to Luxembourg in reaction to a new withholding tax in Germany. Today 49 German banks represent the largest single group of foreign financial institutions.

Why did rich Germans turn to Luxembourg and not to secrecy-promising and tax-free Switzerland? The answer is that German banks had a presence in Luxembourg allowing them to enjoy confidentiality and at the same time sparing them the cost and inconvenience of opening a new account. The Germans are not alone: there are another 120 mostly foreign institutions offering private banking services for high net-worth individuals in Luxembourg – including 13 Swiss banks.

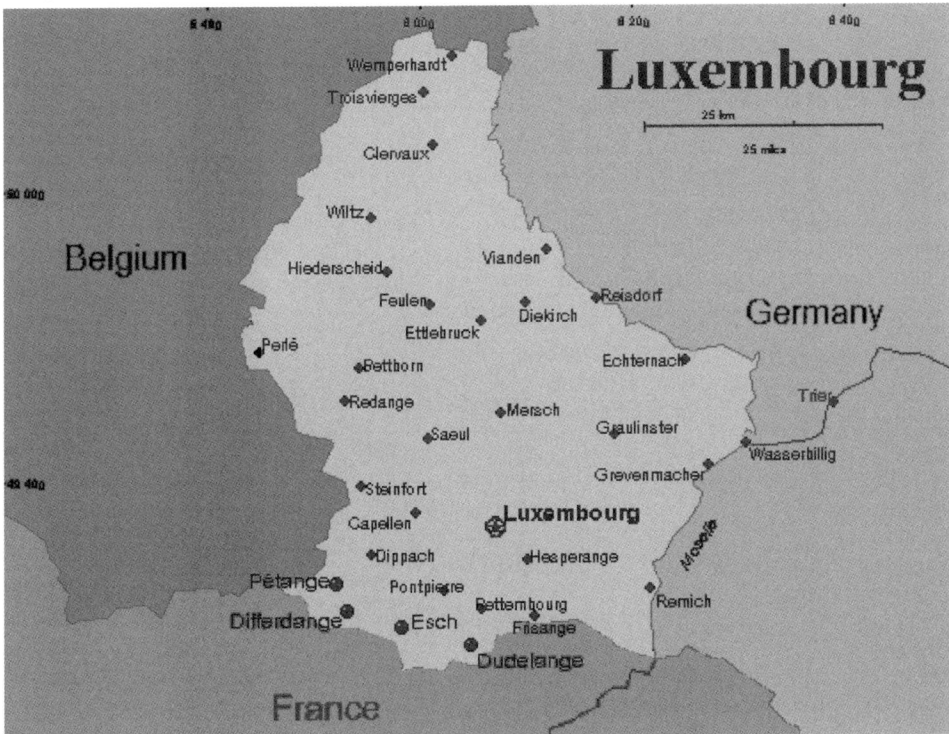

Figure F.1   Luxembourg

One of Luxembourg's strongholds is the investment fund sector. Luxembourg is the European Number Two in the industry which held a market share of 23% (France 24%, Germany 20%) in 2004. The same year, the value of funds under management in Luxembourg was €1034 billion. In 2001, there were 1908 funds, and the number of portfolios on offer to investors was 7519 fund units. Almost one-third of the funds were legally able to market their units freely throughout the European Union. Net assets of bond funds were €360.7 billion, the value of assets in pure equity funds was €337.3 billion. Funds of Swiss origin were the Number One, followed by American funds. One of Luxembourg's latest rivals in this business in Europe is Ireland. Previously a base for institutional funds, Dublin is recently pursuing retail business and is well placed to exploit new opportunities in more innovative products.

The fund industry has grown virtually from scratch over little more than a decade. Traditionally, Luxembourg's success as a financial centre was based on its ability to transpose European directives more rapidly than potential rivals in other EU states, which was facilitated by a compact legislature of only 60 members allowing fast enactment of laws. In 1985, a directive was passed allowing funds based in one European country to be marketed and sold throughout the Community. Luxembourg was the first to implement the directive in 1988 which was facilitated by the fact that a mutual fund sector of sorts had already existed in the country.

As the EU drives ahead with financial liberalisation, Luxembourg expands beyond its traditional banking activities. Beside the *niches of sovereignty* that allowed the country to benefit from national legislation by offering financial services unavailable in other countries, it is now searching for *niches of competence* profiting from the specialisation, know-how and experience of its banking sector. The country passed a law allowing fund investment in asset-backed securities, reduced subscription tax on assets for some classes of funds and opened the way for pension pooled vehicles. However, one hindrance for cross-border pension funds is the still incomplete EU single market in pensions and existing tax barriers. An additional advantage is the ability for hedge funds to list cheaply in Luxembourg – in particular with regard to pension funds that do not buy unlisted companies. In 2004, the country was home to about 100 hedge funds with more than €30 billion in assets.

Luxembourg's performance is threatened by the loss of tax haven status. A withholding tax is levied which in accordance with an agreement reached between the country and other EU governments will be

- 15% from 15 January 2005 to 31 December 2007;
- 20% from 1 January 2008 to 31 December 2010; and
- 35% from 1 January 2011.

However, products are affected by the tax in different ways (Table F.1). For instance, savings portfolios with less than 40% in bonds are exempt from the tax which, in principle, makes it possible for holders to simply shift assets from bonds to stocks to circumvent it.

Table F.1 Financial products affected by the withholding tax

Product		
Monetary products	Issued before 1 March 2001	Issued after 1 March 2001
Bonds		Issued after 1 March 2001
Investment fund governed by Luxembourg law	If a dividend is paid	In case of sale or redemption
Bond fund	If a dividend is paid	In case of sale or redemption
Balanced fund		
From 40%	If a dividend is paid	In case of sale or redemption
From 15 to 40%	If a dividend is paid	–
Less than 15%	–	–
Equity fund	–	–

Source: Financial Times.

In the negotiations with its EU partners Luxembourg insisted that its main rivals in private banking in Europe had to follow suit. As a consequence, a withholding tax also applies in Switzerland, Andorra, Monaco, Liechtenstein, the Cayman Islands and the Channel Islands. However, other competitors worldwide are standing in line to benefit from the new regulation. There are estimates that the tax will cause €1000 billion to flow out of Luxembourg and Switzerland and into Asian tax havens such as Singapore and Hong Kong.

Appendix G
Nonlinearities

In the 1990s, new technologies and computing facilities led to a renewed interest in certain 'anomalies' in the statistical properties of financial time series which had been well known for many years but largely due to computational limits had not been studied in depth. Financial data show some characteristic *stylised facts* that taken together raise doubts on the validity of linear equilibrium models of determinants of financial market prices and the respective assumption underlying empirical studies that these prices are normally distributed fluctuating around a mean which represents the theoretically found equilibrium value.

The first hints to existing 'anomalies' date back to the 1960s when *Benoît Mandelbrot* published a paper on 'The Variation of Certain Speculative Prices'. In his work, Mandelbrot focused on two peculiarities which, referring to the Old Testament, he called the Joseph and the Noah effect. These are an extremely long-range persistence in the data and a non-constant variance, respectively.

The *Joseph effect* points to the biblical story of the seven fat and seven lean years. It describes *very long-run dependencies* with large positive or negative values tending to be followed by large values of the same sign. Under the influence of the Joseph effect the time series seems to go through a *succession of cycles*, including very long ones with a wavelength extending over the total sample size. However, a closer look reveals that these cycles are mere *artefacts*. This can be demonstrated by means of spectral analysis.

In *spectral analyses*, stochastic processes are *decomposed* into a number of components. For example, these may be seasonal, cyclical and trend factors and – although spectral analyses do not depend on the specification of a model – ideally each of them is associated with a theoretically well-founded frequency. Then, the *power spectrum* shows the contribution of each component to the total variance of the process.

Figure G.1 shows the typical spectral shape of a speculative price variable. A concentration at low frequencies as in this case typically indicates the importance of an influence with a wavelength just equal to, or greater than, the length of the series.

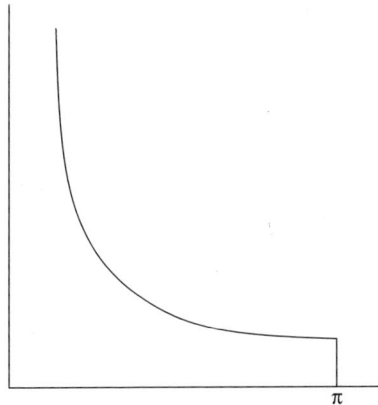

Figure G.1   Long-run persistence

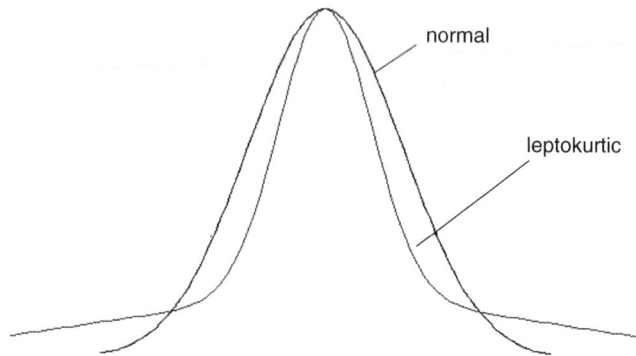

Figure G.2   Fat tails

However, the striking observation is that for many financial prices this shape can be found regardless of the number of observations and regardless of whether, for example, monthly, weekly or daily data are studied. The data exhibit a kind of *self-similarity* in that, except for a scale factor, the variations roughly show *recurring patterns*. Apparently, they go through cycles as indicated by the spectrum, but these *cycles are not stable*. Whenever the length of the series is widened or shortened the cycle length changes as well. The conclusion drawn from this observation was that there are very long-run *non-periodic dependencies* influencing price movements.

One implication of the Joseph effect is that the normal distribution hypothesis, although still *justified for short series* where the long-run persistence is not so manifest, appears no longer valid with the lengthening of the sample period.

The *Noah effect* refers to the emergence of unusually high outliers coming and going like a spring tide. Different samples of the same series of prices appear different because under this effect sample variances vary erratically and nothing like 'the' population variance can be estimated. Compared to a normal distribution there are too many small variations while at the same time the price jumps observed are too large, a phenomenon also discussed in the literature as *leptokurtosis* or *fat tails*. In Figure G.2, the black line illustrates a normal curve and the red line a leptokurtic one with fewer observations of smaller price changes and more observations of higher ones.

If both effects come together the implications for the statistical modelling of financial prices are severe. While under the Joseph effect for short time periods both the assumption of normal distribution and the traditional linearity assumption of standard economic models are still valid, the existence of a non-constant variance allows keeping the latter only by sacrificing the former. For series that exhibit both effects the linearity assumption has to be given up once and for all, as Mandelbrot puts it, 'for the sake of coexistence'.

This result, if taken literally, is a big challenge to both economic theory and empirical modelling:

- Self-similarity and scale invariance of a series make the distinction between the short run and the long run flawed when, on the one hand, deterministic effects of any length overlap, building upon one another like cascades, thereby making prices fluctuate independent of any stochastic interference and, on the other, smallest influences are persistent affecting the behaviour of the series for a long time.
- Traditional statistical methods are not of much use in these cases. For example, for existing alternatives to the normal distribution least-square estimates are not reliable; they give too much weight to outliers and are too dependent on the sample chosen.
- Time series models assuming finite processes such as ARMA (autoregressive moving average) models remain unsatisfactory because, usually, they assume finite processes while the Joseph effect can be thought of as an influence passed on to infinity.

- Spectral analyses offer no solution either. They decompose a series into a sum of periodic harmonic components while the Joseph effect stands for an infinite long dependence with the appearing individual cycles being mere artefacts.

In financial economics, the reactions to these findings were divided. A small group of scholars concentrated their research efforts on – almost exclusively empirical – studies searching for traces of nonlinear *deterministic* behaviour in financial prices. However, without theory, i.e. an underlying knowledge of the 'true' relations driving market prices, the search for 'chaos' (as this sort of phenomenon became known in a wide variety of disciplines) in financial data is like looking for a needle in a haystack. Accordingly, with few exceptions, it was given up quickly.

The larger group decided to neglect the implications of self-similarity and scale invariance for the distinction of short term and long term, and of stochastic and deterministic, and consider the acknowledged nonlinear nature of financial prices as a *stochastic* phenomenon which can be grasped by modelling the variance of the process, for example, by assuming some kind of GARCH process. Although regarded as extremely useful by applicants of these models in the markets, the approach must appear somewhat unsatisfactory to the purist who cannot help feeling that here an opportunity to develop an understanding of the processes driving market volatility has been missed.

Additional Links and References

The Mandelbrot citation is from:

Mandelbrot, Benoît (1969) Long-run linearity, locally Gaussian process, H-spectra and infinite variances, *International Economic Review*, 1, 82–111.

For the typical spectral shape not only of financial prices but also many other economic variables see:

Granger, C.W.J. (1966): The typical spectral shape of an economic variable, *Econometrica*, **34**(1), 150–61.

A general overview of deterministic nonlinearities in economic time series is given in:

Frank, M. and T. Stengos (1988) Chaotic dynamics in economic time series, *Journal of Economic Surveys*, **2**, 103–33.

One rare approach trying to explain chaotic dynamics in foreign-exchange rates is:

De Grauwe, Paul, Hans Dewachter and Mark Embrechts (1993) *Exchange Rate Theory: Chaotic Models of Foreign Exchange Markets*, Oxford: Blackwell.

One of the first authors applying chaos theory and related statistical concepts to a variety of financial markets was:

Peters, Edgar E. (1991) *Chaos and Order in the Capital Markets*, New York: John Wiley & Sons, Inc.

and from the same author

Peters, Edgar E. (1994) *Fractal Market Analysis*, New York: John Wiley & Sons, Inc.

A recent approach which interprets financial markets as nonlinear systems exhibiting complex dynamics and which explains stock market crashes as critical events is presented in:

Sornette, Didier (2004) *Why Stock Markets Crash – Critical Events in Complex Financial Systems*, Princeton, NJ: Princeton University Press.

Appendix H
Value at Risk

Value at risk (VAR) is a *price sensitivity analysis* which measures how the potential losses in a portfolio's total value vary under changing market conditions. This instrument was developed as an alternative to traditional asset-and-liabilities management (ALM) where future estimated earnings are projected periodically under assumed market scenarios with the results reported according to generally accepted accounting principles, mostly on an accrual basis. With the growing use of off-balance-sheet instruments, such as options, ALM became less reliable.

Options differ in many respects from other cash and derivative instruments. Option contracts are *contingent claims* based on the insurance principle that makes the calculation of the stream of future cash flows impossible. Further, the distribution of risks between the contracting parties is not symmetric as for other derivatives where the risk of loss for the one mirrors the chance of profit for the other. In addition, their sensitivity to changes in market conditions is different. In contrast to other instruments, the relationship between a price change of the underlying instrument and the derivative is not linear but depends on the interplay of a variety of determinants that leave broad room for interpretation. Furthermore, those influences may change very rapidly thereby adding to the existing uncertainties.

There is no generally accepted model for *options pricing*. Most approaches are in one form or another based on the Black–Scholes method giving a formula in which the price of an option is determined by the current price of the underlying instrument, the option's exercise price, its remaining life time, the interest-rate level and the projected volatility of the underlying instrument. In contrast to most other financial instruments, these factors combine in a way that the relation between position value and market rate does not allow expected changes in value to be estimated by multiplying expected price changes by a given constant sensitivity of the position to changes.

The increasing use of off-balance-sheet instruments was only one driving force for the development of a new concept for measuring financial risks. Another was the desire to build a consistent framework that accounts for *interdependencies* between markets and instruments, different probabilities of returns and losses for different financial products and the risk-reducing capacities of *diversification strategies*.

VAR analysis has its roots in portfolio theory, which does not focus on the performance of an individual financial instrument but on the interaction between different risks and returns. Also known as *mean-variance approach* it assumes that investors choose between portfolios on the basis of expected returns and their volatility with the standard deviation or variance of returns as risk measure. Taking into account return *correlations*, portfolio diversification maximises the expected return for a given standard deviation of the portfolio or minimises the standard deviation for any given expected return. The implicit or explicit assumption behind most versions of this approach is that returns are *normally distributed*. The existence of other, mathematically less tractable, stochastic behaviours of many financial instruments is acknowledged in accompanying textbooks and manuals, but in practice the consequences are rarely accepted.

What does a typical VAR model look like, what are its main components and how is the final result (denoting the amount of capital needed to cover potential losses) derived? The rationale behind the VAR approach can be demonstrated by a widely used system developed by the US investment bank JP Morgan, *RiskMetrics*.

When RiskMetrics was made available to the public in 1994 it offered information on rates and volatilities, and over 100,000 correlations between more than 300 financial instruments in 15 markets. The model consists of several *building blocks* that distinguish between various kinds of positions,

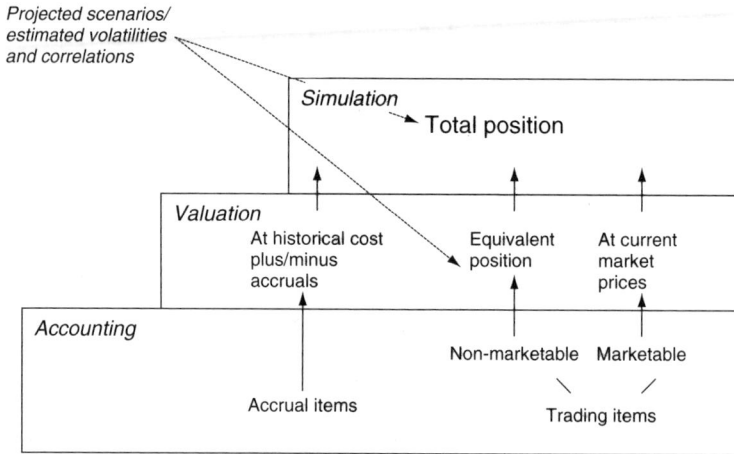

Figure H.1   Stages of risk analysis

which differ in their valuation treatment. Calculation of the VaR proceeds in three steps, from accounting to valuation to simulation (Figure H.1).

At the *accounting level* a line is drawn between accrual items – all those positions that are still measured at historical costs plus/minus accruals – and trading items, with the latter further divided into marketable and non-marketable instruments. At the *valuation level* those items for which a liquid secondary market exists are valued at the current value quoted in this market. Transactions for which no market value exists, but which can be decomposed into parts that do have a market value, are treated as a combination of cash flows from these parts and than mapped into so-called equivalent positions. Here, the value is approximated as the sum of market values of the component cash flows.

What happens with non-marketable items such as *options*? In these cases, an option-pricing model is used to revalue the portfolio over a set of postulated price changes. Those price changes, in turn, are gained either from a scenario approach or a simulation method. While the former focuses on a more limited number of specific price movements, the latter covers a more continuous range of changes and their effects on the entire portfolio.

For option valuation itself, two broad alternatives exist. One is the *full valuation* method where the potential loss is the difference between the value of the portfolio at potentially changed rates and at the original rate with the portfolio being continuously revalued at each price change. The other is *delta valuation* calculating the sensitivities of the positions to changes in rates multiplied by the potential changes in rates. Then the delta value is the net portfolio value given as the arithmetic sum of the deltas of all instruments and transactions in the portfolio. There are several possible modifications to increase the accuracy of the approach such as by incorporating the gamma value in addition taking into account the risk that the delta changes with variations of the price of the underlying instrument or by considering the effects of volatility changes on option prices.

The last step is the *simulation* of the effects of expected changes in market rates and prices on the value of the entire portfolio. Again, there are two alternatives. The potential price and rate changes are calculated either by designing specific scenarios or by using estimated volatilities and correlations. In those cases where the value of a position is affected only by a single rate, depending on the approach chosen, the change in value of that position is a function either of the rates in each of the projected scenarios or of the volatility of that rate estimated by a model. If the potential change in value depends on multiple rates it is a function of either the combination of those rates in each scenario or of each volatility and each correlation between all pairs of volatilities.

Market characteristics

Price distribution:

- normal
  $\Rightarrow$ volatilities,
  correlations

- non-normal
  $\Rightarrow$ scenarios

Functional relation:

- linear
  $\Rightarrow$ sensitivity
  analysis

- non-linear
  $\Rightarrow$ simulations

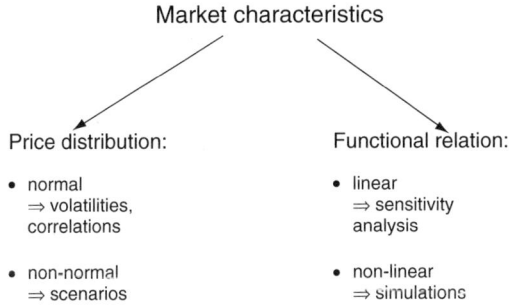

Figure H.2   Analysis tools and market environment

RiskMetrics does not propagate a uniform approach to risk estimation but acknowledges the need to *combine* diverse concepts to account for different market conditions and environments. The latter can be divided into two main categories (Figure H.2). First, *distributions* of rate and price movements may differ. Estimating volatilities and correlations with traditional statistical means is the best method in cases where rate and price movements can be statistically described as normally distributed, but they become unreliable if the normality assumption does not hold. Then the danger of sudden unexpected market movements should be taken into account explicitly with the help of scenarios. Another aspect is the *functional relationship* between the value of a position and changes in rates and prices. If this relation is approximately linear, the position value can be best calculated by means of sensitivity analyses. However, for changes in non-linear positions, such as options, simulations are considered a more effective tool.

RiskMetrics is not the only VAR approach, and since its introduction many other systems have been developed. Not all of them are based on portfolio theory. Some exclusively, or in addition, use other risk measurement techniques. In general, several components of the VAR methodology can be distinguished:

- The *variance–covariance approach* based on portfolio theory and the assumption of normally distributed returns. Its advantage is mathematical tractability.
- The *historical simulation* approach based on historical data to construct the distribution of portfolio returns from which the VAR is read off. The advantage is that the method does not rely on a particular distribution assumption. The disadvantage is that its result depends strongly on the data set used.
- The *Monte Carlo simulation* where the distribution is derived from a large number of simulated random paths that returns could follow. The assumption is that with a sufficiently large number of simulations the resulting distribution, from which the VAR is inferred, will converge towards the unknown true distribution of portfolio returns. The advantage is that the technique is very powerful and able to handle almost any kind of position. The drawback is that it is very difficult and time consuming.
- *Stress testing* or scenario analysis. This is not part of the actual VAR estimation but rather complements it in order to account for the vulnerability of portfolios to unusual events. Value at risk is a measure of potential losses due to 'normal' market movements, which must fail in times of financial turmoil. However, stress tests have two major drawbacks. One is the entirely subjective nature of the scenarios and assumptions. The second is the often poor handling of correlations as these tests tend to focus on the effects of a large move in one or few variables.

In recent years, the VAR methodology has been extended to other risk categories, in particular *credit risk*. Traditionally, credit risk was treated as the likelihood of default for individual borrowers. The new approach tries to estimate the volatility of the value of a credit portfolio due to changes in overall credit quality taking into account correlations and changes in value resulting not only from possible default events but also from up- and downgrades in creditworthiness. Similar to the case of market risk, a portfolio approach to credit risk management is chosen in order to systematically address *concentration risk*. The latter is defined as the additional portfolio risk caused by an increased exposure to individual borrowers, industries or regions.

There are four practical reasons given for adopting this approach instead of limiting the analysis to the individual borrower.

1. The increasing *complexity* of financial products including derivatives, which imposes additional challenges to the management of credit risk.
2. The proliferation of *credit enhancement mechanisms* such as third-party guarantees, posted collateral, margin arrangements and netting that call for an assessment of the related risks at the portfolio level in addition to the individual level.
3. The opportunities for more active *management of credit risk* created by improved liquidity in secondary cash markets and the emergence of credit derivatives.
4. The explicit value innovative *new credit instruments* derive from correlation estimates or credit events such as up- and downgrades and defaults.

Market and credit risk differ in several respects. While market risk management focuses on rates and prices, credit risk management has to pay additional attention to default probabilities, recovery rates in defaults and the identity of counterparties. Market risk management considers relatively short time horizons, credit risk usually exists over a much longer horizon. The normality assumption is even less valid for credit risk analysis than for market risk evaluation, since on the one hand it is harder to justify over longer horizons and on the other the occurrence of events is less frequent in the case of credit risk. Controlling market risks means trying to impose limits on individual behaviour within the organisation, while the control of credit risk refers to another party, the counterparty, taken as a whole. In contrast to market risk, credit risk is surrounded by legal uncertainties such as the legal status of netting agreements or the ownership of collateral in default.

Additional Links and References

The VAR concept and its applications to different financial instruments and portfolios are explained in:

Dowd, Kevin (1998) Beyond Value at Risk, Chichester: John Wiley & Sons, Ltd.
Jorion, Philippe (1997) *Value at Risk: The New Benchmark for Controlling Market Risk*, Chicago: Irwin.

A detailed discussion of VAR concepts can be found in the technical documents of JP Morgan for various risk categories:

http://www.riskmetrics.com/techdoc.html

There is a website by Barry Schachter on many aspects of VAR providing additional information, links and references:

http://www.gloriamundi.org/about.asp

Appendix I
Legend to the FESE Diagram of the European Exchanges

(SE = Stock Exchange) June 2004

Cash Markets

EU – EEA – EFTA

AMS	Euronext Amsterdam	LIS	Euronext Lisbon	STO	Stockholmsbörsen
ATH	Athens Exchange	LJU	Ljubljana Stock Exchange	STU	Stuttgart Stock Exchange
BAR	Barcelona Stock Exchange	LON	London Stock Exchange	SWX	SWX Swiss Exchange
BER	Berlin Stock Exchange	LUX	Luxembourg Stock Exchange	TAL	HEX Tallinn
BIL	Bilbao Stock Exchange	MAD	Madrid Stock Exchange	VAL	Valencia Stock Exchange
BME	Bolsas & Mercados Españoles	MAL	Malta Stock Exchange	VIE	Wiener Börse AG
BRA	Bratislava Stock Exchange	MUC	Munich Stock Exchange	VIL	Nat. SE of Lithuania (Vilnius)
BRE	Bremen Stock Exchange	OSL	Oslo Stock Exchange	Virt-X	Virt-X (UK)
BRU	Euronext Brussels	PAR	Euronext Paris	WAR	Warsaw Stock Exchange
BUD	Budapest Stock Exchange	PRG	Prague Stock Exchange		
COP	Copenhagen Stock Exchange	RIG	HEX Riga		
CYP	Cyprus Stock Exchange				
DEU	Deutsche Börse AG				
DUS	Düsseldorf Stock Exchange				
ENXT	Euronext				
HAM	Hamburg Stock Exchange				
HAN	Hannover Stock Exchange				
HEX	Helsinki Exchanges				
HEXIM	HEX Integrated Markets				
ICE	Iceland Stock Exchange				
IRE	Irish Stock Exchange				
ITA	Italian Exchange				

Appendix I (Continued)

Central, Eastern and Southern Europe

BEL	Belgrade SE (Yugoslavia)	MAC	Macedonian SE (Skopje)	SAR	Sarajevo SE (Bosnia-Herz.)	VAR	Varazdin SE (Croatia)
BjL	Banja Luka SE (Bosnia-Herz.)	MOL	Moldova SE (Chisinau)	SOF	Bulgarian SE (Sofia)	ZAG	Zagreb SE (Croatia)
BUC	Bucharest SE (Romania)	MON	NEX Montenegro (Podgorica)	TIR	Tirana SE (Albania)		
IST	Istanbul SE (Turkey)	RUS	Various Russian Exchanges	UKR	Ukrainian SE (Kiev)		

Derivatives Markets

EDX Lon	EDX-Equity Deriv. Exchange	IDEM	Italian Derivatives Market	LIFFE	Euronext LIFFE	MEFF	Spanish Deriv. Exchange
		IPE	International Petroleum Exch.	LME	London Metal Exchange	OM Lon	OM London

Clearing and Settlement (CSD = Central Securities Depository, CCP = Central Counterparty)

APK	Finnish CSD	CC&G	Cassa di Compens. & Garanzia	MoTit	Monte Titoli (Italy)	SIS	Sega Intersettle (Switzerland)
3xBalt	CSDs in Eston., Latv., Lith.	LCH	London Clearing House	NCSD	Nordic CSD (project)	VPC	Swedish CSD

Non-European Exchanges, Clearing Houses etc.

ArcaEx	Archipelago Exchange (US)	CME	Chicago Mercantile Exchange	JSE	Johannesburg SE (RSA)	NQLX	Euronext US Futures Market
BM&F	Sao Paolo Comm. & Fut. Exch.	DJ	Dow Jones (News Service)	LAT-AM	(several) Latin American Exch.	SGX	Singapore Exchange
BOVISPA	Sao Paolo SE (Brazil)	DTCC	Depos. Trust & Clearg Corp. (US)	LATIBEX	Mkt for Lat-Am Equ. (Madrid)	SydFE	Sydney Futures Exchange
CBOT	Chicago Board of Trade			MONTR	Montreal SE (Canada)		

References

Abu-Lughod, Janet L. (1989) *Before European Hegemony – The World System A.D. 1250–1350*, New York: Oxford University Press.

Adam, Klaus, Tullio Jappelli, Annamaria Menchini, Mario Padula and Marco Pagano (2002) Analyse, compare, and apply alternative indicators and monitoring methodologies to measure the evolution of capital market integration in the European Union, CESF, University of Salerno, 28 January, http://europa.eu.int/comm/internal_market/en/update/economicreform/020128_cap_mark_int_en.pdf

Akerlof, George A. (1970) The market for 'lemons': quality uncertainty and the market mechanism, *Quarterly Journal of Economics*, **84**, August, 488–500.

Allen, Franklin and Douglas Gale (2001) *Comparing Financial Systems*, Cambridge, MA: MIT Press.

Allen, Franklin and Douglas Gale (2001) Comparative financial systems: a survey, http://fic.wharton.upenn.edu/fic/.

Allen, Franklin and Anthony M. Santomero (1996) The theory of financial intermediation, Wharton Financial Institutions Center Working Paper 96–32, http://fic.wharton.upenn.edu/fic/papers/96/9632.pdf.

Arthur, W. Brian (1994) Self-inforcing mechanisms in economics, in W. Brian Arthur (ed.), *Increasing Returns and Path Dependence in the Economy*, Ann Arbor, pp. 111–32.

Augar, Philip (2001) *The Death of Gentlemanly Capitalism*, London: Penguin Books.

Axelrod, Robert (1984) *The Evolution of Cooperation*, New York: Basic Books.

Balassa, Bela (1964) The purchasing-power parity doctrine: a reappraisal, *Journal of Political Economy*, **72**(6), 584–96.

Bank for International Settlements (1998) *Annual Report*, Basle.

Bank for International Settlements (2001) Triennial central bank survey: foreign exchange and derivatives market activity in 2001, Basle, March, http://www.bis.org.

Bank for International Settlements (2004) Triennial central bank survey of foreign exchange and derivatives market activity – preliminary global results, Basle, September, http://www.bis.org.

The Banker, various issues: http://www.thebanker.com/.

Bank of England (2004) The UK foreign exchange market and over-the-counter derivatives market in April 2004, 28 September, http://www.bankofengland.co.uk/.

Bank of England (2004) Finance for small firms, April http://www.bankofengland.co.uk/fin4sm11.pdf.

Barro, Robert J. and Xavier Sala-i-Martin (2003) *Economic Growth*, Cambridge, MA: MIT Press.

Basel Committee (1988): International convergence of capital measurement and capital standards, http://www.bis.org/publ/bcbs04A.pdf.

Basel Committee (1996): Amendment to the capital accord to incorporate market risks, http://www.bis.org/publ/bcbs24.pdf.

Basel Committee (2001): The New Basel Accord, press release, 16 January, www.bis.org/press/p010116.htm.

Basel Committee on Banking Supervision (2003) The New Basel Capital Accord, Third Consultative Paper, 29 April, http://www.bis.org/bcbs/bcbscp3.htm.

Baygan, Günseli (2003) Venture capital policy review: United Kingdom, OECD STI Working Paper 2003/1, http://www.oecd.org/dataoecd/41/58/2491240.pdf.

Bean, Charles (2003) Asset prices, financial imbalances and monetary policy: are inflation targets enough? BIS Working Paper No. 140, September, http://www.bis.org/publ/work140.pdf.

Benston, George J. and George G. Kaufman (1996) The appropriate role of bank regulation, *Economic Journal*, **106**, 688–97.

Bernanke, Ben S. and Mark Gertler (2001) Should Central Banks Respond to Movements in Asset Prices? www.princeton.edu/~bernanke/asset.doc.

Bodie, Zvi, Alex Kane and Alan J. Marcus (2002) *Investments*, New York: McGraw-Hill/Irwin.

Bundesverband deutscher Banken (2002) Übersicht über das Bankgewerbe im Euro-Währungsgebiet, http://www.bdb.de.

Cantor, Richard and Frank Packer (1996) Determinants and impact of sovereign credit ratings, *Federal Reserve Bank of New York Economic Policy Review*, October, 37–53, http://www.newyorkfed.org/research/epr/96v02n2/9610cant.pdf.

Castells, Manuel (1996) *The Rise of the Network Society*, Oxford: Blackwell.

Caviglia, Giacomo, Gerhard Krause and Christian Thimann (2002) Key features of the financial sectors in EU accession countries, in Christian Thimann (ed.) (2002) *Financial Sectors in EU Accession Countries*, http://www.ecb.int/pub/pdf/other/financialsectorseuaccessionen.pdf.

Clearstream International and Deutsche Börse Group (2002) Cross-border equity: trading, clearing and settlement in Europe, White Paper, http://www1.deutsche-boerse.com/INTERNET/EXCHANGE/zpd.nsf/PublikationenID/AKLS-58TMV6/$FILE/White-Paper_online_d.pdf?OpenElement.

Committee on Payment and Settlement Systems of the Central Banks of the Group of Ten Countries (CPSS) (1996) Settlement risk in foreign exchange transactions, CPSS Publications No. 17, March, http://www.bis.org/publ/cpss17.pdf.

Committee on Payment and Settlement Systems of the Central Banks of the Group of Ten Countries (CPSS) (2004) Statistics on payment and settlement systems in selected countries – Figures for 2002, CPSS Publications No. 60, March, http://www.bis.org/publ/cpss60.htm.

Cootner, Paul H. (1964) *The Random Character of Stock Market Prices*, Cambridge, MA: MIT Press.

Copeland, Laurence S. (2000) *Exchange Rates and International Finance*, London: Prentice Hall.

Crang, Mike (1998) *Cultural Geography*, London: Routledge.

CSFI (2002): Banana Skins 2002, http://www.csfi.org.uk.

Daniels, Peter and William F. Lever (eds) (1996) *The Global Economy in Transition*, Essex: Addison Wesley Longman.

Darbar, Salin M., R. Barry Johnston and Mary G. Zephirin (2003) Assessing offshore financial centers, *Finance & Development*, September, 32–5.

Davis, Glyn (2002) *A History of Money: From Ancient Times to the Present Day*, Cardiff: University of Wales Press.

Dawes, Robyn M. (1988) *Rational Choice in an Uncertain World*, Orlando, FL: Harcourt Brace Jovanovich.

De Grauwe, Paul, Hans Dewachter and Mark Embrechts (1993) *Exchange Rate Theory: Chaotic Models of Foreign Exchange Markets*, Oxford: Blackwell.

De Roover, Raymond (1974) What is dry exchange? A contribution to the study of English mercantilism, in Julius Kirshner (ed.) *Business, Banking, and Economic Thought in Late Medieval and Early Modern Europe – Selected Studies of Raymond de Roover*, Chicago: University of Chicago Press.

Deutsche Bank Research (2002) EU financial market special, *Frankfurt Voice*, June, http://www.dbresearch.com.

Deutsche Bundesbank (2001) The New Basel Capital Accord (Basel II), in *Deutsche Bundesbank: Monthly Report*, April, pp. 15–41, http://www.bundesbank.de/vo/download/mba/2001/04/200104mba_art01_baselaccord.pdf.

Dicken, Peter (2003) *Global Shift*, New York: Guilford Press.

Di Noia, Carmine (1998) Competition and integration among stock exchanges in Europe: network effects, implicit mergers and remote access, http://fic.wharton.upenn.edu/fic/papers/98/9803.pdf.

Dosi, Giovanni (1997) Opportunities, incentives and the collective patterns of technological change, *Economic Journal*, **107**, 1530–47.

Dow, Sheila C. (1996) Why the banking system should be regulated, *Economic Journal*, **106**, 698–707.

Dowd, Kevin (1996) The case for financial laissez-faire, *Economic Journal*, **106**, 679–87.

Dowd, Kevin (1998) *Beyond Value at Risk*, Chichester: John Wiley & Sons, Ltd.

Dufey, Gunter and Ian Giddy (1994) *The International Money Market*, Englewood Cliffs, NJ: Prentice Hall.

The Economist (2004) Pocket world in figures, London.

Edwards, Jeremy and Klaus Fischer (1994) *Banks, Finance and Investment in Germany*, Cambridge: Cambridge University Press.

Einzig, Paul (1970) *The History of Foreign Exchange*, London: Macmillan.

Elster, Jon (1984) *Ulysses and the Sirens – Studies in Rationality and Irrationality*, Cambridge: Cambridge University Press.

Euromoney, various issues: http://www.Euromoney.com/.

European Central Bank (2003) *Statistics Pocket Book*, September, http://www.ecb.de/pub/pdf/stapobo/spb200309en.pdf.

European Central Bank (2004) *The Monetary Policy of the ECB 2004*, http://www.ecb.int/pub/pdf/other/monetarypolicy2004en.pdf.

Fama, Eugene F. (1965) The behavior of stock market prices, *Journal of Business*, **1**, 34–105.

Fama, Eugene F. (1970) Efficient capital markets: a review of theory and empirical work, *Journal of Finance*, **25**(2), 383–417.

Favier, Jean (1998) *Gold and Spices: The Rise of Commerce in the Middle Ages*, New York: Holmes & Meier.

Ferguson, Niall (2001) *Cash Nexus – Money and Power in the Modern World 1700–2000*, London: Penguin Books.

Folkerts-Landau, David *et al.* (1997) *International Capital Markets – Developments, Prospects, and Key Policy Issues*, Washington, DC: International Monetary Fund.

Frank, M. and T. Stengos (1988) Chaotic dynamics in economic time series, *Journal of Economic Surveys*, **2**, 103–33.

Galati, Gabriele and Kostas Tsatsaronis (2001) The impact of the euro on Europe's financial markets, BIS Working Paper No. 100, July, http://www.bis.org/publ/work100.pdf.

Gilli, Manfred and Evis Kellezi (2003) An application of extreme value theory for measuring risk, Preprint, 8 February, http://www.unige.ch/ses/metri/gilli/evtrm/evtrm.pdf.

Giordano, Francesco (2002) Cross-border trading in financial securities in Europe: the role of central counterparty, European Capital Markets Institute, December, http://www.ecmi.es/files/giordano.pdf.

The Giovannini Group (2001) Cross-border clearing and settlements arrangement in the European Union, November, http://europa.eu.int/comm/economy_finance/publications/giovannini/clearing1101_en.pdf.

The Giovannini Group (2003) Second report on EU clearing and settlements arrangements, April, http://europa.eu.int/comm/economy_finance/publications/giovannini/clearing_settlement_arrangements140403.pdf.

Goldberg, Linda, John Kambhu, James M. Mahoney, Lawrence Radecki and Asani Sarkar (2002) Securities trading and settlement in Europe: issues and outlook, *Federal Reserve Bank of New York: Current Issues in Economic and Finance*, **8**(4), April.

Gorton, Gary and Andrew Winton (2002) Financial intermediation, NBER Working Paper No. 8928, May, http://www.nber.org/papers/w8928.

Granger, C.W.J. (1966): The typical spectral shape of an economic variable, *Econometrica*, **34**(1), 150–61.

Grether, David M. and Charles R. Plott (1979) Economic theory of choice and the preference reversal phenomenon, *American Economic Review*, **69**(4), 623–38.

Gros, Daniel and Karel Lannoo (2000) *The Euro Capital Market*, New York: John Wiley & Sons, Inc.

Hall, Peter (1998) *Cities in Civilization*, London: Weidenfeld & Nicolson.

Hamilton, Adrian (1986) *The Financial Revolution*, Harmondsworth: Penguin.

Hartmann, Philipp, Angela Maddaloni and Simone Manganelli (2003): The euro area financial system: structure, integration and policy initiatives, European Central Bank, Working Paper No. 230, http://www.ecb.int/pub/wp/ecbwp230.pdf.

Heinemann, Friedrich (2002) The benefits of creating an integrated EU market for investment funds, ZEW Discussion Paper No. 02-27, ftp://ftp.zew.de/pub/zew-docs/dp/dp0227.pdf.

Held, David *et al.* (1999) *Global Transformations*, Stanford: Stanford University Press.

Herring, Richard and Nathporn Chatusripitak (2001) The case of the missing market: the bond market and why it matters for financial development, Wharton Financial Institutions Center Working Paper 01-08, http://fic.wharton.upenn.edu/fic/papers/01/0108.pdf.

Hirata de Carvalho, Cynthia (2004) Cross-border securities clearing and settlement infrastructure in the European Union as a prerequisite to financial market integration – challenges and perspectives, HWWA Discussion Paper No. 287, http://www.hwwa.de/Publikationen/Discussion_Paper/2004/287.pdf.

HM Treasury, Financial Services Authority (FSA), Bank of England (2003) *The EU Financial Services Action Plan: A Guide*, http://www.bankofengland.co.uk/publications/FSAP-guide.pdf.

Hogarth, Robin M. and Melvin W. Reder (eds) (1987) *Rational Choice – The Contrast between Economics and Psychology*, Chicago: University of Chicago Press.

Horvath, Julius (2003) Optimum currency area theory: a selective review, Bank of Finland, Institute for Economies in Transition (BOFIT) Discussion Paper No. 15, http://www.bof.fi/bofit/fin/6dp/03abs/pdf/dp1503.pdf.

Huh, Chan (1990) The equity-risk premium puzzle, *FRBSF Weekly Letter*, 13 April, http://www.frbsf.org/publications/economics/letter/1990/el90-15.pdf.

Huizinga, Harry and Gaetan Nicodème (2002) Deposit insurance and international bank deposits, European Commission, Directorate General for Economic and Financial Affairs, Economic Papers, No. 164, February, http://europa.eu.int/comm/economy_finance/publications/economic_papers/2002/ecp164en.pdf.

Hull, John C. (2002) *Options, Futures, and Other Derivatives*, London: Prentice Hall.

International Financial Services London (IFSL) (2003) International financial markets in the UK, http://www.ifsl.org.uk.

International Monetary Fund (1997) *International Capital Markets – Developments, Prospects and Key Policy Issues*, Washington, DC.

International Monetary Fund (2000) Offshore financial centers, IMF Background Paper, June 23, http://www.imf.org/external/np/mae/oshore/2000/eng/back.htm#table2.

Jackson, Patricia (2001) Bank capital standards: the new Basel accord, *Bank of England Quarterly Bulletin*, Spring, 55–63, http://www.bankofengland.co.uk/qb/qb010101.pdf.

Jackson, Patricia (2002) Bank capital: Basel II developments, *Bank of England: Financial Stability Review*, December, http://www.bankofengland.co.uk/fsr/fsr1art3.pdf.

Jorion, Philippe (1997) *Value at Risk: The New Benchmark for Controlling Market Risk*, Chicago: Irwin.

Kenen, Peter (1969) The theory of optimum currency areas: an eclectic view, in Robert A. Mundell and Alexander K. Swoboda (eds) *Monetary Problems of the International Economy*, Chicago: University of Chicago Press, pp. 41–60.

Kettell, Brian (2000) *What Drives the Currency Markets*, London: Prentice Hall.

Kiff, John and Ron Morrow (2000) Credit derivatives, *Bank of Canada Review*, autumn, 3–11, http://www.bank-banque-canada.ca/publications/review/r005-ea.pdf.

Kindleberger, Charles P. (1993) *A Financial History of Western Europe*, Oxford: Oxford University Press.

Knight, Frank H. (1921) *Risk, Uncertainty and Profit*, Boston: Houghton Mifflin, http://www.econlib.org/library/Knight/knRUP6.html#Pt.III, Ch.VII.

Knight, Frank H. (1944) Diminishing returns from investment, *Journal of Political Economy*, **52**, March, 26–47.

Kolb, Robert W. (2002) *Futures, Options, and Swaps*, New York: Blackwell.

Kreditanstalt für Wiederaufbau (KfW) (2002) Private equity in Germany and Great Britain – A comparison of market structures (in German), http://www.kfw.de/DE/Research/Sonderthem68/Beteiligun15/Cambridge_Vergleich_Beteiligungsmaerkte.pdf.

Krugman, Paul R. and Maurice Obstfeld (1997) *International Economics – Theory and Policy*, Reading, MA: Addison-Wesley.

La Porta, Rafael, Florencio Lopez de Silanes, Andrei Shleifer and Robert W. Vishny (1999) Investor protection and corporate governance, http://ssrn.com/abstract=183908.

Levich, Richard M. (1998) *International Financial Markets – Prices and Policies*, Boston: Irwin McGraw-Hill.

Lintner, John (1965) The valuation of risky assets and the selection of risky investments in stock portfolios and capital budgets, *Review of Economics and Statistics*, **47**, February, 13–37.

Llewellyn, David (1996) Banking in the 21st century: the transformation of an industry, http://www.rba.gov.au/PublicationsAndResearch/Conferences/1996/Llewellyn.pdf.

Loriaux, Michel (2003) France: a new 'capitalism of voice'? in Linda Weiss (ed.) *States in the Global Economy – Bringing Domestic Institutions Back In*, Cambridge: Cambridge University Press, pp. 101–20.

Machina, Mark J. (1987) Choice under uncertainty: problems solved and unsolved, *Journal of Economic Perspectives*, **1**(1), 121–54.

Machina, Mark J. (1989) Dynamic consistency and non-expected utility models of choice under uncertainty, *Journal of Economic Literature*, **27**(4), 1622–68.

Malkiel, Burton G. (2003) The efficient market hypothesis and its critics, *Journal of Economic Perspectives*, **17**(1), 59–82.

Malthus, Thomas (1798) *An Essay on the Principle of Population: A View of its Past and Present Effects on Human Happiness; with an Inquiry into Our Prospects Respecting the Future Removal or Mitigation of the Evils which It Occasions*, published: London: John Murray, 1826. Sixth edition, available online at: http://www.econlib.org/library/Malthus/malPlong.html.

Mandelbrot, Benoît (1969) Long-run linearity, locally Gaussian process, H-spectra and infinite variances, *International Economic Review*, **1**, 82–111.

Mankiw, N. Gregory (1995) The growth of nations, *Brookings Papers on Economic Activity*, **1**, 275–310.

Markowitz, Harry M. (1952) Portfolio selection, *Journal of Finance*, **7**, March, 70–91.

Mastroeni, Orazio (2001) Pfandbrief-style products in Europe, BIS Paper No. 5, October, http://www.bis.org.

McAndrews, James and Chris Stefanadis (2002) The consolidation of European stock exchanges, *Federal Reserve Bank of New York: Current Issues*, **8**(6), http://www.newyorkfed.org/research/current_issues/ci8-6.pdf.

McKinnon, Ronald (1963) Optimum currency areas, *American Economic Review*, **53**, 717–25.

Melvin, Michael (2004) *International Money and Finance*, Boston: Pearson Addison Wesley.

Mishkin, Frederic S. and Stanley G. Eakins (2000) *Financial Markets and Institutions*, Reading, MA: Addison Wesley Longman.

Mossin, Jan (1966) Equilibrium in a capital asset market, *Econometrica*, **34**, October, 768–83.

Mundell, Robert A. (1961) A theory of optimum currency areas, *American Economic Review*, **51**, 657–65.

Nison, Steve (1991) *Japanese Candlestick Charting Techniques*, New York: Simon & Schuster.

OECD: Financial Market Trends, various issues, http://www.oecd.org/.

OECD (2002) Risk capital in OECD countries: recent developments and structural issues, *Financial Market Trends*, No. 82, June.

O'Rourke, Kevin H. and Jeffrey G. Williamson (1999) *Globalization and History – The Evolution of a Nineteenth-Century Atlantic Economy*, Cambridge, MA: MIT Press.

Pakko, Michael R. and Patricia S. Pollard (2003) Burgernomics: A Big Mac guide to purchasing power parity, *Federal Reserve Bank of St. Louis Review*, December, http://research.stlouisfed.org/publications/review/03/11/pakko.pdf.

Peters, Edgar E. (1991) *Chaos and Order in the Capital Markets*, New York: John Wiley & Sons, Inc.

Peters, Edgar E. (1994) *Fractal Market Analysis*, New York: John Wiley & Sons, Inc.

Ramsey, Frank (1928) A mathematical theory of saving, *Economic Journal*, **38**, December, 543–59.

Reinicke, Wolfgang H. (1998) *Global Public Policy – Governing without Government?* Washington, DC: Brookings.

Reisen, Helmut and Julia von Maltzan (1998) Sovereign credit ratings, emerging market risk and financial market volatility, HWWA Discussion Paper No. 55, http://www.hwwa.de/Publikationen/Discussion_Paper/1998/55.pdf.

Reszat, Beate (1998) Emerging financial centres, HWWA Discussion Paper No. 52, http://www.hwwa.de/Publikationen/Discussion_Paper/1998/52.pdf.

Reszat, Beate (2002) Information technologies in international finance and the role of cities, *GaWC Research Bulletin 74*: http://www.lboro.ac.uk/gawc/publicat.html, 26th February.

Reszat, Beate (2003) Financial reform in Germany, in Maximilian J.B. Hall (ed.) *The International Handbook of Financial Reform*, Cheltenham: Edward Elgar, pp. 88–112.

Ricardo, David (1817) *On the Principles of Political Economy and Taxation*, published: London: John Murray, 1821. Third edition, available online at: http://www.econlib.org/library/Ricardo/ricP.html.

Rodriguez, L. Jacobo (2002) International banking regulation – Where's the market discipline in Basel II? *Policy Analysis*, No. 455, 15 October, http://www.cato.org/pubs/pas/pa-455es.html.

Rogoff, Kenneth (2003) A vote against grandiose schemes, *Finance & Development*, **40**(1), http://www.imf.org/external/pubs/ft/fandd/2003/03/rogo.htm.

Sallard, Delphine (1999) Risk capital markets, a key to job creation in Europe. From fragmentation to integration. Euro Paper No. 32, Brussels: European Commission, http://Europa.eu.int/comm/economy_finance/publications/Euro_papers/2001/eup32en.pdf.

Samuelson, Paul (1964) Theoretical notes on trade problems, *Review of Economics and Statistics*, **46**(2), 145–54.

Santillán, Javier, Marc Bayle and Christian Thygesen (2000) The impact of the euro on money and bond markets, European Central Bank Occasional Paper No. 1, July, http://www.ecb.int/pub/pdf/scpops/ecbocp1.pdf.

Sargent, Thomas J. (1995) *Bounded Rationality in Macroeconomics*, Oxford: Oxford University Press.

Sassen, Saskia (1991) *The Global City – New York, London, Tokyo*, Princeton, NJ: Princeton University Press.

Sato, Setsuya and John Hawkins (2001) Electronic finance: an overview of the issues, http://www.bis.org/publ/bispap07a.pdf.

Setty, Gautam and Randall Dodd (2003) Credit rating agencies: their impact on capital flows to developing countries, Financial Policy Forum, Derivatives Study Center, Special Policy Report No. 6, http://www.financialpolicy.org/FPFSPR6.pdf.

Schelling, Thomas (1978) *Micromotives and Macrobehavior*, New York: W.W. Norton.

Schich, Sebastian and Gert Wehinger (2003) Prospects for stock exchanges, *OECD: Financial Market Trends*, No. 85, October.

Schumpeter, Joseph (1934) *The Theory of Economic Development*, Cambridge, MA: Harvard University Press.

Sen, Amartya (1982) Behaviour and the concept of preference, reprinted in Amartya Sen (ed.) *Choice, Welfare and Measurement*, Oxford: Oxford University Press, pp. 432–49.

Sharpe, William F. (1964) Capital asset prices: a theory of market equilibrium under conditions of risk, *Journal of Finance*, **19**, 425–42.

Shiller, Robert J. (2001) *Irrational Exuberance*, Princeton, NJ: Princeton University Press.

Smith, Adam (1776) *An Inquiry into the Nature and Causes of the Wealth of Nations*, published: London: Methuen and Co., Ltd., ed. Edwin Cannan, 1904. Fifth edition, available online at: http://www.econlib.org/library/Smith/smWN.html.

Sornette, Didier (2004) *Why Stock Markets Crash – Critical Events in Complex Financial Systems*, Princeton, NJ: Princeton University Press.

Spufford, Peter (2002) *The Merchant in Medieval Europe*, London: Thames & Hudson.

Steinherr, Alfred (2000) *Derivatives – The Wild Beast of Finance*, Chichester: John Wiley & Sons, Ltd.

Study Group on Fixed Income Markets (2001) The changing shape of fixed income markets, BIS Paper No. 5, October, http://www.bis.org.

Thaler, Richard H. (1994) *The Winner's Curse*, Princeton, NJ: Princeton University Press.

Thiel, Michael (2001) Finance and economic growth – a review of theory and the available evidence, European Commission, Directorate-General for Economic and Financial Affairs, Economic Paper No. 158, July.

Turner, Philip (2001) Bond markets in emerging economies: an overview of policy issues, BIS Papers No. 11, December, http://www.bis.org.

Walmsley, Julian (1996) *International Money and Foreign Exchange Markets: An Introduction*, Chichester: John Wiley & Sons, Ltd.

Walter, Ingo and Roy Smith (2000) *High Finance in the €uro Zone – Competing in the New European Capital Market*, London: Prentice Hall.

Watson, James L. (ed.) (1997) *Golden Arches East – McDonald's in East Asia*, Stanford: Stanford University Press.

Wolf, Martin (2002) Misplaced hopes in Tobin's tax, *The Financial Times*, 20 March.

Young, Allyn (1928) Increasing returns and economic progress, *Economic Journal*, **38**, 527–42.

Index

Index compiled by Annette Musker